THEIOS ANER IN HELLENISTIC–JUDAISM:
A Critique of the Use of This Category in
New Testament Christology

SOCIETY OF BIBLICAL LITERATURE
DISSERTATION SERIES

edited by
Howard C. Kee
and
Douglas A. Knight

Number 40

THEIOS ANER IN HELLENISTIC–JUDAISM:
A Critique of the Use of This Category in
New Testament Christology

by
Carl R. Holladay

SCHOLARS PRESS
Missoula, Montana

THEIOS ANER IN HELLENISTIC-JUDAISM:
A Critique of the Use of This Category in New Testament Christology

by
Carl R. Holladay

Published by
SCHOLARS PRESS
for
The Society of Biblical Literature

Distributed by

SCHOLARS PRESS
Missoula, Montana 59806

THEIOS ANER IN HELLENISTIC–JUDAISM:
A Critique of the Use of This Category in New Testament Christology

by

Carl R. Holladay

Library of Congress Cataloging in Publication Data
Holladay, Carl R.
   Theis aner in Hellenistic-Judaism

   (Dissertation series - Society of Biblical Literature ;
No. 40 ISSN 0145-2770)
   Originally presented as the author's thesis, Yale.
   Bibliography: p.
   Includes index.
   1. Jesus Christ—History of doctrines—Early church,
ca. 30–600. 2. Josephus, Flavius. 3. Philo, Judæus.
4. Artapanus. I. Title. II. Series: Society of
Biblical Literature. Dissertation series ; no. 40.
BT198.H64 1977   232'.09'015   77-20712
ISBN 0-89130-205-0 pbk.

Printed in the United States of America
1 2 3 4 5

Printing Department
University of Montana
Missoula, Montana 59812

5560 UM Printing Services

FOR MY FATHER AND MOTHER

TABLE OF CONTENTS

PREFACE

The decision to investigate a single aspect of
Christology against the background of Hellenistic-Jewish apologetic reflects the influence of three of my teachers, to each
of whom I am profoundly indebted. Professor C. F. D. Moule,
whose interest in Christology kindled and nurtured the
Christological aspect of this study, has supervised the bulk
of my research; his critical eye and penetrating insight
have often saved me from a multitude of sins, most of them
unforgivable, but his patient encouragement has always been
forthcoming, nevertheless. Dr. Ernst Bammel, under whose
supervision I worked for three terms, provided highly informed
and stimulating guidance through the Hellenistic-Jewish
sources. Professor A. J. Malherbe, (now) of Yale University,
to whom I owe an incalculable and manifold debt, first
suggested to me Hellenistic-Jewish apologetic as an area
worthy of further mining.

Each of these has contributed in his own way to my work
and development, and traces of their respective interests and
influence are easily discernible. Although the degree to which
I have been influenced by them, and many others, in my thinking
and in the formation of my conclusions is clearly visible, this
study is the result of my independent research into both the
primary and secondary literature, and for its content and conclusions I alone am responsible.

I must also express thanks to the Trustees of the Hort
Memorial Fund for a grant making it possible for me to visit
Münster in the summer of 1973 in order to work at the
Institutum Judaicum Delitzschianum, where Professor K. H.
Rengstorf very kindly made available to me the files of the
Josephus concordance. I must also say a word of thanks to his
staff, especially Dr. Jürgen Schwark, for their most cordial
assistance and valuable consultation.

Finally, to my parents, Mr. & Mrs. Ben R. Holladay, I
am inutterably grateful for their generosity, patience, and

encouragement. But, most of all, to my wife and two sons I am
indebted beyond measure, especially for their patience with an
often preoccupied and unavailable husband and father.

Cambridge
July 1974

The typing of this manuscript was made possible by an A.
Whitney Griswold Award granted by the Council on the Humanities
of Yale University. I also wish to acknowledge the care and
skill with which Nona Jenkins typed the manuscript. At an
earlier stage, Colin Hemer and Harold Dressler rendered
invaluable assistance in proofreading and in providing helpful
suggestions. I make all these acknowledgements with gratitude.

New Haven
September, 1977

ABBREVIATIONS

I. Collections, Periodicals, Reference Works, etc.

BGU	Berliner griechische Urkunden (Ägyptische Urkunden aus den Königlichen Museen zu Berlin)
BJRL	Bulletin of the John Rylands Library
BZAW	Beihefte zur Zeitschrift für die alttestamentliche Wissenschaft
CAH	Cambridge Ancient History
CBQ	Catholic Biblical Quarterly
CQ	Classical Quarterly
E Jud	Encyclopaedia Judaica
FGrH	F. Jacoby, Die Fragmente der griechischen Historiker
FHG	C. Müller, Fragmenta Historicorum Graecorum
FRLANT	Forschungen zur Religion und Literatur des Alten und Neuen Testaments
FVS	H. Diels-W. Kranz, Die Fragmente der Vorsokratiker
GCS	Die griechischen-christlichen Schriftsteller der ersten drei Jahrhunderte
GGL	W. Schmid-O. Stählin, Geschichte der griechischen Literatur
GGR	M. P. Nilsson, Geschichte der griechischen Religion
HDB	J. Hastings (ed.), Dictionary of the Bible
HERE	J. Hastings (ed.), Encyclopaedia of Religion and Ethics
HTR	The Harvard Theological Review
HUCA	Hebrew Union College Annual
JBL	Journal of Biblical Literature
JE	The Jewish Encyclopedia

JETS	Journal of the Evangelical Theological Society
JQR	The Jewish Quarterly Review
JR	Journal of Religion
JTS	The Journal of Theological Studies
JThC	Journal for Theology and the Church
LSJ	H. G. Liddell, R. Scott, H. S. Jones, & R. McKenzie, A Greek-English Lexicon
NT	Novum Testamentum
NTS	New Testament Studies
OCD[2]	The Oxford Classical Dictionary, 2nd edition
OGIS	W. Dittenberger (ed.), Orientis Graeci Inscriptiones Selectae
PL	J. Migne, Patrologia latina
PWRE	W. Pauly-G. Wissowa, Realencyclopädie der klassischen Altertumswissenschaft
RAC	Reallexikon für Antike und Christentum
RGG[3]	Die Religion in Geschichte und Gegenwart, 3. Auflage
Rev. Hist. Rel.	Revue de l'histoire des religions
SBL	Society of Biblical Literature
SJT	Scottish Journal of Theology
SVF	H. von Arnim, Stoicorum Veterum Fragmenta
TDNT	G. Kittel-G. Friedrich (edd.), Theological Dictionary of the New Testament, Trans. G. Bromiley
ThLZ	Theologische Literaturzeitung
TU	Texte und Untersuchungen zur Geschichte der altchristlichen Literatur
TWNT	G. Kittel-G. Friedrich (edd.), Theologisches Wörterbuch zum Neuen Testament
ZKG	Zeitschrift für Kirchengeschichte
ZNW	Zeitschrift für die neutestamentliche Wissenschaft und die Kunde der älteren Kirche

ZTK	Zeitschrift für Theologie und Kirche
ZWT	Zeitschrift für wissenschaftliche Theologie

II. Individual Authors Frequently Cited.

A. Philo:

Abr.	De Abrahamo
Aet.	De aeternitate mundi
Agr.	De agricultura
Alex.	Alexander (de animalibus)
Cher.	De Cherubim
Conf.	De confusione linguarum
Cong.	De congressu eruditionis gratia
Decal.	De decalogo
Det.	Quod deterius potiori insidiari soleat
Ebr.	De ebrietate
Flacc.	In Flaccum
Fuga	De fuga et inventione
Gig.	De gigantibus
Heres	Quis rerum divinarum heres sit
Hyp.	Hypothetica
Immut.	Quod Deus sit immutabilis
Jos.	De Josepho
Leg. All.	Legum Allegoriae
Leg. ad Gaium	Legatio ad Gaium
Migr.	De migratione Abrahami
Mut.	De mutatione nominum
Opif.	De opificio mundi
Plant.	De plantatione
Post. C.	De posteritate Caini
Praem.	De praemiis et poenis
Prob.	Quod omnis probus liber sit
Prov.	De providentia
Qu. Ex.	Quaestiones in Exodum
Qu. Gen.	Quaestiones in Genesim
Sacr.	De sacrificiis Abelis et Caini
Sobr.	De sobrietate
Som.	De somniis
Spec. Leg.	De specialibus legibus
Virt.	De virtutibus
V. Contempl.	De vita contemplativa
V. Mos.	De vita Mosis

(Taken, with slight modification, from Chapter 8 in
The Cambridge History of Later Greek and Early
Medieval Philosophy. Ed. A. H. Armstrong.)

B. Josephus:

Ant.	Antiquitates Judaicae
Ap.	Contra Apionem
Bel.	Bellum Judaicum
Vit.	Vita

C. Generally, for classical authors the abbreviations listed in Liddell-Scott-Jones, xvi–xxxviii, have been used.

III. Note: The method of citation generally used for secondary literature in the footnotes is as follows: volume and page separated by full stop; page and note separated by colon. Thus, 2. 3:4 = volume 2, page 3, note 4.

CHAPTER ONE

THE THEIOS ANER DEBATE

In contemporary New Testament scholarship the expression _theios aner_ is used more and more frequently to explain certain features of early Christianity; in fact, frequently enough to make it possible to speak of an emerging _theios aner_ debate. On the one hand, there are those who regard the expression _theios aner_ as a legitimate and useful category for analyzing New Testament passages which are said to portray Jesus as a _theios aner_ and who thus speak with confidence of a "_theios aner_ Christology,"[1] either as an orthodox viewpoint from which

---

[1]So, H. D. BETZ, "Jesus as Divine Man," in _Jesus and the Historian_ (Philadelphia, 1968) 114-33, who classifies miracle pericopae from the Gospels according to the degree to which they exhibit a "_theios aner_ Christology," which he defines as "a Christology that presents the earthly Jesus of Nazareth by making use of motifs from the Hellenistic concept of the Divine Man" (116). According to Betz, Mark reinterprets this Christology but does not fully reject it as do Paul and Q; Matthew develops his own version of it; Luke goes a further step in Acts and portrays the apostles as _theioi andres_; John begins with a _theios aner_ Christology in his source materials and combines it with the motif of pre-existent Mediator of creation and Logos-revealer. H. KOESTER, "The Structure of Early Christian Beliefs," in _Trajectories Through Early Christianity_ (Philadelphia, 1971) 216ff., analyzes "Jesus, the Divine Man," as one of four Christologies whose parallel development is discernible in the earliest decades of Christian history. Though Jesus himself understood his miracles as "evidence of an eschatological event... , as soon as these great works of Jesus became the objects of Christian faith, they became part of a divine man Christology." Cf. also "GNOMAI DIAPHOROI: The Origin and Nature of Diversification in the History of Early Christianity," "One Jesus and Four Primitive Gospels," in _Trajectories_, 151f., 187ff. L. E. KECK, "Mark 3: 7-12 and Mark's Christology," _JBL_ 84 (1965) 341-58, classifies the Marcan pericopae 3:7-12; 4:35-5:43; 6:31-52; 6:53-56 as a single complex of traditions notable because of the lack of Jewish-oriented features, e.g. conflicts with Judaism, Sabbath, etc.; "Instead, all these stories tell of miracles that result from the supranatural power resident within Jesus in a way as to make him different from other men, as indicated in the query, 'Who is this?' (4:41). These miracles have no stated connection with the kingdom of God, or with the forgiveness of sins. They are direct manifestations of the Son of God, and in a

(cont.)

1

particular way--the theios aner." According to Keck, this
stream of tradition is incorporated into Mark's Gospel "relatively unrelated to Jesus' message," and stands "under the
stamp of the hellenistic theios aner whose divine power is
manifested on earth" (349ff.). P. ACHTEMEIER, "The Origin and
Function of the Pre-Markan Miracle Catenae," JBL 91 (1972) 198-
221, analyzes two sets of pre-Marcan miracle catenae and argues
that they originally formed part of a Eucharistic liturgy whose
theological foundation, i.e. its "epiphanic" emphasis, was
connected with a "theios aner Christology," i.e. "a theology
which saw in Jesus a glorious theios aner who manifested himself as such by his deeds during his earthly life, and who is
present in his wondrous powers at the eucharistic celebration"
(218); cf. also "Toward the Isolation of pre-Markan Miracle
Catenae," JBL 89 (1970) 265-91; "Gospel Miracle Tradition and
the Divine Man," Interpretation 26 (1972) 174-97; Further
examples could be multiplied from, among others, the following:
G. P. WETTER, Der Sohn Gottes (Göttingen, 1916); H. WINDISCH,
Paulus und Christus (Leipzig, 1934); R. BULTMANN, History of
the Synoptic Tradition (Oxford, 1972. ET of 2nd German ed.
1931) 218ff.; Theology of the New Testament (New York, 1951),
1. 128ff.; The Gospel of John (Oxford, 1971. ET of 1964 ed.)
101f., 104, 106, 116f., passim; L. BIELER, THEIOS ANER: Das
Bild des "Göttlichen Menschen" in Spätantike und Frühchristentum (Wien, 1: 1935; 2: 1936; repr. Darmstadt, 1967) 1. 25ff.,
40, 138ff.; H. BRAUN, "The Meaning of New Testament Christology"
(1957), JThC 5 (1968) 89-127; A. KUBY, "Zur Konzeption des
Markus-Evangeliums," ZNW 49 (1958) 52-64; J. SCHREIBER, "Die
Christologie des Markusevangeliums: Beobachtungen zur Theologie
und Komposition des zweites Evangeliums," ZTK 58 (1961) 154-83;
Theologie des Vertrauens (Hamburg, 1967); F. HAHN, Titles of
Jesus in Christology (London, 1969. Abbreviated ET of 1968
German ed.) 288ff.; D. GEORGI, Die Gegner des Paulus im 2.
Korintherbrief (Neukirchen-Vluyn, 1964) 282ff., passim.; P.
VIELHAUER, "Erwägungen zur Christologie des Markusevangeliums,"
in Zeit und Geschichte (Tübingen, 1964) 155-69; R. H. FULLER,
Foundations of New Testament Christology (London, 1965) 68ff.,
97f., 227ff.; U. LUZ, "Das Geheimnismotiv und die markinische
Christologie," ZNW 56 (1965) 9-30; J. M. ROBINSON, "Kerygma and
History in the New Testament" (1965), in Trajectories, 48, 55f.;
S. SCHULZ, Die Stunde der Botschaft (Hamburg, 1967) 64-79; H-D.
KNIGGE, "The Meaning of Mark," Interpretation 22 (1968) 53-70;
T. J. WEEDEN, "The Heresy That Necessitated Mark's Gospel," ZNW
59 (1968) 145-58; Mark: Traditions in Conflict (Philadelphia,
1971) 70ff.; E. GRÄSSER, "Jesus in Nazareth (Mark VI. 1-6a),"
NTS 16 (1969) 1-23; J. BECKER, "Wunder und Christologie," NTS
16 (1970) 130-48; N. PERRIN, What Is Redaction Criticism?
(London, 1970) 55; "The Christology of Mark: A Study in Methodology," JR 51 (1971) 173-87; Christology and a Modern Pilgrimage (Claremont, 1971) 55; M. SMITH, "Prolegomena to a Discussion of Aretalogies, Divine Men, The Gospels and Jesus," JBL
90 (1971) 174-99; W. H. KELBER, The Kingdom in Mark (Philadelphia, 1974) 47. I am indebted to E. LEMCIO for pointing me to
several of these references.

the Gentile Son of God Christology developed,[2] or as a heretical viewpoint in which the image of Jesus as a miracle-worker was central and which was being opposed in certain New Testament writings, e.g. 2 Corinthians and Mark.[3] In this same category

---

[2]Especially, WETTER, Sohn Gottes, 186f., "Andererseits fliesst doch die Sohn-Gottes-Vorstellung mit einer im Hellenismus viel allgemeineren zusammen: dem theios anthropos, oder was dafür unter den Christen gesagt wird: ὁ ἄνϑρωπος τοῦ ϑεοῦ;" cf. also 82f. H. BRAUN, "New Testament Christology," 100ff., in explaining how Son of God developed as a fundamental Christological title in the Hellenistic community, says, "Jesus appears as the Son of God in the sense of the hellenistic-oriental thaumaturge, the theios aner. On occasion, as at the beginning of the Gospels of Matthew and Luke, the miraculous manner of his conception and birth can be especially emphasized. Both concepts, the Pauline, which has little interest in the earthly career of Jesus aside from his death, and the Marcan concept of theios aner, which is consequently also found in the other synoptics and John, have this one thing in common: the Son of God gains victory over death in his resurrection or in his ascension." Cf. also BULTMANN, New Testament Theology, 1. 128ff.; HAHN, Titles, 288ff.; FULLER, Foundations, 227ff.

[3]Some confusion prevails as to who is responsible for first employing theios aner to designate aberrational Christological tendencies. KOESTER, Trajectories, 189:106, evidently because of such statements as those in the expanded notes to DIBELIUS, Formgeschichte (Tübingen, [6]1971), 313f., attributing to him the linking of Mark's sources with a theios aner Christology, disclaims credit for connecting the opponents in 2 Cor. with the theology of Mark's and John's miracle sources, bowing instead to GEORGI, whose Heidelberg dissertation (Die Gegner; cf. note 1 above) was completed in 1958. While it is true that Georgi assigns to the 2 Cor. opponents a theios aner Christology which provides partial grounds for their pneumatically oriented view of discipleship, and that he also sees a similar Christology in Mark (and Luke) as well as in the pre-literary traditions at his disposal, as far as I can determine, he does not evaluate these traditions, either before or after Mark's incorporation and reinterpretation of them, as aberrational. Instead, Mark (and Luke) remains for Georgi an exponent of a theios aner Christology: "Markus und Lukas folgen im Aufriss ihres jeweiligen Evangeliums der vorgetragenen christologischen Anschauung. Sie stellen auf Schritt und Tritt den wunderbaren Habitus des Christus heraus. Es ist interessant, dass Matthäus dieser Tendenz nicht folgt" (214). In contrast, KOESTER, art. "Häretiker im Urchristentum," RGG 3 (1958, fascicle) 3. 18f., significantly, discussing the theios aner Christology under "Häretiker," implies that these Gospel traditions are aberrational, and that the Evangelists consciously resisted this theological tendency: "Gleiche Tendenzen (to transform the historical Jesus into a divine wonder-worker (theios aner) and discipleship into an imitation of this Christological image, i.e. a pneumatic-power oriented

(cont.)

are scholars who use the term positively to describe persons other than Jesus, such as Jewish or Christian missionaries who regarded themselves as singularly affiliated with the divine.[4] On the other hand, there are those who question the appropriateness of the expression _theios aner_ as a category in which to discuss Christ, much less the apostles, and who mention it only to reject it.[5]

---

style of discipleship) haben auch teilweise den Erzählungsstoff der Evangelienüberlieferung geprägt. Das zeigen nicht erst die apokryphen Evangelien und Apostelgeschichten. Schon gewisse Schichten der älteren Tradition sind von dieser Theologie beherrscht, wie die Traditionen des MkEv und die σημεῖα (=Zeichen) Quelle des JohEv, ebenso schon manche Stücke der kanonischen Apg. ... Dass diese Aufgabe (for this _theios aner_ theology to take root and grow) von den Evangelisten bewältigt wurde, ist eine nicht zu unterschätzende Leistung in der Entwicklung zur Rechtgläubigkeit." Cf. further _Trajectories_, 152, 189. Regardless of who qualifies as εὑρετής, this line of interpretation has gained popularity. Cf. SCHREIBER, "Christologie," 154-83; LUZ, "Geheimnismotif," 9-30; SCHULZ, _Botschaft_, 64-79; KNIGGE, "Mark," 53-70; ACHTEMEIER, "Origin and Function," 198, 210, esp. 218ff.; R. H. FULLER, Review of G. MINETTE DE TILLESSE, _Le secret messianique dans l'evangile de Marc_, CBQ 31 (1969) 109-12; GRÄSSER, 1-23; WEEDEN, "Heresy," 145-58; _Mark_, _passim_.; though, cf. KELBER, _Kingdom_, 63.

[4]GEORGI, _Gegner_, 220ff.; KOESTER, _Trajectories_, 153, 191; ACHTEMEIER, "Gospel Miracle Tradition," 192ff., 195f.

[5]Thus, W. MANSON, _Jesus the Messiah_ (London, 1943) 45, taking issue with BULTMANN, stresses: "The form of all the healing narratives answers to that which we find in stories of miraculous cures recorded by secular writers of the period except that, as has been already indicated, Jesus is not like Apollonius of Tyana a _theios anthropos_, a virtuoso in divine science, whose acts point to the numen in himself, but is throughout a witness to the God of Israel and to the nearness of His kingdom and righteousness." Cf. also p. 36. H. C. KEE, _Jesus in History_ (New York, 1970) 134, objects: "It is almost surely too much to claim that there was a fixed type, the _theios aner_, to which Mark conformed the image of Jesus. This notion, which arose in the heyday of the history of religions school, has been repeated so often that it has come to be accepted as a fact. But in truth, except for a widespread fondness for apotheosis of great men, there is no set type or model of _theios aner_." Cf. also Kee's review of HAHN, _Christologische Hoheitstitel_ in JBL 83 (1964) 191-93; also "Terminology of Mark's Exorcism Stories," NTS 14 (1967-68) 232-46; "Aretalogy and Gospel," JBL 92 (1973) 402-22. Dissenting opinions have also been expressed by O. CULLMANN, _Christology of the New Testament_ (London, 1959. ET of 1957 German ed.) 272; K. PRÜMM, "Zur Früh- und Spätform der religionsgeschichtlichen Christusdeutung von H. Windisch," _Biblica_ 42 (1961) 391-422;

(cont.)

In one sense, the debate is centuries old, since comparisons between Jesus and similar religious figures were already
made in antiquity.[6] But, in another sense, the debate belongs
to the 20th century. The real beginnings of the modern awareness of the pluralistic religious setting in which Christianity
arose and spread can be said to stem largely from the catalytic
influence of the History-of-Religions School which emerged
during the early decades of the 20th century.[7] After R.
Reitzenstein published his two seminal works Hellenistische
Wundererzählungen (1906) and Die Hellenistischen Mysterien-
religionen (1910) and succeeded in forcing Biblical scholarship
for the first time to take serious notice of other ancient
religious traditions and the mutual interpenetration of these
traditions with the Judaeo-Christian tradition, it was no
longer possible to treat the origin and development of
Christianity in isolation from the many diverse religious and

---

43 (1962) 22-56; W. VON MARTITZ, art. υἱός, TWNT (1967,
fascicle) 8. 337-40; E. SCHWEIZER, art. υἱός, TWNT (1967) 8.
378f.; Jesus (London, 1971. ET of 1968 ed.) 127; "Neuere Markus-
forschung in USA," Evangelische Theologie 33 (1973) 533ff.;
P. STUHLMACHER, Das paulinische Evangelium I. Vorgeschichte
(Göttingen, 1968) 191f.; A M. AMBROZIC, The Hidden Kingdom.
A Redaction-Critical Study of the References to the Kingdom of
God in Mark's Gospel (Washington, D.C., 1972) 95ff.; O. BETZ,
"The Concept of the So-Called 'Divine Man' in Mark's Christ-
ology," in Studies in New Testament and Early Christian Litera-
ture [Wikgren Festschrift] (Leiden, 1972) 229-40; D. L. TIEDE,
Charismatic Figure as Miracle Worker (Missoula, Montana, 1972);
H. WEINACHT, Die Menschwerdung des Sohnes Gottes im Markus-
evangelium: Studien zur Christologie des Markusevangelium
(Tübingen, 1972); W. L. LIEFELD, "The Hellenistic 'Divine Man'
and the Figure of Jesus in the Gospels," JETS 16 (1973) 195-205.
Cf. also C. H. DODD, Interpretation of the Fourth Gospel
(Cambridge, 1953) 250ff.; A. D. NOCK, Early Gentile Christianity
and Its Hellenistic Background (New York, 1964) 44ff. Also,
for a sketch of another group of dissenters "fleeing to pseudo-
orthodoxy," cf. SMITH, "Prolegomena," 192ff.

[6]Justin Martyr, I Apol. 21-27; 54; Origen, C. Cel. 2.
49ff.; 3. 3, 42f.; 6. 8-11; 7. 9, 53; etc.; Jerome, Breviarum
in Psalmos, Ps. 81 end (Migne PL 26. col. 1130). References
cited in SMITH, "Prolegomena," 188:95-96. Cf. also Acts of
Pilate I (Hennecke-Schneemelcher 1. 449ff.).

[7]Cf. SMITH, "Prolegomena," 188ff., for his admittedly
abbreviated survey of the history of the problem. Also, TIEDE,
242ff. for the History-of-Religions influence on New Testament
studies; cf. W. G. KÜMMEL, The New Testament: The History of
the Investigation of Its Problems (London, 1973) 245ff.

philosophical streams flowing into the ongoing river of man's
religious history.

The impossibility of understanding the _theios_ _aner_ apart
from its connection with the History-of-Religions School is
evidenced by the fact that even after the expression became
integrated into the history of Biblical scholarship, it still
retained a primary History-of-Religions function by being
employed almost exclusively in discussions analyzing certain
features of the Judaeo-Christian tradition _vis à vis_ other
religious traditions.[8] This is graphically illustrated by the
simple fact that the expression _theios_ _aner_ never occurs in
either the Greek Old Testament or in the New Testament, but
derives instead from the alien world of Hellenism. In spite of
the recognition that within each separate religious tradition
of antiquity there could be found prominent religious figures
who possessed numerous traits in common, when the term _theios_
aner is employed in scholarly discussions today, almost without
exception it is understood to refer to an essentially _Hellenis-_
tic phenomenon. This tacit assumption that _theios_ _aner_ constitutes a pure strain, as it were, accounts for its function as a
constant against which variables are measured, specifically its
function in measuring relative degrees of Hellenization, i.e.
the process in which a clearly defined constant (Hellenism)
influences a clearly defined variable (e.g. Judaism). The very
term Hellenization, of course, presupposes a one-way movement
in the direction of the influence, and in the process the constant is assumed to be active, the variable passive. The
theios _aner_ question, therefore, at its core is a History-of-
Religions question, dealing not with intramural relationships
within the Judaeo-Christian tradition, but instead with the
extramural relationships between the Judaeo-Christian tradition
and _one_ other tradition, Hellenism. It is primarily concerned
with the nature and extent of the latter's influence upon the
former.

Although the expression _theios_ _aner_ never occurs in the
New Testament, the implications of the _theios_ _aner_ question for

---

[8]Thus, the subtitle of WINDISCH'S _Paulus_ _und_ _Christus_
was: "Ein biblisch-religionsgeschichtlicher Vergleich."
Numerous other examples could be cited.

New Testament studies cannot be adequately measured by the mere
occurrence or non-occurrence of the expression either in the
original sources or in contemporary discussions. The issues
arising out of the _theios_ _aner_ expression are broader than the
term itself, but whatever else the term does it serves as a
focal point at which these issues meet; in fact, it acts as a
kind of prism into which certain questions can be focused, the ✓
resultant diffraction serving to expose more vividly the inner
fabric of the questions and thereby inviting fresh and more
scrutinizing examinations.

Perhaps it will be worthwhile to delineate briefly some
of these issues.

Christology.

When the ordinate of Jesus' miracles and the abscissa of
his divinity (either his own claim or a claim made of him) are
plotted on a graph in contemporary scholarship, more often than
not, many scholars are finding _theios_ _aner_ at the point of
intersection, for it is chiefly in respect to these two foci of
Christological investigation that the expression seems to be
most frequently employed.

(1) Miracles.

It is significant that the presence of miracle traditions within the Gospels has provided the major rationale for
New Testament scholars to incorporate _theios_ _aner_ into their
discussions of Jesus and the Gospel tradition, a point that can
be easily documented by simply noticing that not only in the
earlier form critical studies,[9] but even in contemporary discussions[10] virtually without exception the _theios_ _aner_ is appealed
to in conjunction with discussions of miracles and miracle
traditions. D. L. Tiede correctly observes that one of the two
major ways in which the _theios_ _aner_ question has come to affect

---

[9]E.g., BULTMANN, Synoptic Tradition, 218ff.; DIBELIUS,
Tradition, does not employ the term _theios_ _aner_, but appeals to
the miracle traditions about contemporary miracle-workers in
explaining various features of the Gospel tradition. Cf.
Tradition, 75, 94ff. Similarly, BOUSSET, Kyrios Christos (ET)
100ff.

[10]E.g., KECK, "Mk. 3:7-12," 349ff.; H. D. BETZ, "Divine
Man," 114ff.; ACHTEMEIER, "Gospel Miracle Tradition and the
Divine Man," 174ff.; BULTMANN, John, 101f., passim.; to mention
only a few.

New Testament studies is in relation to redaction critical treatments of the Gospels.[11] While this is true, it is nevertheless striking that the common denominator of virtually all the redaction critical treatments of the Gospels which he surveys is their common preoccupation to interpret the _miracles_ and _miracle traditions_ within the Gospels.[12] Thus, that which really provides grist for the redaction critics' mill is the presence of miracle traditions in the Gospels.

Important though it is to notice the _fact_ of the occurrence of _theios aner_ in critical studies, it is equally important to notice the _function_ which it plays in such discussions, viz. its role in establishing a Hellenistic origin[13] not only of many of the Gospel miracle stories themselves but also of numerous motifs which are felt to have been added to originally Palestinian miracle stories.[14] In addition to the question of the provenance of the Gospel miracle traditions, _theios aner_ raises in its most acute form the question of the exact purpose of miracles and miracle traditions in early Christianity, not only in the Gospels but elsewhere in the New Testament, i.e. whether they were intended to authenticate a metaphysically understood divine sonship and thus were in closer proximity with Hellenistic miracle traditions, or whether, in closer proximity with Old Testament modes of thought, they were regarded as a means of demonstrating God's continuous intervention and activity in salvation-history.[15]

---

[11] TIEDE, 253f.

[12] So VIELHAUER, WEEDEN, KECK, GEORGI, H. D. BETZ, KOESTER, ROBINSON, BULTMANN, KÄSEMANN.

[13] BUTLMANN, _Synoptic Tradition_, 240, " ... the Hellenistic miracle stories offer such a wealth of parallels to the Synoptic, particularly in style, as to create a prejudice in favour of supposing that the Synoptic miracle stories grew up on Hellenistic ground." Further, "In Mark he (Jesus) is a _theios anthropos_, indeed more: he is the very Son of God walking the earth .... But this distinction between Mark and Q means that in Q the picture of Jesus is made essentially from the material of the Palestinian tradition, while in Mark and most of all in his miracle stories Hellenism has made a vital contribution" (241).

[14] BULTMANN, _Synoptic Tradition_, 239.

[15] Cf. W. MANSON, _Jesus the Messiah_, 33ff., who disagrees

In other words, when signs and wonders occur, what precisely do
they attest--the divinity of the miracle worker, the authenticity of the claim concerning the deity whom the miracle worker represents, the breaking in of the eschaton, or what? Not
that these were the only alternatives, even mutually exclusive
ones, but they do serve to illustrate the point. A related
question has to do with the role of miracles and miracle
traditions in Christian propaganda--how far did miracles performed by missionaries serve to validate the kerygma either in
missionary preaching or in edification of Christians? This
entire network of questions stems from the virtually unexcept-
ional association of theios aner and miracle-worker, which
raises all the more sharply such questions as whether such a
one-to-one correspondence existed within the Hellenistic-Jewish
apologetic tradition, and the function of miracles and miracle
traditions within these sources.

(2) Son of God.

Directly, if not inseparably, related to the problem of
miracle traditions is the Christological question concerning
Jesus' divinity, particularly those titles such as υἱὸς θεοῦ
which are thought to have been designations of his divine
personhood. Again, if one simply notices the contexts in which
theios aner is invoked in contemporary discussions, one finds
that it is usually in those sections of books on New Testament

---

with BULTMANN on these very grounds: " ... the emphasis in
both statements (Acts 2:22; 10:38) is on God and on acts of
God attending Jesus and investing him outwardly and visibly
with revelational significance. There is no reference in these
summaries to any manifestation of God made through the doctrine
of Jesus. Jesus the Messiah is accredited in this form of the
kerygma not by appeal to the divine truth of his teaching or to
the transcendent greatness and quality of his person, but
externally and phenomenally by the halo of divine signs attending him and authenticating him to Israel as the Deliverer sent
by God." Cf. also G. W. H. LAMPE, "Miracles in the Acts of the
Apostles," in Miracles, Ed. C. F. D. Moule (London, 1965) 163-
78, who analyzes Acts within the framework of these two
alternatives: "Luke's point of view ... is not that of a
writer describing the incredible performances of Hellenistic
wonder-workers. It is much closer to that of the Old Testament,
and especially Deuteronomy, the Deuteronomic Psalms and the
prophets. To these writers 'signs and wonders' are the manifest operations of God, his mighty works for the salvation of
his people" (166).

theology[16] and Christology[17] which deal with Jesus as Son of
God. Naturally, this question belongs hand in glove with discussions of miracle traditions, but it does constitute a
separate problem in some respects. In most discussions, after
the relative paucity of Old Testament and Jewish references to
υἱὸς θεοῦ applied to individuals is noticed, the focus shifts
to divine paternity and divine sonship in non-Jewish thought,
theios aner serving again as one of the near equivalents from
Hellenistic thinking. Its synonymity, if not identity, with
similar terms, e.g. υἱὸς θεοῦ, ἄνθρωπος θεοῦ, is usually
tacitly assumed, as the evolution of Christological development
from Palestinian to Hellenistic soil is traced. The function
of theios aner in explicating the emergence and blossoming of
υἱὸς θεοῦ is similar to its function in explaining miracle
traditions--to explain how and why the latter arose and
developed in the Hellenistic church. The shift to a more
metaphysical understanding of υἱὸς θεοῦ in contrast to the
more personalistic nuances of Old Testament thought is usually
detected within this emergence of theios aner within Christian
thought. It is in connection with the Christological question,
more strictly speaking, that theios aner plays a crucial role,
because of its ostensibly more direct conceptual similarity
with υἱὸς θεοῦ. Moreover, it is at this point that the development of theios aner in Hellenistic-Jewish thought emerges as a
crucial consideration, for the tendency of Jews to ascribe
divinity to their heroes is thought to have emerged within this
tradition of thought, and the direct continuity of this development with those aspects of the early Christian tradition in
which Jesus is asserted to be ὁ υἱὸς τοῦ θεοῦ is assumed. Thus
the question is raised as to the precise relationship between
the two expressions theios aner and υἱὸς θεοῦ, e.g. whether
theios aner is an appropriate category for discussing Jesus'

---

[16]BULTMANN, New Testament Theology, 1. 128ff.; H.
CONZELMANN, Outline of the Theology of the New Testament (New
York, 1969) 78, 129; A. RICHARDSON, Introduction to the
Theology of the New Testament (New York, 1958) 147ff., esp.
150.

[17]CULLMANN, Christology, 272; HAHN, Titles, 284ff.;
FULLER, Foundations, 68ff. Especially WETTER, Sohn Gottes;
BRAUN, "Christology," 100ff.

divine sonship. Or, the wider question of how far the expression theios aner even in Hellenistic thought denoted divinity
either exclusively or even primarily, as well as whether the
theios aner = υἱὸς θεοῦ equation is as patent in Hellenistic
thought as is often assumed, which is to say, how far is one
justified in translating theios aner by "divine man" and using
these terms interchangeably without further qualifications?
The investigation therefore inevitably becomes terminological
and forces a further look at the mutual relationship of such
expressions as υἱὸς θεοῦ, ἄνθρωπος θεοῦ, θεῖος ἀνήρ (= θεῖος
ἄνθρωπος), and a host of related expressions resulting when
such synonyms as ἔνθεος, δαιμόνιος, θεσπέσιος are juxtaposed
with ἀνήρ.

Historiography.

The History-of-Religions function of theios aner in
current discussions has been briefly alluded to, especially its
function in establishing a Hellenistic provenance for certain
features of the Gospel tradition. If we can return to the
analogy of a graph, it can be observed that the expression
theios aner is usually discovered in the quadrant designated
"Hellenistic Christianity," or sometimes "Hellenistic-Jewish
Christianity," that is to say, non-Palestinian Jewish Christianity. The reason for this is that theios aner is felt to
connote something distinctively Hellenistic, as opposed to
Jewish, and therefore functions in explaining Christological
conceptions within Sitze im Leben in which essentially non-
Jewish modes of thought are felt to have predominated.
Consequently, it does not normally function as a conceptual
framework for discussing Old Testament notions, e.g. prophet,
nor for discussing Christological thinking carried on within
an essentially Jewish matrix, although it often serves a
transitional function by providing a conceptual bridge for
interpreting how certain basically Jewish Christological conceptions came to be transformed into basically Greek categories.

At its very heart the expression theios aner embodies
Tertullian's question--if we can be allowed to lift it from its
context--"What has Jerusalem to do with Athens?" It was introduced into Biblical discussions when scholars presupposed a
dichotomistic view of the ancient Mediterranean world in which

one could speak with relative clarity--and confidence--of
Hellenism and Judaism as two separate, definable entities, and
in which the answer to Tertullian's question was "Very little,
if anything." In that setting theios aner proved useful as a
term to denote a concept belonging essentially to that half of
the world known as Hellenism, and consequently was regarded as
an inappropriate designation for describing anything or anyone
in Judaism. It thus functioned as a sort of control for contrasting these two distinct worlds. The degree to which a
concept from Judaism resembled theios aner, to that degree it
could be said to be Hellenized. A half-century of scientific
research has shattered this oversimplified picture of the
ancient world, and in addition to our knowing considerably more
about Jerusalem, we know now that Jerusalem had far more to do
with Athens than previously imagined.[18] Thus while the map has
been redrawn, the expression theios aner lingers and serves as
a constant reminder of how much contemporary New Testament
scholarship is still based upon the old map. Current discussions involving theios aner still reveal the tensions caused
by the simultaneous use of these two maps.[19]

Thus we become confronted with what James M. Robinson
calls the "crisis of categories":

> The current crisis at the basis of New Testament
> scholarship moves through the whole spectrum of
> its presuppositions and categories, from such
> empirical items as the correlated categories
> "Palestinian" and "Hellenistic" (presupposing a
> nonexistent correspondence between geographical
> and cultural boundaries) to the most abstract
> presuppositions of scholarship, its metaphysical
> (or antimetaphysical) assumptions.[20]

------

[18] S. LIEBERMAN, Hellenism in Jewish Palestine (New York,
1950); E. R. GOODENOUGH, Jewish Symbols in the Greco-Roman
World (New York, 1953-68), esp. vols. 2 & 3; M. SMITH, "The
Image of God. Notes on the Hellenization of Judaism with
especial reference to Goodenough's work on Jewish symbols,"
BJRL 40 (1958) 473-512; V. TCHERIKOVER, Hellenistic Civiliza-
tion and the Jews (Philadelphia, 1966); M. HENGEL, Judentum und
Hellenismus (Tübingen, 21973). Also, review by A. MOMIGLIANO,
JTS N.S. 21 (1970) 149-53; P. WENDLAND, Die hellenistische-
römische Kultur (Tübingen, 41972) 192-211.

[19] Cf. I. H. MARSHALL, "Palestinian and Hellenistic
Christianity: Some Critical Comments," NTS 19 (1973) 271-87.

[20] ROBINSON, Trajectories, 8.

The sheer difficulty of using such categories as "Hellenistic,"
"Hellenistic-Jewish," "Hellenistic-Jewish Christian," "Jewish,"
in discussing theios aner only underscores the pressing nature
of the inquiry. If it is no longer possible to speak with any
degree of confidence about what constituted being "Jewish,"[21]
how useful is theios aner as a term for measuring the degree of
Hellenization which Jewish notions underwent? Or, if, as M.
Hengel asserts, all Judaism, both in Palestine and the Diaspora,
of the Graeco-Roman period is to be understood as Hellenistic-
Judaism,[22] how far does theios aner perform a useful function
in illustrating the process of Hellenization in the Diaspora?
Even further, how useful is the expression in Christological
discussions? If it was useful in History-of-Religions and form
critical studies of the Gospels in the early part of this century in providing a means of accounting for the occurrence and
proliferation of miracle traditions, or in explaining how υἱὸς
Θεοῦ became a prominent feature of the Gospel tradition only
insofar as one could presuppose a sharp dichotomy between the
Palestinian and Hellenistic church, or even insofar as one
allowed intermediate subclassifications such as "Hellenistic-
Jewish Christianity"--and if the ground has shifted, how useful
is it today as a concept for Christological discussions? Does
the term need to be redefined to account for such a shift? Or,
does merely the function of the term in the scholarly discussions need to be altered?

Heresies.

The complexion of doctrinal aberrations within early
Christianity is yet a third question which comes to the fore in
theios aner discussions. The impetus for connecting certain
heresies and theological tendencies which ran counter to the
majority positions, at least from the viewpoint of the present
canon, is largely traceable to D. Georgi's provocative study
Die Gegner des Paulus im 2. Korintherbrief, in which theios
aner figures prominently in his analysis of the opponents of
Paul in 2 Corinthians. Of late, heresy-hunts have been

---

[21] TIEDE, 107.

[22] HENGEL, Judentum, 1.

extended to other parts of the New Testament, most notably
Mark's Gospel, where theios aner has been detected in the
theology of Mark's miracle source, which he reinterprets and
therefore corrects to bring it into line with the true implications of the cross.[23] These investigations represent a second
stage in the development of the theios aner hypothesis in that
they build upon the foundations of those analyses in which
theios aner has been applied to Jesus, especially as a miracle-
worker, and seek to trace the movement of this Christological
perspective as it works itself out, in these instances, in
aberrational rather than theologically acceptable positions.

Missionary Preaching.

A fourth area of New Testament research directly
affected by the theios aner question has to do with the early
Christian missionary preaching, both its content and method.
Again, the problem is freshly focused by Georgi, who strongly
emphasizes that Jewish missionaries in the Diaspora not only
propagandized in behalf of the Jewish faith by presenting their
heroes as theioi andres, i.e. "divine men" whose status was
authenticated by their miraculous powers, but also that they
themselves were theioi andres who employed pneumatic demonstrations of power to authenticate their own preaching activity.
The overall impression left by Georgi's analysis is that
pneumatic activity was a major feature of Hellenistic-Jewish
propaganda as well as that the depiction of Israel's heroes as
theioi andres and the enhancement of their status as miracle
workers was a major theme of such propaganda. Again, tracing a
direct line of continuity between Hellenistic-Jewish missionary
preaching and early Christian missionary preaching, he argues
that the same was true of Hellenistic-Jewish Christian
missionaries in the Diaspora, except that they also had added
Christ to their list of theioi andres. As late as 1969 he
could still speak with confidence of one type of early
Christian mission theology in which theios aner played a

---

[23]Cf. note 3 above. R. JEWETT, "Enthusiastic Radicalism
and the Thessalonian Correspondence," SBL Proceedings (Los
Angeles, 1972) 1. 181-232, esp. 212ff., uses theios aner in
analyzing the Thessalonian situation.

central role.[24]

The Theios Aner Hypothesis.

Although the debate usually focuses on specific New Testament issues, it should be remembered that the theios aner question insofar as it bears upon the New Testament is only part of a larger network of arguments whose general shape has been evolving since the turn of the century. A fairly clearly defined position has emerged and may be schematized as follows: (1) That within the Hellenistic world the theios aner was a widespread and popularly known figure who possessed a recognizable set of traits, the most prominent and recurrent of which were his divinity (or at least his uniquely conceived affiliation with the divine), itinerancy, and miracle-working; other distinguishing marks might also include prophesying, oracular and ecstatic utterances, wisdom, and rhetorical ability.[25]

---

[24]D. GEORGI, "The Form-critical Assessment of Miracle Stories," cited in TIEDE, 264.

[25]The classic example is Apollonius of Tyana of whom many studies have been made, including: F. C. BAUR, Apollonius von Tyana und Christus (Tübingen, 1832); J. HEMPEL, Untersuchungen zur Überlieferung von Apollonius von Tyana (Leipzig/Stockholm, 1920); H. D. BETZ, Lukian von Samosata und das Neue Testament (Berlin, 1961) is the most comprehensive recent treatment, including extensive bibliography; also, G. PETZKE, Die Traditionen über Apollonius von Tyana und das Neue Testament (Leiden, 1970). To date, BIELER still remains the sourcebook of pagan passages regarded as evidence for theios aner, though BETZ, Lukian, 100-44, provides a useful treatment of the position regarding the theios aner concept. Numerous other thumbnail sketches of theios aner have appeared. PFISTER, art. "Kultus," PWRE 11.2 (1922) 2106-2192, esp. 2125-38:" ... theioi andres, den Männern, die mit einem besonderen Charisma begabt sind und zu denen auch der Priester gehört" (2125); " ... theioi anthropoi ... Gottmenschen, die auf Erden wandelten und Wunder verrichteten. Schon die Sagen, die sich um die alten Heroen rankten, erzählten von ihren wunderbaren Fähigkeiten, Kenntnissen und Taten, so vom Zauberer und Arzt Cheiron, von Melampus und vielen anderen. Die Reihe dieser Wundertäter ist niemals abgerissen. Von Abaris und Aristeas berichtete man Ähnliches, von Pythagoras und Empedokles, Apollonios von Tyana, Alexander von Abunoteichos, Peregrinus Proteus, Simon Magus u.a. Der König Pyrrhos heilte wie der Kaiser Vespasian und Christus wie die Apostel" (2127). ACHTEMEIER, "Pre-Markan Miracle Catenae," 209f., "The characteristics of the theios aner can be summarized briefly: a wondrous birth, a career marked by the gift of overwhelmingly persuasive speech, the ability to perform miracles, including
(cont.)

(2) That within Jewish life and thought, especially as reflected in the Old Testament, the notion of a "divine man" was a contradiction in terms and therefore the expression theios aner is an inappropriate designation for such Old Testament figures as priests, prophets, judges, kings, and other "men of God."[26]

(3) That within Jewish thought, owing to the impact of Hellenization, a perceptible conceptual transformation begins to occur in the Hellenistic era as Jews, particularly in the Diaspora, in their efforts to propagate the Jewish faith (either by "missionary preaching" or "apologetic") begin to reinterpret and remodel their ancient Biblical heroes, most notably Moses, to conform to the image of the Hellenistic theios aner, so that by the first century A.D. it was not uncommon for Jews to conceive of and present their heroes to

---

healing and foreseeing the future, and death marked in some way as extraordinary;" similarly, "Gospel Miracle Tradition," 186f.; also cf. H. D. BETZ, "Jesus," 116. Also worth mentioning is M. NILSSON, Geschichte der griechischen Religion (München, 1950) 2. 505: "Wie gotterfüllte Bildnisse gab es auch gotterfüllte Menschen. Die Wundermänner der Spätantike waren moderner als diejenigen der archaischen Zeit, welche etwas den Schamanen ähnelten; sie waren auch nicht des Schlages der phönizischen und palästinensischen Propheten, die Celsus, wohl um Christus zu verringern, erwähnt (C. Cel. VII. 9) und die sich Götter oder Söhne eines Gottes oder das göttliche Pneuma nannten, Busse und das nahe Ende der Welt prophezeiten und Rettung denjenigen versprachen, die an sie glaubten. Die griechischen Wundermänner der Kaiserzeit waren ausgesprochen oder wenigstens halbwegs Philosophen; sie predigten eine höhere Gotteserkenntnis, eine strengere Moral, gerechte und strenge Lebensführung, sie verrichteten daneben auch Wunder, heilten Kranke, erweckten sogar Tote, offenbarten sich an entlegenen Plätzen. Sie waren theioi andres. Der berühmteste von diesen Männern war der am Ende des ersten nachchristlichen Jahrhunderts lebende Apollonios von Tyana ..." Cf. also K. PRÜMM, Religionsgeschichtliches Handbuch für den Raum der altchristlichen Umwelt (Rome, 1954) 458ff., esp. 54f. for extensive bibliography; OEPKE, art. ἀποκαλύπτω, TDNT 3. 567f.; O. WEINREICH, "Antikes Gottmenschentum," Neue Jahrbücher für Wissenschaft und Jugendbildung 2 (1926) 633-51; C. HABICHT, Gottmenschentum und griechische Städte (München, [2]1970); H. LEISEGANG, "Der Gottmensch als Archetypus," Eranos Jahrbuch 18 [Jung Festschrift] (Zürich, 1950) 9-45.

[26]Cf. quotation from NILSSON, note 25 above; HAHN, Titles, 289; WINDISCH, 90; BIELER, 2. 24f.; J. JEREMIAS, art. Μωυσῆς, TDNT 4. 849:5, "But we must not forget the basic distinction between the OT ἄνθρωπος θεοῦ, who is always God-related, and the deified Hellenistic theios aner."

non-Jews as "divine men" in this Hellenistic sense.[27]
(4) That since this change within Jewish thinking had already
occurred, or at least had been set in motion prior to the first
century A.D. and developed concurrently with Christianity during the first century A.D., it not only paved the way for but
made possible and stimulated early Christian conceptualizations
of Jesus especially in those areas of the church strongly
influenced, if not dominated by more Hellenistic as opposed to
Jewish modes of thought.

    Diagrammatically, this hypothesis may be sketched as
follows:

```
(1) Hellenistic
    Theios Aner
                    ↘
                     →  (3) Hellenistic Judaism  →  (4) Early Christianity
                    ↗        (Moses=theios aner)        (Jesus=theios aner)
(2) OT-Jewish Heroes
    ("Men of God")
```

    This study is concerned primarily with the middle
section (3) of the diagram, Hellenistic-Judaism, not because
the other three components are any less important--for each
would constitute a major study in its own right[28]--but because
of the crucial role it plays in the overall argument, and
ironically enough, because of its relative neglect in the
secondary literature on the subject.[29] The specific focus of
our inquiry is upon the nature and function of the theios aner
motif within Hellenistic-Jewish propaganda. An attempt will be
made to adduce and assess the relative evidence from two of the
major representatives of Hellenistic-Judaism, Josephus and
Philo, as well as a minor Hellenistic-Jewish author, Artapanus,
which bears upon the theios aner question. The inquiry will be
set within the larger context of the role which the theme of

---

[27]Cf. below, pp. 24ff.

[28]And, in some cases, has, e.g., on (1), BIELER, BETZ,
Lukian.

[29]E.g., out of 270pp., BIELER devotes 15 pp. to
Hellenistic-Jewish sources; WINDISCH, 15pp. out of 314 pp.;
HAHN, Titles, 288, depends upon BIELER and WINDISCH; FULLER
follows HAHN.

Israel's heroes plays within Hellenistic-Jewish propaganda with
a view to determining the relationship of the theios aner motif
within this larger context, i.e. whether its role is major or
minor, central or peripheral.

The decision to focus the investigation upon the question of theios aner insofar as it relates to Hellenistic-
Judaism, far from implying that the New Testament sources are
of secondary importance in addressing the question, arises out
of the conviction that any clear understanding of theios aner
depends to a large extent upon a clearer perception of how the
concept was used and understood in Hellenistic-Judaism. Moreover, it is only because the theios aner question has come to
impinge upon several crucial New Testament issues that such an
intensive concentration upon a single aspect of the question
can be justified. Thus, in one sense, this investigation per
se is a prolegomenon as it relates to New Testament studies,
but to the extent that it serves to clarify certain features of
early Christianity, it is hoped, to that extent it will illumi-
nate our understanding of the New Testament.

Protests.

Not surprisingly, the theios aner hypothesis has not
been without its critics. Having arisen under the impulse of
the History-of-Religions School, it was bound to catch some of
the opposition directed against the school as a whole.[30] The
fact that some of the most active proponents of the theios aner
hypothesis provided classic examples of the excesses of the
school only served to intensify the protests. The prodigious
effort to collect parallels from various religious traditions,
admirable though it was, often succeeded in composing the
character sketch of the theios aner by indiscriminately crossing chronological and geographical boundaries.[31] Of L.

---

[30]C. COLPE, Die religionsgeschichtliche Schule.
Darstellung und Kritik ihres Bildes vom gnostischen Erlösermythus (Göttingen, 1961); cf. E. R. DODDS, Pagan and Christian
in an Age of Anxiety (Cambridge, 1968) 31:1, 34:1; cf. KÜMMEL,
New Testament: History, 309ff. Also, K. HOLL, The Distinctive
Elements in Christianity, Trans. N. V. Hope (Edinburgh, 1937)
1ff.

[31]Of BIELER's THEIOS ANER, NILSSON, GGR, 2. 505:3, says,
(cont.)

Bieler's THEIOS ANER, M. Smith complains, "it was somewhat careless; the references were sometimes false and the texts sometimes misinterpreted; the choice of sources was questionable."[32] In a similar vein, Windisch's Paulus und Christus came under attack from M. Lagrange and C. A. A. Scott, both of whom called in question the excesses of the method he had employed. Scott wrote:

> He assumes that they (Paul and Christ) both belong to the type described in Hellenic literature as theioi andres and in the Old Testament as men of God, and the first third of the book is devoted to an interesting and exhaustive examination of the usage and significance of these two phrases, with a view to suggesting that both Jesus and Paul conform to these types. Here the author appears, at least in regard to the former of these phrases, to prove too much for his purpose. The illustrations he has collected, especially from Plato, are so copious and were used to decorate so many types of excellence that the phrase loses all technical significance, all connexion with its etymology.[33]

But the most comprehensive and damaging critique has come only recently in D. L. Tiede's The Charismatic Figure as Miracle Worker,[34] the major thrust of which is to demonstrate the diversity of ways in which charismatic figures were authenticated as divine, both in Jewish and non-Jewish traditions prior to the 3rd century A.D., and thereby question the common assumption that miracle-working traditions were the primary, if not the only, means of authenticating claims of divinity. By employing a more precise method of analysis which constantly reflects an awareness of such diversity, he illustrates what he rightly regards as a superior methodological approach which, if heeded, raises serious questions about the appropriateness of

---

"Ausführungen und Interpretation, ist eine typologische Darstellung, die auch die ältere Zeit und grosse geschichtliche Persönlichkeiten, von denen Wundertaten berichtet werden, heranzieht, die zeitlichen und örtlichen Verschiedenheiten aber beseite (sic) lässt."

[32]SMITH, "Prolegomena," 192.

[33]C. A. A. SCOTT, Review of WINDISCH, JTS 36 (1935) 85f.; M.-J. LAGRANGE, "Socrate et N. S. Jésus-Christ," Revue Biblique 44 (1935) 5ff.

[34]Cf. note 5 above. Also reviews by ACHTEMEIER, CBQ 35 (1973) 559-60; M. SMITH, Interpretation 28 (1974) 238f.

using the expression _theios_ _aner_ to signify a generally static
category under which are grouped traditions which were originally discrete as well as its function in serving as a means by
which these traditions are arranged in a linear sequence to
demonstrate historical continuity. He finds that the divine
wise man of the Greek philosophical tradition exercised greater
influence upon Jewish writers than a divine miracle-worker
motif.

Another group of works critical of this point of view
concentrated more upon the Christological question of how far
the portrait of Jesus as Son of God in the Gospel tradition has
been influenced by the Hellenistic concept of _theios_ _aner_. All
of the protests listed in M. Smith's review of the history of
the problem[35] fall into this category, whether they are trying
to show that υἱὸς θεοῦ in the Gospels is to be understood primarily in its Jewish milieu as opposed to its Hellenistic
milieu,[36] or whether they endeavor to demonstrate the phenomenological and theological differences between Jesus the
miracle-worker and other thaumaturges of antiquity.[37] Tiede
also concentrates on the question of miracle-working, but
instead of trying to demonstrate phenomenological differences
between Jesus and other miracle workers, denies the common
assumption that miracle-working was the primary, or even
necessarily an important means of authenticating claims to
divinity.[38] In this same vein, E. Schweizer still remains

---

[35]SMITH, "Prolegomena," 192f.

[36]So, W. GRUNDMANN, Die Gotteskindschaft in der
Geschichte Jesu und ihre religionsgeschichtlichen Voraus-
setzungen (Weimar, 1938); "Sohn Gottes," ZNW 47 (1956) 113-33;
J. BIENECK, Sohn Gottes als Christusbezeichnung der Synoptiker
(Zürich, 1951); C. MAURER, "Knecht Gottes und Sohn Gottes im
Passionsbericht des Markusevangeliums," ZTK 50 (1953) 1-38; J.
JEREMIAS, "Abba," ThLZ 79 (1954) 213f.; T. DE KRUIJF, Der Sohn
des lebendigen Gottes (Rome, 1962).

[37]H. PREISKER, Wundermächte und Wundermänner (Halle-
Wittenberg, 1952/3).

[38]TIEDE, 241, " ... the primary concern of this study
has been to document the nature of the _diversity of ways_
(emphasis mine) in which charismatic figures in the concentric
Hellenistic and Hellenistic Jewish spheres were authenticated
as having divine status ..." Further, "Because of the greater
(cont.)

unconvinced that the miracle-worker as a common type of figure
played a significant role in the Graeco-Roman world before the
second century A.D.[39] The M. Smith-H. C. Kee debate[40] falls
into this same category, although the focus of the question
shifts slightly from attention to υἱὸς θεοῦ or miracle traditions to the question of what is the most appropriate conceptual framework in which to interpret the Gospels, Mark in
particular, whether patterned after the Hellenistic lives of
divine men, i.e. aretalogies (Smith) or within the framework of
Old Testament/Jewish apocalyptic (Kee).

   Growing out of both types of protests is what may be
termed a lexicographical critique, lodged by W. von Martitz in
the TWNT article on υἱός.[41] Here was the first real attempt to
respond to the lexicographical imprecision of Bieler's work,[42]

---

availability of literary sources, the most clearly defined
stream of tradition that this study has identified is that of
the depiction of the heroes of moral virtues in the philosophical traditions. Whether the figure in question is Plato's
Socrates, Dio of Prusa's Diogenes, Plutarch's Alexander, or
Philo's Moses, the elevated or even divine status of the
charismatic figure rests upon his characterization as a sage
and possessor of virtue who can serve as a paradigm for moral
edification" (291).

[39]SCHWEIZER, Jesus, 127, cautiously argues that miracle-
workers found in the vicinity of Palestine, e.g. Syria,
probably provided the models for early Christian reflections
on Jesus as a miracle worker. Significantly, he refrains from
designating them theioi andres, evidently because of the
fluidity of the term: "The connection between these figures
(i.e. Hellenistic wonderworkers) and the Greek 'divine man' is
a matter of dispute. The divine man was originally only a
philosopher, poet, or statesman inspired by God, while the
figure of the miracle-worker does not appear in written sources
until the second half of the second century. It seems more
likely, therefore, that the picture of Jesus was shaped by the
miracles performed by Old Testament men of God, as depicted by
Hellenistic Judaism following the Old Testament, and by all
sorts of magical figures in Egypt and Syria" (127:10). Cf.
TDNT, 8. 378f.

[40]In a literal sense. Their respective papers which
appear in JBL 90 (1971) and JBL 92 (1973) were originally
presented across the same table at an SBL meeting in October,
1970, where their two essentially different viewpoints were
discussed.

[41]TDNT, 8. 335ff.

[42]TDNT, 8. 338:23, "The generous use of theios (cont.)

and the corresponding imprecision which resulted in Christological discussions in utilizing theios aner as an equivalent
or near-equivalent of υἱὸς θεοῦ.[43]

Focusing the Problem.

As mentioned earlier, this study seeks to clarify only
one aspect of the theios aner hypothesis so that the contours
of the larger question can be more sharply focused.

Having noticed some of the points at which the theios
aner question intersects New Testament studies, it may be
worthwhile to look at the other three components of the hypothesis (cf. diagram, p. 17).

There can be no doubt about the distinctly Hellenistic
texture of the expression theios aner nor that actual historical figures existed for whom the expression was an appropriate
and evidently accurate description. Nor can there be any doubt
about the relative ease, as compared with Old Testament thought,
with which the divine and human realms tended to merge within
Hellenistic thought, although facile explanations about Greek
conceptions of divinity and humanity have been rendered
impossible by the research of W. K. C. Guthrie in The Greeks
and Their Gods.[44]

---

aner in Bieler, passim gives the wrong idea that there was a
designation and fixed concept in this early period. Even with
aner or anthropos, theios is predicative; it is not a technical
term (emphasis mine)."

[43]TDNT, 8. 339f., "As regards the question whether
divine sonship is connected with the Hellenistic idea of the
theios aner it is thus to be noted that theios aner is by no
means a fixed expression at least in the pre-Christian era.
Theios is mostly used predicatively. Some are called theioi
without any ascription of a charismatic character. Others have
this character but never in the tradition are they called
theios. The term is not, then, an essential element in these
notions. One cannot tell from the material even that such
theioi are usually sons of gods .... When, therefore, divine
sonship is associated with description as theios this is quite
accidental. The conceptual spheres of divine sonship and
theios may well be related, but the terminology does not
support this association."

[44]GUTHRIE'S basic thesis is that there existed side by
side two diametrically opposed streams within Greek religion.
In one stream, "there was a great gulf between mortal and
immortal, between man and god, and that for man to attempt to

(cont.)

But whether the expression _theios aner_ was in any sense a technical term[45] and whether it denoted a fixed, definable sociological type is now regarded as a highly debatable, if not tenuous, assumption.[46] Apollonius of Tyana is still cited as the classic example of the Hellenistic _theios aner_ in the sense of an itinerant, miracle-working prophet, with Peregrinus running a close second. Although the expression occurs much earlier, e.g. in the Greek philosophical tradition, representatives of philosophical schools are seldom cited as examples of the _theios aner_. The most notable exception would be Pythagoras, especially as he came to be understood in some Neo-Pythagorean circles.

Nor can there be any doubt about the inappropriateness of the expression _theios aner_ to designate sociologically similar Old Testament figures, as evidenced by the non-occurrence of the term in the Greek Bible.

Given these two parallel streams, one is left with a limited number of options. Either the streams remained parallel, and thus never intersected, in which case _theios aner_ would be automatically excluded from New Testament discussions, since Christianity was unmistakably primarily an outgrowth of Judaism rather than Hellenism. Or, these two

---

bridge it was _hybris_ and could only end in disaster;" the other stream held "that there was a kinship between human and divine, and that it was the duty of man to live a life which would emphasize this kinship and make it as close as possible" (114). Guthrie's analysis demands more precision from statements about "_the_ Greek conception of the gods," such as ACHTEMEIER, "Gospel Miracle Tradition," 186f., who speaks of "the ease (in Greek religion) with which the divine passed into human form and became involved in the affairs of men (and of women!) .... This simply meant that the Hellenistic world was convinced that contemporary men, like the heroes of old, could be and were endowed with divine powers and ultimately could themselves become gods."

[45]VON MARTITZ, _TDNT_, 8. 338:23. Cf. note 42.

[46]TIEDE, 238, "To a large extent, the thrust of this study has been a negative evaluation of the interpretative significance of the generalized portrait of the _theios aner_ which has been extensively defended by Ludwig Bieler, among others." Further, " ... many scholars have been operating under the false impression that the term _theios aner_ was a fixed concept in the Hellenistic world" (289). Cf. STUHLMACHER, _Evangelium_, 191f.

24

streams converged, at which point(s) the Jewish viewpoint could
conceivably have been significantly altered, if not transmogri-
fied.

Of these two alternatives, the latter is more often
asserted to have occurred. The point of convergence is
generally taken to be Hellenistic-Judaism, which in turn is
thought to have acted as the midwife which brought the concept
from the womb of Hellenism into the world of Christianity.

It is this mediating role of Hellenistic-Judaism that
invites a closer investigation, and since it will be the primary focus of this study, some attention should be given to
elaborating more fully its function in the overall hypothesis.
(1) Reitzenstein.

The basic outline of the hypothesis can already be
detected in Reitzenstein, who begins his treatment of the
mysteries by distinguishing two basic types of religion in the
Near East:

> On the one hand, the more sober view held a more
> superficial, external connection between the divine
> and the human: the deity was felt to have created
> or elected a particular people and cared for it,
> especially for its representative, the king, i.e.
> so long as he remained faithful. Yet the deity's
> providential care was related only to the earthly
> life; no common substance or hope for another life
> bound man to him. The purest example of this
> viewpoint is to be found in the Babylonian and
> older Israelite religion. The other viewpoint
> holds that the soul, at least that of the legiti-
> mate members of the tribal religion, was essentially
> related to God, and therefore immortal. Man and God
> are thus infinitely much closer. The Iranian and
> Indian religions exemplify this point of view.[47]

Out of the Hellenistic world there emerges the conception of
the theios aner:

> A general conception of the theios anthropos, the
> God-man, begins to emerge. It bound together the
> deepest power of knowledge, prophecy, miracles and
> a form of personal holiness. Without positing
> such a conception, the appearance of such a preacher
> and wonderworker as Apollonius of Tyana or the seer
> and religious founder Alexander of Abonuteichos
> remains incomprehensible. Already previous to this,
> eminent Romans made it a practice to employ along
> with philosophers (or, instead of them) oriental
> prophets and ministers, as, for example Sergius

[47] REITZENSTEIN, Hell. Myst. (3. Aufl.), 5f.

Paulus in Acts, as well as Memmius, the patron of
Lucretius. It is regarded as a matter of course in
the literature that such men can know the future in
advance, heal the sick or can even raise the dead
again back to life, at least temporarily. In actual
life, the title of respect for such a person is
"prophet," while "trickster" (Goët) is the title of
derision. The explanation is apparently provided by
the character of oriental religion as such. For the
Stoic Chaeremon, the teacher of Nero, Egyptian
religion consisted of an astrologically oriented
nature-cult, plus magical prayers, by means of which
the spell of the stars could be broken. This is
conceivable if we realize that in the Day-cult of
the Egyptian priests every cult activity is essentially magic, and, if we realize that the inextric-
able connection between supernatural knowledge and
miraculous power, at this time regarded as self-
evident in Hellenism, finds its simplest explanation
in the basic viewpoint of the mysteries that union
with God is accomplished through supernatural knowledge and miraculous power, and that in the process
the prophet or miracle-worker actually becomes God.
Indeed we encounter everywhere the view that only
through this union can the magician do his miracles
and the seer or teaching-prophet see the future, or
the secrets of God; indeed, we discover that this
union with God entails the logical consequence that
while one performs magic or learns the future, one
becomes immortal.[48]

Once the notion theios aner had become initiated into the

mysteries, it became possible for him to take on all the traits

which, strictly speaking, could be documented from the

mysteries themselves, ecstasy, for example, and the resultant

union with God:

Ecstasy constituted the climax of the religious
life, and reached its fullest and most infallible
expression in the mysteries. If therein man could
become united with God, then it only followed that
he gained a direct knowledge, independent of
everything previously experienced, and that God,
from then on, would speak through his servant
dedicated to him. And thus for the believer this
becomes a new message, equally on par with, indeed
superior to the earlier messages.[49]

Proof of this viewpoint Reitzenstein finds in the Hermetic

literature in which Gnosis is regarded as seeing God, and where

such "seeing" and experiencing of God enables one to become

divine, i.e. attain salvation. Such a gift from God enlightens

---

[48] REITZENSTEIN, Hell. Myst. (1. Aufl.), 12f.

[49] Ibid., 18f.

men, in fact changes their substance; it pulls them through the body into the supra-sensual world, forming a new life, variously conceived of as the highest perfection of the soul, liberation from the body, the way to heaven, the means of salvation, true worship of God, and piety. In short, one becomes divine: "He who has Gnosis or is said to stand in Gnosis, that one is already as a man theios." (Cf. Corp. Herm. X. 9, ὁ γνοὺς ... ἤδη θεῖος; cf. XI. 355B.)

But, so far, we are still in the world of Hellenism. Where does this composite theological position penetrate Judaism? Reitzenstein's answer: Philo.

> It will be remembered that Philo of Alexandria, who always wanted this higher knowledge he spoke of to be understood as direct communication of the soul with God, correspondingly called certain passages of his published writings "mysteries," which should be read only by one who had been initiated; in fact, they could only be understood by such a one in any case. This view cannot be merely a conventional phrase, deduced from Plato and developed further. Philo's entire religious position and self-evaluation depends upon this; even less can this viewpoint be deduced from Judaism, since it does not acknowledge such communication with God, at least in its official form of theology. Hellenistic theology, which more and more has as its aim the intimation of the secrets (μυστήρια) of God, or to preach these secrets, and which attributes its knowledge to direct communication with God, provides the only explanation. And, here I see a further confirmation of the view that already in Philo's time there existed a literature similar in basic character to the one outlined above (i.e. the mystery literature). As a kind of magical instruction becoming a kind of devotional literature, it seeks to awake within those standing afar off the reality of the power of God who is at work within religion, and within those already converted it seeks to enhance the awe for the preacher of such secrets. Thus, in doing so, it follows the form of ancient secret literature, although unintentionally, and it acquiesces to the conviction (or fiction) that the power of God also of this new revelation can become perceptible only to the one who is called or determined beforehand by God.[50]

(2) Windisch.

The same basic schema is adopted by Windisch, reflected, among other things, in the method of arranging his material.

---

[50]REITZENSTEIN, Hell. Myst. (1. Aufl), 37f.

His first chapter is devoted to "Die theioi andres der
griechischen-römischen Antike," followed by a chapter on "Die
israelitischen Gottesmänner und ihre hellenistische Interpretation." His enthusiasm for finding theioi andres everywhere
is clearly apparent in his analysis of the Old Testament
materials. At the outset, he concedes that Israelite theology,
with its belief in the transcendence of God, precluded the
notion of a man's becoming divine,[51] a caveat which, if taken
seriously, would have largely undercut his interpretation.
Yet, he contends that the Old Testament heroes had many traits
in common with Hellenistic theioi, and in essence proceeds with
his investigation as if the Old Testament notion ἄνθρωπος θεοῦ
and the Hellenistic notion theios aner were identical:

> Thus the Old Testament "men of God" and "men of
> the Spirit" are actually Israel's theioi andres.
> Standing closest to the genuine theioi of the
> Greeks (the seers, oracle-priests, and inspired
> persons) are the old nabhis, the fortune-tellers,
> the ecstatic, the "corybants" of Samuel's time,
> the Nasireans, the small and great seers, also
> Balaam, the prophetic poets, and in another
> category are the priests with their taboos, their
> cultic powers and privileges, and their oracles;
> also the magicians, the necromancers, and
> diviners--an important group of old Greek theioi--
> are found in Israel, indeed are derided, condemned,
> and banned as illegitimate by the Law and by the
> genuine prophets of Yahweh (Num. 23:23)--not an
> unimportant difference between Greek and Israelite
> religion. Also, those "men of God" whose image in
> the tradition became embroidered with miracle-
> legends have their counterpart in the "divine"
> wonderworker of Greek antiquity. I am thinking of
> Pythagoras, Empedocles, Apollonius of Tyana on the
> one hand, and Moses, Elijah, Elisha on the other.[52]

Still, like Reitzenstein, Windisch maintains the essential
differences between the Hellenistic and Israelite traditions:

> The Greek and Israelite "man of God," as similar
> as they are to each other, have nevertheless not
> been mutually influenced in their formation;
> though, they might possess some common roots in
> the pre-historical popular religion and in the
> oriental cult of the kings. But both developments
> and lines of tradition were bound to converge. Philo
> of Alexandria performed their first synthesis.[53]

---

[51]WINDISCH, Paulus und Christus, 90.

[52]Ibid., 92f.   [53]Ibid., 101.

Again, like Reitzenstein, Windisch sees the crucial point of convergence in Hellenistic-Judaism:

> (Philo) looked up not only to the exalted patri-
> archs, to Moses and the prophets, but also
> recognized the Stoic wise man as an ideal as
> well as the image of the ecstatic who penetrated
> to the true vision of God. The theioi in the
> Torah and the Prophets and the theioi of the Stoa
> and the mysteries are both holy and living tradi-
> tions to him. He thus interprets the figures of
> the Bible in the context of the teaching of
> deification as understood by the Stoa and the
> teachings of the mysteries. This synthesis is
> already seen in the fact that he employs both of
> the typical titles ἄνθρωπος θεοῦ and (more seldom)
> theios.[54]

Windisch is not completely unaware of the weak links in his chain of argument, such as his rather telling concession that "one might get the impression that Philo avoids the predicate theios." Yet even if the term is absent, the idea is present, Windisch affirms, as seen not only in Philo's use of the Stoic notion of the ideal wise man, but also in his use of θεσπέσιος ἀνήρ, a clear proof that he has moved beyond the Jewish "man of God" to the Greek "divine man":

> Thus Philo has encompassed Greek and Biblical-
> Jewish teaching by his equation of thespesios
> aner and theios aner. If he had any qualms about
> using the traditional term theios too often, then
> the more frequently employed thespesios is per-
> fectly congruent in terms of the meaning which it
> contains. It is interesting to see how many
> individual types of the Greek theios-tradition
> his thespesioi andres encompass: the divine
> singer, the divine lawgiver, the ecstatic, the
> exegete of the inspired oracles, the wise man,
> and the philosopher. The list is almost
> exhaustive.[55]

The clearest example of theios aner in Philo is provided by the description of Moses' death in Vita Mosis 2. 288ff., which Windisch takes to be a description of his apotheosis:

> No further proof is required to show that in this
> description of the deified and divine Moses there
> reverberates the entire Greek teaching of the
> theios aner, multi-faceted though it is. Moses
> is the divine ruler, lawgiver, seer, fortune-teller,
> divine philosopher, logos, mystic and hierophant;

---

[54]WINDISCH, Paulus und Christus, 101.

[55]Ibid., 111f.

he is Pythagoras, Empedocles (the "god"), Lycurgus, Plato, Chrysippus, Augustus--all in one; he is God for mankind. Philo also emphasizes that Moses actually unites in himself every conceivable representative of the deified man. Thus, the Moses of Philonic speculation appears as the most grandiose summary of the Greek-Biblical theios concept.[56]

His final assessment of the mediating role of Philo:

Philo stands in the middle between Judaism and early Christianity, just as he is also the middle-man between Biblical and Greek-syncretistic religion. This applies also to the development of the Biblical-Hellenic idea of theios. Philo fuses the theios of Greek religion, mystery teachings, and philosophy with the Biblical "man of God." The great figures of the Old Testament, Abraham and Moses, the prophets and high priests, appear in him as the theioi of Plato, the Stoa, the mysteries. He describes not only their god-like, mediating nature, but also the process of their deification.[57]

Further,

In Philo the men of God of the Old Testament tradition have become Hellenistic-syncretistic theioi.[58]

The other representative of Hellenistic-Judaism, Josephus, serves as Windisch's second witness to testify to the "Hellenizing of the Biblical concept of prophecy."

(Josephus) describes the nature and work of the old prophets with the expressions of the Greek mantis. Although he is well acquainted with the Jewish doctrine of the distance between God and man (cf. Bellum 7. 344), he nevertheless uses the word theios as an attribute for Moses and the prophets. Whoever understands the furnishings of the tabernacle and the garments of the high priest and their significance will recognize in the lawgiver a theion andra (Ant. 3. 180). History exhibits the many τεκμήρια τῆς ὑπὲρ ἄνθρωπον δυνάμεως αὐτοῦ (Ant. 3. 318). Moses was for Josephus more than a mere man, more than ψιλὸς ἄνθρωπος, as Christianity later said of him. Similarly, everyone acknowledges that the prophet Isaiah is called θεῖος καὶ θαυμάσιος τὴν ἀλήθειαν (Ant. 10. 35). Saul is called ἔνθεος, which has the same meaning as theios (Ant. 6. 76). In Bellum, as in the conclusion of Antiquitates, Josephus reports of fortunetellers whose predictions were fulfilled, and of "prophets" who were imposters (γόητες). In particular, does he tell of ecstatics

---

[56]WINDISCH, Paulus und Christus, 106.

[57]Ibid., 112.   [58]Ibid., 112.

and prophets, thus of <u>theioi</u>, who appeared
shortly before the destruction of Jerusalem,
above all of that Jesus, who cried out continu-
ally like a maniac his "Woe Jerusalem" until he
perished in battle with a "Woe is also me." And,
Josephus considered himself to be one of these
genuine fortunetellers, since, shortly prior to
his imprisonment he had received a prophecy in an
ecstatic trance which was fulfilled miraculously
in Vespasian (<u>Bell</u>. 3. 350ff.) .... In every case,
from a Hellenistic standpoint, he is also a <u>theios</u>,
a little Moses, similar to the Maccabean leader
John Hyrcanus, who according to his report was not
only priest and king but prophet.[59]

Windisch can thus conclude by saying:

Thus, like Philo, Josephus is a middle link between
Judaism and Hellenism, also between Hellenistic-
Judaism and early Christianity. Although one must
disregard his hypocritical character, nevertheless,
there are some features about him that can be said
to be similar to features of Paul, indeed Jesus as
well, in spite of the contrasts which are obvious
in such comparisons.[60]

(3) <u>Bieler</u>.

As suggested by the subtitle "Das Bild des 'Göttlichen
Menschen' in Spätantike und Frühchristentum," L. Bieler's
THEIOS ANER, strictly speaking, belongs to the history-of-ideas.
It is an attempt primarily to prove the existence of <u>an</u> idea--
that there existed in late antiquity and early Christianity a
well defined conceptual type (<u>Typus</u>), the <u>theios aner</u>--as well
as in some measure to elucidate its content--i.e. compose a
character sketch of the <u>theios aner</u> personality (pp. 22-140 of
vol. 1). Intentionally, <u>Bieler primarily treats neither the
idea within history nor the history of the idea</u>; it is, as it
were, a quest for the Platonic form of the <u>theios aner</u>,[61]
although unlike Plato, Bieler does not admit the possibility
of a single αἰσθητός <u>theios aner</u> ever possessing all the traits
of the νοητός <u>theios aner</u>.

---

[59]WINDISCH, <u>Paulus</u> <u>und</u> <u>Christus</u>, 113.

[60]<u>Ibid</u>., 114.

[61]BIELER, 1.4, "Sie (this study) will vielmehr den
Gesamttypus, gewissermassen die platonische Idee des antiken
Gottmenschen schauen lassen, der sich, mag der einzelne <u>theios</u>
gleich nie und nirgends alle wesentlichen Züge in letzter
Vollkommenheit lückenlos in sich vereinigen, doch in jedem
seiner Vertreter, bald mehr, bald weniger ausprägt."

The fundamental differences between the Hellenistic and the Biblical thought-worlds stand in an uneasy, and in some respects, unresolved tension throughout the work. The historical and conceptual continuity of the Old Testament and New Testament, and the discontinuity of both of these to Hellenistic thought (and Far Eastern thought) calls for some explanation by Bieler in view of the fact that all three traditions yield essentially identical formal portraits of the theios aner personality within their respective traditions. For all practical purposes, the solution follows the lines set forth by Reitzenstein and Windisch, albeit slightly modified and more tightly argued. Like Windisch, Bieler analyzes the Old Testament heroes with the theios aner category, while at the same time conceding fundamental differences between Old Testament theioi andres and Hellenistic theioi andres:

> Their most striking difference as compared with the Hellenic (theioi andres) is the fact that Judaism knows of no heroization of men in the ancient (Hellenic) sense, and therefore of no hero-cult: Old Testament theocracy draws a sharp line of demarcation between God and man, which is illustrated even in the names used for the "God-sent" individual: he is never called theios anthropos, but only ἄνθρωπος θεοῦ. And this designation is as well established (in the Old Testament tradition) as theios aner is in classical antiquity.[62]

The implications of this fundamentally different viewpoint are worked out in two directions. On the one hand, in a strong attachment of the prophet to God, manifested, for example, in the fact that God is the real subject of the actions performed by the prophet, be they prophesying or miracle-working; on the other hand, in a keen awareness of the limitations of humanity:

> (the Old Testament "man of God") ... remains man in the fullest sense--man especially in his sinfulness--a self-conscious awareness that was particularly high among Jews, almost unknown in classical antiquity: Moses' despondency and punishment, Samson's weakness, Saul's fall, David's sin and repentance are a few examples.[63]

Hellenistic-Judaism, for Bieler, sees the merger of these two viewpoints:

---

[62]BIELER, 2. 24.   [63]Ibid., 2. 25.

The Diaspora provided opportunities for more and
more contacts with Hellenism. Also, it invited
comparisons with respect to religious leaders,
which naturally stimulated types of thinking which
sought to prove that those persons within one's
own religious heritage who were regarded as
specially elected by God were of equal stature to
pagan heroes--indeed, superior to them. It thus
became easy for one's own prophet to be modelled
more and more in the style and in the colors of
the Hellenistic theioi andres. Philo and Josephus
provide us the best examples of this.[64]

.... Hellenistic-Judaism soon saw its great men,
its prophets, heroes and kings as theioi andres in
the Hellenistic sense. Thus, Josephus, Antiq. 3.
180 says that whoever takes a look at the splen-
dour of the holy garments and vessels will see τὸν
... νομοθέτην (εὑρήσει) θεῖον ἄνδρα. More instructive
is a comparison of a passage of the LXX with its
counterpart in Josephus. The LXX describes the
impression left by the famous decision of King
Solomon (3 Kms. 3:28) thus: καὶ ἤκουσαν πᾶς Ἰσραὴλ
τὸ κρίμα αὐτοῦ ὃ ἔκρινεν ὁ βασιλεύς, καὶ ἐφοβήθησαν
ἀπὸ προσώπου τοῦ βασιλέως, ὅτι εἶδον ὅτι φρόνησις
θεοῦ ἐν αὐτῷ τοῦ ποιεῖν δικαίωμα. In contrast,
Josephus, Ant. 8. 34 says κἀξ ἐκείνης τὸ λοιπὸν τῆς
ἡμέρας ὡς θεῖαν ἔχοντι διάνοιαν αὐτῷ προσεῖχον.
The Biblical text is still in view, Solomon is not
directly called theios aner, but the entire manner
of expression has nevertheless moved in the direction of the Hellenistic God-man.[65]

Further evidence for Josephus' bending of the Old Testament
heroes towards Hellenistic theioi andres Bieler detects in the
depiction of Abraham as Kulturbringer (following Artapanus),[66]
various Haggadic embellishments of Old Testament characters,
the enhancement of miracle-working activity in narrating
various Old Testament stories, and most especially in the
propensity to give "secularized" explanations of Old Testament
events, the main consequence of which is to push God more and
more into the background. His overall treatment of Moses in
Antiquitates 2-3, being propagandistically motivated, indicates
that "he wants to achieve his aim above all so that he conforms
the figure Moses to the general syncretistic type of theios
aner as much as he possibly can."[67]

In contrast to Josephus, Philo, according to Bieler,

---

[64]BIELER, 2. 24.   [65]Ibid., 1. 18f.

[66]Ibid., 2. 26.   [67]Ibid., 2. 30.

... does not want to boast that the proud civilized nations of the West are indebted to the Jews for their knowledge, nor does he want to out-trump their holy books and engage in a contest with reference to their contents as to the deeds of a theios aner; he is instead interested in proving the religious worth and the philosophical depth of the holy tradition. Filled with religious conviction and possessing a philosophical bent, and equally conversant with Jewish revelation and Greek thought, he seeks the unity of both along the path which religious faith had always trod: for him it was certain that all genuine human wisdom was contained implicitly in the divine revelation. Thus, in Νόμοι ἄγραφοι, from which the periods about Abraham and Joseph are preserved he almost never goes beyond what the Old Testament contains: the direct enlightenment by God is retained in the story of Joseph, for example, exactly as in Genesis (cf. Jos. 90, 107, 110), and whereas Josephus calls him σωτὴρ τοῦ πλήθους (Ant. 2. 94), Philo only speaks of the πνεῦμα θεῖον within him. Occasionally, in contrast to Josephus, the specifically religious motivation is highlighted even stronger than in the Old Testament.... It is in harmony with Philo's nature to emphasize especially the ethical element (in narrating Biblical events) ...68

Thus, at least in one respect, and also in the description of Old Testament figures, Philo comes much closer to the Greeks than Josephus ever managed to do, in spite of some external embellishments by the latter.69

In his Vita Mosis Philo depicts the lives of the patriarchs as νόμοι ἄγραφοι, although this time he has in view the outside world when he portrays Moses as a Greek philosopher dressed as a Jewish prophet. In a manner very similar to Iamblichus' Life of Pythagoras, Philo singles out Moses' precocity as a child as well as taking note that he received philosophical training of a Platonic character, and as a result embodied ὁ σοφός. As a reward, God gave him true riches, κοινωνὸν τῆς ἑαυτοῦ λήξεως, which included powers over the cosmos. As the giver of the law he is νόμος ἔμψυχος. Thus,

This Moses is not the prophet of the Old Testament, nor is he the usual theios of Hellenism, the typical hero of miracle-addicted aretalogies. To be sure, the ideal of the Greek φιλόσοφος of the classical stamp, in the last analysis, does not remain any less strange to him, even if there is an attempt to capture the essence of his personality by using the Stoic ideas and formulae. Instead, he is the

---

68BIELER, 2. 29.   69Ibid., 2. 30.

πνευματικός, in whom centuries later the pagan
as well as Christian Gnosis saw the perfect man--
that Gnosis which is already announced so
impressively in Philo.[70]

(4) Georgi.

Although the special focus of Georgi's investigation is
the problem of Paul's opponents in 2 Corinthians, the subtitle
Studien zur religiösen Propaganda in der Spätantike indicates
the real thrust of the book, and even though his interpretation
of the Corinthian problem has not gained full acceptance,[71] the
extended middle section comprising a History-of-Religions
analysis of Jewish, pagan, and Christian missionary methods and
motivations is still often referred to as something of a defi-
nitive treatment of the subject, primarily because of his
evident perusal of the original sources bearing on the question.
The length of the section (pp. 82-213!) as well as its location
in the center of his treatment illustrates the crucial role it
plays in the overall movement of the book. Stated briefly,
Georgi holds that Paul's opponents in 2 Corinthians are linked
with Diaspora synagogue circles and that their mission theology,
indeed their theology as a whole, stands in direct continuity
with Hellenistic-Jewish theology as worked out in a Diaspora
Sitz im Leben during the Hellenistic era, and that this
theology can be reconstructed with some degree of certainty, in
fact a high degree of certainty, from the literary remains that
have come to be known as Hellenistic-Jewish apologetic. The
distinctive features of this theology included a Hellenized
metaphysical viewpoint which made it easier for a Jew to conceive of his being able to share in the divine than was otherwise possible on Old Testament presuppositions.[72] Evidence of
this basic theological-philosophical shift is to be detected in
the heightened awareness of the cosmic order in which every man
to some degree participated, although not to so intense a
degree as those persons who regarded themselves or were regarded by others as singularly in tune with the divine. Movement

---

[70]BIELER, 2. 36.

[71]Cf. C. K. BARRETT, "Paul's Opponents in II
Corinthians," NTS 17 (1971) 233ff.

[72]GEORGI, Gegner, 140ff.

between the divine and human realm, conceptually, came to be
regarded in dynamic terms, thus as a process, whereas formerly
more static categories had dominated conceptions of the universe and the divine order. The more frequent occurrence of
δύναμις within the sources bears witness to this shift from
static to dynamic categories. The impact of this metaphysical
shift enabled Jews for the first time to conceive of persons,
who were either especially elected by God or regarded as hold-
ing a particularly close relationship with Him, as sharing in
the divine, and thence to view these persons, either past or
present, as receptacles of the cosmic δύναμις--in other words,
as theioi andres whose hallmark was the ability to work
miracles.[73] Pneumatic activity therefore came to play an
increasingly crucial role in propaganda, both as a means of
authenticating a Jewish missionary's message as well as a
category into which Biblical heroes could be recast so as to
make them, and therefore the Jewish faith, more attractive and
convincing to outsiders. Theios aner thus becomes a self-
conscious category in which Jewish missionaries begin to conceive of themselves and their former heroes, primarily for
propagandistic reasons.

Hellenistic-Jewish Christianity, i.e. Christianity whose
basic roots were grounded in Diaspora synagogues, became heirs
of this Hellenistic-Jewish theology, and the particular blend
combatted by Paul in 2 Corinthians represents the amalgamation
of a theological viewpoint dominated by a loyalty to Jewish
tradition as mediated by its more Hellenized interpreters,
combined with a pneumatic self-consciousness, with which has
been fused a Christology and resultant understanding of
Christian faith informed by those aspects of the Christian
tradition favorable to such a viewpoint, viz., the thaumaturgic
Jesus traditions and pneumatic activity as a proof of God's
δύναμις, i.e. the mission theology reflected in Mark and Luke-
Acts which highlights the power of the kingdom. Thus the
opponents which Paul combats in 2 Corinthians are Hellenistic-
Jewish Christian missionaries who preach ἄλλος ᾿Ιησοῦς, Jesus
the theios aner, the thaumaturge, and who possess a view of the

---

[73]GEORGI, Gegner, 145ff.

Christian ministry which allows them to view themselves as
theioi andres who are preoccupied with demonstrating their
δύναμις by performing signs and wonders--a view most conducive
to boasting. In both respects they are undercutting Paul's
foundational work and his continuing relationship with the
Corinthian church. His response necessarily is framed in terms
of reiterating and further delineating his fundamentally anti-
thetical view of a theologia crucis in which the suffering of
Christ is central and which gives rise to a view of Christian
ministry authenticated by suffering and dying daily with
Christ, which has no room for boasting.

Even though Georgi's analysis of Hellenistic-Judaism
depends heavily upon the research of E. R. Goodenough, who
everyone admits successfully questioned the sharp dichotomy
between Palestinian Judaism (i.e. normative, orthodox, undiluted Judaism) and Hellenistic Judaism (i.e. aberrant, hererodox,
impure Judaism) which had served as the presuppositional framework within which earlier scholarship had worked,[74] one can
detect a certain tension throughout Georgi's analysis created
by his tacit approval of the dichotomistic categories which
underlay the investigations carried on during the earlier part
of the twentieth century, especially by the History-of-
Religions School. The Judaism Reitzenstein analyzed, Philo in
particular, has radically changed in complexion over the last
half-century, and ironically Georgi's Judaism is in many
respects more similar to Reitzenstein's than to Goodenough's.
In fact, Georgi's large section devoted to missions in
antiquity has a pervasive Reitzensteinian complexion. This is
particularly evident not only in his basic equation of
Hellenistic-Judaism and Diaspora Judaism (though not always an
unqualified equation), but also in his easy identification
between the propaganda tactics of the mystery religions and
those of Hellenistic-Jews. Reitzenstein's original statement
about the missionary activities of the mystery religions could
serve as a succinct summary of Georgi's understanding of
Hellenistic-Jewish missionaries:

---

[74]GOODENOUGH, Symbols, vols. 2-3. Also, reviews by A.
D. NOCK, in Essays on Religion and the Ancient World (Oxford,
1972) 2. 877ff.

> The rapid spread of those cults into remote cities
> scarcely touched by regular trade and commerce
> cannot be understood if we fail to keep in sharp
> focus those few notices concerning the activity of
> wandering ministers of individual oriental deities.
> I would not--and have never been able to see those
> persons as being official priests who were employed
> by particular sanctuaries of the homeland. But
> they nevertheless functioned as priests and prophets
> and authenticated their proclamation by the ecstatic
> spirit (Geist) of their speech, as well as by pro-
> phesying and miracles.[75]

In at least two other respects is the similarity also striking:
first, the depiction of Jewish missionaries as theioi andres.
Reitzenstein had emphasized that in the mysteries there could
be experienced true Gnosis, the union of the initiate with God,
and to the priests and prophets of the mysteries was given
direct revelation of the heavenly secrets:

> Even up until the final demise of paganism,
> revelation and direct visions remained for the
> priest the effect and climax of the true cult;
> he saw the deity and the deity spoke (from) out
> of him; only thus could one choose the Greek
> designation prophet for the highest priestly
> class.[76]

The second important feature has to do with the process by
which missionaries ignited the divine force within themselves
by which they qualified as theioi andres, viz. exegesis of the
sacred books. This, for Georgi, is most important, since his
analysis depends heavily upon his being able to move from the
assertion that missionaries depicted their heroes as theioi
andres to the claim that they themselves were theioi andres.[77] ✓
Thus the miraculous power sparked by reading and interpreting
the holy books, which Georgi finds to be the essential earmark
of Diaspora synagogue theology, Reitzenstein saw in the
mysteries:

> Whoever published the writing about regeneration
> as a book, expected that the reader, if God would
> give him grace, would feel the same effect by
> his reading as Tat did allegedly when listening;
> the miraculous power of divine revelation works

---

[75] REITZENSTEIN, Hell. Myst. (1. Aufl.), 11f.

[76] Ibid., 19.

[77] GEORGI, 168ff.

from the written word (printed page) too.[78]

This whole package which included a view of the cult as
a mystery in which union with God, i.e. true Gnosis, was
experienced, and which was propagated by priests and prophets
whose distinguishing characteristics were itinerancy, possession of miraculous powers, variously designated as miraculous,
pneumatic, ecstatic, and prophetic, all of which served to
confirm the message they preached--is alleged to have been
mediated to Christianity via Hellenistic-Judaism. The transfer
takes place not in Palestine, but in the Diaspora, the homeland
of Hellenistic-Judaism, where this Hellenistic apparatus had
already been incorporated into Judaism and thus becomes
Christianized when members of Diaspora synagogues become
Christians and begin to spread their message as they had previously done. In the overall movement of the argument, theios
aner acts as the shuttle shooting the Hellenistic thread of the
woof through the Jewish threads of the warp so that in the end
it shows up in every square inch of the tapestry.

In many respects, therefore, Georgi's work resembles
that of his predecessors, such as in his assumption that
Hellenistic-Judaism is the crucible in which the alien Hellenistic theios aner becomes mixed with the Jewish tradition.
Yet, his work represents a major step in the development of
the theios aner hypothesis for several reasons. Formerly, when
theios aner was used in explaining Christological development,
its incorporation into Christianity, say through υἱὸς θεοῦ, was
regarded as a legitimate synthesis of modes of thought which
lay ready to hand. In other words, it functioned as a means of
explaining legitimate Christological development. In Georgi,
theios aner becomes the property of heretics.[79] The opponents
in 2 Corinthians possess a theios aner Christology, but it is
heretical, at least to Paul's way of thinking. Or, even if the
Christology reflected in Mark and Luke-Acts also reflects a
theios aner Christology, it nevertheless has all the potential
for becoming transformed into an aberrant Christology which can
undercut a theologia crucis. In either case, the debate has

---

[78]REITZENSTEIN, Hell. Aufl. (1. Aufl.), 36.

[79]Cf. note 3 above.

moved beyond the stage of conventional discussions of Christological development. Another distinctive feature of Georgi's
treatment is the comprehensive analysis of theios aner against
the background of Hellenistic-Jewish apologetic. Hellenistic-
Judaism as the locus at which the alien Hellenistic theios aner
concept was naturalized in the Jewish tradition, as we have
seen above, had been stated earlier, but only stated. Windisch
and Bieler, for example, had adduced various passages from
Philo and Josephus as proof that they were bending Old Testament heroes in the direction of the Hellenistic theios aner,
but Georgi is the first, to my knowledge, to attempt a comprehensive explanation of the theological and metaphysical shift
within Hellenistic-Jewish thought that both enabled and
stimulated the development of the theios aner concept. While
others had noticed that something different was happening within Hellenistic-Jewish authors, Georgi attempted to explain
what was happening, and why. His analysis of the theological
basis of the Jewish mission is actually an explanation of the
points at which the theology of Hellenistic-Jewish apologetic
diverged from Old Testament (or Palestinian theology) which
made it possible for Jews not only to begin to conceive of
their past heroes, but themselves as well, as theioi andres,
i.e. if they qualified in any sense as special spokesmen for
God. Here we come to the third significant feature of Georgi's
treatment, his insistence that all (Diaspora) Jewish missionaries were, potentially at least, theioi andres and that they
were standard equipment in Diaspora synagogues. This feature
of his analysis represents the culmination of Reitzenstein's
treatment of the mysteries. The itinerant priests and prophets
of mystery cults whom Reitzenstein saw as essential in explaining their phenomenal spread in antiquity now have their
counterpart in the Hellenistic-Jewish missionaries whom Georgi
regards as the bearers of the glad tidings of the Jewish gospel
in which Judaism was held to be the religion of mankind, and
who, having become Christians, preach essentially the same
message, only Christianized. From this treatment of the
Hellenistic-Jewish mission movement derives the fourth significant feature of Georgi's work, the application of this
background to explaining Paul's opponents. Their message is

distorted Christologically, but their heretical Christology is
not the cause, but the result of their mission theology which
they had inherited from Hellenistic-Jewish apologetic. Thus,
identifying the opponents as representatives of this particular
stream of Jewish thought and explaining their anti-Pauline
posture against the theological framework of Hellenistic-Jewish
apologetic was new.

We can see, then, that the theios aner hypothesis as
diagrammed on p. 17 above is implicit rather than explicit in
Georgi's treatment. Only brief attention is paid to the
Hellenistic notion of theios aner, relatively speaking (pp.
187-205), nor does he dwell upon the conceptual difference
between Old Testament modes of conceiving of Israel's great men
and that of Hellenistic-Jewish apologetic; he is content merely
to notice that the one prepares the way for the other. Even
so, the importance of the Hellenistic-Jewish section of the
theios aner hypothesis is attested by the sheer length of this
large section of his work, and possibly stems from his acknow-
ledgement of the difficulty with which Jews seem to have
adopted the theios aner concept into their thinking:

> Those inspired persons were regarded as filled
> by God and designated ἔνθεοι (in Hellenistic-
> Jewish apologetic). It was only consistent that
> finally the expression theios aner came to be
> employed as a designation for those pious persons
> elected by God. Occasional scruples against such
> a use of this idea intimate certain inhibitions
> from a faith based upon the Old Testament, but
> they did not constitute any basic resistance to
> the ongoing movement (die einmal eingeschlagene
> Richtung) of apologetic theology and its develop-
> ment. It was difficult to raise a basic objection
> because the apologists were concerned with inter-
> preting the Scripture. The theioi andres whom
> they had in mind were not just any men, but first
> and foremost the great heroes of their own history.
> Thus one could speak for the greater honor of
> Judaism and consequently ad maiorem gloriam dei.[80]

(5) F. Hahn and P. Achtemeier.

The use of the theios aner hypothesis in explicating the
double Christological foci of Jesus' divinity and his miracles
may be illustrated in the work of F. Hahn and P. Achtemeier
respectively, not necessarily because these two scholars are

---

[80]GEORGI, Gegner, 147.

identified in any exclusive way with this particular point of
view, but mainly because they serve as concrete examples of
the position.

Significantly, the notion of the theios aner is incorporated into Hahn's treatment of Christological titles in his
chapter on Son of God and occurs in the subsection dealing with
the Son of God in Hellenistic-Jewish Christianity. Although he
regards υἱὸς θεοῦ as having originally been connected with
royal messianism in the Palestinian church and there having had
eschatological overtones, he still feels that significant
changes occurred in the use of the term in the Hellenistic
church where it came to be used as a title of exaltation signi-
fying the Son adopted and raised to the heavenly office.

Unlike Windisch and Bieler, Hahn thinks it inadmissible
to use theios aner as a category for classifying the Old
Testament "men of God":

> There tell against that two characteristics which
> distinguish the old Israelitish nebiism fundamen-
> tally from all Graeco-Hellenistic thought about
> phenomena of a similar kind: on the one hand,
> there is here no sort of participating by man in
> what is divine, but only complete subordination
> to God; on the other hand, the special abilities
> of the "men of God" are carried back to the action
> of the divine Spirit; accordingly, these abilities
> are understood not as signs of an ἐνθουσιασμός but
> as χαρίσματα. Quite definitely the constitutive
> element of the theios aner-conception, the divinity
> of man or the possibility of his participating in
> what is divine, indeed of his deification, is
> unthinkable in the Old Testament, and for that
> reason this concept is not at all suited to des-
> cribe the Old Testament circumstances.[81]

Yet, on the other hand, it is impossible, in explaining the
development of the Son of God conception in Hellenistic
Christianity, to hold that the Hellenistic theios aner concept
penetrated Christianity directly from paganism:

> If indeed we mean to sketch a history of the Son
> of God conception in Hellenistic Christianity,
> it is inadmissible to refer at once to the
> pronouncedly pagan cast of the theios aner-idea.[82]

Instead, Hellenistic-Judaism is the "not unessential interven-
ing link," for therein "Hellenistic ideas of various sorts were
actually accepted and transformed in order to render feasible

---

[81]HAHN, Titles, 289.   [82]Ibid., 288.

an association of them with the Biblical tradition."[83]
Hellenistic-Judaism (in the Diaspora) thus prepared the soil
for the Christians in the Hellenistic church to ascribe divinity or divine sonship to Jesus. The evidence for discovering
how Jews began to reinterpret their heroes as theioi andres,
admittedly sketchy, is sufficient to see the trend setting up.
Such evidence Hahn finds in Ep. Arist. 140, Josephus and Philo.
Although Josephus avers in one place that fellowship with the
divine is an impossibility for mortals, he nevertheless applied
theios to Moses and the prophets. Although Philo seems consciously to avoid using the expression theios aner, using
instead θεσπέσιος ἀνήρ, in him "Abraham and Moses and also the
prophets are no longer men of this earth," although there is
"no thought ... of a divinity that is a natural endowment of
these specially elected men."

In P. Achtemeier's treatment of the miracle catenae in
the Gospel of Mark the mediatory role of the Hellenistic-Jewish
understanding of theios aner is also graphically illustrated.[84]
In discussing parallel phenomena which could serve as possible
counterparts for the Gospel miracles, he appeals on the one
hand to the Hellenistic miracle stories, and on the other hand
to Rabbinic miracles, the tacit assumption being that these are
the two chief alternatives, therefore automatically excluding
looking to the Old Testament for possible prototypes. Of these
two options, the Gospel miracles are felt to resemble the
Rabbinic miracle stories less than the Hellenistic miracle
stories, the latter being distinguished as "epiphanic."[85] Once
the argument is set up in this manner, and once it is made
imperative to look to the Hellenistic stories as the most
fruitful source for explaining the Gospel miracle stories,
assuming that the early Christian tradition did not borrow them
directly from paganism, it must be asked where they had already
elsewhere penetrated the Jewish tradition. The answer:
Hellenistic-Judaism:

---

[83] HAHN, Titles, 288f.

[84] ACHTEMEIER, "Gospel Miracle Tradition," 174ff.

[85] ACHTEMEIER, "Pre-Marcan Miracle Catenae," 205.

The manner in which Hellenistic Judaism began to
interpret its own religious history bears out the
statement that for a religion to be understood in
that milieu, it had to make use of the interpretative device of divine man. Thus in the
Hellenistic-Jewish religious propaganda designed
for that world, the inspired figures of Jewish
history came to be described as, and on occasion
identified as, divine men, theioi andres. Abraham,
Moses, Elijah, Solomon, and many others, came to
be identified in these terms. Thus Solomon,
according to Josephus, was the originator of the
magical devices and incantations by means of which
demons could be exorcised and his inheritance was,
Josephus tells us, still used effectively, and he
himself had once observed. But the greatest divine
man of them all was Moses, not only because of the
miracles he performed in Egypt and during the exodus
but also because of his godlike wisdom as lawgiver.
Even his death apparently was interpreted by some
Hellenistic Jews as a kind of apotheosis. Thus, the
Jewish divine man shares in God's power over the
cosmos; a power which, in typical Hellenistic
fashion, the Jewish apologists see as giving that
divine man the power to perform miracles. Such wonders are, in turn, the way a divine man can
legitimate himself. Miracle and divine law were
thus two manifestations of the same reality for
Hellenistic Judaism it would appear, and logically
enough, if the law be divine, then those who
interpret the law must themselves in some sense be
divine men. Interpreting Jewish tradition and law,
these men also shared in a power transcending the
merely human and could themselves thus qualify for
the designation theios aner.[86]

Following this occurs an analysis of how the early Christian
tradition came to do what Hellenistic-Jews had done, viz.
interpret their leader using the category of the Hellenistic
divine man in order to make him more palatable to pagan ears.

Summary.

No attempt has been made to sketch even this single
aspect of the theios aner hypothesis comprehensively. Our only
aim has been to document the manner in which the Hellenistic-
Jewish section of the argument has functioned in explaining
various features of primitive Christianity. For this reason it
has been felt necessary to quote from these representative
scholars at some length, although in what may appear to be
unnecessarily overlapping detail. The scholars have been

[86]ACHTEMEIER, "Gospel Miracle Tradition," 187f.

allowed to speak for themselves not only to demonstrate the recurrent crucial function of the Hellenistic-Jewish under-standing of _theios aner_ but also to allow the slight modifica-tions to become visible, if for no other reason than to show that a fairly coherent position has emerged in spite of these individual differences. A certain degree of historical continuity, even genetic dependence, between these positions has been affirmed, justifiably, we think, as a look at the footnotes of the various works cited will indicate. Even though no attempt has been made to give a comprehensive cover-age, we have nevertheless tried to select what appear to be some of the major mountain peaks in the overall range, for it is felt that only when those peaks have been isolated and have become identifiable can the other lesser peaks be viewed in perspective.

This introductory survey has pointed up two things: the importance of clarifying precisely the nature and role of the _theios aner_ concept within Hellenistic-Judaism as well as the implications for this in terms of providing a corresponding clarification of those New Testament questions which relate to the _theios aner_. Moreover, it is hoped that the survey of positions has demonstrated the paradox that this crucial middle link in an ever increasingly popular hypothesis has been repeatedly based upon the same few bits of data, conspicuous not only for their paucity but also for their ambiguity. In a sense, herein lies the rationale for this study: to concen-trate upon this single section of the _theios aner_ hypothesis and explore it as thoroughly as possible in direct proportion to its cruciality in the overall argument.

We are thus concerned with the following questions:
(1) What is the nature and role of the expression _theios aner_ in Hellenistic-Jewish literature, specifically in Hellenistic-Jewish propaganda addressed to Gentiles?
(2) How useful is the expression _theios aner_ in explaining conceptual developments within Hellenistic-Judaism relating to ways in which Israel's heroes were elevated in their status relating to God?
(3) What is the precise relationship, if any, between the expression _theios aner_ and miracle-working in Hellenistic-

Judaism?

(4) How did Jews begin to reinterpret and remodel their heroes for propagandistic reasons <u>vis</u> <u>à</u> <u>vis</u> Gentiles, and what are the contours of this propaganda in this single respect?

(5) How far did these reinterpretations affect primitive Christianity?

CHAPTER TWO

JOSEPHUS

Although there is something to be said for examining the
Hellenistic-Jewish evidence chronologically, that approach will
not be followed here, primarily because of the nature of the
evidence. If theios aner were a frequently used expression in
these sources, such an approach would perhaps be justified, for
then it would be possible to presuppose some historical continuity in the development of the concept. But as it is, the
term is infrequently used, and since we are concerned to
inquire whether Israel's heroes came to be understood as theioi) &
andres, we must first examine those places where there is an
explicit and undeniable application of the term theios aner, or
a similar expression, to one of Israel's heroes, and proceed
from there, allowing the questions to arise out of the material
rather than superimposing questions upon the material. Accordingly, the most logical place to begin turns out to be
chronologically the latest: Josephus.

Antiquitates 3. 180.

In Ant. 3. 179-87[1] Josephus takes up his apologetic pen
to respond to the charge frequently made by pagans that Jews
are irreligious.[2] In this passage he rejects the standard
apologetic answers[3] and composes instead one of the most
puzzling passages in the whole of his writings. Part of the
puzzlement stems from the suddenness with which the passage

---

[1]The Loeb edition, edited by H. St. J. Thackeray, R.
Marcus, A. Wikgren, and L. H. Feldman, has been used in this
study.

[2]Cf. I. HEINEMANN, art. "Antisemitismus," PWRE, Suppl. 5
(1931) 3-43, esp. 19ff. for references to pagan sources.

[3]The most extensive treatment of these is M. FRIEDLÄNDER,
Geschichte der jüdischen Apologetik als Vorgeschichte des
Christentums (Zürich, 1903) 328-427; also. P. KRÜGER, Philo
und Josephus als Apologeten des Judentums (Leipzig, 1906).

interrupts a rather prosaic description of the tabernacle and its furnishings, the priests and vestments, purification rites, and the various feast days.[4] Equally remarkable is the occurrence of the hapax legomenon theios aner to designate ὁ νομοθέτης. The passage is further distinguished by the highly unusual symbolic description of the tabernacle, which, though mentioned briefly elsewhere by Josephus,[5] if anything, appears to be more Philonic than Josephan, an observation which raises several complex questions about Josephus' relationship to Philo which must be postponed for the moment. These three features combine to make this passage one of the cruces interpretum of the Josephan corpus.

History of Interpretation.

The passage has become important within recent years primarily because of the second of these three features, the mention of theios aner. Citing this passage as evidence of how the divine and cosmic processes came to be fused in certain Old Testament heroes, Georgi understands theios aner as "divine man" in the so-called Hellenistic sense:

> One wanted to show that especially in Judaism divine things had also come to expression. One hoped that unbiased and sensible pagans would agree at this point—a characteristic expectation for the attitude of Jewish missionaries toward pagan rationality. The decisive trump-card which one could play was the possession of a theios aner in one's own tradition. Josephus proves the divinity of Moses (die Göttlichkeit des Mose) by the cosmic character of the laws given by him. They portrayed cosmic things and would lead to a cosmic religiosity.[6]

Georgi was by no means the first so to interpret the passage; we have already noticed that Windisch appealed to this passage nearly thirty years earlier in his Paulus und Christus.[7]

Although this is certainly an obvious, even defensible line of interpretation, the meaning of the expression theios

---

[4] Ant. 3. 102-294.

[5] Ant. 3. 123; Bel. 5. 212f.

[6] GEORGI, Gegner, 152.

[7] WINDISCH, Paulus und Christus, 113. Cf. above, p. 29.

aner in this passage has baffled Josephan scholars for centuries. As early as 1531 the German translator Caspar Hedion
realized the difficulty when he chose to render τὴν νομοθέτην
... θεῖον ἄνδρα in Ant. 3. 180 as "den heiligen gsatzgeber."[8]
Two centuries later Johann Baptist Ott softened the German
translation even further by inserting "fromm," thus "ein
heiliger frommer Mann."[9] In the same year that Ott's one-
volume edition appeared (1736),[10] Johann Friderich Cotta published his edition with the completely different phrase "ein
Mann Gottes."[11] In striking contrast to his predecessors, R.
Martin opted for "ein göttlicher Mann."[12] Into the 20th
century both lines of interpretation continued: standing close
to Hedion and Ott, M. Friedländer chose "ein heiliger Mann,"[13]
whereas A. Schlatter's "ein göttlicher Mann"[14] placed him in
the same tradition with Martin. Demonstrating far greater
consistency, the French translators of Josephus uniformly chose
"un homme divin," beginning as early as Francois Burgoing's
1558 edition[15] and continuing through the magisterial edition
produced under the supervision of Reinach,[16] thus maintaining a

---

[8]Josephus Teütsch. (Strassburg, 1531) 2 pts. Book 3,
p. 3 of chapter 6, line 6 from bottom.

[9]Jos. Fl. Sämtliche Wercke (Zürich, 1736), p. 60.

[10]According to SCHÜRER, Gesch. jüd. Volkes, 1. 101,
Ott's work first appeared in six "Octavbänden" in Zürich in
1735, then as an enlarged single folio volume in 1736.

[11]Jos. Fl. Sämmtliche Wercke (Tübingen, 1736), p. 85.

[12]Die jüdischen Alterthümer des Flavius Josephus
übersetzt und mit Anmerkungen versehen. 2 Bde. (Köln, 1852),
vol. 1, p. 171.

[13]Geschichte der jüd. Apol., p. 340 (cf. note 3 above).

[14]Die Theologie des Judentums nach dem Bericht des
Josefus (Gütersloh, 1932), p. 60.

[15]Histoire de Fl. Iosèphe Sacrificatevr Hebriev (Lion,
1558), vol. 1, p. 80.

[16]Thus, G. GENEBRARD (trans.), Histoire de Fl. Josèphe
..., Mise en francois. Reueuë sur le Grec ... (Paris, 1588),
p. 69; (Paris, 2 1616), p. 94; M. ARNAULD D'ANDILLY (trans.),
Histoire des Ivifs Ecrite par Flavius Ioséph. Sous le Titre de
Antiqvitez Ivdaiqves. Troisième Ed. (Paris, 1670), p. 94; Ibīd.,
(cont.)

single line of interpretation for over 300 years. Whether the
Germans were more painstaking translators than the French, and
therefore more diverse in their results, is difficult to say.
Whatever the case, the English opted for German inconsistency
over French uniformity. It appears that the first person to
translate Josephus into English was a man named Morisyn,[17]
whose work has eluded the major libraries of Great Britain.
More popular, and possibly the first complete English translation, was that of Thomas Lodge, which underwent seven printings
and four editions between 1602 and 1670.[18] Lodge translated
the phrase "a man of diuine spirit," which was maintained,
albeit with an updated spelling, in the later editions.[19] The
anonymous edition of 1676 "with great diligence revised and
amended according to the excellent French translation of M.
Arnauld D'Andilly" followed suit,[20] although D'Andilly's French

---

rev. ed., 1680, vol. 1, p. 175; Ibid., newly rev. ed., 1700, p.
73; R. P. GILLET (trans.), Nouvelle Traduction de L'Histoire
Joseph (Paris, 1756-67). 4 Tome. vol. 1, p. 280; J. WEILL
(trans.), OEuvres complètes de Flavius Josèphe, traduites en
Francais. Ed. Th. Reinach. (Paris, 1900-32), vol. 1 (1900), p.
184.

[17]Preface, p. iv., of J. COURT (trans.), The Works of
Flavius Josephus (London, 1733). This is generally overlooked
by historians of Josephus. Thus, JOANNES A. FABRICIUS,
Bibliotheca Graeca, Ed. G. C. Harles. 4th ed. (Hamburg, 1796),
37, "Primus Anglis Iosephi antiquitates vernaculas dedisse
dicitur Thomas Lodge ..." HENRY STUBBINGS, drawing on
Fabricius, continues the error in his introductory essay to
Josephus, "Thomas Lodge, who combined in himself the several
characters of poet and physician, was the first who attempted
the task (i.e. translating Josephus into English" (cf. Kregel
Publications ed. (Grand Rapids, 1969), p. xxi.). Cf.
HENRIETTA R. PALMER, List of English Editions and Translations
of Greek and Latin Classics Printed Before 1641 (London, 1911),
pp. 65f., lists Lodge's 1602 translation as the first English
translation: "Between 1601 and 1610 appeared six translations.
These included Josephus by T. Lodge, 1601."

[18]Cf. British Museum General Catalogue of Printed Books
to 1955. Compact Edition (New York, 1967) 13. 795.

[19]T. LODGE (trans.), The Famous and Memorable Workes of
Josephus, A Man of Much Honour and Learning Among the Jews
(London), 1602; 1609; 1620; 1632; 1640; 1655; 1670), p. 65 in
each printing.

[20]The Works of Flavius Josephus. With great diligence
... (London, 1767; 1683; 1693), p. 88 in each printing. The
(cont.)

translation of 1670 (the 3rd edition) read "un homme divin."
The turn of the century saw the appearance of another anonymous
translation, Works of the Learned and Valiant Josephus Epitomi-
zed from the Greek Original (1701), but it omitted this passage
along with many others. A year later, Sir Roger L'Estrange
published his translation, acknowledging the assistance of John
Hudson, Chief Librarian of the Bodleian, "for the pains he has
been pleased to take in revising and comparing the translation
with the Greek"[21] as well as for his critical annotations.
Diverging from his predecessors, Sir Roger plumped for "a pious
man" as the correct translation.[22] Hudson's Greek and Latin
edition of 1726 throws no light on the question except for
providing virum divinum as the Latin equivalent.[23] "A pious
man" was retained by L'Estrange in his later editions,[24] and
satisfied his successors including James Wilson (1740),[25]
Ebenezer Thompson and William C. Price (1777),[26] who in their
preface pay tribute to L'Estrange's "excellent translation of
Josephus," and George H. Maynard (1785).[27] Though establishing
something of a tradition which lasted through the 18th century,

------

preface of this edition indicates that it is a revision of
Lodge's translation.

[21]The Works of Flavius Josephus (London, 1702), preface.

[22]SIR ROGER L'ESTRANGE, The Works of Flavius Josephus
(London, 1702) p. 66.

[23]JOANNIS HUDSONI, Flavii Josephi. Opera Omnia. Graece
et Latina. 2 vols. (Amsterdam, et al., 1726). This edition
does include an interesting footnote on our passage, "Mosen
ipsum ἄνδρα appellat. Num ergo Jesum Mosi praetulit de hoc
dubitans an ἄνδρα dicere ipsum fas sit? Id testimonium
Josephi de Christo suspectum reddit. REL. (=Hadriani Relandi)."

[24]Cf. 1766 ed. published in Dundee.

[25]A Collection of the Genuine Works of Flavius Josephus
(London, 1740), p. 133.

[26]The Works of Flavius Josephus. 2 vols. (Dondon, 1777),
vol. 1, p. 142.

[27]The Genuine and Complete Works of Flavius Josephus,
The Celebrated Warlike, Learned & Authentic Jewish Historian
(London, 1785; New York, 1792; Philadelphia, 1795), p. 41 in
each edition.

L'Estrange's "a pious man" by no means held a monopoly among
English translators. The 1733 edition of J. Court, "translated
from the original Greek according to Dr. Hudson's edition,"
broke new ground with "a man of divine virtue,"[28] but it
appears that no one after him was fond enough of the phrase to
borrow it. The lone English dissenter, whose convictions on
other matters cost him the Lucasian chair of Mathematics at
Cambridge, in which he had succeeded Sir Isaac Newton,[29] was
William Whiston, the first English translator daring enough to
render theios aner as "divine man."[30] Whiston's name became a
household word for the next 2 1/2 centuries, and his edition is
still the standard English translation for many. Even if the
history of translating theios aner tells us more about the
theology of the various translators than about the theology of
Josephus, this can hardly be the case with H. St. J. Thackeray,
praised by George F. Moore as "a skillful translator,"[31] and
whose thorough and perceptive lexicographical work on Josephus
has only been surpassed by the recent publication of the
Josephus concordance by the Institutum Judaicum Delitzschianum
under the editorship of K. H. Rengstorf.[32] Thackeray dissents
from Whiston, choosing to remain true to the general English
tradition, although his "a man of God" is innovative in this
tradition, finding its closest kin in Cotta's "ein Mann Gottes."
His extensive and scrutinizing analysis of the language of
Josephus lends a certain weight to his authority, but unfortunately it is impossible to let him explain his reasons since

---

[28]Op. cit., p. 62 (cf. note 16).

[29]MANSFIELD D. FORBES (ed.), Clare College, 1326-1926
(Cambridge, 1928), vol. 1, p. 154.

[30]The Genuine Works of Flavius Josephus the Jewish
Historian. Trans. from the original Greek according to
Havercamp's edition. (London, 1737), p. 81.

[31]In preface to H. ST. J. THACKERAY, Josephus, The Man
and the Historian (New York, 1929).

[32]H. ST. J. THACKERAY & RALPH MARCUS, A Lexicon to
Josephus [4 pts. 1: 1930; 2: 1934; 3: 1948; 4: 1955] (Paris,
1930-55). K. H. RENGSTORF (ed.), A Complete Concordance to
Flavius Josephus. Vol. 1: A - Δ. (Leiden, 1973); vols. 2-4
forthcoming. Supplement vol. by A. SCHALIT, Namenwörterbuch
zu Flavius Josephus (Leiden, 1968).

his lexicon of Josephus, even though carried on posthumously
with the help of Ralph Marcus, remains incomplete, reaching
only to ἐμ. A. Schalit's Hebrew translation איש אלהים instead
of tipping the balance in favor of one line of interpretation,
only serves to point up the difficulty of our inquiry by
illustrating how that in Hebrew איש אלהים must do double duty
for both Greek expressions ἄνθρωπος θεοῦ and theios aner.[33]
The Dutch "een godlyk man"[34] is equally elusive, though
probably more equivalent to "divine" than "pious."

Generally, then, two lines of interpretation have
emerged over the last four centuries. On the one hand are
those who see theios aner as an expression of Moses' piety or
religiousness; on the other hand are those who regard it as an
expression of his divinity or divine nature. Possibly "a man
of God" qualifies as a third line of interpretation, its
subtlety lying in its deliberate ambiguity which allows the
interpreter to see it either as an expression of piety or
divinity, or both. Deciding between these three options
thrusts the interprcter into the very heart of Josephus'
thought,[35] indeed into the very heart of Hellenistic-Jewish

---

[33] יוסף בן מתתיהו [פלביוס יספוס] קדמוניות היהודים.
(Jerusalem/Tel Aviv, 1955), vol. 1, p. 92.

[34] W. SEWEL, Alle De Werken van Flavius Josephus
(Amsterdam, 1704), p. 69.

[35] The most thorough treatment of Josephus' thought is
SCHLATTER, Theologie (cf. note 14 above; also the review by
S. S. COHON, "Theology of Judaism according to Josephus," JQR
N.S. 26 (1935-36) 152-47). G. HÖLSCHER, art. "Josephus," PWRE
9.2 (1916) 1934-2000, is devoted mainly to source critical
questions. R. LAQUEUR, Der jüdische Historiker Flavius
Josephus. Ein biographischer Versuch auf neuer quellenkritischer Grundlage (Giessen, 1920) is an attempt to prove
that the Vita was Josephus' earliest work, not the latest, as
most scholars think; THACKERAY, Josephus (cf. note 30), as it
says, treats "the man and the historian," paying little attention to his thought. It contains the best statement of his
theory of "Greek assistants," cf. pp. 100-25. F. J. FOAKES-
JACKSON, Josephus and the Jews. The Religion and History of the
Jews as Explained by Flavius Josephus (London, 1930) is a busy
man's Josephus, devoting only 30 pages to the "life and faith
of Flavius Josephus." Some of the best treatments are those in
encyclopedias: BENEDICTUS NIESE, art. "Josephus," HERE (Edinburgh, 1914) 7. 569-79; E. SCHÜRER, art. "Josephus,"
Realencyclopaedie f. prot. Theol. u. Kirche (³1901) 9. 377-86;
(cont.)

thought. If Josephus intends by the expression to attribute
divinity to Moses, he is departing radically from Old Testament
thought which regarded no human being as divine,[36] a conviction
which accounts for the Jews' unyielding resistance to emperor
worship. Yet, if this is not his intention, why does he employ
the expression theios aner instead of the LXX designation of
Moses ἄνθρωπος θεοῦ?[37]

Our interest extends beyond this passage, for we are
interested in finding out how Josephus, a Hellenistic-Jewish
author, felt about the question of attributing deity to human
beings, and particularly whether the deification of Israel's
heroes played any significant role in his apologetic for
Judaism. Within the immediate context of this passage the
inquiry has to do with Moses, but it cannot be limited to him.
The question must be viewed against the background of Josephus'
treatment of Israel's other heroes before any true assessment
can be made. Since the passage has an explicit polemical
thrust, the inquiry must be set within the context of Josephus'
wider apologetic aims in order to determine whether what he
says here is to be interpreted in the light of or independently
of these aims. In other words, although the problem is perhaps
at its clearest focus in this passage, the question extends
beyond this passage and beyond Josephus' treatment of Moses.
Since, however, this passage is the only place where Josephus
ever uses the expression theios aner, it will be used both as
the point of departure and the framework for investigating the
larger problem of the relationship between theios aner and
Josephus' thought.

H. ST. J. THACKERAY, art. "Josephus," HDB (Edinburgh, 1904) 5.
461-73; A. EDERSHEIM, art. "Josephus," Dictionary of Christian
Biography (London, 1882) 3. 441-60. G. A. WILLIAMSON, The
World of Josephus (London, 1964). Cf. also KRÜGER, Philo u.
Josephus als Apologeten (note 3 above). J. A. MONTGOMERY, "The
Religion of Flavius Josephus," JQR N.S. 11 (1920-21) 277f.,
compiles a list of older works treating Josephus' theology.

[36]SCHLATTER pays particular attention to Josephus'
Pharisaic background, though he does not make this particular
point, to my knowledge. Cf. G. DELLING, "Josephus und die
heidnischen Religionen," Klio 43-45 (1965) 263-69.

[37]Deut. 33:1.

<u>Analysis</u>.

θαυμάσειε δ' ἄν τις τῶν ἀνθρώπων τὴν πρὸς
ἡμᾶς ἀπέχθειαν, ἣν ὡς ἐκφαυλιζόντων ἡμῶν
τὸ θεῖον ὅπερ αὐτοὶ σέβειν προῄρηνται
διατετελέκασιν ἐσχηκότες. εἰ γάρ τις τῆς
σκηνῆς κατανοήσειε τὴν πῆξιν καὶ τοῦ ἱερέως
ἴδοι τὴν στολὴν τά τε σκεύη, οἷς περὶ τὴν
ἱερουργίαν χρώμεθα, τόν τε νομοθέτην εὑρήσει
θεῖον ἄνδρα καὶ ματαίως ἡμᾶς ὑπὸ τῶν ἄλλων
τὰς βλασφημίας ἀκούοντας· ἕκαστα γὰρ τούτων
εἰς ἀπομίμησιν καὶ διατύπωσιν τῶν ὅλων, εἴ
τις ἀφθόνως ἐθέλοι καὶ μετὰ συνέσεως σκοπεῖν,
εὑρήσει γεγονότα.

But one may well be astonished at the hatred
which men have for us and which they have so
persistently maintained, from an idea that we
slight the divinity whom they themselves pro-
fess to venerate. For if one reflects on the
construction of the tabernacle and looks at
the vestments of the priest and the vessels
which we use for the sacred ministry, he will
discover that our lawgiver was a man of God
and that these blasphemous charges brought
against us by the rest of men are idle. In
fact, every one of these objects is intended
to recall and represent the universe, as he
will find if he will but consent to examine
them without prejudice and with understanding.[38]

The extended description of the tabernacle beginning in
<u>Ant</u>. 3. 102 evidently provides Josephus with a choice oppor-
tunity to answer the critics of the Jews, though he is well
aware that few of his detractors are going to give a close look
at his tabernacle allegory.[39] Even so, if it could only be
assumed that they would give studied consideration to the
make-up of the tabernacle and observe closely the priestly
vestments, as well as the equipment used in the religious services, Josephus is confident that a twofold discovery will
result. First, it would be seen that the Jewish lawgiver was a
<u>theios aner</u>; second, that all these charges of ἀσέβεια brought
against the Jews are devoid of substance. Of these two discoveries, the latter is primary, although the former is not
thereby unimportant.[40]

---

[38]<u>Ant</u>. 3. 179-80. Trans. H. St. J. Thackeray (Loeb).

[39]Note the large number of optatives used in the entire
pericope, 3. 179-87.

[40]On the τε ... καί construction in 3. 180, cf. H. W.

(cont.)

There is a certain illogicality in Josephus' argument in at least two respects. First, with regard to who is being defended. His comments are presumably motivated by τῶν ἀνθρώπων τὴν πρὸς ἡμᾶς ἀπέχθειαν arising from the charge ἐκφαυλιζόντων ἡμῶν τὸ θεῖον ὅπερ αὐτοὶ σέβειν προῄρηνται mentioned in 3. 179. It is therefore the Jews as a whole who are under attack,[41] but, strangely, it is not they who are defended, at least directly. There is no attempt to deny the charge outright nor to extol the virtues of Judaism as there is, for example, in Ap. 2. 145ff. Instead of fitting his response to the charge, Josephus takes the more unusual course (unusual for him, at least) of elaborating on the symbolic significance of the tabernacle, the priestly vessels, and the tabernacle vessels.

Second, with regard to the structure of the response. It is very difficult to see how Ant. 3. 180 should, in any sense, follow what is said in 3. 179. It is not immediately obvious why a studied consideration of the tabernacle, etc., even if seen as allegory, should result in this twofold discovery. Even if it were, the first discovery seems superfluous, since 3. 180 would make equally good, if not better sense if the words τόν ... νομοθέτην ... θεῖον ἄνδρα καὶ ... were deleted. The Jews, not Moses, are the object of scorn. If they are being accused of impiety, what would it matter if Moses were a theios aner? This raises the whole question of the logic and structure of the response. Are the two discoveries to be treated as independent of each other, and thus both serving equally to refute the charge of impiety? Is Josephus saying that if one grasps the cosmic significance of the tabernacle, one will make two discoveries, both of which equally disprove the charge of impiety brought against the Jews? Or, does the τε ... καί construction indicate that one

---

SMYTH, Greek Grammar (Cambridge, Mass., 1956) par. 2974, who remarks, "τὲ ... καί often serves to unite complements both similars and opposites. τὲ ... καί is not used when one clause is subordinate to another. The two words or clauses thus united may show a contrast, or the second may be stronger than the first. ... τὲ ... καί is weaker than καί ... καί, and will not easily bear the translation "both ... and."

[41] N.B. ἡμᾶς, ἡμῶν in 3. 179-80.

discovery is subordinate to the other, so that it is either
there by accident, and thus serves no real purpose, or is there
to substantiate the major discovery? Does the discovery that
the lawgiver was theios aner serve to substantiate the second
discovery, which in turn refutes the charge, in which case the
theios aner would be a subordinate argument; or, alternatively,
is the second discovery intended to reinforce the theios aner
discovery, which in turn refutes the charge of impiety, in
which case the theios aner discovery would be the crucial link
in the overall chain of argument? It is not altogether clear
why either of these two discoveries should result from one's
perceiving the cosmic significance of the tabernacle, but
granting Josephus' logic for the moment, the second of the two
discoveries is more directly germane to the charge of impiety.
If so, why, then, does he even introduce the lawgiver=theios
aner equation into the passage? If it is to be taken as only
one of two unrelated discoveries connected by καί and thus does
not reinforce the second discovery, its presence is all the
more an unexplained intrusion. That is to say, conceivably the
theios aner discovery is there for no reason and thus plays no
integral role in the argument. It is not picked up again later
in the passage unless it is to be connected with the mention of
τὴν ἀρετὴν τοῦ νομοθετοῦ in 3. 187. It is not explicitly
integrated into the symbolic interpretation of the tabernacle.
And yet, of the two members of the pair of discoveries, it is
placed conspicuously first rather than added as an afterthought.
Furthermore, since hapax legomena are usually either highly
significant or totally insignificant, its prominent position
within the sentence would tend to suggest significance rather
than insignificance. We are forced, then, to examine in more
detail the expression theios aner.

Lexicographical Considerations.

The difficulty of determining what Josephus means by
theios aner is partly accounted for by the elusiveness of the
adjective theios. Scholars, such as F. M. Cornford, have long
recognized that it is a very slippery term, and has at least
four shades of meaning:

> The epithet 'divine' (theios) has a wide range
> of meaning. It could be taken literally, as when

Pythagoras or Plato was supposed to be the son of a god. In the context of the belief in metempsychosis, it could denote the condition of a soul which had achieved purification and was destined to escape further reincarnation and to join the company of the gods. This may be what is meant by saying that 'among rational creatures there are gods and men and beings like Pythagoras' (Aristotle, frag. 192). At the least, 'divine' signified 'divinely inspired' and was so applied to the seer and to the poet. At bottom, the word recognizes the existence of a class of men whose wisdom is not derived from ordinary experience in the light of common day but from access to a world of gods and spirits or a timeless reality however conceived.[42]

Taking these four categories as a point of departure, we can eliminate the second at the outset as being alien to Josephus' thought. But, if we take the other three possibilities as options open to us, it means that Josephus by designating Moses, the lawgiver, as theios aner, can mean at least one of three things, viz. that he is:

(1) υἱὸς θεοῦ, i.e. divine, in the most literal sense;

(2) ἔνθεος, or (divinely) inspired;

(3) ἄριστος, or, extraordinary, or excellent.

Unfortunately, these distinctions, for the most part, have been overlooked by scholars who have interpreted Ant. 3. 180 and other theios aner passages as they relate to Biblical scholarship. It is often assumed, without qualification, that theios has only one meaning--"divine" in Cornford's first sense, and hence theios aner is assumed to be equivalent to υἱὸς θεοῦ, or understood as a category in which the notion of divinity is primary and fundamental.[43] Of course, this interpretation of the expression cannot be rejected a priori, but neither can it be accepted as a foregone conclusion. Josephus' intention can only be discovered, first by looking at his use of theios, its

---

[42] F. M. CORNFORD, Principium Sapientiae. The Origins of Greek Philosophical Thought. Ed. W. K. C. Guthrie (New York, 1965; orig. pub. 1952) 108; also, cf. R. S. H. BLUCK, Plato. Meno (Cambridge, 1961) 428, remarks on Meno 99c-d; also, J. KLEIN, A Commentary on Plato's Meno (Chapel Hill, N.C., 1965) 254-55; A. H. ARMSTRONG, "Plotinus," in Cambridge History of Later Greek and Early Medieval Philosophy (Cambridge, 1967) 222.

[43] As, e.g. HAHN, Titles, 289; cf. above, p. 41. Cf. A. D. Nock's criticism of Wetter, in NOCK, Essays, 1. 85:152.

cognates and synonyms.

The substantival use of theios, particularly in the singular, can be dispensed with since it is not really germane to this inquiry.[44] The plural form is a general expression whose meaning can hardly be more specifically delimited than by rendering it "divine things" or "divine matters," as when he mentions "things human and divine" (ἀνθρωπίνων ... καὶ θείων).[45] Perhaps the meaning is more concrete when he mentions the first Greek philosophers to speak of "celestial and divine subjects" (περὶ τῶν οὐρανίων τε καὶ θείων ...).[46] Things directly related to or originating from God can be called τὰ θεῖα, such as the laws of Moses (or is it the topics which the law of Moses deals with?),[47] prophetic events,[48] or the temple vessels.[49] More pertinent to this inquiry is the adjectival use of theios, particularly to describe God, as when Josephus speaks of "the divine Ally" (τὴν θείαν συμμαχίαν).[50] Often θεία δύναμις takes on a quasi-personal dimension when it is used as a substitute for ὁ θεός, although it is probably simply another way of saying πρόνοια θεοῦ, as when Josephus says that "it was through some divine intervention (ἔκ τινος θείας δυνάμεως) that Claudius enjoyed exemption from the mad fits of Gaius,"[51] or when he allows that Alexander the Great had made his expedition under "divine guidance" (θείᾳ πομπῇ).[52] In this same category belong those instances where theios describes either an aspect of God (e.g. θεία φύσις[53]), an activity of God, or an object or event resulting from His activity. A

_____

[44]Josephus' use of τὸ θεῖον as an alternative expression for ὁ θεός is too frequent to document. Rengstorf's concordance gives over 150 such uses.

[45]Ant. 6. 264. [46]Ap. 1. 14.

[47]Ant. 12. 112. [48]Ant. 15. 379.

[49]Bel. 5. 564.

[50]Bel. 6. 41; cf. Ap. 2. 160 var.: God is Moses' σύμβουλον θεῖον.

[51]Ant. 19. 69.

[52]Ant. 11. 335; cf. Ant. 4. 157; 9. 58; 10. 214; 18. 197.

[53]Ant. 8. 107.

φωνὴ θεία promises Abraham a blessed progeny.[54] Isaac reckons
that Rebekah's presence at the well was ὑπὸ θείας ἐπιφανείας.[55]
Jacob christens Bethel as "God's hearthstone" (θεία ἑστία).[56]
Joseph's brethren reckon that he had come to them κατὰ θείαν
βούλησιν.[57] The ground around the burning bush is _theios_;[58]
God's anger against those who flout his commands is χόλος
θεῖος.[59] The path through the Red Sea provided by God is θεία
ὁδός.[60] The food sent by God from heaven is θεῖον ... καὶ
παράδοξον.[61] Balaam is prevented from prophesying θείᾳ
προνοίᾳ.[62] Samuel favored aristocratic government, the type
ordained by God, "accounting it divine (θείας) and productive
of bliss to those who adopted it."[63] He also reproaches Saul
after the Amalekite fiasco by reminding him that "change and
reversal of judgment were the part of human frailty and not of
divine power" (θείας ἰσχύος).[64] The ploy by which Elisha
captured the Syrians, because they were ensnared θείᾳ δυνάμει,
is θεῖον καὶ παράδοξον πρᾶγμα.[65] Describing Sodom, Josephus
mentions that "vestiges of the divine fire (τοῦ θείου πυρός)
and faint traces of five cities are still visible."[66] Agrippa
reminds the Jews that wars are begun either θείᾳ ... ἢ
ἀνθρωπίνῃ βοηθείᾳ.[67] The laws, since they are from God, are
οἱ πάτριοι καὶ θεῖοι λόγοι,[68] and their "divine and awful
nature" (διὰ τὸ θεῖαν αὐτὴν εἶναι καὶ σεμνὴν ...)[69] is the

---

[54] _Ant_. 1. 185; cf. 8. 352.

[55] _Ant_. 1. 255.

[56] _Ant_. 1. 284; cf. LXX οἶκος θεοῦ.

[57] _Ant_. 2. 20.   [58] _Ant_. 2. 267.

[59] _Ant_. 2. 292.   [60] _Ant_. 2. 339.

[61] _Ant_. 3. 30.   [62] _Ant_. 4. 157.

[63] _Ant_. 6. 36.   [64] _Ant_. 6. 153.

[65] _Ant_. 9. 58.   [66] _Bel_. 4. 483-84.

[67] _Bel_. 2. 394.   [68] _Bel_. 7. 343.

[69] _Ant_. 12. 111.

reason given by Demetrius of Phalerum (sic)[70] for their not having been translated into Greek.[71] By extension, things relating to the temple are θεῖος: the treasures (τὰ κειμήλια),[72] the pavement (τὸ ἔδαφος),[73] the precincts (οἱ περίβολοι),[74] and the worship performed there[75]--in fact, the worship of any deity, true or false, can be called θεία θρησκεία.[76] In these instances, the meaning of theios tends to shade off into ἱερός.[77] On several occasions the Spirit of God is called τὸ θεῖον πνεῦμα;[78] it is said to impel Balaam's ass to speak,[79] to impel Balaam to speak divine utterances to Balak;[80] it passes from Saul to David and enables him to prophesy;[81] it is the possession of a true prophet,[82] and also of Daniel the dream-interpreter.[83] In a slightly different category is the use of theios to designate an ἄγγελος of God.[84] At the other end of the scale, Josephus can use theios in a manner almost devoid of "divine" content to describe the paradisal fertility of the land near Jericho: "it would be no misnomer to describe as 'divine' (θεῖον) this spot in which the rarest and choicest plants are produced in abundance."[85] Perhaps "heavenly" would be an apt translation.

Less frequently, Josephus uses theios in reference to persons, and when he does so, the references are often too oblique to be taken as ascriptions of divinity. In his

---

[70]Josephus is here perpetuating the fictional account of Epistle of Aristeas.

[71]Cf. Ant. 11. 123 var.: τοῦ θείου νόμου. Cf. Ap. 1. 38 τὰ βιβλία θεῖα; Ap. 1. 211 var. τοῦ νόμου θείου.

[72]Bel. 2. 321.   [73]Bel. 4. 201.

[74]Bel. 5. 18; ὁ χῶρος, Bel. 5. 402.

[75]Ant. 18. 15.   [76]Ant. 5. 101.

[77]Cf. Ant. 4. 285.   [78]Cf. SCHLATTER, 58.

[79]Ant. 4. 108.   [80]Ant. 4. 118.

[81]Ant. 6. 166; cf. 6. 222.   [82]Ant. 8. 408.

[83]Ant. 10. 239.

[84]Ant. 1. 189, 219, 332; 4. 108.

[85]Bel. 4. 469.

narration of the siege of Masada, he includes a speech placed
in the mouth of Eleazar which is replete with Greek philosophical themes concerning the immortality of the soul. Adopting
the σῶμα-σῆμα viewpoint, Eleazar says that it is unfitting for
anything theios, i.e. ψυχή, to have fellowship with anything
θνητός, i.e. σῶμα.[86] Twice a pagan is called theios, but each
time in a quotation from a pagan which Josephus has chosen to
include in his narrative. Augustus is called ὁ θεῖος Σεβαστός
in an edict of Claudius,[87] and in an excerpt from Manetho, a
certain Amenophis, son of Paapis, is said to have had θεία
φύσις, on account of his wisdom and knowledge of the future.[88]
Neither of these two instances says anything of Josephus' own
point of view, although they do illustrate a use of theios, in
Cornford's first sense, applied to persons. Three times
Josephus uses theios in reference to Moses. Thermuthis tells
her father Pharaoh that Moses is a παῖς μορφῇ τε θεῖον καὶ
φρονήματι γενναῖον.[89] He reminds Manetho and Apion that the
Egyptians regard Moses as ἀνὴρ θαυμαστὸς ... καὶ θεῖος.[90]
Then, there is the passage under consideration in which Moses
is theios aner.[91] Twice Solomon is attributed "divine understanding,"[92] a logical description of his God-given σοφία and
φρόνησις.[93] The prophet Jadon (unnamed in the Old Testament
account),[94] who rebukes Jeroboam at Bethel, possesses θεία
πρόγνωσις,[95] and is called by Jeroboam θεῖον ἀληθῶς καὶ
προφήτην ἄριστον.[96] The corpse of Elisha is said to have had

---

[86] Bel. 7. 344.   [87] Ant. 19. 289.

[88] Ap. 1. 232.

[89] Ant. 2. 232. Cf. Ex. 2:2, MT: ותרא אתו כי־טוב הוא
Also, cf. Acts 7:20.

[90] Ap. 1. 279.   [91] Ant. 3. 180.

[92] Ant. 8. 34: θεία διάνοια; Ant. 8. 187: θεία ἐπίνοια.

[93] Ant. 8. 42; cf. 8. 23-24.

[94] Cf. 1 Kings 12:32ff.; 13:1ff.; MT: איש אלהים; LXX:
ἄνθρωπος τοῦ θεοῦ.

[95] Ant. 8. 234.

[96] Ant. 8. 243.

θείαν δύναμιν,[97] a reference to the legend mentioned in 2 Kings
13:20f. The prophet Isaiah is θεῖος καὶ θαυμάσιος.[98] Daniel's
ability to interpret Nebuchadnezzar's dream and the handwriting
on the wall is described as τὸ σοφὸν καὶ θεῖον.[99] Josephus
himself claims to possess the prophetic ability to predict
accurately the course of political events, and when his predictions come true, they are called θεῖος.[100] Once the Old
Testament prophets are referred to collectively as θεῖοι
προφῆται in the Testimonium Flavianum.[101]

The significant fact that emerges from this collection
of passages is that Josephus, in his own narrative, rarely
attached theios to an individual.[102] It is far more usual for
him to use theios of an individual's activity or of an aspect
of his personality. He knows a use of theios denoting divinity
in the most literal sense.[103] But, it is even more significant
to notice that the activity he singles out most often as being
worthy of the designation theios, almost without exception, is
the prophetic activity. It is by virtue of θεῖον πνεῦμα[104]
that Daniel's ability to interpret dreams and signs is
theios.[105] The prophetic activity is the process in which
θεῖον πνεῦμα possesses the prophet and uses him as a channel
for conveying the divine message,[106] and this is the reason
that the prophetic utterances are themselves designated

---

[97] Ant. 9. 183.   [98] Ant. 10. 35; cf. 10. 32.

[99] Ant. 10. 241.

[100] Bel. 4. 625. Although Josephus never calls himself
προφήτης, he does describe his activity as ἔνθεος (Bel. 3.
353). Cf. FASCHER, ΠΡΟΦΗΤΗΣ, 152:1.

[101] Ant. 18. 64.

[102] Ant. 2. 232; 3. 180; Ap. 1. 279; Ant. 8. 243; 10. 35;
18. 64. Cf. Ant. 19. 289; Ap. 1. 232.

[103] Ant. 19. 289. Possibly, Ap. 1. 232; also Ap. 1. 279.

[104] Ant. 10. 239.   [105] Ant. 10. 241.

[106] Ant. 4. 118; 6. 166; 6. 222; 8. 408; cf. Ant. 4. 108.
On Josephus' concept of prophecy, cf. SCHLATTER, Theologie,
57ff.; also FASCHER, ΠΡΟΦΗΤΗΣ, 161ff.

theios,[107] especially when they turn out to be true.[108] In these three cases, the best translation of theios is "inspired," since the meaning is clearly that the person so named, being a prophet of God, has spoken accurately the Word of God.

Theios was not the only word Josephus had at his disposal had he wanted to refer to a person as "divine." Possibly a more likely choice would have been δαιμόνιος[109] which in Bel. 6. 429 is used as an antonym of ἀνθρώπινος.[110] At times it appears to be an exact equivalent of theios, as for example, when Josephus speaks of "the wind veering as if by a divine providence" (ἐκ δαιμονίου προνοίας).[111] Since δαίμων was a more general term than θεός, it is not surprising that the same type of elusive diversity obtains in the cognate forms. Josephus displays the same diversity in his use of δαίμων as did classical Greek authors, using it to denote a/the deity,[112] or in the plural as a designation of "spirits" or "ghosts" of the dead,[113] and either of "good genii"[114] or "evil spirits."[115] Similarly, τὸ δαιμόνιον can mean "the Divinity" or "divine Power,"[116] "spirit" or "genius" (of Socrates),[117] and "evil spirit."[118] Even though the adjective is used almost exclusively in Bellum, and therefore unquestionably for Greek consumption, it exhibits a similar diversity as used by Josephus in Antiquitates. Frequently he chooses it to identify

---

[107]Ant. 8. 234; 15. 379; cf. 15. 373.

[108]Ant. 8. 243; 10. 35.

[109]Here I am dependent upon THACKERAY-MARCUS, Lexicon, Fasc. 2, p. 119.

[110]Cf. Bel. 1. 373, 376.   [111]Bel. 7. 318.

[112]Ant. 13. 415; 14. 291; Bel. 1. 556, 628; 4. 41; Vit. 402.

[113]Ant. 13. 317, 416; Bel. 1. 521, 599, 607.

[114]Bel. 6. 47.   [115]Ant. 8. 45.

[116]Ant. 16. 76; 19. 60; Bel. 1. 69, 84, 613.

[117]Ap. 2. 263.

[118]Ant. 6. 166; 8. 45ff.; Bel. 7. 185.

πρόνοια.[119] It is consistently used to describe concepts and events: τέρας,[120] συμφορά,[121] πληγαί,[122] κακόν,[123] μήνιμα,[124] συνεργία,[125] προθυμία,[126] θύελλα,[127] φάσμα,[128] φθορά,[129] χαρά,[130] χορηγία.[131] Only twice is it used in reference to human beings, once to describe Vespasian's "supernatural intrepedity" (δαιμόνιον τὸ παράστημα τῆς ψυχῆς),[132] and once in a speech by Josephus when he refers to the "superhuman exploits of your fathers" (πατέρων ἔργα δαιμόνια),[133] i.e. the Jewish figures of the past. Even in both these cases, the adjective is not used directly of the persons themselves but of activities performed by the persons. On this showing, Josephus seems to be more reluctant to attribute divinity to persons in Bellum, a document addressed explicitly to non-Jews, than in Antiquitates.[134]

As to other possible terminology available to Josephus to attribute divinity to human beings, it is interesting to note that he does not use θεσπέσιος nor any of his cognates. He consistently uses ἔνθεος for describing a prophet or prophetic activity.[135]

In summary it can be said that the most significant fact that emerges from these observations is that Josephus, with but rare exception, uses theios to describe objects, phenomena, concepts, or events, not persons, especially named individuals.

---

[119] Ant. 13. 314; Bel. 2. 457; 4. 217, 622; cf. 4. 501; 5. 502; 6. 59 (252), 303.

[120] Bel. 1. 331. [121] Bel. 1. 370.

[122] Bel. 1. 373. [123] Bel. 1. 376.

[124] Bel. 2. 455. [125] Bel. 3. 341.

[126] Bel. 3. 485. [127] Bel. 4. 76.

[128] Bel. 6. 296. [129] Bel. 6. 429.

[130] Bel. 7. 120. [131] Bel. 7. 159.

[132] Bel. 4. 34. [133] Bel. 5. 377.

[134] Cf. THACKERAY, Josephus, 24, 27; in a sense, this is a false dichotomy, since Antiquitates was not intended solely for Jews; cf. Ant. 1. 5ff.; 16. 174; 20. 263. Cf. NIESE, "Josephus," HERE, 7. 572.

[135] Bel. 3. 353; 4. 33, 4. 388; Ant. 6. 56; 6. 76; 8. 346; 9. 35.

And, when he does, he does so most often in connection with
prophets. Even then, it is more usual for him to call the
prophet's work, especially if successful, theios, rather than
the prophet himself. Moreover, the fact that in Bellum there
is even less of a tendency to portray Israel's heroes as divine
raises serious questions about the validity of the view that
Hellenistic-Jews tended to portray their heroes as divine
before Greek audiences. What is even more striking is the
absence of this tendency in C. Apionem, perhaps the best
example we have of Hellenistic-Jewish apologetic, where, certainly, if this had been a major theme of Hellenistic-Jewish
apologetic, it would at least have appeared in some form.

The results are not wholly negative, however, since this
analysis has suggested a possible line of interpretation which
explains the meaning of theios aner in Ant. 3. 180. These
lexicographical observations have suggested that theios for
Josephus, when applied to persons, should be interpreted in
the context of his understanding of prophecy, assuming, of
course, that it is to be interpreted uniformly in the passages
in question. The danger of uniformly interpreting a multi-
valent term by only one of its meanings must be avoided, and
there is no compelling reason why he could not have used theios
in another sense in Ant. 3. 180. At the same time, however, if
it is used only rarely in the entirety of his writings to refer
to persons, and most of those uses are explicitly related to
prophets, the odds are weighted fairly heavily in favor of this
line of interpretation. If prophecy is the interpretative key,
Cornford's third meaning would most naturally fit, so that
theios aner is to be interpreted as "a divinely inspired man."
The crucial question is whether this interpretation of the term
results in a more meaningful explanation of Ant. 3. 179-87 in
the light of its context as well as Josephus' overall apologetic aims.

When we test ἔνθεος in Ant. 3. 180, however, we are
still left puzzled. This meaning of theios would perhaps make
sense of the first illogicality; presumably, the possession of
an inspired lawgiver in one's religious heritage could be
adduced to offset the charge of impiety, although the logic is
still, strictly speaking, a bit disconnected. But, even less

clear is why one, after inspecting the tabernacle, etc., would deduce that the lawgiver was a divinely inspired person. Thus, even though this line of interpretation has firm lexicographical support, it still is not fully satisfactory to the sense of the passage.

Looking at the third alternative, ἄριστος, we are left with the same feeling. Certainly, this interpretation is conceivable, but must be rejected. Proving that Moses was an extraordinary man as an apologetic device seems an incredibly weak argument, and hardly seems to be an intelligible deduction from the cosmic interpretation of the tabernacle.

We are left, then, with the first alternative, υἱὸς θεοῦ, and since it is the meaning which has often been equated with theios aner, and which is often felt to illustrate the shift in Jewish thought seen particularly in Hellenistic-Judaism, we must consider it in some detail.

Theios Aner and υἱὸς θεοῦ.

It has already been noticed that Josephus knows a use of theios in its literal sense of "divine,"[136] but to determine whether he is making the same claim of the lawgiver Moses we must investigate two interlocking questions: (1) Josephus' attitude towards deifying mortals, especially Israel's heroes, and (2) the contours of his reinterpretation of Israel's heroes for apologetic purposes, i.e. to determine whether assigning deity to them, or whether the tendency to elevate them to suprahuman status, is indicative of and consonant with his overall apologetic. We shall examine them in reverse order.

(1) Josephus' Interpretation of Israel's Heroes.

(a) Moses.

One of the best examples of the way Josephus takes the Biblical narrative and reshapes it along Hellenistic lines is his portrait of Moses.[137] Unlike Philo, who explicitly sets

---

[136] Ant. 19. 289; Ap. 1. 279.

[137] On the question of Hellenistic influence at work upon Josephus, cf. NIESE, "Josephus," HERE, 7. 573; also SCHLATTER'S final chapter on "Freisinn;" B. BRÜNE, Flavius Josephus und seine Schriften in ihrem Verhaltnis zum Judentume, zur

(cont.)

out the categories in which he intends to portray Moses,[138]
Josephus presumes simply to unfold the Biblical narrative, but

griechisch-römischen Welt und zum Christentume ... (Gutersloh,
1913) par. 52-4; L. H. FELDMAN, "Hellenizations in Josephus'
Portrayal of Man's Decline," in Religions in Antiquity
[Goodenough Festschrift] (Leiden, 1968) 336-53.
    The question of Hellenistic influences discernible in
Josephus inevitably raises the question of his Greek assistants,
and how much of the Hellenizing tendency is traceable to them
instead of Josephus. THACKERAY detected two such assistants, a
"Sophoclean," and "Thucydidean" assistant, who are responsible,
respectively, for Books 15-16 and Books 17-19 of Antiquitates.
He thinks that the remainder of Antiquitates was written with
little assistance (cf. his remarks in Loeb, vol. 2, p. xv),
although he does find traces of the "Sophoclean" assistant in
Books 1 & 2 (cf. Loeb, vol. 4, p. xv). R. J. H. SHUTT, Studies
in Josephus (London, 1961) attempts, unconvincingly, to disprove Thackeray's theory by arguing that Josephus follows
Nicolaus of Damascus in those places where stylistic peculiari-
ties are discernible. For another critique of Thackeray's
theory, cf. G. C. RICHARDS, "The Composition of Josephus'
Antiquities," CQ 33 (1939) 36-40. In private conversation H.
SCHRECKENBURG also expressed doubts about Thackeray's theory of
assistants, noting that he has observed, in connection with his
work on the Josephus concordance, more stylistic unity on the
part of Josephus than is generally supposed.
    As far as our inquiry is concerned, Thackeray does not
provide enough examples from the earlier parts of Antiquitates
(where our investigation is concentrated) to warrant explaining
the Hellenistic complexion of these books as due to assistants.
Thus, in this study, I am assuming that Josephus is responsible
for the text as we have it, especially in Books 1-9 of
Antiquitates, if not in toto, at least as the final editor, so
that conclusions drawn from the text can be used in interpreting the thought of Josephus himself.
    D. L. TIEDE, The Charismatic Figure as Miracle Worker
(Missoula, Montana, 1972) 207-24, treats Josephus, primarily
from the standpoint of how the Hellenistically colored portrait
of Moses the Lawgiver did not include the thaumaturgic motif as
a means of documenting his divine status. He rightly emphasizes the influence of the Stoic Sage motif upon Josephus. His
analysis does not treat the question of whether and how
Josephus conceived of Moses as divine. Unlike most treatments,
Tiede exercises considerable caution in his discussion of
Josephus' portrait of Moses: " ... He idealizes Moses as a
supreme Sage who approaches divinity in virtue ..." (237).
"Subsequent scrutiny of crucial texts where Josephus speaks of
Moses' divine or semi-divine nature will show that Josephus is
very cautious about calling Moses divine, usually attributing
such statements to persons other than himself" (229).

    [138]Cf. V. Mos. 2. 2ff.

in the process weaves his tapestry with at least six dis-
tinguishable threads: (1) legislative,[139] (2) prophetic,[140]
(3) mediatory,[141] (4) thaumaturgic,[142] (5) military, and (6)
sophistic. With the first four Josephus is on solid Biblical
ground, for the most part, but with the last two, it is another
matter altogether, for they illustrate different degrees of
departure from the Biblical text.

(aa) Military role.

   In the Biblical narrative Moses performs military tasks,
but they are neither conceived nor described in military terms.
In the LXX Moses is never called στρατηγός, or even ἡγεμών,
whereas στρατηγός[143] is one of Josephus' most frequently used
descriptive titles. Josephus also links another distinctly
Hellenistic concept, ἐλευθερία, with the military role of
Moses. Ἐλευθερία as an essential ingredient of the state was
axiomatic in Greek thought,[144] and the gradual emergence of
Israel in Josephus' account of her history as a nation who
embodies ἐλευθερία as one of its ideals cannot be accidental.
From the outset Josephus emphasizes the subjugation of the
Egyptian hegemony[145] and conceives of the Exodus as motivated
by a desire for ἐλευθερία. He does not hesitate to tell of the
Jews' own resistance to the realization of this noble ideal[146]
and devotes a large part of Book 4 to narratives illustrating
that στάσις is the perennial enemy of all states.[147]

---

[139]Cf. Ant. 1. 95, 240; 3. 286; 4. 193; 5. 98; 7. 384;
8. 120; 9. 2; 17. 159; Ap. 1. 238, 250; 2. 154, 156, passim.

[140]Cf. Ant. 2. 327; 3. 75ff., 87-88; 4. 303; 5. 20, 40,
69.

[141]Cf. Ant. 3. 33ff., 66ff., 316; 4. 194, 321, passim.

[142]Cf. Ant. 2. 270ff.; 277-80, 283, 284-92, 293-313; cf.
TIEDE, 227f.

[143]Cf. below, pp. 70f.

[144]H. SCHLIER, art. ἐλεύθερος, TDNT, 2. 488.

[145]Ant. 2. 216, 234-36.

[146]Ant. 2. 327; 3. 5ff., 20f., passim.

[147]Ant. 4. 11-66, 141-55.

'Ελευθερία is achieved nevertheless,[148] and Moses speaks of it
at least twice as an accomplished fact,[149] although it should
be emphasized that it is a gift from God. The obstinacy of
the Jews to their own pursuit of ἐλευθερία is exceeded only by
Moses' determination to achieve it, since, like all great
leaders he was able to perceive what was good for the people
and strove for it even when they were blind to it.[150] Moses is
the crucial agent in helping Israel achieve her ἐλευθερία and
he has forsaken the good life to help her do so.[151] He accomplishes this extraordinarily difficult feat as στρατηγός of the
Jews in the face of Egyptian military strength, Canaanite
opposition, repeated internal insurrection, not to mention the
Jews' own nearsighted obstinacy. By incorporating the
Ethiopian legend,[152] Josephus lays added groundwork for establishing Moses' military prowess by showing that even the
Egyptians owed their ἐλευθερία to his military gallantry.[153]
With the threat of an Ethiopian invasion Pharaoh persuades his
daughter to let Moses serve as στρατηγός of the Egyptian
army,[154] but then becomes jealous of Moses' στρατηγία and turns
the tables against him by lending support to a plot to murder
him.[155] When Moses later returns to Egypt, he reminds the new
Pharaoh of his former military efforts in behalf of the
Egyptians,[156] but this time he is a στρατηγός seeking not
Egyptian, but Israelite ἐλευθερία.[157] Particularly in the
wilderness does Moses' role as στρατηγός become prominent,[158]
since there the Israelites are a nation in their own right.
The trying circumstances of the wilderness prove the mettle of
Moses the στρατηγός and affords Josephus ample opportunity to
interpret Moses' military role in terms which recall the

---

[148]Ant. 3. 64.

[149]Ant. 3. 44, 300; 4. 2.

[150]Ant. 2. 290.

[151]Ant. 4. 42.

[152]Ant. 2. 239ff.

[153]Ant. 2. 252.

[154]Ant. 2. 241.

[155]Ant. 2. 255.

[156]Ant. 2. 281-83.

[157]Ant. 2. 281.

[158]Ant. 3. 2, 11, 28, 65, 67, 78, 102.

Cynic-Stoic ideal of the σοφός-βασιλεύς.[159] It is he who
always remains unperturbed in the midst of turbulence, always
encouraging and emboldening his troops by his words and
actions. In celebrating the victory over the Amalekites,
Raguel praises the gallantry of the στρατηγός Moses and cites
his ἀρετή as the reason for victory.[160] The σύνεσις of Moses
praised in Ant. 2. 244 is his military sagacity, and repeatedly
it is this aspect of his ἀρετή which Josephus underscores.
Raguel rewards the beneficence (εὐεργέτημα) and charity
(εὐποιΐα) of Moses for his gallant rescue of the maidens from
ruffians.[161] Moses dares to approach the unapproachable holy
spot of the burning bush because of his courage (θάρσος),
where the voice commissions him to act as στρατηγός and ἡγεμών
of the Hebrews, assuring him that he will accomplish this
seemingly impossible feat through his σύνεσις.[162] At Elim,
the Israelites are ready to stone Moses when they forget the
ἀρετή and σύνεσις of their στρατηγός.[163]

By depicting Moses in this military role, Josephus is
taking a basically Biblical thread--Moses as the leader of the
Jews--and dyeing it another color--a Hellenistic color--as he
weaves it into his tapestry portrait of Moses.

(bb) Sophistic role.

On the basis of the foregoing analysis, it would be
easy to conclude that the military ἀρετή of Moses plays a far
greater role in Josephus' depiction of Moses than philosophic
ἀρετή, and that Josephus has in mind the military ἀρετή of
Alexander the Great, the successful general, rather than the
sophistic ἀρετή of Socrates the brilliant philosopher as he
narrates the exploits of Moses. But such a conclusion comes
to grief when we come to look at Josephus' final eulogy of
Moses in Ant. 4. 327-31, in which he all but gives the sophistic role exclusive coverage, while dismissing the military role
with a mere five words: καὶ στρατηγὸς μὲν ἐν ὀλίγοις.[164]

---

[159]Cf. discussion below, pp. 108ff.

[160]Ant. 3. 65.   [161]Ant. 2. 258-63.

[162]Ant. 2. 267-69.   [163]Ant. 3. 12.

[164]Ant. 4. 329.

What cannot be denied, however, is the thoroughly Hellenistic
color of the dye Josephus uses to describe Moses the στρατηγός.

If the military role is a Biblical thread dyed a different color, the sophistic role in which Josephus depicts Moses
can only be called an external thread which he weaves into the
portrait. The Moses Josephus wants to leave with his readers
is the Moses of <u>Ant</u>. 4. 327-31, a Moses who has been baptized
in the waters of Hellenism. The old man has not entirely
passed away; the prophetic and legislative roles are still
prominent; but there has been a new creation. The note on
which he ends--ἀρετή[165]--recalls his earlier promise to dwell
at length upon the ἀρετή of the lawgiver.[166] That he succeeds
is attested by the sheer frequency with which the term ἀρετή
is used to describe Moses. Prior to his birth an Egyptian
scribe predicted that he would surpass all men in ἀρετή,[167]
and with this trait Josephus punctuates every stage of his
life.[168] In fact, he successfully incorporates virtually every
Stoic virtue into Moses' life. His grandeur of intellect and
contempt of toil (φρονήματός τε μεγέθει καὶ πόνων καταφρονήσει)
qualified him as the noblest Hebrew of them all.[169] He was
endowed with an extraordinary measure of σύνεσις which became
the hallmark of his life: συνέσει τε τοὺς πώποτ' ἀνθρώπους
ὑπερβαλὼν ... .[170] He possessed beauty,[171] a generous
spirit,[172] valor,[173] power of endurance,[174] beneficence,[175]

---

[165]<u>Ant</u>. 4. 331.   [166]<u>Ant</u>. 3. 187.

[167]<u>Ant</u>. 2. 205.

[168]Cf. <u>Ant</u>. 2. 257, 262; 3. 12, 65, 69, 74, 97, 187,
188, 192, 317, 322.

[169]<u>Ant</u>. 2. 229.

[170]<u>Ant</u>. 4. 328; cf. 2. 230, 244, 269; 3. 12.

[171]<u>Ant</u>. 2. 225, 231, 232.

[172]<u>Ant</u>. 2. 232.   [173]<u>Ant</u>. 2. 252, 262.

[174]<u>Ant</u>. 2. 256.   [175]<u>Ant</u>. 2. 261.

courage,[176] rhetorical ability,[177] a cool head,[178] a benevolent
spirit,[179] willingness to undergo danger,[180] and complete
mastery of the passions.[181]

(b) Abraham.

Important as Moses is in Josephus' apology, he is not
the only link in the chain. In fact, we find that the other
heroes are reshaped in similar ways consistent with his apologetic aims. Traces of the concept of ἀρετή appear regularly,
for example, in his depiction of Abraham, who is introduced
into the narrative as "a man of ready intelligence on all
matters, persuasive with his hearers, and not mistaken in his
inferences" (δεινὸς ὢν συνιέναι τε περὶ πάντων καὶ πιθανὸς τοῖς
ἀκροωμένοις περί τε ὧν εἰκάσειεν οὐ διαμαρτάνων).[182] Like
Moses, he is interpreted by Josephus in terms of ἀρετή: "Hence
he began to have more lofty conceptions of virtue (ἀρετή) than
the rest of mankind, and determined to reform and change the
ideas universally current concerning God."[183] This last statement is no doubt an effort on the part of Josephus to enter
Abraham into competition with Greek philosophers; that he wins
the competition hands down is owing to the fact that he was the
first (πρῶτος) to promulgate a monotheistic view of God, thus
upstaging Pythagoras, among others.[184] His sophistic eminence
continues as he emigrates to Egypt κατὰ βούλησιν καὶ βοήθειαν
τοῦ θεοῦ,[185] where he wants to learn what the priests there
said about gods,[186] his aim of course being to convert them to
his view. In Egypt he becomes renowned for his extraordinary
ἀρετή: "... and Abraham consorted with the most learned of the
Egyptians, whence his virtue (ἀρετή) and reputation became
still more conspicuous;"[187] his sagacity and persuasive ability

---

[176]Ant. 2. 267; 3. 65.   [177]Ant. 3. 13; 4. 328.

[178]Ant. 3. 13ff.   [179]Ant. 3. 188.

[180]Ant. 3. 188.   [181]Ant. 4. 328.

[182]Ant. 1. 154.   [183]Ant. 1. 155.

[184]Ant. 1. 155.   [185]Ant. 1. 157.

[186]Ant. 1. 161.   [187]Ant. 1. 165.

in particular, are singled out.[188] Josephus' eulogy of Abraham
continues in the same vein: "a man in every virtue supreme"
(ἀνὴρ πᾶσαν ἀρετὴν ἄκρος),[189] although he is still well on Old
Testament ground when he mentions that "(Abraham) received from
God the due meed of honour for his zeal in His service,"[190] as
he is elsewhere when he speaks conventionally of Abraham as the
forefather of the Jewish race.[191] Only once does Josephus
slightly interpret Abraham in the prophetic role.[192]

(c) Joseph.

Even though Joseph strikes a slightly different pose as
a result of the presence of the dream-interpreter motif in the
Old Testament narrative,[193] Josephus still manages to interpret
him sophistically:

> Ἰώσηπον ἐκ Ῥαχήλας πεπαιδοποιημένος Ἰάκωβος
> διά τε τὴν τοῦ σώματος εὐγένειαν καὶ διὰ ψυχῆς
> ἀρετήν, φρονήσει γὰρ διέφερε, τῶν ἄλλων πλέον
> υἱῶν ἠγάπα.

> Joseph, whom Jacob begat by Rachel, was beloved
> of his father above all his sons, alike for the
> beauty of person that he owed to his birth and
> for virtuous qualities of soul, for he was
> endowed with exceptional understanding.[194]

As would be expected, the Potiphar's wife incident is interpreted as proof of Joseph's ἀρετή.[195] In prison he impressed the
king's cupbearer by his σύνεσις[196] and pled his innocence to
the butler by saying:

> οὐδὲν γὰρ ἐξαμαρτόντες ἐν δεσμοῖς γεγόναμεν, ἀλλ'
> ἀρετῆς ἕνεκα καὶ σωφροσύνης τὰ τῶν κακούργων
> ὑπομένειν κατεκρίθημεν, οὐδέ γε μετ' οἰκείας ἡδονῆς
> τὸν ταῦθ' ἡμᾶς ἐργασάμενον ὑβρίσαι θελήσαντες.

---

[188]Ant. 1. 167. [189]Ant. 1. 256.

[190]Ant. 1. 256.

[191]Ant. 2. 269, 318; 3. 87; 7. 67; 14. 255; Bel. 4. 531.

[192]Ant. 1. 154.

[193]On Josephus' Hellenistic portrait of Joseph, cf. H.
SPRÖDOWSKY, Die Hellenisierung der Geschichte von Joseph in
Ägypten bei Flavius Josephus (Greifswald, 1973); also M. BRAUN,
History and Romance in Graeco-Oriental Literature (Oxford, 1938).

[194]Ant. 2. 9. Trans. Thackeray (Loeb).

[195]Ant. 2. 40. [196]Ant. 2. 63.

For it was no crime that brought me into these
bonds: nay, it was for virtue's sake and for
sobriety that I was condemned to undergo a
malefactor's fate, and because even the lure
of my own pleasure would not induce me to dis-
honour him who has thus treated me.[197]

It is his extreme sagacity (σύνεσιν ἱκανώτατος)[198] that
recommends him to Pharaoh, who later names him Psonthomphanechos
"in view of his amazing intelligence" (πρὸς τὸ παράδοξον τῆς
συνέσεως).[199] The incident of the brothers' return to Egypt is
interpreted as an illustration of Joseph's φιλανθρωπία.[200]
Josephus' eulogy provides a neat summary of his overall portrait of Joseph: "a man of admirable virtue, who directed all
affairs by the dictates of reason and made but sparing use of
his authority" (... θαυμάσιος τὴν ἀρετὴν γενόμενος καὶ λογισμῷ
πάντα διοικῶν καὶ τὴν ἐξουσίαν ταμιευόμενος ...).[201] The
closest Joseph comes to being called theios is in the choice of
titles Josephus uses to describe his role as Pharaoh's protégé:
σωτὴρ τοῦ πλήθους,[202] Αἰγύπτου κύριος,[203] but these are clearly
devoid of any religious significance. It should also be
noticed that πρόνοια θεοῦ is likewise an integral motif in the
Joseph story.[204]

(d) David.

Josephus devotes the greater part of two books to David,
in which a similar pattern occurs, though with some variations.
If anything, David is presented in more distinctly Hellenistic
terms than Moses. From the beginning of his career to the end
of his life, he is the paragon of the Greek virtues. When
Samuel mistakenly thinks Jesse's oldest son should be king, God
replies:

ἀλλὰ σὺ μὲν εἰς τὸ κάλλος ἀπιδὼν τοῦ νεανίσκου
καὶ δὴ τοῦτον ἡγῇ ἄξιον τοῦ βασιλεύειν εἶναι,
ἐγὼ δ' οὐ σωμάτων εὐμορφίας ἔπαθλον ποιοῦμαι τὴν

---

[197] Ant. 2. 69. Trans. Thackeray (Loeb).

[198] Ant. 2. 80; cf. 2. 87.

[199] Ant. 2. 91.   [200] Ant. 2. 101.

[201] Ant. 2. 198.   [202] Ant. 2. 94.

[203] Ant. 2. 174; cf. 3. 87.

[204] Ant. 2. 60, 107, 116, 122, 160-66.

βασιλείαν ἀλλὰ ψυχῶν ἀρετῆς, καὶ ζητῶ ὅστις ταύτης
ἐστὶ τελέως εὐπρεπής, εὐσεβείᾳ καὶ δικαιοσύνῃ καὶ
ἀνδρείᾳ καὶ πειθοῖ, ἐξ ὧν τὸ τῆς ψυχῆς συνίσταται
κάλλος, κατακεκοσμημένος.

"Nay, thou, looking upon this young man's beauty,
thinkest none other than him worthy to be king; but
I make not of the kingdom a prize for comeliness of
body, but for virtue of soul, and I seek one who in
full measure is distinguished by this, one adorned
with piety, justice, fortitude and obedience, qualities whereof beauty of soul consists."[205]

His ἀρεταί are singled out repeatedly;[206] he is δίκαιος,[207] ὁ
ἀγαπῶν τὴν ἀλήθειαν,[208] θεοσεβής,[209] εὐχάριστος,[210]
φιλόστοργος,[211] ἀνδρεῖος,[212] all of which are compactly pulled
together in Josephus' eulogy.[213] In turn, when David comes to
give paternal advice to Solomon, he does so in exactly the same
terms.[214]

Josephus' portrait of David is also revealing in two
other aspects. First, he heightens David's prophetic role,
while at the same time making his contact with God less direct
than it is in the Old Testament. Several times David is made
to prophesy (προφητεύειν) in Josephus' narrative when there is
no comparable mention in the LXX.[215] Yet, at the same time
when in the LXX he addresses God directly, in Josephus' account
he does so through a third party.[216] Secondly, he underscores
the piety of David by calling attention to God's πρόνοια over
all his affairs[217] and his corresponding response. The four
cardinal virtues, as we have already noticed above, Josephus

---

[205]Ant. 6. 160. Trans. Thackeray & Marcus (Loeb). Cf.
Philo, V. Mos. 1. 156. Cf. discussion below, pp. 108ff., esp.
113.

[206]Cf. Ant. 6. 206.   [207]Ant. 7. 110, 130, 269.

[208]Ant. 7. 110, 269.   [209]Ant. 7. 130, 153.

[210]Ant. 7. 111.   [211]Ant. 7. 252.

[212]Ant. 7. 300.   [213]Ant. 7. 390-91.

[214]Ant. 7. 338-40, 381, 384-85.

[215]Ant. 6. 166; 7. 334; 8. 109.

[216]Ant. 7. 71ff.

[217]Ant. 6. 181, 196, 203, 280; 7. 65, 71ff., 90, 122,
153.

significantly alters by substituting εὐσέβεια and πειθώ for
σωφροσύνη and φρόνησις, and both distinctly Jewish virtues are
interwoven into his portrait of David, which makes the
Bathsheba-Uriah incident all the more painful for Josephus to
include, but he does so nevertheless--indeed amplifies it.
David's piety is defined in terms of his response to God and
becomes one of the main features of ἀρετή which he recommends
to Solomon and which his successors imitate.[218] Moreover, it
is gauged according to his response to πρόνοια.[219]

(e) Solomon.

Solomon, as would be expected, exhibits the same sophistic traits, though surprisingly, not to the extent which the
Biblical account legitimately warrants. The transition from
David to Solomon is made by David's prayer for Solomon to have
"a sound and just mind, strengthened by all virtuous qualities"
(διάνοιαν ὑγιῆ καὶ δικαίαν καὶ πᾶσι τοῖς τῆς ἀρετῆς μέρεσιν
ἐρρωμένην).[220] In the farewell charge of David to Solomon,
εὐσέβεια and δικαιοσύνη towards his subjects are emphasized
more than the sophistic qualities.[221] But Josephus does call
attention to his wisdom,[222] and mentions the famous request for
wisdom instead of wealth.[223] Josephus' only use of the
language of deification in connection with Solomon occurs in
the statement that he makes after the tale of the two mothers
claiming the same child, when he notes that from that day on
the multitude "hearkened to him as to one possessed of a god-
like understanding" (ὡς θείαν ἔχοντι διάνοιαν αὐτῷ
προσεῖχον).[224] Bieler takes this passage as evidence that
Josephus has bent Solomon in the direction of the Hellenistic
God-man,[225] but, surely, this passage is but another way of
stating that Solomon's wisdom was God-given, as in Ant. 15.
398: κατ' ἐπιφροσύνην τοῦ θεοῦ. Josephus also includes the
celebrated visit of the Queen of Sheba who heard of his

---

[218]Ant. 8. 315; cf. 10. 49.

[219]Ant. 7. 338.   [220]Ant. 7. 381.

[221]Ant. 7. 383-85.   [222]Ant. 8. 21.

[223]Ant. 8. 22.   [224]Ant. 8. 34.

[225]Cf. above, p. 32.

ἀρετὴ καὶ φρόνησις,[226] and the exchange of conundrums with
Hiram of Tyre who regarded him as ἀνὴρ σοφὸς καὶ πᾶσαν ἀρετὴν
ἔχων.[227] In spite of the reports which circulated heralding
his ἀρετὴ καὶ σοφία,[228] Josephus candidly reports that he came
to an inglorious end.[229]

(f) Summary.

The generally uniform mold into which Josephus recasts
each of these Biblical figures is the most striking feature of
the preceding analysis. In the end, they all turn out looking
about the same, having been transformed into images reflecting
the Hellenistic ideal of the virtuous (wise) man. Many of
these characteristics are common to the Stoic Wise Man, but one
wonders whether they can be identified that precisely. Is it
not likely that we are seeing here what was probably popular,
possibly philosophical or semi-philosophical ethics, which was
more or less common property of the age?

What is undeniable is that Josephus is reflecting non-
LXX imagery and terminology in these portraits. He has
willingly absorbed the atmosphere of his day, and, in fact, is
probably providing us a good mirror of his day. He has not
moved completely beyond the LXX, for his Biblical heritage is
still dominant enough within him for him to emphasize repeatedly the importance of εὐσέβεια, in fact to change the four
cardinal Greek virtues to suit his Jewish piety.

Finally, what is also undeniable is the absence of any
tendency for him to deify these heroes, or even to elevate them
to supra-human status. He is more than willing to reinterpret
them in contemporary categories, but in this survey we only
found three instances, two in reference to Josephus,[230] one in
reference to Solomon,[231] where there was anything that even

---

[226] Ant. 8. 165-67.

[227] Ant. 8. 53; cf. 142-43, 147-49; Ap. 1. 109-11, 113-15.

[228] Ant. 8. 182; cf. 11. 90.

[229] Ant. 8. 196, 211.

[230] Ant. 2. 94; 2. 174; cf. 3. 87.

[231] Ant. 8. 34.

resembled language of deification, and these turned out to be
slight and insubstantial. Certainly, in no instance is <u>theios</u>
used of any of these figures in the sense that it is attached
to Augustus in <u>Ant</u>. 19. 289, and in none of these is there any
suggestion of a transformation into υἱὸς θεοῦ.

(2) <u>Josephus' Estimation of Pagans</u> and <u>Non-Biblical Jewish Heroes</u>.

When we come to look at Josephus' treatment of persons
besides Israel's heroes, we find that he displays a similar
reluctance in his handling of kings and other figures whom
pagans regard as divine. Augustus is called "the Lord of all
men" (ἐπὶ τῷ πάντων δεσπότῃ Καίσαρι),[232] "the Lord of the
universe" (ὁ τῆς οἰκουμένης προστάτης Καῖσαρ),[233] and the
"saviour of all mankind" (ἐπὶ τὸν πάντας σῴζοντα),[234] but each
time in a speech by a participant in the narrative, not by
Josephus himself. The responsibility for attributing deity to
kings Josephus always shifts to someone else: Antiochus II
Theos is "Antiochus, the grandson of Seleucus, called Theos <u>by
the Greeks</u>" (ὁ παρὰ τοῖς Ἕλλησιν θεὸς λεγόμενος).[235] For
lesser figures the same rule holds. Herod Agrippa I is
addressed as a god by his flatterers (οἱ κόλακες),[236] and
refers to himself as a god ("ὁ θεὸς ὑμῖν ἐγώ ..."),[237] whereas
Josephus' own assessment of him is considerably more restrain-
ed.[238] Costobarus, governor of Idumaea, was believed to be a
god <u>by the Idumaeans</u> (θεὸν δὲ τοῦτον Ἰδουμαῖοι νομίζουσιν).[239]
Herod the Great calls Eurycles, the Lacedaemonian flatterer,
"saviour and benefactor" (σωτῆρα καὶ εὐεργέτην),[240] but this
hardly qualifies as an attribution of divinity. Vespasian,
whom Josephus praises only less highly than his own son and
successor Titus, when caught in a perilous position, "like one
inspired (ὥσπερ ἔνθους γενόμενος),[241] linked his comrades

---

[232]<u>Ant</u>. 16. 118.

[233]<u>Bel</u>. 1. 633.

[234]<u>Ant</u>. 16. 105.

[235]<u>Ant</u>. 12. 125.

[236]<u>Ant</u>. 19. 345.

[237]<u>Ant</u>. 19. 347.

[238]<u>Ant</u>. 19. 330-31.

[239]<u>Ant</u>. 15. 253.

[240]<u>Bel</u>. 1. 530.

[241]<u>Bel</u>. 4. 33.

together ...," but this can hardly qualify as an attribution of
divinity since Josephus felt that πρόνοια θεοῦ guided the
military and imperial endeavors of Roman leaders.[242]   When he
comes to Gaius, perhaps the least tactful and therefore most
hated Roman ruler the Jews had, Josephus' attitude is both
consistent and unsympathetic.   At first Gaius ruled with
moderation, according to Josephus,

> προϊὼν δ᾽ ἐξίστατο τοῦ ἀνθρωπίνως φρονεῖν ὑπὸ
> μεγέθους τῆς ἀρχῆς ἐκθειάζων ἑαυτὸν καὶ τὰ
> πάντα ἐπ᾽ ἀτιμίᾳ τοῦ θείου πολιτεύειν ἦρτο.
>
> But as time went on, he ceased to think of him-
> self as a man and, as he imagined himself a god
> because of the greatness of his empire, he was
> moved to disregard the divine power in all his
> official acts.[243]

Later, he says that Gaius "would also have deified himself and
demanded from his subjects honours that were no longer such as
may be rendered to a man" (ἐξεθείαζέν τε ἑαυτὸν καὶ τὰς τιμὰς
οὐκέτ᾽ ἀνθρωπίνως ἠξίου γίνεσθαι παρὰ τῶν ὑπηκόων αὐτῷ).[244]
He had the audacity to address Jupiter as brother and drove his
chariot over a pontoon bridge--a way of travelling befitting a
god (θεῷ).[245]   It is not surprising that he expected to be
hailed as a god,[246] nor is it any more surprising that the Jews
saw the matter differently.[247]   To them he was only a man whom
they adamantly refused to address as θεός.[248]   Josephus' eulogy
of Gaius, understandably enough, is only lengthy, not compli-
mentary.[249]

        If Josephus was hesitant to call Biblical persons θεῖος
or δαιμόνιος, and if he judiciously refrained from leaving any
impression that he agreed with the pagan estimation of certain
persons being regarded as divine, he can hardly be expected to
have used more lavish terms for the non-Biblical Jewish heroes.
On the whole, the Maccabean struggle produced examples of
bravery rather than divinity.   In the case of John Hyrcanus,

---

[242]Cf. Bel. 4. 501.

[243]Ant. 18. 256.   Trans. L. H. Feldman.

[244]Ant. 19. 4.   [245]Ant. 19. 6.

[246]Bel. 2. 184.   [247]Bel. 2. 195.

[248]Ant. 19. 284.   [249]Ant. 19. 201-11.

Josephus underscores his extraordinary cleverness,[250] whereas
Judas Maccabaeus is singled out primarily for his courage and
bravery.[251] In neither case does Josephus intimate that they
are divine in any sense, unless the allusion to Judas' ability
to foresee the outcome of events should be taken as an indication that he possessed the prophetic gift. During the Zealot
uprising the high priest Matthias begs Simon, son of Gioras, to
enter Jerusalem to rid it of the Zealots, whereupon he is
"acclaimed by the people as their savior and protector" (σωτὴρ
... καὶ κηδεμών ...).[252] This same Matthias was appointed high
priest on the recommendation of his brother Jonathan: πάσης
καὶ πρὸς τὸν θεὸν ἁμαρτίας καὶ πρὸς σέ, βασιλεῦ, καθαρὸς
ἀδελφὸς ἔστι μοι,[253] a description which resembles Philo's
definition of a theios aner as one who is sinless, but πρὸς
τὸν θεὸν ἁμαρτίας ... καθαρὸς ... is not equivalent to τὸ
μηδὲν συνόλως ἁμαρτεῖν,[254] the former referring to cultic
cleanliness, the latter to moral purity. Josephus' assessment
of the tax-collector Joseph, father of Hyrcanus, is more typical of the way he describes eminent non-Biblical persons:
ἀνὴρ ἀγαθὸς γενόμενος καὶ μεγαλόφρων.[255] In fact, ἀνὴρ καλὸς
καὶ ἀγαθός seems to have been a stock phrase used in praising
men.[256] If a king is being praised, δίκαιος is substituted,
and the phrase becomes something like ἀνὴρ ἀγαθὸς καὶ
δίκαιος.[257]

(a) Summary.

The foregoing analysis is extremely important to our
inquiry for the following reasons:
(1) It demonstrates the interconnection between Josephus'
Hellenizing tendency and his overall apologetic aims, which in

---

[250] Ant. 12. 190-98.

[251] Ant. 12. 284, 339, 352, 433-34.

[252] Bel. 4. 575.   [253] Ant. 19. 315.

[254] Virt. 177. Cf. discussion below, pp. 173ff.

[255] Ant. 12. 224.

[256] Ant. 13. 260; 14. 249, 251; cf. Ant. 18. 117.

[257] Ant. 9. 216, 236, 260.

turn explains why his portraits of all Israel's heroes fall
into a similar pattern.

(2) There is no indication that Josephus' propensity to recast
Israel's heroes into Hellenistic molds resulted in a corresponding tendency to portray them as divine. The evidence, if
anything, suggests an indirect ratio. Josephus' willingness to
Hellenize, even if it meant deleting embarrassing features of
the Biblical narrative, is matched not by a corresponding
willingness to portray Israel's heroes as divine, but by a
consistent reluctance to do so, a tendency matched by his
treatment of pagans who were regarded as divine and also of
non-Biblical Jewish heroes.

(3) On the basis of this evidence there is no compelling
reason why _theios_ in _Ant_. 3. 180 must be interpreted in Cornford's first sense, i.e. "divine," in its most literal sense.

(3) The Tabernacle Allegory.

        One other feature of the passage to be considered in
connection with determining whether _theios aner_ must be
rendered as equivalent to υἱὸς θεοῦ has to do with the
allegorical/symbolic interpretation of the tabernacle. We
have already briefly alluded to the novelty of this allegory.
Even though Josephus admits that Moses expresses some things in
allegories,[258] he himself rarely allegorizes, especially compared with Philo. The use of allegory as an apologetic device
is even more surprising, since he sharply criticizes the Greeks
who used allegory to circumvent problems they found in
Homer.[259] As mentioned earlier, his use of the tabernacle
allegory, in particular, is striking. It is similar to the
tabernacle allegory of Philo in terms of particular items and
symbols, but in Philo it is interpreted moralistically and is
not attached to a specific polemical setting as it is in
Josephus.[260]

----

[258]_Ant_. 1. 24.   [259]_Ap_. 2. 255.

[260]There is insufficient evidence that Josephus has
borrowed his allegory of the tabernacle from Philo (cf. _V_. _Mos_.
2. 74-140; _Spec_. _Leg_. 1. 71-97), as is supposed by C.
SIEGFRIED, _Philo von Alexandria als Ausleger des Alten Testa-
ments_ (Jena, 1875) 279-80. FRIEDLÄNDER, _Geschichte jüd. Apol_.,
(cont.)

In _Ant_. 3. 181ff., having called attention to the tabernacle, etc., Josephus launches into an uncharacteristically
detailed, albeit tentatively stated,[261] symbolic interpretation
of the tabernacle and its related features.[262] Simply stated,

---

340, simply says that Josephus is dependent upon Jewish-
Hellenistic modes of Scripture-interpretation. THACKERAY, art.
"Josephus," _HDB_, 5. 471, follows Siegfried. There are certain
features common to both Josephus' and Philo's treatments, but
the differences both in content and function are too great.
The similarities which are present are more likely due to the
common traditions underlying both, and they are probably
Palestinian traditions at that. (Thus, SCHÜRER, _Gesch. jüd._.
Volkes, 1. 702; cf. L. GINZBERG, "Allegorical Interpretation,"
_JE_, 1. 403-4; also E. R. GOODENOUGH, _Light_, 99, doubts that
Josephus is dependent upon Philo here; cf. NIESE, "Josephus,"
HERE, 7. 573. HÖLSCHER, "Josephus," _PWRE_, 1960-61, believes
that Josephus and Philo draw upon a common tradition, but that
it is an Alexandrian tradition.

[261]Note οἶμαι, 3. 184.

[262]The composite nature of Josephus' symbolic interpretation of the tabernacle makes it impossible to detect all the
sources upon which he is drawing. (Cf. R. PATAI, _Man and_
Temple in Ancient Jewish Myth and Ritual [New York, 1947] 105-
39, upon whom I depend for references and quotations from
Rabbinic sources cited below in this note.) Some features are
stock symbolic interpretations, e.g., the most holy place-holy
place = heaven-earth & sea (_Ant_. 3. 123; Jellinek, _Beth_
Hamidrash, 3. p. xxxiv); the four-part veil = four elements
(_Bel_. 5. 212-13; Philo, _V. Mos._, 2. 88); seven branches of
candlestick = seven planets (_Bel_. 5. 217; Philo, _V. Mos._ 2.
102; _Mid. Tadše_); tunic of high priest = four elements (Philo,
Spec. Leg. 1. 93-94). There was also great flexibility in the
interpretation of some items. Philo is aware that some interpret the two cherubim as the two hemispheres, but he prefers to
see them as symbols of the two "potencies," the creative and
the kingly (_V. Mos._ 2. 98-99. Colson, Loeb, vol. 6, p. 609,
remarks on par. 117-35, also notes other differences.). The
twelve stones on the high priest's garment can represent either
the twelve months or the twelve constellations, i.e., the
zodiac (so, _Ant_. 3. 186); Josephus is content to leave it at
that. The tentativeness of his language, e.g. οἶμαι, _Ant_. 3.
184, δέ μοι δοκεῖ, _Ant_. 3. 186, indicates that some of his
suggestions are his own creations.
   In spite of the fluidity of the tabernacle symbolism,
for the most part Josephus seems to be dependent upon a Palestinian hermeneutical tradition. That some Rabbis engaged in
allegorization is indisputable (cf. R. P. C. HANSON, _Allegory_
and Event, A Study of the Sources and Significance of Origen's
Interpretation of Scripture (London, 1959) 23ff., and the
literature cited therein, esp. J. Z. LAUTERBACH, "The Ancient
Jewish Allegorists, in Talmud and Midrash," _JQR_ N.S. 1 (1910-
11) 291-333; 503-31), but the line between symbolism and
(cont.)

the tabernacle, its equipment, and the priestly vestments are

---

allegory is exceedingly difficult to draw, if indeed it can be
drawn at all. L. GINZBERG, "Allegorical Interpretation," JE,
1. 403f., attempts to solve the problem by distinguishing two
modes of allegorical interpretation: (1) symbolic or typologi-
cal, and (2) philosophical or mystical, the former deriving
from Palestinian Jews, the latter from Alexandrian Jews, but
this is inadequate because typology is yet another phenomenon,
and, besides, his second type was practised in Palestine,
although not extensively (cf. LAUTERBACH's article cited above;
also STRACK-BILLERBECK, 3. 385-99). His suggestion that
Josephus was engaging in symbolical explanations is in the
right direction. I would distinguish the two by the presence
or absence of Scripture as the point of departure, symbolism
arising from the proclivity to see cultic objects as symbolic
of another object or event, allegory being an exercise in which
a (sacred) text is seen to have another meaning besides the
literal, for whatever reason. Rabbinic interpretations such as
"... the court which encompassed the tabernacle as the sea
encompasses the world" (Num. Rab. 13, 19; cf. also B. Suk. 51b;
Midr. Ps. 90, 18), or the statement by R. Jehuda b. Salom that
the great laver symbolized the waters of the sea, the golden
candlestick the light of the firmament, the cherubim the birds
flying in the heavens (Jalk. Sim. 719), or Num. Rab. 4, 13:
"The (position of the terrestrial) Sanctuary corresponds with
that of the heavenly Sanctuary and the (position of the) ark
with that of the heavenly Throne. He made a cover above it to
symbolise the seraphim which stand above Him. He made two
cherubim, which were precious as symbolising the heaven and
earth ... This (the cherubim facing each other) corresponded to
the Throne of Glory which was directly opposite the Holy One
..." (cf. also Num. Rab. 12, 11; 12, 12; 12, 13), or the quotation attributed to R. Pinhas b. Ya'ir (2nd cent.): "The
Tabernacle was made to correspond to the Creation of the world.
The two Cherubs over the Ark of the Covenant were made to
correspond to the two holy names (of God: Yahweh and Elohim).
The heaven, the earth and the sea are houses with bolts. The
house of the Holy of Holies was made to correspond to the
highest heaven. The outer Holy House was made to correspond
to the earth. And the Courtyard was made to correspond to the
sea. The eleven hangings of the Tabernacle were made to
correspond to the highest heaven. The table was made to
correspond to the earth. The two shew-breads were arranged to
correspond to the fruit of the earth. 'In two rows, six in a
row' (were set the twelve cakes) to correspond to the months of
summer and winter. The laver was made to correspond to the sea
and the candlestick was made to correspond to the lights (of
heaven). 'and he set up the pillars.' ... Jachin and Boaz,
Jachin (i.e. 'he will establish') corresponding to (the moon as
it is written), 'It shall be established for ever as the moon,'
for it is the moon which establishes the feasts for Israel, as
it is written 'He appointed the moon for seasons.' And Boaz
corresponds to the sun which comes out in power and in strength,
as it is written, 'it (the sun) rejoiceth as a strong man to
run the course" (as cited in PATAI, Man and Temple, 108-9)

(cont.)

said to have had cosmic significance, and that this was so
_____

are, strictly speaking, symbolism, for they reflect traditions
which sought to find symbolic meanings to these features of the
cult. These symbolic interpretations were foreshadowed in the
Old Testament, but the passages suggested (Isa. 41:1ff.; 1 Kn.
8:27; Isa. 66:1) by E. KÖNIG, art. "Tabernacle," JE, 11. 656,
hardly qualify; a more likely candidate is Ps. 78:69. These
symbolic interpretations were very early incorporated into
exegetical traditions, but the movement was from symbolism to
Scripture. The symbolic significance of the tabernacle which
had arisen in popular legends, or cultic circles, is then
justified by finding Biblical passages to which it can be
attached. This is quite a different phenomenon from allegory,
in which the interpreter begins with a text and looks for
symbolic meanings behind it (cf. PATAI, Man and Temple, 111-12).

      Allegory, by contrast, was not as common within the
Palestinian tradition because it was felt to be more directly
tampering with the sacred text and more easily liable to
excesses. R. Akiba (d. 135), who interpreted the Song of
Solomon as an expression of the mystical relationship between
God and Israel (cf. J. C. JOOSEN and J. H. WASZINK,
"Allegorese," RAC, 1. 287), was engaging in allegory as a means
of interpreting an otherwise inexplicable passage, and was more
in the tradition of Aristobulus, the first Jew to attempt to
allegorize the Old Testament according to Greek philosophical
methods, a process which reached its culmination in Philo.

      Of these two traditions, Josephus is more akin to the
former. He is incorporating traditions in which the symbolic
significance of the tabernacle flourished (cf. J. WEILL
(trans.), OEuvres complètes de Flavius Josèphe (ed. T. Reinach),
vol. 1, note on Ant. 3. 180, for references to similar traditions in Midrashim and Samaritan liturgy.) These traditions
have been influenced by Greek thought, e.g., the four-elements
motif (cf. R. MEYER, Hellenistisches in der rabbinischen
Anthropologie. Rabbinische Vorstellungen vom Werden des
Menschen (Stuttgart, 1937) 122-27, esp. 126, "Allerdings darf
man aus diesem Tatbestand kaum schliessen (i.e. Josephus'
Palestinian background compared with Philo's Hellenistic back-
ground), dass der Pharisäismus sich grundsätzlich gegen die
Naturvorstellungen der Griechen gewehrt habe und dass Josefus'
Aussagen gleichsam Konzessionen an seine hellenistische
Leserschaft darstellen. Denn so wenig verarbeitet diese
Gedanken bei Josefus auch sein mögen, ebensowenig sind sie aus
seinem ihm zur Verfügung stehenden weltanschaulichen
Vorstellungen hinwegzudenken." H. WENSCHKEWITZ, "Die
Spiritualisierung der Kultusbegriffe: Tempel, Priester und
Opfer im Neuen Testament," ΑΓΓΕΛΟΣ, Archiv für neutestament-
liche Zeitgeschichte und Kulturkunde 4 (1932) 87, overstates
the case when he says, "Die stark griechische Formulierung
(with regard to Bel. 5. 458-59) scheint schriftstellerische
Redaktion des Josephus zu sein, zumal da dieser eine
allegorisierende Ausdeutung des Tempels auf die Welt und der
Teile des Tempels auf die Teile des Kosmos kennt" (citing Ant.
3. 123, 181ff.; Bel. 5. 213ff.). He does reinterpret the
traditions in keeping with his apologetic aims which are
Hellenistically conditioned, but there was no doubt some
(cont.)

intended by Moses himself.[263] Or, more accurately, when the
Lawgiver instituted these features of Jewish worship he did so
with the intention of their representing some part of universal
nature. Accordingly, the most holy place corresponds to
heaven, being accessible to God alone, whereas the two outer
courts correspond to the earth and sea, since they are accessible to everybody. The four-part tapestry within the tabernacle
represents the four elements of the universe, etc.

If Josephus is here dependent upon the Alexandrian
exegetical tradition,[264] even minimally, this places him in
more direct contact with the Greek philosophical tradition of
allegorical interpretation. It would thus have been more
likely that he knew about the centuries-old debate between the
philosophers and poets, in which allegory had functioned as the
crucial means for exonerating Homer and the poets.[265] It was
by no means a dead issue in the time of Josephus. In the
Quaestiones Homericae Heracleitus, an older contemporary of
Josephus,[266] vigorously defends Homer in a manner strikingly

---

Hellenistic influence which had already permeated the Palestinian traditions before Josephus used them. Even with the
Hellenistic influence, these symbolic traditions which Josephus
employs are unlike both Alexandrian and Palestinian allegory,
which relegated the literal meaning to a secondary level of
importance, or even of total unimportance. If Josephus is
engaging in allegory at all, it is at the most elementary level.
For further discussion of the cosmological symbolism in Ant. 3.
179ff., cf. U. FRÜCHTEL, Die kosmologischen Vorstellungen bei
Philo von Alexandrien. Ein Beitrag zur Geschichte der Genesis-
exegese (Leiden, 1968) 98ff.; also J. DANIÉLOU, "La symbolique
du temple de Jérusalem chez Philon et Josephe," in Le
symbolisme cosmique des monuments religieux (Rome, 1957) 83-90;
also Philon d'Alexandrie (Paris, 1958), 130, where he notes
that the cosmic interpretation of temple(s) is a Stoic theme,
frequent in Cicero, Seneca, traceable no doubt to Aristotle;
cf. FESTUGIÈRE, Le dieu cosmique, 230ff.

[263]Cf. Plutarch, De Is. et Osir. 382b-d, especially the
remarks concerning the vestments of Isis.

[264]Cf. DANIÉLOU, Philon, 102ff., for a condensed sketch
of the Alexandrian exegetical tradition.

[265]Cf. G. BARDY, art. "Apologetik," RAC, 1. 533ff.

[266]Cf. K. REINHARDT, art. "Herakleitos," PWRE 8.1 (1912)
508-10, who dates him in the period of the Augustan or Neronian
era. Cf. also SCHMID-STÄHLIN, GGL, 1. 367-69. The edition of
(cont.)

similar to what we find in <u>Ant</u>. 3. 179-87. Homer has been
accused of ἀσέβεια, primarily by Plato and Epicurus because of
his supposed contempt for the Deity (περὶ τῆς εἰς τὸ θεῖον
ὀλιγωρίας).[267] As a means of defense, Heracleitus appeals to
allegory, arguing that Homer is indeed guilty of ἀσέβεια <u>if</u>
what he says is to be taken literally: πάντα γὰρ ἠσέβησεν, εἰ
μηδὲν ἠλληγόρησεν.[268] The bulk of the work consists of examples of allegorical exegesis, including some rather far-fetched
ones, resulting in a transformation of the poem "if not into a
highly metaphysical chat about the weather, at least into a
rationalistically conceived scientific and historical account
of the seige of Troy."[269] His first line of defense is outright denial: Τίς οὖν ἐπὶ τούτοις Ὅμηρον ἀσεβῆ λέγειν
τολμᾷ;.[270] Then follow two passages from the <u>Iliad</u> to illustrate Homer's adoration for Zeus,[271] cited as examples of "the
pious intentions of Homer" (τῆς Ὁμήρου θεοσεβοῦς προαιρέσεως).
Then follows this remarkable statement: ὅτι πάθεσιν ἐξαιρέτοις
ἅπαν νεωκορεῖ τὸ δαιμόνιον, ἐπεὶ καὐτός ἐστι θεῖος.[272] Later,
while explaining a passage about the gods fighting, he exclaims,
with almost visible exasperation:

> Ὅμως δ᾽ οὖν πάντα ταῦτα κατ᾽ἀρχὰς μὲν οὐδ᾽ ὅλως
> σφόδρα πείθειν δύναται τοὺς πολλούς. Εἰ δ᾽
> ἐθελήσοι τις ἐνδοτέρω καταβὰς τῶν Ὁμηρικῶν
> ὀργίων ἐποπτεῦσαι τὴν μυστικὴν αὐτοῦ σοφίαν,
> ἐπιγνώσεται τὸ δοκοῦν αὐτῷ ἀσέβημα πηλίκης μεστόν
> ἐστι φιλοσοφίας.

> Nevertheless, therefore, all these things from
> the beginning are indeed not able to persuade
> most (people) very fully. But, if one were only
> willing, having plumbed the depths of the Homeric
> mysteries, to attain to his mystic wisdom, one
> will recognize how full of philosophy is that
> which seems to him to be impiety.[273]

Heracleitus used in the following analysis is that of F.
BUFFIÈRE (ed. and trans.), <u>Héraclite</u>, <u>Allégories</u> D'Homère
(Budé) (Paris, 1962).

[267] <u>Qu</u>. <u>Hom</u>. 1. 1. Contrast the trial of Socrates, who
was also accused of impiety.

[268] <u>Qu</u>. <u>Hom</u>. 1. 1.

[269] HANSON, <u>Allegory</u> <u>and</u> <u>Event</u>, 56.

[270] <u>Qu</u>. <u>Hom</u>. 3. 1.   [271] <u>Il</u>. 2. 412; 3. 277-80.

[272] <u>Qu</u>. <u>Hom</u>. 3. 1.   [273] <u>Qu</u>. <u>Hom</u>. 53. 1-2.

The similarities between this passage from Heracleitus and <u>Ant</u>. 3. 179-80 are obvious, but the crucial question, insofar as our inquiry is concerned, is whether the ascription of <u>theios</u> to a celebrated historical figure who has been accused of impiety was an established apologetic device, and if so, whether Josephus is utilizing it in <u>Ant</u>. 3. 179-80. This line of interpretation is extremely attractive as a possible framework in which to interpret <u>Ant</u>. 3. 179-80, if for no other reason, because the structural combination of motifs found in Heracleitus would provide an example of what is otherwise an inexplicable combination in Josephus. Josephus' response in 3. 179-87 is unique both in terms of its content and function. He does not normally respond to anti-Jewish polemics with allegory; and, this particular allegory is never employed, even by writers besides Josephus, as an apologetic device. The <u>theios aner</u> motif is, of course, unique by its very appearance at all. Yet, the Heracleitus quotations combine all three: the polemical setting, the ascription of <u>theios</u> to Homer, and allegory as an apologetic device.

Attractive as it is, the argument only has to be laid out for the differences to become apparent:

1. Statement of charge: Homer is ἀσεβής.
2. Refutation of charge:
   a. Denial: Homer is εὐσεβής (examples cited).
   b. Affirmation of divinity:[274] Homer is <u>theios</u>.
   c. Apparent impieties must be allegorized: Homer ἠλληγόρησεν.
   d. Deeper insight is the key to true interpretation: εἰ δέ ...

The one is concerned with an individual, Homer; the other with a people, the Jews. The charges are ostensibly the same--ἀσέβεια--Homer's impiety is his irreverent description of the gods. But, in reality, they are not the same. Homer is more strictly ἀσεβής; the Jews' action is more accurately ἄθεος.[275]

---

[274]Assuming, of course, that <u>theios</u> carries this meaning even here. BUFFIERE seems to think so as he refers to CUMONT, <u>Symbol. funer</u>., 313ff., "on the divinization of Homer."

[275]Cf. the distinction made in Diogenes Laertius 7. 119, θείους τ᾽ εἶναι· ἔχειν γὰρ ἐν ἑαυτοῖς οἱονεὶ θεόν. τὸν δὲ φαῦλον ἄθεον. διττὸν δὲ εἶναι τὸν ἄθεον, τόν τ᾽ ἐναντίως τῷ θείῳ λεγόμενον καὶ τὸν ἐξουθενητικὸν τοῦ θείου· ὅπερ οὐκ εἶναι (cont.)

Moreover, the allegory is substantially different. Heracleitus allegorizes a text, the Homeric narrative, now moralistically, now physically, now historically; it is debatable whether the Josephus passage is anything more than cosmic symbolism. The tabernacle (Temple) has not been attacked for its ludicrousness, nor has Moses been ridiculed for his irreverent conception of God. In other words, the allegory in Josephus does not arise out of the accusation, as is the case in Heracleitus. Instead, it is an external device brought into a foreign situation.

There is, therefore, no compelling reason why we must interpret theios aner as υἱὸς θεοῦ in Ant. 3. 180 on the basis of Heracleitus, Quaestiones Homericae, 3. 1 and 53. 1-2, even if one assumes that by theios Heracleitus means "divine" in its literal sense.

We are left then with having excluded the three possibilities open to us as possible interpretations of theios aner without having reached a fully satisfactory solution. Briefly, our dilemma is this: the context of Ant. 3. 179ff., both with respect to the charge of ἀσέβεια in 3. 179 and with respect to the appeal to the tabernacle, etc., seems to demand that theios aner be taken to mean ἀνὴρ εὐσεβής, or something similar; and yet, theios is not really a synonym of εὐσεβής; at least, in those instances where Josephus applies theios to persons, it does not carry this meaning. Even so, this is the most plausible meaning, not only from the context, but also from the mention in Ant. 3. 187 of τὴν ἀρετὴν τοῦ νομοθέτου. We shall proceed to show, therefore, that taking theios aner in Ant. 3. 180 to mean "holy man" or "pious man" fits with Josephus' overall portrayal of Moses in light of his apologetic task.

(4) Moses as εὐσεβής.

Stated in the broadest possible terms, Antiquitates is an apology for Judaism,[276] even if it is likely that Josephus'

περὶ πάντα φαῦλον. The Jews, of course, were accused of ἀσέβεια; cf. S. S. COHON, "The Unity of God. A Study in the Hellenistic and Rabbinic Theology," HUCA 26 (1955) 428.

[276]NIESE, art. "Josephus," HERE, 7. 576-77, "... the leading motive of all that he writes is that of the apologist."

audience was largely apathetic, if not antipathetic to the
Jewish cause. It is unlikely that a non-Jew, particularly from
the upper classes, living outside Palestine (and possibly
Alexandria) in the last decade of the first century A.D. had
much substantial first-hand knowledge of Judaism.[277] Even if
he did, ethnic stereotypes abounded, and true to form, were
usually uncomplimentary. Anti-Jewish polemics flourished but
can hardly be called propaganda in the sense of an organized
attack upon Jews qua Jews. For all their social progress, they
were still a hated race. The obvious distinctive features of
their religion, such as the Sabbath and some of the cultic
observances, were known, but, as H. St. J. Hart has remarked,
Vespasian must have puzzled over the scrolls of the Law which
he brought back to Rome and deposited in the palace.[278]

Josephus' apology for Judaism has two foci: ὁ θεός and
ὁ νόμος. His section devoted to Moses is bracketed by this
bifocal theme (it is really one inseparable theme). Already in
the preface to Ant. these two foci are singled out, restated,
and woven together, as seen in a very important passage, Ant.
1. 14-16. Similarly, at the end of the section on Moses, the
farewell speech which Josephus attributes to him reiterates
these same two concerns: "... and leaving in your memory the
thought that it behoves you to revere and honour Him, and to
observe His laws."[279] This bifocal perspective, then, is the
overarching view against which Josephus' treatment of Moses
must be viewed.

(a) ὁ θεός.

The first focus explains the theological preoccupation
of what is supposedly an historical work. Josephus is both
historian and apologist, in reverse order. Unlike Bellum and
C. Apionem, which are self-styled attempts to narrate correctly
events which have been falsely reported, Antiquitates is not
conceived by Josephus as an effort to set the record straight;
it is not refutation apologetic so much as it is affirmation
apologetic. The preface indicates that Josephus is in less of

---

[277]Cf. J. GAGER, Moses in Greco-Roman Paganism (New
York, 1972), esp. 162.

[278]Bel. 7. 150, 162.   [279]Ant. 4. 318.

a defensive posture. He brings to the center of the stage the cardinal doctrines of Judaism, especially belief in God, which is the single most important ingredient conditioning his concept of history, and therefore his historiography. He openly admits that he does not intend merely to write history, but history from a theologically determined, moralistic point of view.[280] He unreservedly alerts his readers to the fact that the featured character of Antiquitates is God.[281] Only in the light of this fundamental theological concern can the other features of his history be seen in any balanced perspective. It is always possible, of course, for an author to fall short of his stated aims, but at least one should take note of what these intended aims are and, for a start, view the work in light of those aims. Given this overriding theological preoccupation, the characters of his narrative take on a subordinate importance owing to their being part of a larger argument. Josephus does not focus attention upon Moses, nor even upon his brilliance as a lawgiver as ends in themselves, but only insofar as they bear upon the validity of his conception of God. He would like to launch directly into an extended discourse on the nature of God, but defers such a "profoundly and highly philosophical" inquiry until a later work.[282] In his opinion the strongest case for Judaism can be made by letting Jewish history speak for itself, albeit with some Josephan reshaping, by comparing Moses' account of God, i.e. the Biblical account, with that of other lawgivers, and arguing that the former is not only more ancient, but more accurate and attractive, and, if one grants his moralistic presuppositions, more rewarding.

But, like all apologists, Josephus has to seek common ground on which to meet his readers. His attempt to make the Jewish God more palatable to pagans is evidenced by the use of less strictly Jewish titles such as τὸ θεῖον and ὁ θεὸς τῶν ὅλων.[283] More subtle is his decision to employ the widely known concept of πρόνοια as the interpretative framework by

---

[280]Ant. 1. 14. [281]Ant. 1. 15.

[282]Ant. 1. 25; 20. 268.

[283]Cf. SCHLATTER, Theologie, 2ff.; FRIEDLÄNDER, Gesch. jüd. Apol., 333.

which to unfold Old Testament history, indeed the whole of
Jewish history. Behind this decision lay the awareness that
few, if any, pagans would concede that ὁ θεὸς τῶν ὅλων was to
be identified with ὁ θεὸς τῶν 'Ιουδαίων. Josephus capitalizes
upon the historical development that had occurred in the understanding of πρόνοια, originally an abstract notion, which by
his time was regarded by many as a personal force.[284] Πρόνοια
θεοῦ becomes the apologetic device by which Josephus seeks to
show that his God is the true God. The Biblical stories are
told in order to document the presence of πρόνοια θεοῦ as an
integral and demonstrable feature of Israel's history.[285] Once
this point is granted, Josephus is then able to argue that the
θεός in the phrase πρόνοια θεοῦ is none other than ὁ θεός at
work within Jewish history, i.e. ὁ θεὸς τῶν 'Ιουδαίων.[286]
Πρόνοια θεοῦ is thus redefined to conform to Josephus' first
apologetic focus, ὁ θεός. It is no longer grounded metaphysically in the Stoic view of φύσις, but historically in the
experience of Israel.

Josephus' preoccupation with this theme in his treatment
of Moses is seen most noticeably in the speeches ("speeches"
here includes prayers) which he inserts at crucial points in
his narrative. Since he is ostensibly narrating Israel's
history as recorded by Moses, the Old Testament can serve as a
measuring-stick by which to examine Josephus. The speeches in
particular serve as windows through which the real Josephus can
be seen, for in them it is possible to see how he alters the
Old Testament narrative.[287] Sometimes he creates speeches ex
nihilo, sometimes he expands brief speeches into much longer
discourses, while at other times he radically condenses

---

[284]Cf. J. BEHM, art. προνοέω, etc., TDNT, 4. 1012ff.

[285]Cf. J. A. MONTGOMERY, "The Religion of Flavius
Josephus," JQR, N.S. 11 (1920-21) 285ff.; G. DELLING, "Josephus
und das Wunderbare," in Studien zum Neuen Testament und zum
hellenistischen Judentum (Göttingen, 1970) 139, notes Josephus'
tendency to rationalize πρόνοια.

[286]On the difference between the Old Testament and Stoic
concepts of πρόνοια, cf. BEHM, TDNT, 4. 1014.

[287]Cf. B. GÄRTNER, The Areopagus Speech and Natural
Revelation (Uppsala, 1955) 24:4; also KRÜGER, Philo und Jos.,15.

several Old Testament discourses, but in all his modifications, the same themes recur. Diagrammatically, his modifications look this way:

	Antiq.		Parallel OT Reference
1.	2. 330-33	Moses' speech to Jews before crossing Red Sea	Ex. 14:13-14
2.	2. 335-37	Moses' prayer to God before crossing Red Sea	Ex. 14:15-Prayer by Mos. only alluded to.
3.	3. 84-88	Moses' speech to Jews after 1st Sinai ascent	Ex. 19:8-Only mentions that Mos. spoke words of Lord to people.
4.	3. 300-02	Moses' speech to Jews before they enter Canaan	Num. 13:1 - No speech mentioned.
5.	4. 25-34	Moses' speech to Korah	Num. 16:8-11
6.	4. 40-50	Moses' prayer for God to intervene in Korah affair	Num. 16:15
7.	4. 114-17		Num. 23:7-10
8.	4. 119-23	Balaam's trilogy of speeches	Num. 23:18-24 / Num. 24:3-9 — Balaam's 4 oracles
9.	4. 127-30		Num. 24:15-19 / Num. 24:20-24 — Miscel. Oracle
10.	4. 177-93	Moses' speech at age 120	Deut. 31:2-6 -Jos. condenses the 3 Deut. discourses into one.
11.	4. 315-19	Moses' final speech	Deut. 31:16-21-God to M. / Deut. 32:1-43-Song of M.

In all the speeches πρόνοια θεοῦ emerges as the central theme.[288] Even in those speeches where the term πρόνοια is absent, the theme is present.[289] In these speeches πρόνοια θεοῦ means that God is able to keep his promises,[290] as well as to perform his will.[291] Even the Egyptians come under the scope of God's will.[292] A corollary of πρόνοια θεοῦ is δύναμις θεοῦ; the events of Israel's history—both her vicissitudes and her successes—are demonstrations of God's δύναμις and

---

[288]Ant. 2. 329, 330, 332; 2. 336; 4. 40, 42, 47; 4. 114, 117; 4. 128; 4. 184; 4. 316.

[289]Ant. 3. 88; 3. 302; 4. 28, 32; 4. 121.

[290]Ant. 2. 329, 331.

[291]Ant. 2. 333; 4. 40; 4. 47.

[292]Ant. 2. 335.

ἰσχύς.[293] Failure to perceive these manifestations of God's
δύναμις is to be blind to his πρόνοια, and is failure to comprehend who he really is. Πρόνοια θεοῦ is historically
grounded in the successive events of Israel's past,[294] abundant
testimony that He is their ally and helper[295] who actively
cares for their welfare.[296] All attempts to thwart God's purposes come to a bad end.[297] It is clear that God's πρόνοια,
δύναμις, ἰσχύς, μελέτη, θέλημα, and βούλησις[298] form a nexus,
seen for example by the way all these motifs cluster in two
important passages: Ant. 2. 329-33 and 4. 315-319.

(b) ὁ νόμος.

The other focus of Josephus' apology, ὁ νόμος, also
figured prominently in Jewish history, and even in Josephus'
time was the force cementing the many Judaisms into any
semblance of homogeneity, especially after the Temple was
gone.[299] Pagans would readily acknowledge the need for order-
ing their lives by νόμος, even ὁ νόμος τοῦ θεοῦ, or νόμος
θεῖος, as Epictetus calls it.[300] They would not so readily
acknowledge that ὁ νόμος τῶν ᾿Ιουδαίων and ὁ νόμος τοῦ θεοῦ
were the same thing, and here arose the second aspect of
Josephus' apologetic task. Once again he wisely seeks common
ground and draws upon a familiar Hellenistic-Roman popular-

---

[293]Ant. 2. 332, 333; 2. 336, 337; 4. 32; 4. 117; 4. 121;
4. 180; 4. 318.

[294]Ant. 3. 86-7; 4. 43-5; 4. 316-17.

[295]Ant. 2. 334; 3. 302; 4. 114; 4. 182.

[296]Ant. 3. 88; 4. 123.

[297]Ant. 4. 44, 47, 50; 4. 117; 4. 190-91; 4. 319.

[298]SCHLATTER, Theologie, 27, observes Josephus' reluctance to speak of βούλησις θεοῦ, particularly in Bellum, since
he is addressing Greeks. This points up all the more clearly
why Josephus must link βούλησις θεοῦ etc., with a more Greek-
colored concept, e.g. πρόνοια or δύναμις, and accounts for his
attempt to make them all virtually interchangeable concepts.

[299]SCHLATTER, Theologie, 27, comments on the centrality
of νόμος in Palestinian Judaism.

[300]Epictetus, Diss., 1. xxix, 4, 13, 19; 2. xvi, 28;
3. xxiv, 42; cf. 1. xiii, 2; 3. xxiv, 110; 4. iii, 12; 4. vii,
35.

philosophical notion, ἀρετή, and uses it as the interpretative
key for bridging the ideological gap between himself and his
pagan readers. Briefly stated, he wants to show that ὁ νόμος
τῶν 'Ιουδαίων is the true path to virtue, but the fact that
many of the Jewish laws and regulations were odious to Greeks
meant that recasting the pursuit of ἀρετή as the equivalent of
obeying the Law of Moses was no easy matter. Josephus accomplishes this by a fairly intricate series of interrelated
arguments. First, he affirms that God himself embodies
ἀρετή,[301] and that whoever seeks ἀρετή must emulate God, i.e.,
obey his will. Second, he holds that this God who embodies
ἀρετή is the author of οἱ νόμοι τῶν 'Ιουδαίων, which means that
the divine origin of οἱ νόμοι has more than academic interest
for Josephus. Third, he portrays each of Israel's heroes,
especially Moses, as the quintessence of ἀρετή, so that in the
process, a second redefinition occurs; by shifting the point of
reference of ἀρετή from φύσις (in the Stoic view) to θεός (in
the Jewish view), he manages to redefine ἀρετή as εὐσέβεια.[302]
Israel's heroes, in Josephus' view, are paradigms of ἀρετή
precisely because of their obedience to οἱ νόμοι τοῦ θεοῦ.

(c) The Integration of These Two Foci in Moses' Life.

        The integration of these two themes πρόνοια θεοῦ and
ἀρετή, is illustrated most notably in Moses, whose life is
blessed with πρόνοια from birth. Attempts to kill the infant
Moses are futile because they are attempts to thwart πρόνοια
θεοῦ.[303] God's πρόνοια over Moses' life is attested time and
again in the events of his miraculous escape from death and
subsequent adoption by Pharaoh's daughter.[304] But Moses is not
completely passive as the object of this πρόνοια. The life
Josephus unfolds is a life always sensitive to the workings of
πρόνοια θεοῦ, always demonstrating unshakeable confidence in
πρόνοια, and herein lies the proof of his ἀρετή. One of the
most vivid contrasts used by Josephus to illustrate this is to
be seen in the handling of the Pharaoh-Moses confrontation.
Pharaoh and Moses are contrasted by their respective responses

---

[301]Cf. Ant. 1. 23.   [302]Cf. Ap. 2. 170.

[303]Ant. 2. 209.

[304]Ant. 2. 236; cf. 2. 215, 218-25, 229, 231-32.

to πρόνοια θεοῦ. When Moses tells Pharaoh of the burning bush
incident, he beseeches him not to attempt to obstruct God's
purpose (ἡ τοῦ θεοῦ γνώμη),[305] assuring him that his miracles
proceed from God's πρόνοια and δύναμις.[306] A second time he
warns him not to oppose God's will.[307] Pharaoh's refusal to
release the Israelites is evaluated by Josephus in terms of his
response to πρόνοια θεοῦ: "Thus he did but exasperate God the
more in thinking to impose upon His providence,[308] and he per-
sists in matching himself against God.[309] His recalcitrant
behavior, because it is totally oblivious to πρόνοια θεοῦ,
enables Josephus to portray him as the Stoic fool who rejects
σωφροσύνη,[310] who acts on the basis of fear rather than wisdom
(φόβῳ μᾶλλον ἢ φρονήσει),[311] who has to be forced to listen to
reason (λογισμός),[312] and who embodies κακία.[313] In fact, in
Ant. 2. 307 Josephus gives us a virtual summary of all the
marks of the Stoic fool, relating them directly to Pharaoh, who
is the antithesis of ὁ σοφός precisely because he refuses to
acknowledge God's πρόνοια which explains why he so audaciously
and foolishly opposes it.

Set in vivid contrast to Pharaoh is Moses who has everything which Pharaoh lacks, most notably an unshakeable faith in
πρόνοια θεοῦ. His commission at the burning bush is headed by
these words: "To mistrust, O Lord, thy power (δύναμις), which
I venerate myself and know to have been manifested to my fore-
fathers, were madness too gross, I trow, for my mind to
conceive."[314] His unwavering confidence in God's promises is
the recurrent feature typical of his life,[315] and he is con-
tinually cast in the role of trying to persuade Pharaoh to
follow suit. Moses' ἀρετή consists in his responsiveness to
πρόνοια θεοῦ.

---

[305]Ant. 2. 283.   [306]Ant. 2. 286.

[307]Ant. 2. 291.   [308]Ant. 2. 302.

[309]Ant. 2. 304, 307, 309, 320.

[310]Ant. 2. 296.   [311]Ant. 2. 299.

[312]Ant. 2. 301.   [313]Ant. 2. 307.

[314]Ant. 2. 270-71.   [315]Cf. Ant. 2. 275-76.

Josephus portrays a similar contrast, and thus makes the
same point, in his depiction of the respective behavior of
Moses and the Israelites. Their well-known experiences from
the Exodus onward are presented as instances of their inability
to see πρόνοια θεοῦ at work. In each case, by contrast, Moses
is able to perceive God's purpose at work, and is therefore
always able to remain unperturbed by their obduracy. Even when
they inveigh against him, he trusts in God,[316] and addresses a
speech to them on the subject of πρόνοια θεοῦ,[317] after which
he utters a prayer replete with the same theme.[318] This
pattern is repeated at each crisis: the Israelites fail to
perceive God's πρόνοια at work and murmur, while Moses
resolutely believes in God's πρόνοια and remains steadfast;
this can be seen in the following diagram:

Israelites	Moses
1. Mar (Ant. 3. 1-4) -murmur for water	. makes the sufferings his own (3.5) . beseeches God . demonstrates that God heard him
2. Elim (Ant. 3. 9-32) - murmur	. before angry mob, M is confident in God (τῷ θεῷ θαρρῶν, 3.13) . pacifies their wrath with his poise and rhetorical ability (3.14) . is able to see that distress is a means of God's testing their ἀρετή (3.15) . reminds them of all the acts attesting God's πρόνοια (3.17-21) . prays to God, gets response (3.22ff.)
3. Raphidin (Ant. 3. 33-8) - murmur	. beseeches God (Ant. 3. 33) . admired because he is so highly esteemed by God (Ant. 3. 38)
4. Amalekite threat (Ant. 3. 39-62) - fearful	. encourages (παρακαλεῖν) Israelites (3.44) . reminds them that God is their ally (3.45) . emboldens all the troops
5. Esermoth (Ant. 3. 295-9) - murmur	. emboldens Israelites (3. 298) . assures them that he (and God) will never cease efforts on their behalf
6. Korah sedition (Ant. 4. 11-66)	. holds no grudge against Israelites even though they threatened to stone him (4.12) . M's πρόνοια had saved them (4.13)

[316]Ant. 2. 329.   [317]Ant. 2. 330-33.

[318]Ant. 2. 335-37.

. unafraid (4.24)
. displays rhetorical ability (4.25)
. speech: unthinkable that Korah could
    resist God (4. 25-34)
. prays to God:
    . acknowledges will of God (4.40)
    . forsook good life to endure
        tribulation for his people (4.42)
    . underwent great dangers (4.42)
    . reiterates instances showing God's
        δύναμις (4. 43-45)
    . did not pervert justice (4.46)
    . did not pursue wealth (4.46)
    . did not neglect common good (4.46)
    . calls for another proof of God's
        πρόνοια (4.47)
    . wants to be vindicated as a faithful
        minister of God (4.49)

Josephus makes the same point negatively in the Zambrias
incident,[319] particularly in the speech which he puts into the
mouth of Zambrias,[320] who accuses Moses of tyrannical
behavior[321] (τυραννικῶς) in pretending to promise the Israelites ἐλευθερία under the pretext of "νόμοι" and "ὁ θεός,"
while in fact establishing his own sovereignty as a tyrant.
Instead of responding directly, Moses judiciously avoids a
direct confrontation and lets Zambrias meet his deserved fate
through the hands of Phinees. He had earlier demonstrated
similar wisdom in the advice he gave to the offenders.[322]

In all these crises, whether they involve the inability
of the Israelites to cope with their circumstances or seditious
attempts to undermine Moses' leadership, the main difference
between Moses and the Israelites is his consistent ability to
perceive πρόνοια θεοῦ and act accordingly; consequently, he is
able to exhibit all the characteristics of ἀρετή.

By reinforcing Moses' sensitivity to God and his
πρόνοια, Josephus is basically redefining ἀρετή as εὐσέβεια,
which was an integral ingredient of ἀρετή, according to the
Stoics. Moses always acknowledges God, especially his πρόνοια
and δύναμις[323] and therefore relies upon him and appeals for

---

[319]Ant. 4. 141-55.   [320]Ant. 4. 145-49.

[321]Ant. 4. 146; cf. 149.   [322]Ant. 4. 143-44.

[323]Ant. 2. 270, 275-76, 330, 334, 349; 3. 13, 17, 44.

his help in every circumstance.[324] He acts at his behests[325] and never fails to render thanks for his gracious aid.[326] He is unswerving in his constancy and service to God.[327] In turn, he imitates God, participating in his ἀρετή and himself providing (προνοέω) for the Israelites, particularly in trying to persuade them (and others) of πρόνοια θεοῦ.[328] It is also significant that the signs (σημεῖα) certify God's δύναμις and πρόνοια not Moses' ἀρετή; his ἀρετή consists in being able to recognize πρόνοια θεοῦ and respond accordingly. Moses as the quintessence of ἀρετή becomes a testimony to πρόνοια θεοῦ.

There can be little doubt that Josephus' Moses is made over in the image of the Stoic concept of ἀρετή which included the ability to take a "comprehensive view of what has happened in each individual instance,"[329] and this involved the capacity to perceive the work of God. The related virtues magnanimity (μεγαλοψυχία),[330] courage (ἀνδρεία),[331] patient endurance (καρτερία),[332] coupled with σύνεσις enable one with ἀρετή to keep from being perturbed (ἐξίστημι), troubled (ταράσσω), and distressed (ὀδυνηρός).[333] Adverse circumstances are seen as opportunities to prove one's καρτερία and γενναιότης.[334] To be blind to this σύνεσις leads to fear (τρέμω), lamenting (ὀδύρομαι), grieving (πενθέω), and groaning (στένω), in a word, murmuring[335]--all of which, because they blind one to ὁ θεός,

---

[324]Ant. 2. 329, 330; 3. 5-7, 22, 33; 4. 40, 42.

[325]Ant. 2. 331; 4. 165.

[326]Ant. 2. 253; 3. 25; 4. 316.

[327]Ant. 3. 13, 69, 212.

[328]Ant. 2. 283, 291-93, 309, 329; 3. 298.

[329]Epict., Diss. 1. vi, 1.

[330]Epict., Diss. 1. vi, 28.

[331]Epict., Diss. 1. vi, 28.

[332]Epict., Diss. 1. vi, 29.

[333]Epict., Diss. 1. vi, 29.

[334]Epict., Diss. 1. vi, 34.

[335]Epict., Diss. 1. vi, 38.

lead to ἀσέβεια.[336] Particularly did the ideal king embody these theological qualities of ἀρετή, seen by the way Dio Chrysostom places εὐσέβεια at the head of the list of ideals for the king.[337] The king is not only to acknowledge the deities, but to imitate them.[338] He is also obligated to provide for the welfare of his subjects,[339] which entails care and anxiety (ἐπιμέλεια and φροντίς) for his subjects,[340] preferring toil to pleasures and wealth.[341]

Neither can it be doubted that Josephus has radically altered the Stoic notion of ἀρετή by linking it with ὁ νόμος τῶν Ἰουδαίων through the concept of πρόνοια θεοῦ. His preoccupation to show that Moses epitomizes the pious, devoted leader is a crucial part of his apologetic. He is true to the Stoic ideal: he believes in God, in His providence, that nothing is hidden from Him; he has perceived what God is like and then emulates God as he cares for his people. His behavior in every respect stems from the fact that he correctly perceives God, His πρόνοια, δύναμις, θέλημα, etc., and effects a corresponding orientation in his life.

(5) Concluding Remarks.

We have seen that, even though Josephus has certainly bent the Old Testament portrait of Moses in the direction of the Hellenistic Wise Man, he has at the same time redefined Hellenistic ἀρετή in terms of ὁ θεὸς τῶν Ἰουδαίων and ὁ νόμος τῶν Ἰουδαίων, so that his Moses is, like the Stoic Wise Man, εὐσεβής, but on his own Jewish-Old Testament terms. The same tendency has been detected in his portraits of other Jewish figures, such as David.[342] Within this overarching framework

---

[336]Epict., Diss. 1, vi, 39; cf. 1. vi, 41-42.

[337]Dio Chrysostom, Orat. 1. 15b-16; 3. 51-54.

[338]Dio Chrysostom, Orat. 1. 38; cf. Epict., Diss. 2. xiv, 13.

[339]Dio Chrysostom, Orat. 1. 17.

[340]Dio Chrysostom, Orat. 1. 21.

[341]Dio Chrysostom, Orat. 1. 21.

[342]Cf. above, pp. 75f.

of εὐσέβεια, defined with respect to the two foci of his
apologetic, Moses is to be seen and understood. Thus, when
Josephus decides to respond to his antagonists who have charged
the Jews with ἀσέβεια, he adduces the tabernacle, etc. as evidence that the Lawgiver was a theios aner, i.e. ἅγιος or
εὐσεβής, and that all these charges are without substance.
This interpretation of theios is demanded not only by the
context of the passage, as well as by the overall thrust of
Josephus' apologetic, but is further supported by an observation made earlier that theios in Josephus sometimes tends to
shade off into a meaning equivalent to ἱερός, or ἅγιος,[343]
which seems to be the shade of meaning which best fits our
passage.

Two final questions remain. First, why employ theios
aner, a hapax legomenon, rather than an expression such as
ἄνθρωπος θεοῦ? Although this is an almost impossible question
since it demands an argument from silence, the short answer is
that ἄνθρωπος θεοῦ said less, or perhaps more, than he wanted
to say. Perhaps, it is to be explained because of his anti-
Samaritan sentiments.[344]

---

[343]SCHLATTER, Theologie, 58, remarks, "πνεῦμα ἅγιον hat
Josephus gemieden aus demselben Empfinden heraus, das ihm
verbot, θεὸς ἅγιος, ἄγγελος ἅγιος, νόμος ἅγιος, βιβλία ἅγια,
πόλις ἅγια zu sagen. Da, wo die Palästiner ihr קדוש brauchten,
sagte Josephus θεῖος.

[344]On Josephus' anti-Samaritan feelings, cf. THACKERAY,
Josephus, 59. JOHN MACDONALD, The Theology of the Samaritans
(London, 1964) 147-222, discussing the prominent place of Moses
in Samaritan theology, says of the title Man of God
(איש האלהים): "Another title, based on Deut. 33:1, that is
fundamental to the Samaritan evaluation and description of
Moses, is the title 'Man of God' or 'his Man.' Although the
Judaists and Christians too have the Pentateuch as part of
their sacred literature, they do not emphasize this attribute
of Moses. It is in Samaritanism alone that the title receives
prominence. Perhaps this pre-eminence derives from the fact
that no other Pentateuchal figure was so called" (157). As to
what they meant by the title, "What they understood by the
title 'Man of God' is best demonstrated in Markah's Memar
(VI.6). He does not explain it; he expounds it, stating that
the Man of God was possessed of his power and that power was
manifest in all his actions during his earthly life. Thus
Moses was God's Man as distinct from other humans. God's Man
meant the man, out of all men, through whom God manifested himself, i.e. through whom he declared his will for men. Thus
(cont.)

102

Second, how does the symbolic interpretation of the
tabernacle in <u>Ant</u>. 3. 181-87 fit into the overall pericope?
The answer must be directly related with the fact that the
Hellenistic era had witnessed the extension of the notion of
νόμος to cosmic proportions, especially since the Stoics
regarded νόμος as the expression of ὁ κόσμος. Man, being
κοσμοπολίτης, must order his life by this cosmic νόμος, or
universal law.[345] Aware of this cosmic understanding of law,
Josephus invites the Greek detractor to investigate the tabernacle, etc. as evidence to refute their accusation. He is
confident that if a Greek would but consent to do this, he
would see in the tabernacle, not an incomprehensible maze of
strange religious paraphernalia, but rather the deeper meaning
intended by the lawgiver, i.e. that the tabernacle was actually
symbolic of the universe. Josephus hoped this would ring a
bell in the mind of the Greek inquirer, who, when he once com-
prehended the significance of the tabernacle imagery, would
conclude that these are not the laws of some backward nation
in the hinterland of the Empire, but rather the laws of the
God of the Universe, because they have cosmic dimensions. The
symbolic interpretation of the tabernacle, therefore, enables
Josephus to show that the Jews, by following the Law of Moses,
are following not a national law-code, but a cosmic law code,
and this refutes any charge of ἀσέβεια brought against them.

God's Man was the most "select" of men, in a figure of speech,
the pre-existent among men. As the first created being,
materialized from his pre-existent bodiless state, born and
dead with cosmic repercussions in both cases, Moses spelled
humanity in the sense that Jesus for many is Man with a capital
'M'" (158). In other words, the prominence of "Man of God" in
Samaritan may have induced Josephus to opt for the alternative
expression <u>theios aner</u>. Cf. further J. MACDONALD, <u>Memar Marqah</u>
2 vols. BZAW 84 (1963); "The Samaritan Doctrine of <u>Moses</u>," <u>SJT</u>
13 (1960) 149-62.

[345]Cf. H. KLEINKNECHT, art. νόμος, <u>TDNT</u>, 4. 1032f.

CHAPTER THREE

PHILO[1]

Philo plays a crucial role in the theios aner hypothesis
because he is regarded as the representative par excellence of
a Hellenized Judaism in which the middle wall of partition
between God and man has broken down, thereby enabling the
emergence and development of the notion of a "divine man" in

---

[1]For this study I have used primarily the following
works: J. DRUMMOND, Philo Judaeus. The Jewish-Alexandrian
Philosophy in Its Development and Completion (London, 1888) 2
vols.; E. ZELLER, Die Philosophie der Griechen in ihrer
geschichtlichen Entwicklung (Leipzig, 41903) 3.2, 385-467;
T. H. BILLINGS, The Platonism of Philo Judaeus (Chicago, 1919);
E. BRÉHIER, Les idées philosophiques et religieuses de Philon
d'Alexandrie (Paris, 21925); E. R. GOODENOUGH, By Light, Light.
The Mystic Gospel of Hellenistic Judaism (New Haven, 1935;
repr. Amsterdam, 1969); An Introduction to Philo Judaeus
(Oxford, 21962); H. LEISEGANG, art. "Philon," PWRE 20.1 (1941)
1-50; M. POHLENZ, "Philon von Alexandreia," Nachrichten von
der Akademie der Wissenschaften in Göttingen [Philologisch-
historische Klasse] Fasc. No. 5 (Göttingen, 1942) 409-87;
H. A. WOLFSON, Philo. Foundations of Religious Philosophy in
Judaism, Christianity, and Islam (Cambridge, Mass., 1947)
2 vols.; A. J. FESTUGIÈRE, La révélation d'Hermès Trismégiste.
Tome 2: Le dieu cosmique (Paris, 1949) 519-85; J. DANIÉLOU,
Philon d'Alexandrie (Paris, 1958); R. ARNALDEZ, "Introduction
Générale," in Les oeuvres de Philon d'Alexandrie (Paris, 1961)
1. 17-112; L. FELDMAN, Studies in Judaica. Scholarship on
Philo and Josephus (1937-62) (New York, 1962); H. CHADWICK,
"St. Paul and Philo of Alexandria," BJRL 48 (1965-66) 286-307;
"Philo," Chapter 8 in Cambridge History of Later Greek and
Early Medieval Philosophy ed. A. H. Armstrong (Cambridge, 1967)
137-57; S. SANDMEL, Philo's Place in Judaism. A Study of
Conceptions of Abraham in Jewish Literature (New York, 21971).
        Editions and Translations: J. B. AUCHER, Philonis
Judaei. Sermones Tres Hactenus Inediti (Venice, 1822); C. D.
YONGE, The Works of Philo Judaeus (London, 1854-55) 4 vols.
(= Yonge); L. COHN & P. WENDLAND, Philonis Alexandrini opera
quae supersunt Editio maior (Berlin, 1896-1930) 7 vols.
(= C-W); H. LEISEGANG, Indices ad Philonis Alexandrini (Berlin,
1926); L. COHN, I. HEINEMANN, M. ADLER, W. THEILER, Philo von
Alexandria. Die Werke in deutscher Übersetzung (Breslau, 1909-
38. repr. Berlin, 1962; Bde.7, 1964) (= Werke); F. H. COLSON,
G. H. WHITAKER, R. MARCUS, Philo with an English Translation
[Loeb series] (London/Cambridge, Mass., 1949-61) 12 vols.
(=Loeb); R. ARNALDEZ, J. POUILLOUX, C. MONDÉSERT, Les oeuvres
de Philon d'Alexandrie [Lyon ed.] (Paris, 1961-) (=Lyon).

Jewish thought.[2] And, indeed, when we examine his writings, we detect a far greater willingness to stretch the categories of the Old Testament into different shapes than in Josephus, for example. This is not to say necessarily that he is any more willing to play fast and loose with Biblical traditions at his disposal; it is only to say that he is more at home in Hellenistic philosophy and is far more willing to recast his Biblical theology into Greek philosophical categories.

Most discussions of theios aner in Philo begin by observing his conspicuous reluctance to use the term theios even when seemingly opportune occasions present themselves. Windisch, for example, so observes, but argues that Philo uses θεσπέσιος and other synonyms instead and thus that theios aner is still present in Philo albeit under a different guise.[3] The inescapable fact remains that the exact expression theios aner occurs rarely in the entire Philonic corpus. Equally inescapable is the fact that, so far as I can determine, it is never applied to Moses, nor to any other Jewish figure.[4] In spite of this, commentators still insist upon using it as a category for interpreting Philo. E. R. Goodenough, on the basis of Spec. Leg. 1. 116, believes that Philo remodels the high priest Aaron into a "theios anthropos, the man who is between the human and divine natures because he shares in both, and who is hence in a position to mediate the salvation of God to men."[5] The character-sketch is filled out further:

> A marked part of this tendency was the increasing regard for what was called the theios anthropos, the human being who had by his virtue raised himself, or been raised by God or the gods, to

---

[2]Especially REITZENSTEIN, WINDISCH, and BIELER. (Cf. above, pp. 24ff.). This is particularly well illustrated in H. LEISEGANG, "Der Gottmensch als Archetypus," Eranos-Jahrbuch 18 [Jung Festschrift] (Zürich, 1950) 9-45, in which Philo's portrayal of Moses provides the example of the theios aner Archetypus in antiquity, treated midway between the Hellenistic portrayals of Pythagoras, Empedocles, and Plato on the one hand, and Jesus of the canonical Gospels on the other.

[3]Cf. quotations from WINDISCH, p. 28 above.

[4]Cf. discussion of Virt. 177, pp. 173ff.

[5]GOODENOUGH, Light, 110.

relations with deity so far beyond those of
ordinary people that he had become in a sense
divine. Such men were inspiring as models, but
still more useful in popular eyes as mediators
and saviors for other men.[6]

Moses, it is claimed, becomes the quintessential theios aner
in Philo:

Moses is equated more explicitly (in Philo) with
such current conceptions as the ideal king and
the Hellenistic theios anthropos than was done
in the case of the other patriarchs.[7]

If theios aner were merely a useful conceptual category
for explaining certain Philonic data, the problem would be
relatively unimportant. But this is hardly the case. For, on
the one hand, we find one stream in Philo which would seem to
suggest that for him the notion of theios aner (taking theios
in its most literal sense, "divine") would be a contradiction
in terms. He appears to agree with Josephus that "fellowship
with the divine does not befit a mortal,"[8] as seen particularly
in his polemic against emperor worship[9] and other supposed
demigods,[10] where, in each case his disapproval of both is as
uncompromising as it is unremitting. In these passages it
appears inconceivable for him to concede that a man can in any
sense become a god. The fundamental premise with which he
works--that God is not as man[11]--further illustrates this
stream of his thought, and in fact becomes something of a
cliché in his writings.[12] He believes that "God would sooner
change into a man than man into god."[13] If it is objected that
these passages occur primarily in polemical contexts and that

---

[6]GOODENOUGH, Light, 126.   [7]Ibid., 181.

[8]Bel. 7. 344, κοινωνία γὰρ θείῳ πρὸς θνητὸν ἀπρεπής
ἐστι.

[9]Leg. ad Gaium 114, 118, 154, 162, 198, 201.

[10]V. Contemp. 6; cf. Ebr. 110.

[11]Cf. Num. 23:19.

[12]V. Mos. 1. 283; 2. 194; Leg. ad Gaium 118; Immut. 53;
Ebr. 30; Migr. 42; Decal. 32; Gen. Gk. frag. 1. 55 (Loeb,
Suppl. 2, p. 184); Gen. Gk. frag. 2. 54 (Loeb, Suppl. 2, p. 202).

[13]Leg. ad Gaium 118.

apologists tend to overstate their convictions when their back
is to the wall, it should be noticed that this conviction also
emerges in non-polemical settings, such as the unidentified
fragment of Qu. Ex. (Loeb, Suppl. 2, p. 258 Marcus = p. 72
Harris) where he says: "in order to 'see' God, man must first
become God--the very thing which is impossible."[14] In a
similar vein, he includes the notion that man can become god
in a list of a priori impossibilities and worries that it might
be blasphemous even to entertain the idea.[15]

Yet, another stream in Philo seems to run completely
counter to this. This stream includes such passages as those
mentioned by Goodenough[16] in which Philo seems more than willing to transform certain historical persons into something more
than (or at least, other than) human. The high priest, we are
told, when he enters the Most Holy Place, does so "not as a
man,"[17] a contention which Philo bases upon a LXX text evidently known only to him, or possibly altered by him to suit his
needs.[18] Or, Moses, when he is taken up into prophetic ecstasy
on Sinai, is said to become "divinized;"[19] and, elsewhere is
referred to as "the divine and holy Moses."[20] Flowing in this
same stream is another group of passages, those in which he
cites or alludes to Ex. 4:16/7:1, where ostensibly the LXX
itself, by designating Moses θεός, ascribes divine status to
him.[21]

One soon learns in dealing with Philo not to be unduly
upset at what appear to be inconsistencies in his thought,
otherwise he becomes even more incomprehensible than he already

---

[14]θεὸν γενέσθαι δεῖ πρότερον--ὅπερ οὐδὲ οἷόν τε--ἵνα
θεὸν ἰσχύσῃ τις καταλαβεῖν.

[15]Mut. 181-82.

[16]GOODENOUGH, Light, 110, 222ff.

[17]Her. 84; Som. 2. 231-32.

[18]Lev. 16:17; cf. below, pp. 171f., esp. n. 313.

[19]Qu. Ex. 2. 40.

[20]Qu. Ex. 2. 54.

[21]Cf. discussion below, pp. 108ff.

is.[22] Yet we have to do here with an inconsistency at the very heart of his thought. The problem is real, not manufactured. Supposedly, one could argue that Philo could polemicize against emperor worship in one breath, and then, blinded by his patriotic zeal, transform Moses into a divine man in the next. Or, it could perhaps be argued that no real contradiction exists, since Gaius' claim to divinity simply belongs to a different category from Philo's ascription of divinity to Moses, the one being a claim in direct competition with the supreme Deity Yahweh, the other not. Certainly, the whole question of emperor worship belongs in a class to itself since the problem was often political, strictly speaking, rather than religious or metaphysical,[23] although Legatio ad Gaium leaves the impression that for Philo and a majority of Alexandrian Jews it was definitely a religious problem. But Philo's blanket assertion about the impossibility of man's becoming a god does not always occur in polemical attacks against emperor worship, and in fact, at times seems to be his firm conviction apart from that particular issue.

It is the presence of these conflicting streams that calls for a closer investigation of those passages in which Philo appears to ascribe divine status to Israel's heroes, Moses in particular.[24]

---

[22]On the problem of consistency in Philo's thought, cf. FELDMAN, Studies, 7, who points to Goodenough's criticism of Wolfson for making Philo too consistent. Cf. Goodenough's review of Wolfson, Philo, JBL 67 (1948) 87-109.

[23]Cf. especially the discussions by W. S. FERGUSON, CAH (1928) 7. 13-22 and A. D. NOCK, CAH (1934) 10. 481-503.

[24]The recent treatment of Philo by D. L. Tiede in The Charismatic Figure as Miracle Worker (Missoula, Mont., 1972) 101ff. does not focus upon the question whether, or in what sense, Philo ascribes divinity to Israel's heroes. It concentrates instead upon the criteria by which Israel's heroes, Moses in particular, are authenticated as "divine men" in Philo. His working assumption--and I believe a correct one--is that the commonly held equation "divine man" = miracle worker can be invalidated once it is demonstrated that (in Philo) "divine man" status was based upon ἀρετή instead of miracle-working. Thus he argues that the possession of moral virtue (ἀρετή), not the ability to work miracles, is "the criterion which Philo uses to document levels of divine presence in men" (p. 132), and that the Stoic concept of ὁ σοφός provides

(cont.)

Ex. 7:1/4:16

The first group of passages to be considered are those in which Philo either cites or alludes to Ex. 7:1, and, less importantly, Ex. 4:16. His handling of these passages, which perhaps come as close as any Old Testament passage to affirming the divinity of a single historical person, should at least provide a window, translucent perhaps, through which to view his convictions on the question of deifying mortals. Moreover, for one keen to transform Israel's heroes into theioi andres there could scarcely be found better Biblical warrant.

(1) V. Mos. 1. 158.

Perhaps the best place to begin is the Philonic passage often cited as evidence that Philo transformed Moses into a Hellenistic theios aner, V. Mos. 1. 158:

Philo the main category for recasting Israel's heroes into "divine men" (pp. 112, 123). Rightly calling attention to Philo's failure to enhance the miracle-working activity of Moses beyond the Exodus narrative, he notices that Philo actually devalues Moses' status as miracle-worker as compared with the Biblical account and other non-Biblical accounts of the plagues.

Thus, while Tiede's claim that moral virtue is the criterion by which such ascriptions are made by Philo (cf. p. 132) needs qualification (cf. Qu. Ex. 2. 29, 40), his work nevertheless represents a significant advance by inviting a closer look at the precise nature of the criteria upon which ascriptions of "divinity" are based.

Although it did not fall within the scope of his work to examine the actual ascriptions themselves, an ambiguity is reflected in his treatment which illustrates the need for a closer investigation of the passages in which such ascriptions are made. On the one hand, he exercises commendable caution in writing "divine man" in quotation marks (pp. 105, 108), or in allowing that his status may be "divine or semi-divine" (pp. 120, 123), or in concluding that ἀρετή documents "levels of divine presence in men" (p. 132). Yet, he can employ the expression, apparently with approval, without quotation marks (pp. 105f.) and can call Philo's account of Moses' death in V. Mos. 2. 288 a description of his apotheosis (p. 122).

Clearly, there is a need to analyse the ascriptions themselves to see whether the ambiguity is itself genuinely Philonic or whether a defensible explanation of the ambiguity may be found. Our main interest, therefore, will be to examine not the grounds for such ascriptions but the nature of the claims themselves.

It should also be noted that in this investigation we shall not be concerned with Philo's celebrated doctrine of the "heavenly man," but rather with historical figures who seem to be elevated to supra-human status.

τί δ'; οὐχὶ καὶ μείζονος τῆς πρὸς τὸν πατέρα
τῶν ὅλων καὶ ποιητὴν κοινωνίας ἀπέλαυσε προσ-
ρήσεως τῆς αὐτῆς ἀξιωθείς; ὠνομάσθη γὰρ ὅλου
τοῦ ἔθνους θεὸς καὶ βασιλεύς·[25]

V. Mos. 1. 148-62 constitutes a digression in Philo's rehearsal
of the Exodus story, following his narration of the Ten Plagues
(1. 96-146). At 1. 148 Philo interrupts his narration of the
Exodus account for the second time[26] and includes what may
accurately be described as a compact περὶ βασιλείας tractate
tailored to fit his portrayal of Moses as the ideal king.[27]
Because this pericope is replete with popular philosophical
themes, it is virtually impossible to isolate precisely the
various components.[28] Its eclectic complexion notwithstanding,
it is possible to get some idea of its function in Philo's
overall portrayal of Moses as the ideal Hellenistic king as
well as to tease out those features which he seems to regard as
crucial to such a portrayal. A clue to the immediate conceptual background at work upon Philo occurs when he tells us in
his recapitulation of Book I, which is devoted entirely to
Moses' "education and career as a ruler,"[29] of his intention to
use the Platonic model of the philosopher-king in depicting
Moses. In a direct reference to Resp. 5. 473d, where Plato
asserts that "states can only make progress in well-being if
either kings are philosophers or philosophers are kings,"[30]
Philo claims to have successfully shown in Book I that Moses
combined both these faculties, the kingly and the philosophical,
into his one life. It is hardly surprising, then, to find a

---

[25]Cf. BIELER, 2. 35; GEORGI, 153ff., 156, 160;
GOODENOUGH, Light, 186.

[26]Cf. V. Mos. 1. 18-33.

[27]Cf. BRÉHIER, 19ff.; E. R. GOODENOUGH, "The Political
Philosophy of Hellenistic Kingship," Yale Classical Studies 1
(1928) 55-102; W. SCHUBART, "Das hellenistische Königsideal
nach Inschriften und Papyri," Archiv für Papyrusforschung 12
(1937) 1-26; O. MURRAY, "Aristeas and Ptolemaic Kingship,"
JTS 18 (1967) 337-71. Also, cf. the "speech" of Macro to
Gaius in Leg. ad Gaium 43-51 reflecting contemporary royal
ideology.

[28]BRÉHIER, 20ff., especially emphasizes the Neo-
Pythagorean strand; followed by GOODENOUGH, "Kingship."

[29]V. Mos. 2. 1.   [30]V. Mos. 2. 2.

110

rather heavy sprinkling of Platonic notions scattered throughout his presentation of Moses. In fact, there is strong reason
to believe that the first major digression, V. Mos. 1. 18-33,
is Philo's attempt to demonstrate that Moses is the embodiment
of Plato's philosopher-king as set out in Resp. 6-7.[31] It is
of course too much to expect exact correspondence between
Plato's character-sketch of the ideal philosopher and Philo's
Moses, but the overall contours of the respective portraits are
so strikingly similar as to exclude the possibility of
coincidence.

Though by no means primarily concerned with the outward
appearance of the philosopher, Plato insisted that he be of
"comely appearance,"[32] a feature which Philo repeatedly singles
out in Moses.[33] Even greater stress is laid upon the necessity
of the philosopher's intellectual precocity, which is only
natural considering the difficulty, if not near impossibility
of one's being able to comprehend "the eternal and unchanging;"[34] thus, he must be quick to learn, possessed of superior
memory.[35] Accordingly, Philo devotes several paragraphs to
Moses' intellectual precocity: it was because the princess saw
that "he was advanced beyond his age"[36] that she became even
more fond of him; teachers gathered from near and far (Greece
is specified), "but in a short time he advanced beyond their
capacities;"[37] in words reminiscent of Meno, we are told that
his extraordinary learning ability is attributed to
ἀνάμνησις:[38] "his gifted nature forestalled their instruction,
so that his seemed a case rather of recollection (ἀνάμνησις)
than of learning, and indeed he himself devised and propounded

[31]Cf. also Leg. 4. 709e-711e.

[32]Resp. 7. 535a; cf. Symp. 209b-c; Phaedr. 252e.

[33]V. Mos. 1. 18; cf. 1. 9. No doubt a reference to Ex.
2:2. Cf. also Acts 7:20; Heb. 11:23.

[34]Resp. 6. 484b.

[35]Resp. 6. 486c-d, 487a, 7. 535c; cf. Leg. 4. 709e.

[36]V. Mos. 1. 19.   [37]V. Mos. 1. 21.

[38]Though, cf. WOLFSON, 2. 9.

problems which they could not easily solve."[39] The curricula
of Plato's philosopher and Philo's Moses are identical, almost
to the point of being listed in the same order.[40] After
receiving primary education, the philosopher receives the ten-
year course of "propaedeutic" studies consisting of arithmetic,[41] geometry,[42] stereometry,[43] astronomy,[44] and harmonics.[45]
In slightly altered order, which may simply reflect the state
of the curriculum in Philo's own day,[46] Philo's Moses is
instructed in "arithmetic, geometry, the lore of metre, rhythm
and harmony, and the whole subject of music ...,"[47] and later
picks up astronomy.[48] The next five years of the philosopher's
life were devoted to dialectic,[49] which seems to have its
counterpart in Philo's description of Moses either in the
statement that the Egyptians "instructed him in the philosophy
conveyed in symbols"[50] or the statement that "the Greeks taught
him "the rest of the regular school course,"[51] probably the
latter. The correspondence also extends to the individual
virtues. At the head of the list was the philosopher's "hatred
of falsehood and love of truth;"[52] similarly, Moses is said to
have "sought only for truth . . . his mind was incapable of
accepting any falsehood."[53] Other similarities may simply be

---

[39]V. Mos. 1. 21.

[40]That Philo is here reflecting the royal ideology and
not merely the educational situation of his day can be seen by
contrasting the traditional order of subjects in Cong. 15ff.

[41]Resp. 7. 522c-526c.   [42]Resp. 7. 526c-527c.

[43]Resp. 7. 527c-528d.   [44]Resp. 7. 528e-530c.

[45]Resp. 7. 530e-531c. Cf. J. Raven, Plato's Thought in
the Making (Cambridge, 1965) 178ff.

[46]On Philo's own education, cf. BRÉHIER, 280ff., who
refers to Cong. 11, 79-80, 140-50, 155-56; Sacr. 78-9.

[47]V. Mos. 1. 23; cf. Qu. Gen. 3. 21.

[48]V. Mos. 1. 23b.   [49]Resp. 7. 531d-534e.

[50]V. Mos. 1. 23.   [51]V. Mos. 1. 23.

[52]Resp. 6. 485c-d; 487a; 7. 535e.

[53]V. Mos. 1. 24.

mentioned with references to their counterparts in Philo: σωφροσύνη;[54] δικαιοσύνη;[55] preoccupation with pleasures of the soul, not pleasures of the body;[56] not a braggart.[57] There is a significant difference in one respect: Plato's emphasis upon the bravery and physical strength of the philosopher, i.e. his soldierly qualities,[58] is lacking in Philo's portrayal of Moses. Instead, beginning with V. Mos. 1. 25ff. Philo's portrayal takes on a different tone, partaking more of the spirit of the Cynic-Stoic diatribe by its heightened ethical quality, specifically the emphasis upon Moses' mastery of sexual desires and his scorn for the life of luxury.[59] Another possible reminiscence of Resp. may occur in V. Mos. 1. 30ff., which records Moses' refusal to regard his people disdainfully, an attitude Plato regards as essential in the life of the philosopher, as the analogy of the cave makes clear.[60]

Our passage only attests the widespread popularity of the Cynic-Stoic σοφός-βασιλεύς ideal during the Hellenistic era which stood in a direct line of continuity with the Platonic conception of the philosopher-king as the guardian of the ideal state.[61] The first four tractates on kingship by Dio Chrysostom, although written later in the first century A.D., may be regarded as typical of this genre and provide illuminating parallels. The kingship tractates as a genre could be considerably more systematized than Plato's discussion of the philosopher-king, although there was considerable overlap

---

[54]Resp. 6. 485e; 487a; 7. 536a; cf. V. Mos. 1. 25.

[55]Resp. 6. 486b; 487a; cf. V. Mos. 1. 24.

[56]Resp. 6. 485d-e; cf. V. Mos. 1. 20; 25-29. Also, note the image Philo uses of Moses' controlling the impulses of the soul "as one would a restive horse;" cf. Phaedr. 247a-250c; 253c-256e; cf. BILLINGS, Platonism, 88ff.

[57]Resp. 6. 486b; cf. V. Mos. 1. 30.

[58]Resp. 6. 486b; 486d; 487a; 7. 536a; 537b.

[59]Though, cf. Resp. 6. 485d-e.

[60]Cf. Resp. 7. 519d-520d.

[61]Cf. R. HÖISTAD, Cynic Hero and Cynic King. Studies in the Cynic Conception of Man (Uppsala, 1948).

between them. Philo has tried to maintain the Exodus narrative
as the skeleton on which to hang his portrait of Moses as the
ideal king, which partially helps explain his modification of
the general kingship tractate form. The thoroughly aretalogical basis for Moses' appointment as king constitutes one of the
most pervasive themes, specifically as opposed to military
might.[62] Virtue as opposed to sheer military might occupies a
similar role in the kingship tractate of the Pythagorean
Diotogenes:

> He must excel the rest in virtue and on that
> account be judged worthy to rule, but not on
> account of his wealth, or power, or military
> strength. For the first of these qualities he
> has in common with all sorts of people, the
> second with irrational animals, the third with
> tyrants, while virtue alone is peculiar to good
> men. So that the king, who is self-controlled
> in pleasure, given to sharing his possessions,
> and is prudent and powerful in virtue, that man
> would be a king in very truth.[63]

The catalog of virtues attributed to Moses in V. Mos. 1. 154 is
distinguished primarily by its all-inclusiveness, pulling together many of Plato's virtues assigned to the philosopher with
many others which show up in Cynic-Stoic ethical lists:[64]

> ταῦτα δ' ἦσαν ἐγκράτειαι, καρτερίαι, σωφροσύναι,
> ἀγχίνοιαι, συνέσεις, ἐπιστῆμαι, πόνοι, κακο-
> πάθειαι, ἡδονῶν ὑπεροψίαι, δικαιοσύναι, προτροπαὶ
> πρὸς τὰ βέλτιστα, ψόγοι καὶ κολάσεις ἁμαρτανόντων
> νόμιμοι, ἔπαινοι καὶ τιμαὶ κατορθούντων πάλιν σὺν
> νόμῳ.

> These treasures were the repeated exhibition of
> self-restraint, continence, temperance, shrewd-
> ness, good sense, knowledge, endurance of toil
> and hardships, contempt of pleasures, justice,
> advocacy of excellence, censure and chastisement
> according to law for wrongdoers, praise and honor
> for well-doers, again as the law directs.[65]

Of prime importance also was the necessity for the king's

---

[62]V. Mos. 1. 148.

[63]Stobaeus 4. 7, 62, cited in GOODENOUGH, "Kingship,"
70.

[64]Cf. HÖISTAD, 150, especially the lists of virtues of
the king, 184ff.

[65]Trans. Colson (Loeb).

appointment to be divinely given and divinely ordained.[66]
Philo's mention of undiluted revulsion for evil recalls the
sharp, uncompromising distinction drawn by the earlier Stoics
between good and evil,[67] and thus here Philo shares the self-
righteousness of many of the Cynic-Stoic preachers of his
day.[68] Upon receiving office as king Moses did not seek his
own self-aggrandizement such as the appointment and promotion
of his own sons to positions of importance, but had only one
aim: to benefit his subjects.[69] Riches and wealth did not
tempt him; he knew, as only a true σοφός could know, that real
wealth--the possession of the virtues--was his.[70] The pericope
ends by noting that Moses has put away luxury, inordinate
sexual desires, profligacy, and the like, the tone of which
sounds very Cynic, but no doubt partially reflects Philo's
Jewish piety as much as anything else.[71]

The allusion to Ex. 7:1 in V. Mos. 1. 158 occurs in the
immediate context where it is claimed that Moses is
κοσμοπολίτης,[72] an obvious effort to underscore the cosmic,
universal scope of his "kingship," a theme woven into the
entire pericope from beginning to end.[73] At the very outset

---

[66]V. Mos. 1. 148; cf. Abr. 261; also V. Mos. 2. 131; Som.
2. 243; Praem. 54; Qu. Gen. 4. 76. Also, Dio. C., Orat. 1.11f.,
45; 3. 55; 3. 62. WOLFSON, 2. 331, calls attention to the distinction between divine appointment and divine personhood of
the king.

[67]Cf. E. ZELLER, Stoics, Epicureans, and Sceptics,
Trans. O. J. Reichel (London, 1880) 272ff.

[68]V. Mos. 1. 149; cf. Dio C., Orat. 3. 53.

[69]V. Mos. 1. 150f.; cf. Dio C., Orat. 1. 11-36, esp.
17ff., 23, 34, 65; 2. 67, 71f., 77; 3. 55, 63ff., 86ff.

[70]V. Mos. 1. 152ff.; also Gig. 36ff. where Philo's
polemic against wealth is reminiscent of the Cynic-Stoic
diatribe; cf. Dio C., Orat., 1. 14, 21, 62; 3. 93; cf. Plato,
Resp. 6. 485e; 7. 521a; also cf. Qu. Gen. 4. 76; Fragment P.
362 E. (= Yonge, 4. 243), "No wicked man is rich, not even
though he should be the owner of all the mines in the whole
world; but all foolish men are poor. Etc."

[71]V. Mos. 1. 160ff.; Dio C., Orat. 1. 13, 21; 2. 55f.;
3. 83f.; 4. 84, 101ff.

[72]V. Mos. 1. 157.

[73]Cf. Plant. 67f.; cf. V. Mos. 2. 12, 20.

we are alerted to the "universal benevolence which he never
failed to shew."[74] In a similar vein the universal reign of
God is related to the (expected) universal reign of Israel as
a nation:

> ... He who presides over and takes charge of all
> things thought good to requite him with the king-
> ship of a nation more populous and mightier, a
> nation destined to be consecrated above all others
> to offer prayers for ever on behalf of the human
> race that it may be delivered from evil and
> participate in what is good.[75]

Beginning with 1. 155 in particular does the cosmic, universal
scope of Moses' reign come into sharper focus: God granted him
"the wealth of the whole earth and sea and rivers, and of all
the other elements;"[76] God gave him the "whole world;"[77] he had
received "the whole earth as his portion;"[78] he was appointed
god and king over the entire race.[79]

There can be little doubt that the portrait at this
point has become decidedly Cynic-Stoic by its heightened
interest in the cosmic scope of Moses' reign. It was a crucial
Stoic theme because of the political situation during the
Hellenistic era no less than for philosophical reasons. For,
according to G. F. Moore:

> Conditions had thus prepared the way for the Stoic
> cosmopolitanism. But it had a philosophical root:
> as those who own one law are citizens of one state,
> so those who live by the universal law are citizens
> of the world, or, as Epictetus expresses it in
> religious terms, all men are brethren, for all
> alike have God for their father.[80]

On one level there were the popular notions of the ideal king
conceived of in world-conquering terms. In Dio's second tractate on kingship we learn that Alexander the Great is not
content with anything less than ruling the whole world,[81]

---

[74]V. Mos. 1. 148. [75]V. Mos. 1. 149.

[76]V. Mos. 1. 155. [77]V. Mos. 1. 155.

[78]V. Mos. 1. 157.

[79]V. Mos. 1. 158; cf. Leg. ad Gaium 8, esp. 43-51.

[80]G. F. MOORE, History of Religions (Edinburgh, 1931)
1. 516; also ZELLER, Stoics, 326ff.

[81]Dio C., Orat., 2. 5-6; 4. 13.

something which everybody already knew, but which the kingship
tractates impressed more deeply upon the popular consciousness.
The image of Heracles was also strong at the popular level:
"he was not only king of Greece, but also held empire over
every land from the rising of the sun to the setting thereof,
aye, over all peoples where are found shrines of Heracles."[82]
At another level, the emerging consciousness of the unity of
mankind kindled the development of the notion of a universal
law, a development not unaffected by the Stoic ethical dictum
"to live according to nature."[83] This grounding of ethical
conduct in universal law can be seen especially clearly in the
following two passages, one from Plutarch, the other from
Diogenes Laertius:

> The Politeia of Zeno ... is directed to this one
> main point, that our life should not be based on
> cities or peoples each with its view of right and
> wrong, but we should regard all men as our fellow-
> countrymen and fellow-citizens, and that there
> should be one life and one order, like that of a
> single flock on a common pasture feeding together
> under a common law. Zeno wrote this, shaping as
> it were a dream or picture of a philosophic, well-
> ordered society.[84]

> Living virtuously is equivalent to living in
> accordance with experience of the actual course
> of nature, as Chrysippus says in the first book
> of his About Ends; for our individual natures are
> parts of the nature of the whole universe. And
> this is why the end may be defined as life in
> accordance with nature, or, in other words, in
> accordance with our own human nature as well as
> that of the universe, a life in which we refrain
> from every action forbidden by the law common to
> all things, that is to say, the right reason
> which pervades all things and is identical with
> Zeus, lord and ruler of all that is.[85]

The same general tendency was reflected when Cleanthes decided
to add τῇ φύσει to Zeno's formula τὸ ὁμολογουμένως

---

[82]Dio C., Orat., 1. 60; cf. 1. 84.

[83]Cf. G. WATSON, "The Natural Law and Stoicism," in
Problems in Stoicism, ed. A. A. Long (London, 1971) 219ff.

[84]Plutarch, De Alexandri Magni Fortuna aut Virtute
329a-b, cited in WATSON, "Natural Law," 220.

[85]Diogenes Laertius 7. 87-8, Trans. R. D. Hicks (Loeb),
cited in WATSON, "Natural Law," 222.

ζῆν,[86] and according to Diogenes Laertius, 7. 89, this represents a significant change:

> By the nature with which our life ought to be in
> accord, Chrysippus understands both universal
> nature and more particularly the nature of man,
> whereas Cleanthes takes the nature of the universe
> alone as that which should be followed, without
> adding the nature of the individual.[87]

Accordingly, when we hear Cleanthes speaking of κοινὸς νόμος in the Hymn to Zeus 1. 20ff., we can legitimately translate it "universal law," the law common to all mankind.[88]

For Philo's portrait of Moses as βασιλεύς to have any appeal at all, it was imperative to demonstrate not only that he embodied the virtues, but that in doing so he had conformed his life to universal law,[89] ὁ κοινὸς νόμος φύσεως. Ultimately, of course, he wants to claim that Moses is νόμος ἔμψυχός τε καὶ λογικός,[90] a claim crucial to his overall apologetic for Judaism, but which remains implicit in this pericope.

According to W. A. Meeks,[91] Philo adduces three grounds on which Moses' election to kingship is based: (1) haggadic,[92] (2) philosophical,[93] and mystical.[94] Closer examination, however, reveals that it would be more appropriate to classify the entire pericope as philosophical in the sense that Moses'

---

[86]Cf. Stobaeus, Ecl. 2. 7.5.

[87]Trans. R. D. Hicks (Loeb).

[88]Cf. C. J. DE VOGEL, Greek Philosophy (Leiden, 1964) 3, p. 134; ZELLER, Stoics, 227ff.; H. KOESTER, "ΝΟΜΟΣ ΦΥΣΕΩΣ. The Concept of Natural Law in Greek Thought," in Religions in Antiquity [Goodenough Festschrift, ed. J. Neusner] (Leiden, 1968) 521-41, esp. 530ff.

[89]Cf. Qu. Ex. 2. 42.

[90]V. Mos. 1. 162; cf. W. RICHARDSON, "The Philonic Patriarchs as Νόμος Ἔμψυχος," Studia Patristica, vol. 1, pt. 1 (Berlin, 1957) 515-25.

[91]W. A. MEEKS, The Prophet-King. Moses Traditions and the Johannine Christology (Leiden, 1967) 108.

[92]V. Mos. 1. 148.

[93]V. Mos. 1. 148ff., i.e., the possession of the virtues.

[94]V. Mos. 1. 158-9.

kingship is established primarily, if not solely, on aretalogical grounds: he is βασιλεύς because he is ὁ σοφός/ὁ σπουδαῖος. Integrally related and philosophically necessary was the grounding of his virtue in universal law; if ὁ σοφός was κοσμοπολίτης--and it was generally conceded that he was--[95] how much more ὁ σοφός/βασιλεύς.

For the Stoics τὸ ὁμολογουμένως ζῆν τῇ φύσει was conceived of on pantheistic presuppositions; since the λόγος within man was part of the universal λόγος, he who lived according to λόγος ὀρθός automatically conformed his life to the universal λόγος, and hence enjoyed "kingship" over the universe.[96] For Philo the matter was not so simple because his adherence to Biblical monotheism forced him to distinguish uncompromisingly between ὁ θεός and everything created,[97] which probably included ὁ λόγος,[98] and certainly ὁ κόσμος.[99] Even if it could be shown that Moses, ὁ σοφός, successfully lived according to λόγος, that did not automatically imply his absolute "kingship" of universal nature, since λόγος for Philo was not supreme. In order to posit this, it was necessary to demonstrate Moses' intimate relationship with ὁ θεός, "the Father and Maker of the universe" (τὸν πατέρα τῶν ὅλων καὶ ποιητὴν ...).[100]

This he accomplishes by drawing upon the φίλος θεοῦ theme, which is first introduced in V. Mos. 1. 155, where it is affirmed that "God judged him worthy to appear as a partner (κοινωνός = φίλος) of his own possessions," and "gave into his hands the whole world (πάντα τὸν κόσμον) as a portion well

---

[95]Diogenes Laertius, 6. 63, 98.

[96]Cf. ZELLER, Stoics, 227f.

[97]Cf. esp. Mut. 122; Spec. Leg. 1. 277; Leg. All. 2. 1-2; passim.

[98]Cf. Her. 205f.; cf. WOLFSON, 1. 271ff.

[99]Spec. Leg. 1. 13, 96, 209; Leg. All. 2. 3; 3. 7, 88; Cher. 127; Abr. 75, 78; Som. 1. 243; Decal. 90. On Philo's polemic against the Stoics, cf. BRÉHIER, 537; BILLINGS, Platonism, 14; contra POHLENZ, "Philon," 447; LEISEGANG, art. "Philon," PWRE, 39.

[100]V. Mos. 1. 158.

fitted for His heir." Significantly, he does not take the
ordinary tack of the Hellenistic kingship tractates, a prominent feature of which was the divine lineage, notably the
divine sonship, of such figures as Heracles,[101] Alexander the
Great,[102] and Minos.[103] Instead, the pre-eminence of Moses is
established by appeal to the φίλος θεοῦ-motif, which was
appropriate for at least three reasons. First, its political
overtones. Alexandria's familiarity with Ptolemaic kingship,
in which οἱ φίλοι had become an established institution in
itself,[104] would have made φίλος θεοῦ a particularly well-
chosen expression for illustrating the unique monarchical role
which Moses shared with the supreme King, Yahweh.[105] Second,
its role in applying the "king-imitate-King" schema to Moses'
relationship to God. Dio C., Orat. 1. 37ff., indicates the
crucial role of this schema in the kingship tractates. Dio
turns to address:

> ...that supreme king and ruler whom mortals and
> those who administer the affairs of mortals must
> always imitate in discharging their responsibili-
> ties, directing and conforming their ways as far
> as possible to his pattern.[106]

---

[101]Dio C., Orat. 1. 59; 2. 78; 69. 1; cf. Epictetus,
Diss., 2. xvi, 44.

[102]Dio C., Orat. 2. 16.

[103]Dio C., Orat. 1. 38; though, cf. Qu. Ex. 2. 6.

[104]Cf. C. B. WELLES, Royal Correspondence in the
Hellenistic Period. A Study in Greek Epigraphy (New Haven,
1934) p. 44, and Nos. 22.9; 25.18; also 6.6; 14.9; 22.13;
25.25; 45.3; 49.2; 75.2. Particularly germane for our inquiry
is the use of φίλος in this sense in 1 Macc. 10:65; 2 Macc.
11:14. Cf. also DITTENBERGER, OGIS, No. 256; 219.40-48; also,
H. KORTENBEUTEL, art. "Philos," PWRE 20.1 (1941) 95-103;
especially, the chapter devoted to οἱ φίλοι in G. CORRADI, Studi
Ellenistici (Torino, 1929) 318-47, also 231-55; also, GEYER,
art. "Lysimachus," PWRE 14.1 (1928) 23f.

[105]Cf. Prob. 44, and discussion below, pp. 129ff.

[106]Cf. also Dio C., Orat. 1. 40, where Zeus is designated βασιλεύς "because of his dominion and power;" also, Orat.
2. 75, where he is "the great king of Kings, who is the common
protector and father of men and gods." On the "king-imitate-
King" schema, cf. GOODENOUGH, "Hellenistic Kingship," 74;
BRÉHIER, 20, notes that it was a favorite Neo-Pythagorean
theme, especially in Diotogenes, Stenides, Ecphantus; also,

(cont.)

The king's κοινωνία with <u>the</u> supreme King only further attested
the degree to which he successfully followed the pattern.
Generally, this schema remains implicit in the pericope, however. Third, the close associations between φιλία θεοῦ and the
Stoic doctrine of οἰκείωσις[107] made it a favorite theme in the
kingship tractates. Friendship with men[108] no less than with
the gods[109] was considered a vital prerequisite for the ideal
ruler, although this by no means had always been regarded as
possible. Aristotle had classified friendship with the gods in
the category of friendship between unequal parties and had
declared:

> This is most manifest in the case of the gods,
> whose superiority in every good attribute is
> pre-eminent; .... It is true that we cannot fix
> a precise limit in such cases, up to which two
> men can still be friends; the gap may go on
> widening and the friendship still remain; but
> when one becomes very remote from the other, as
> God is remote from man, it can continue no
> longer.[110]

Aristotle did agree, however, with the popular proverb κοινὰ
τὰ φίλων,[111] as did Plato before him,[112] and Dio Chrysostom
after him,[113] which, when coupled with <u>Ex</u>. 33:11, where Moses

---

21f., he interprets <u>V. Mos</u>. 1. 158 in terms of this scheme,
"C'est dans la monarchie divine que le roi doit prendre son
modèle. Il est le dieu de ses sujets."

[107]Cf. S. G. PEMBROKE, "Oikeiōsis," in <u>Problems in
Stoicism</u>, ed. A. A. Long (London, 1971) 114ff., esp. 124ff.;
DE VOGEL, <u>Greek Philosophy</u>, 3. p. 128; of the "friendship with
God" motif, cf. H. NEUMARK, <u>Die Verwendung griechischer und
jüdischer Motive in den Gedanken Philons über die Stellung
Gottes zu seinen Freunden</u> (Würzburg, 1937), cited and summari-
zed in ARNALDEZ, <u>Oeuvres Philon</u> (Lyon) 1. 98ff.

[108]Dio C., <u>Orat</u>. 3. 86ff.

[109]Dio C., <u>Orat</u>. 3. 115; 4. 40ff.

[110]<u>Nicom. Eth</u>. VIII 7, 1158b 29 - 1159a 5. Trans. H.
Rackham (Loeb).

[111]<u>Nicom. Eth</u>. VIII 9, 1159b 30f.

[112]<u>Leg</u>. 5. 739c; <u>Lys</u>. 207c; <u>Phaedr</u>. 279c; <u>Resp</u>. 5. 449c.

[113]Dio C., <u>Orat</u>. 3. 110. According to Diogenes
Laertius, 8. 10, the proverb is Pythagorean. Cf. HÖISTAD,
139:3, for additional references. NEUMARK underrates the
(cont.)

is designated the "friend of God," provided Philo with an
irrefutable basis for positing the cosmic extent of Moses'
"kingship," i.e. his mastery of universal nature. The argument
at this point has become thoroughly Cynic and recalls the
doxographic account of Diogenes the Cynic of whom Diogenes
Laertius writes:

> He maintained that all things are the property of
> the wise, and employed such arguments as those
> cited above.[114] All things belong to the gods.
> The gods are friends to the wise, and friends
> share all property in common; therefore all things
> are the property of the wise.[115]

By substituting ὁ θεός for θεοί and equating ὁ σοφός and ὁ
προφήτης, Philo thus gains solid Biblical warrant for asserting
Moses' friendship with God, in the Hellenistic sense, which
entitled him to a share in God's possessions, i.e. universal
nature, and qualified him to be called κοσμοπολίτης.[116]

Seen in this overall context, the puzzling statement in
V. Mos. 1. 156, which has been taken to refer to Moses'
thaumaturgic ability,[117] becomes more intelligible:

> τοιγαροῦν ὑπήκουεν ὡς δεσπότῃ τῶν στοιχείων
> ἕκαστον ἀλλάττον ἣν εἶχε δύναμιν καὶ ταῖς
> προστάξεσιν ὑπεῖκον· καὶ θαυμαστὸν ἴσως οὐδέν·

> Therefore, each element obeyed him as its master,
> changed its natural properties and submitted to
> his command, and this perhaps is no wonder.[118]

Immediately upon mentioning the catalogue of virtues,[119] Philo
says that God gave Moses τὸν πλοῦτον τῆς φύσεως, i.e. mastery
over φύσις, which the Stoics conceived of materialistically.
This applied not only to corporeal substances in the generally
understood sense, e.g. trees and sealing wax, but even to
ostensibly non-material entities, e.g. the soul or God.[120]
Given this metaphysics, virtue and vice were also conceived of

---

role of Plato and Aristotle in the development of the theme;
cf. ARNALDEZ, 99.

[114]Cf. Diogenes Laertius 6. 37.

[115]Diogenes Laertius 6. 72.

[116]V. Mos. 1. 157.   [117]TIEDE, 126.

[118]Trans. Colson (Loeb).   [119]V. Mos. 1. 154.

[120]Cf. references in ZELLER, Stoics, 126f.

as material substances, which meant that the practice of virtue or vice could be described in terms of Stoic physics, which is precisely what Philo does in this passage.[121]

Having sought to establish the cosmic scope of Moses' "kingship" over nature by use of the φίλος θεοῦ-motif, Philo turns to a second supporting argument which is less straight-forward than the first and into which Ex. 7:1 figures prominently. Moses is asserted to be κοσμοπολίτης, since he had received the entire world as his portion, not just a small section of it. Then follows, "Did he not enjoy greater fellowship with the Father and Maker of the universe, seeing that he was deemed worthy to bear the same title? For, he was designated god and king of the entire nation."[122] The mention of κοινωνία picks up again the κοινωνός/φίλος theme from V. Mos. 1. 155 and the superlative quality of the relationship is reinforced by an appeal to (1) Moses' possession of the double title θεὸς καὶ βασιλεύς and (2) his unique vision of the realm of Ideas.

As to the former, the first question that arises is, greater than whom? Possibly this is merely Philo's way of expressing the extraordinary quality of Moses' share in God's kingship. But it appears that at this point he is in dialogue with an unknown interlocuter. Perhaps he is attempting to counter the Hellenistic kingship traditions which regarded such figures as Heracles, Minos, or Alexander the Great as sons of Zeus, and therefore the most intimate associates of God.[123] It was above all important for the Cynic-Stoic ideal king to imitate the gods, but Philo could go a step further and claim that Moses bore the same title.

Two aspects of the double title deserve mention:

---

[121]Contra GEORGI, 153, who uses the passage to establish a connection between miracle-working and the theios aner: "Die nächste Redewendung macht offenbar, dass Philo mit seiner Darstellung eine Diskussion des Problems der Wundertätigkeit von Gottesmännern verbindet: 'Und dies ist vielleicht nicht verwunderlich' (θαυμαστός)." On the Stoic doctrine of the transformation of the elements, cf. ZELLER, Stoics, 199ff.

[122]Passage cited above, p. 109.

[123]Cf. notes 101, 102, 103 above.

(1) its content and (2) its function. Presumably, it functions
as a means of attesting the superlative, if not unique quality
of the κοινωνία, and by extension, its universal scope, since
the object is τὸν πατέρα τῶν ὅλων καὶ ποιητήν. But, if this
were the sole function, why the double title? Why not merely
cite Ex. 7:1 and leave it at that, since the single title θεός
would have been sufficient for this purpose? This immediately
raises the question of the content: how is the presence of the
double title to be explained? Or, as Meeks states the problem:

> The double title 'god and king' is also puzzling.
> The first title, 'god,' Philo takes directly from
> Exodus 7:1, "See, I have made you a god to Pharaoh."
> But the scriptural context has no connection with
> the Sinai theophany, nor does it mention kingship.
> We are left with the question how Philo came to
> connect Moses' installation as ideal king with
> (1) a mystic ascent, read into the Sinai episode,
> and (2) the scriptural report that Moses was called
> 'god'."[124]

Meeks's attempt to resolve the question by adducing Rabbinic
passages where the dual roles of Moses' (mystic) ascent to
Sinai and his kingship are joined, though interesting, is, in
the end, unsuccessful, because the question of how Ex. 7:1 and
"kingship" came to be connected remains unanswered. Moreover,
Philo does not himself connect Moses' receipt of the title θεός
with his so-called mystic vision.[125]

A more tenable solution is to be sought by taking
seriously the overall context of the pericope, realizing that
it is a digression devoted solely to establishing Moses' unique
qualifications as βασιλεύς. Yet, unlike φίλος θεοῦ, this is
precisely the role for which Philo could produce no clear-cut
Biblical warrant! He could only search in vain for passages in
the LXX which spoke of Moses as βασιλεύς, ἄρχων, or ἡγεμών.[126]

---

[124]W. A. MEEKS, "Moses as God and King," in Religions in
Antiquity [Goodenough Festschrift, ed. J. Neusner] (Leiden,
1968) 355; also Prophet-King, 111.

[125]Cf. Midrash on Deut. 33:1, below, p. 125.

[126]An indication of the difficulty of finding prooftexts
for Moses' kingship is seen in Tanḥuma, ed. Buber, IV, 51f.,
cited in MEEKS, Prophet-King, 193, in which the LXX Deut. 33:5,
καὶ ἔσται ἐν τῷ ἠγαπημένῳ ἄρχων, the meaning of which is
debatable, but probably refers to Yahweh (so, von Rad), is

(cont.)

Certainly, Ex. 7:1 did not provide such a text as it stood,
but, as it had come to be understood in certain Jewish circles,
it did provide the key. The fact that Moses is designated θεός
vis à vis Pharaoh, combined with the seeming brazenness of
ascribing the title θεός to Moses, produced one line of interpretation which understood θεός to mean βασιλεύς: for Moses to
be θεός means for him to be βασιλεύς, either over Pharaoh, or
over Israel. This is the use made of Ex. 7:1 in the Tanḥuma
text already referred to:

> Another interpretation: What (does this mean):
> "The Lord of Hosts, he is the King of Glory?"
> (This means that) he apportions some of his
> glory to those who fear him according to his
> glory. How so? He is called "God," and he
> called Moses "god," as it is said, "See, I
> have made you a god to Pharaoh" (Ex. 7:1).[127]

In Targum Onkelos the same tendency is reflected when אלהים
in both Ex. 4:16 and 7:1 is interpreted as רב:

> Ex. 4:16   And thou shalt be to him (Aaron) a rab.[128]
>
> Ex. 7:1   I have appointed thee as a Master (rab)
>   with Pharaoh.[129]

With slightly different emphasis Targum of Jerusalem reads:

> Ex. 4:16   And he shall speak for thee with the people,
>   and be to thee an interpreter and thou to
>   him the principal.[130]
>
> Ex. 7:1   Behold, I have set thee a terror to Pharaoh,
>   as if thou wast his God, and Aharon thy
>   brother shall be thy prophet.[131]

The same tendency can be found in the Samaritan tradition, as
in Memar Marqah 1.2 where אלהים is replaced by תנינו, thus

---

altered and made into a prooftext for Moses' kingship. Thus,
"The Holy One ... said to Moses, 'I have made you a king,' as
Scripture says, 'He became a king in Yeshurun' (Deut. 33:5)."
Cf. WOLFSON, 2. 16:40.

[127]Tanḥuma, ed. Buber, IV, 51f., quoted by MEEKS,
Prophet-King, 193, who refers to 53; Bamidbar R 15. 13.

[128]Targum Onkelos XIII (Trans. J. W. Etheridge, 1. 352).

[129]Targum Onkelos XIV (Trans. J. W. Etheridge, 1.
357f.).

[130]Targum of Jerusalem XIII (Trans. J. W. Etheridge,
1. 453).

[131]Targum of Jerusalem XIV (Trans. J. W. Etheridge,
1. 460).

Ex. 7:1 becomes, "You are my second in the lower world."[132]
But this is sharply contrasted with other Samaritan passages
where the naming of Moses with God's name is elaborated and
emphasized,[133] as well as with Memar Marqah 1.2:

> "Then He said, 'I am the God of your fathers'
> (Ex. 3.6). Take from me divinity (אלהו) and
> with it make your prophethood strong."[134]

Similar to this is the Midrash on Deut. 33:1, where "Moses, the
man of God" is interpreted as "Moses, a man, god":

> "A man, god." 'A man' when he ascended on high,
> 'god' when he descended below. "And Aaron and
> all the sons of Israel saw Moses and behold!
> his face emitted beams of light.[135]

Thus, in spite of the diversity of approaches even within
Rabbinic and Samaritan circles, the fact remains that one line
of interpreting Ex. 7:1 was in terms of Moses' "kingship" over
Pharaoh, and, although it must remain uncertain whether Philo
is drawing upon these traditions,[136] it thus appears that Philo
alludes to Ex. 7:1 primarily because it had come to be understood as a statement about Moses' kingship, and therefore the
βασιλεύς member of the pair of titles is really the part he
wishes to underscore, καὶ βασιλεύς serving as a commentary upon
θεός. What we have here, in embryonic form, is an allegorical
interpretation of θεός, taken to signify βασιλεύς, an interpretation which appears in more developed form elsewhere.[137]

The mention of the double title of Moses prompts Philo

---

[132]Trans. J. MacDonald, p. 12.

[133]M. Marq. 1. 2, 9; 2. 12; 4. 1; 5. 3, 4 = ET, pp. 5,
18, 31, 81, 137, 203, 207. Also, A. E. Cowley, The Samaritan
Liturgy (1909), 1. 32f. Cited in MEEKS, "Moses as God," 359.

[134]Trans. J. MacDonald, p. 5.

[135]Pesikta R. K. 32f., 198b; cf. Debarim R. 11. 4; Midr.
Tehillim 90. 1; cited in MEEKS, "Moses as God," 355.

[136]Could this be one of those instances where Philo
provides evidence of contact with Rabbinic schools of exegesis,
indeed possibly provides evidence of the antiquity of this
particular line of interpretation which later shows up in the
Targums and other Rabbinic literature? Cf. J. BOWKER, The
Targums and Rabbinic Literature. An Introduction to Jewish
Interpretations of Scripture (Cambridge, 1969) 30.

[137]Leg. All. 1. 40; cf. discussion below, pp. 141ff.

to introduce another element into the portrait, Moses' so-
called mystic vision, his entry "into the unseen, invisible,
incorporeal and archetypal essence of existing things" where he
beheld "what is hidden from the sight of mortal nature."[138]   At
this point he seems to have departed from the Cynic-Stoic model
of the ideal king in which the mystic vision of the king played
no significant role. As noted above, Meeks is clearly puzzled
by Philo's introduction of Moses' mystic vision at this point,
and suggests that its incorporation here is owing to the mystic
associations that the kingship motif as applied to Moses had
come to have in Rabbinic schools of exegesis. But in the final
analysis he is unable to produce a Rabbinic text in which Moses'
appointment as king is linked with his mystical vision on
Sinai.[139]

A more plausible explanation is that the introduction of
the vision is prompted by the mention of Moses' title βασιλεύς,
and that Philo is here being influenced by the Platonic notion
that the ideal philosopher-king alone has grasped the reality
of the Idea of the Good and thereby became uniquely qualified
to govern the ideal state. We have already noticed Philo's
heavy dependence upon Resp. 5-7 in his first digression.[140]
Many of the same themes also appear in V. Mos. 1. 148-62, even
if the Cynic-Stoic cast is more pronounced. Plato regarded it
as essential that the philosopher-king should have perceived
the "eternal and unchanging realities,"[141] which of course
included the Supreme Good, in order for him to qualify as the
paradigm for the other citizens of the state.[142] Moreover, he
regarded the contemplation of the Supreme Good as an ecstatic
experience.[143] Accordingly, Philo chooses to describe Moses'

---

[138]V. Mos. 1. 158.

[139]MEEKS, Prophet-King, 194-95.

[140]V. Mos. 1. 19-33; cf. above, pp. 109ff.

[141]Resp. 5. 480a; 6. 484b.

[142]Resp. 7. 540a-b.

[143]Phaedr. 249c-e; Symp. 211. Cf. A. J. FESTUGIÈRE,
Contemplation et vie contemplative selon Platon (Paris, 1936)
224; also BILLINGS, Platonism, 16, "It is sufficient here to
(cont.)

experience in thoroughly Platonic terms:[144] "the darkness
where God was," an obvious reference to the clouds in the
Exodus description of the Sinai epiphany,[145] he regards as
none other than Plato's noumenal world: "the unseen, invisible, incorporeal, and archetypal essence of existing things"
(τουτέστιν εἰς τὴν ἀειδῆ καὶ ἀόρατον καὶ ἀσώματον τῶν ὄντων
παραδειγματικὴν οὐσίαν, τὰ ἀθέατα φύσει θνητῇ κατανοῶν).[146]
A possible reason for his incorporating this theme of the
vision of the Unseen at this point may be connected with the
fact that the "friendship with God" motif had come to be understood mystically in the Hellenistic era.[147] The pervasiveness
of the Platonic imagery, nevertheless, strongly suggests that
Philo wishes to conclude the pericope by presenting Moses as
the σοφός, Plato's philosopher-king, the embodiment of ἀρετή,
who has perceived the realm of Ideas--a rare experience
indeed--and thereby has become the paradigm for the unenlight-
ened, which was exactly the same role Plato's Guardian was to
play in the ideal state.[148]

---

point out that the vision of true being is, for Plato,
attained, not through intellectual activity, but in moments
of divine madness, and under the influence of Eros."

[144]Philo's description of Moses' vision should be compared with Plato's analogies of the sun, divided line, and cave
in Resp. 6-7. In the latter, for example, it will be recalled
that the philosopher, having escaped from the cave, first had
to let his eyes become habituated to the brightness by degrees,
having first looked at shadows and reflections, after which he
was finally able to gaze into the sun, i.e. the Supreme Reality;
cf. Resp. 7. 515e-516b.

[145]Ex. 20:21.

[146]V. Mos. 1. 158. Cf. also Post. C. 14 where he
explicitly identifies the "darkness" of Ex. 20:21 as the realm
of "conceptions regarding the Existent Being that belong to the
unapproachable region where there are no material forms." Cf.
also Qu. Ex. 2. 28.

[147]E. PETERSON, "Der Gottesfreund," ZKG [N.F. 5] 42
(1923) 161-202.

[148]Cf. J. B. SKEMP, "Plato's Concept of Deity," Zetesis
(Antwerp/Utrecht, 1973), 116, "Though the ray of the soul's
vision must be compelled to look at this supreme Object at the
supreme moment of its earthly life (or, at least, this is what
the guardians attain, and they do so, in a sense, for the
benefit of all ..." (emphasis mine). Cf. Resp. 5. 480a; 6.
484b, 486d; 7. 518c, 519d, 520c, 532a.

In summary, Philo appeals to Ex. 7:1 in this miniature
περὶ βασιλείας tractate primarily to document Moses' status as
βασιλεύς. The LXX text taken alone, in certain Jewish circles
had caused considerable offense to the religious sensibilities
of Jews who had consequently attempted to tone down its force
by various lines of interpretation. One such interpretation
appears in Targum Onkelos, the Tanḥuma text, less so in Targum
of Jerusalem, and in Philo. According to this exegetical
tradition, βασιλεύς functioned as a commentary upon θεός: for
Moses to be called θεός meant that God named him βασιλεύς, the
explanation ran. Or, as the Tanḥuma text shows, to be called
θεός means to share God's glory, i.e. His kingship. Thus, when
Philo wishes to document the intimacy of Moses' κοινωνία with
God in conjunction with the φιλία θεοῦ motif introduced in V.
Mos. 1. 156 as well as with the Cynic-Stoic conception of the
σοφός-βασιλεύς, he appeals to an extrabiblical tradition,
primarily because of its designation of Moses as βασιλεύς,
instead of θεός, and it is the βασιλεύς title that sparks the
return to the Platonic philosopher-king model, specifically the
necessity for the king to have perceived the realm of the Ideas,
and occasions the introduction of the ecstatic vision of Moses
described in V. Mos. 1. 158-59. Thus, the introduction of the
so-called mystic vision turns out to be philosophically
motivated.

V. Mos. 1. 148-63, thus, is Philo's portrait of Moses,
ὁ σοφός-βασιλεύς-κοσμοπολίτης,[149] who, significantly, is not
transformed into a heavenly figure,[150] but whose "cosmic kingship" is purely ethical in its scope. The cosmic extent of
Moses' "kingship" is stressed throughout, but only insofar as
it relates to the ethical theme of his successful accomplish-

---

[149]Contra K. HOLL, "Die schriftstellerische Form des
griechischen Heiligenlebens," Neue Jahrbücher für das
klassische Altertum 29 (1912) 421:5, who, in discussing ὁ σοφός
as an ideal in Antisthenes and later in the Pythagoreans,
denies that Philo places Moses in the same tradition: "Philo
gehört nicht in diese Entwicklung herein. In seinen Lebens-
bildern von Abraham, Moses und Joseph folgt er entweder einfach
dem Gang der biblischen Erzählung oder--soweit er eine
Gestaltung des Stoffs versucht--schliesst er sich an das
Muster des ἐγκώμιον an."

[150]So, GEORGI, 152f.

ment of life according to (universal) nature; nowhere is it
stated that he becomes a "heavenly figure;" no appeal to his
divine sonship is made, in sharp contrast to contemporary
Hellenistic kingship tractates. On the contrary, the far less
ambitious claim to φιλία/κοινωνία θεοῦ is made. If our analysis of V. Mos. 1. 156 is correct, there is not even a hint of
thaumaturgic activity on the part of Moses in this sketch.
Moreover, even though Philo had solid Biblical warrant in Ex.
7:1 for asserting Moses' divinity, which would per se surely
document his cosmic status, Ex. 7:1 does not serve this
function for Philo. Instead, he speaks only of Moses' φιλία/
κοινωνία with the Father and Maker of the universe. In other
words, Ex. 7:1 provided Philo ample basis for placing on Moses'
lips Empedocles' claim, ἐγὼ δ' ὑμῖν θεὸς ἄμβροτος, οὐκέτι
θνητός,[151] but he shrinks from this--far from this.

(2) Prob. 42-44.

A further clue to Philo's interpretation of Ex. 7:1 in
V. Mos. 1. 155ff. turns up when we examine the other instances
where he deals with the passage in a tractate indisputably
intended for pagan readers,[152] Prob. 42-44. Quod Omnis Probus
Liber Sit is an excursus, probably dating from his younger
days,[153] devoted to the Stoic paradox that only the wise man is

---

[151]Frag. 112 in H. DIELS, Die Fragmente der
Vorsokratiker (Berlin, ⁵1934) 1. 354.

[152]Although it has become more difficult to identify
with certainty the intended addressees of Hellenistic Jewish
apologetic treatises, the evidence seems to tilt in favor of
Gentile addressees as the intended readers of V. Mos., especially from its opening remarks. Cf. F. H. COLSON, "Introduction," in Loeb, vol. 6, p. xv; also DANIÉLOU, 88; on the whole
question, cf. V. TCHERIKOVER, "Jewish Apologetic Literature
Reconsidered," Eos 48 (1956) 169-93; E. R. GOODENOUGH, "Philo's
Exposition of the Law and his De vita Mosis," HTR 27 (1933)
109-25; Introduction to Philo Judaeus, 33; TIEDE, 106f.; cf.
below, pp. 136ff. On the classification of Philo's writings
into "esoteric" and "exoteric," cf. DANIÉLOU, 22, 85; ARNALDEZ
(Lyon) 1. 88f.

[153]So COLSON (Loeb), "Introduction," vol. 9, p. 2. For
the debate concerning the chronology of Philo's works and the
related question of the development of his thought, cf.
MASSEBIEAU-BRÉHIER, "Essai sur la chronologie de la vie et des
oeuvres de Philon," Rev. Hist. Rel. (1906) 25-64; 164-85; 267-
(cont.)

free, or as Philo states it at the beginning, ὅτι πᾶς ὁ ἀστεῖος
ἐλεύθερος.[154] The use of ἀστεῖος, σπουδαῖος, and similar terms
instead of σοφός in the statement of the paradox reflects the
tendency common in Hellenistic times to define σοφία
ethically.[155] Understanding ἀρετή perfectly as well as
possessing, indeed embodying it, entitled ὁ σοφός to a position
of ἡγεμονία over other mortals, and consequently only he could
be said to be ἐλεύθερος. But, besides defining ἐλευθερία
ethically, another means of proving the paradox consisted of
adducing various examples of instances in which a person found
himself in a subordinate position, situations in which
ἐλευθερία was ostensibly, but not actually precluded, or at
least, for which δουλεία was an inappropriate label. In fact,
Prob. 32-40 corresponds roughly to the threefold Stoic classification of δουλεία into (1) mere absence of independence
(στέρησις αὐτοπραγίας);[156] (2) subordination (ὑπόταξις); and
(3) subordination in which the slave is owned (ἐν κτήσει τε
καὶ ὑποτάξει).[157] Like Dio Chrysostom in his Fourteenth Discourse,[158] Philo is concerned to show that one can still enjoy
ἐλευθερία in all three situations. Even though one is in a
subordinate relationship to another either because of the
extenuating circumstances of war and economic hardship[159]--in

89, who place the Exposition of the laws prior to the allegorical treatises; L. COHN, "Einleitung und Chronologie der
Schriften Philos," Philologus Suppl. 7 (1899) 387-435, reverses
the order. Also, cf. A. D. NOCK, Essays on Religion and the
Ancient World (Cambridge, Mass., 1972) 2. 561.

[154] Our chief source for this doctrine is Dio Chrysostom,
Discourses 14 & 15; cf. also Cicero, Paradoxa Stoicorum V;
Tusc. V; Plutarch, Περὶ εὐγενείας (cf. Fragments 139-141, Loeb,
vol. 15); Epictetus, Diss. 3. xxiv, 67ff., 4. i; also Diogenes
Laertius, 7. 121, [τὸν σοφόν] μόνον τ' ἐλεύθερον, τοὺς δὲ
φαύλους δούλους. Cf. SVF 3. 589ff.

[155] Cf. Dio C., Orat. 14. 18; 69. 4.

[156] Cf. Prob. 21-22, where he deals with αὐτοπραγία; also
Diogenes Laertius, 7. 121.

[157] Cf. Diogenes Laertius, 7. 121-22.

[158] Dio C., Orat. 14. 4ff.

[159] Prob. 32-34.

which there is really no choice but to serve in order to sur-
vive--, because of birth[160]--in which case one must be obedient
to one's parents--, or because of being sold either as a
hostage or a slave[161]--in which being owned by a superior
entails subordination, this does not necessarily preclude
ἐλευθερία, that is, ἐλευθερία properly defined.[162]   From Prob.
41ff. onward, Philo is mainly presenting various arguments to
support his general thesis.[163]   When he states at the outset
that τῷ γὰρ ὄντι μόνος ἐλεύθερος ὁ μόνῳ θεῷ χρώμενος
ἡγεμόνι,[164] he is not affirming anything radically new, for
εὐσέβεια was regarded as an essential Stoic virtue and a prerequisite for ὁ σοφός, and therefore for ὁ ἐλεύθερος.[165]
Nevertheless, since man, even ἀνὴρ σπουδαῖος, indisputably
stood in a subordinate relationship to God(s), it was appropriate for Philo to demonstrate that εὐσέβεια did not by definition preclude ἐλευθερία, but rather produced it; or, to state
it another way, that ὁ σπουδαῖος was ὁ εὐσεβής but not
necessarily ὁ δοῦλος. Instead of adducing ὁ εὐσεβής as an
example, he selects φίλος θεοῦ, an expression that implied far
greater intimacy between man and God, yet still presupposed
that φίλος was subordinate to θεός. This is illustrated
especially clearly in Dio C., Orat. 4. 41-43:

> Once more, when he says that kings are 'nurtured
> of Zeus' ("διοτρεφεῖς") and 'dear unto Zeus'
> ("διιφίλους"), do you think that he means any
> other nurture than the teaching and instruction
> which I called divine? Or do you believe that
> he means that kings are nourished by Zeus as by
> a nurse, on milk and wine and various foods, and
> not on knowledge and truth? And in the same way
> he means that friendship ("φιλίαν") also is
> nothing else than identity of wish and purpose,
> that is, a kind of likemindedness. For this, I
> presume, is the view of the world too: that

---

[160]Prob. 35-36.   [161]Prob. 37-40.

[162]For other examples of the "Stone walls do not a
prison make" principle, cf. Dio C., Orat. 14. 4ff.

[163]N.B. πρὸς τούτοις (42); ἔτι τοίνυν (45); πρὸς τοίνυν
(48), etc.

[164]Prob. 20.

[165]Dio C., Orat. 69. 2; Diogenes Laertius, 7. 119.

friends (οἱ φίλοι) are most truly likeminded and
are at variance in nothing. Can anyone, therefore,
who is a friend of Zeus (Διὶ φίλος) and is likeminded with him by any possibility conceive any
unrighteous desire or design what is wicked and
disgraceful?[166]

Philo thus cites two examples of φιλία θεοῦ, one from Hellenism,[167] the other from Judaism:[168]

(42) And, in addition to this, who would not
agree that friends of God[169] (τοὺς φίλους τοῦ
θεοῦ) are free? For, unless it is conceded that
not only freedom but even dominion belongs to
close companions[170] of kings, inasmuch as they
share in the oversight and management of the realm,
then one must ascribe slavery to those (companions)
of the Olympian gods who, because they are lovers
of God(s) have thereby become loved by God(s),[171]
having been honored in return with goodwill which
is truly justified and are, as the poets say, rulers
of all, indeed, kings of kings.[172]
(43) But, the legislator of the Jews, with even
more audacity, went a step further, as if he were
a naked Cynic (ἅτε γυμνῆς ὡς λόγος ἀσκητῆς φιλο-
σοφίας),[173] and was presumptuous enough to say that
the one who is possessed by divine love[174] and
worships the Existent One--and Him alone--, is no

---

[166]Trans. J. W. Cohoon (Loeb).

[167]Prob. 42.   [168]Prob. 43-44.

[169]Cohn conjectures θεῶν instead of τοῦ θεοῦ, on the
basis of the plurals that follow; cf. Diogenes Laertius, 6. 37;
7. 124.

[170]On the question of οἱ φίλοι as a Hellenistic political institution, cf. note 104 above.

[171]On the θεοφιλής-φιλόθεος doublet, cf. Dio C., Orat.
69. 4; also F. DIRLMEIER, "ΘΕΟΦΙΛΙΑ-ΦΙΛΟΘΕΙΑ," Philologus 90
(1935) 57-77, cited by HÖISTAD, 216.

[172]Cf. Qu. Gen. 4. 76.

[173]Colson (Loeb), "and in the practice of his 'naked'
philosophy, as they called it;" Yonge, "inasmuch as he was, as
it is reported, a student and practiser of plain philosophy;"
Cohn, et al. (Werke), "da er sich der nackten Philosophie, wie
es heisst, befleissigte." Colson, note ad loc., "Possibly
there may be some allusion to the gymnosophists (see par. 93)
but more probably to something which we cannot now recover."
On Moses as "philosopher," cf. A. MÉASSON, Oeuvres Philon
(Lyon), note on Sacr. 1, p. 189f., who refers to Opif. 8, Som.
2. 127; V. Contemp. 26, 28.

[174]Compare ἔρως theme in Plato, Symp.

longer "man" but "god;"[175] but, mind you,[176] a
"god" of men, not a "god" of the natural order,
thereby reserving for the Father of all the
position of being King and God of gods.[177]
(44) Now, I ask you, Does one who has obtained
such a privilege as this deserve to be regarded
as a slave, or as free and free alone? Even if
he has not been deemed worthy of divine status
in his own right,[178] at least, because he was
treated as a friend[179] by God,[180] he was bound
to have absolute and continual happiness.[181]
For God, since he is companionable, is neither
a frail champion nor one who neglects friendship
rights, and he oversees those affairs which per-
tain to his companions.[182]

The link between this passage and V. Mos. 1. 155ff. is that
in both instances Ex. 7:1 is alluded to in connection with the
φίλος θεοῦ theme, and each time has the same function: to
document Moses' status as φίλος θεοῦ, although in V. Mos. 1.
158 the intimacy between Moses and God is described as
μείζονος ... κοινωνίας whereas in Prob. 44 φίλος is used. The
σοφός-βασιλεύς-φίλος θεοῦ scheme of V. Mos. 1. 155ff.[183] is
contrasted with the σοφός-σπουδαῖος-φίλος θεοῦ scheme of Prob.
43-44, where the only reference to βασιλεύς is to

---

[175]Colson (Loeb), "as having passed from a man into a
god."

[176]N.B. adversative force of μέντοι; cf. H. W. SMYTH,
Greek Grammar (Cambridge, Mass., 1968) par. 2917-19; LSJ, s.v.,
B. II. 4.

[177]Compare θεὸς καὶ βασιλεύς in V. Mos. 1. 158.

[178]Possibly, καθ' αὑτόν refers to God, thus "... of
divine status comparable to that One Himself." On κατά in
comparisons, cf. LSJ, s.v., B. IV. 3.

[179]On χρῆσθαί τινι ὡς = "... treat him as ...," cf. LSJ,
s.v., C. IV. a, esp. ὡς φίλοις; cf. Thucyd. 1. 53; Xenophon,
Cyr. 4. 2. 8; or as an expression of intimacy, Xenophon, Hier.
5. 2; Mem. 4. 8. 11.

[180]Conceivably θεῷ stands in apposition with φίλῳ and
thus Philo's allegorical interpretation of θεός in Ex. 7:1;
hence, the phrase would read, "at least, because he was treated
as a friend, that is as "god," ..."

[181]Εὐδαιμονία was an essential feature of the paradox;
cf. Prob. 41; also Seneca, De vita beata 8. 1ff.; Sextus, Adv.
math. 7. 158 (= Adv. Log. 1. 158).

[182]Prob. 42-44.   [183]Cf. Post. C. 138.

134

God;[184] in both instances Ex. 7:1 serves to illustrate the
intimate, and lofty, relationship between Moses and God, but in
V. Mos. 1. 155ff. the overriding concern is Moses ὁ βασιλεύς-
κοσμοπολίτης, whereas in Prob. 43-44 it is Moses ὁ εὐσεβής, he
who is "possessed by divine love and worships the Existent One,
and Him alone." The universal implications of being φίλος θεοῦ,
elsewhere associated with this idea[185] and underscored in V.
Mos. 1. 148ff., are missing in Prob. 42-44, although the νόμος
κοινός theme is hinted at in Prob. 45-47. In many respects
Philo's use of the φίλος θεοῦ motif in Prob. 42-44 is similar
to Dio Chrysostom's allegorical-ethical treatment of the υἱὸς
θεοῦ motif as it applied to Heracles in which Heracles' divine
sonship is interpreted in terms of φίλος θεοῦ and ὁμόνοια πρὸς
τὸν θεόν.[186] In contrast to Dio, however, Philo, immediately
upon mentioning that the true worshipper is designated θεός,
issues two qualifying statements: (1) ἀνθρώπων μέντοι θεόν, οὐ
τῶν τῆς φύσεως μερῶν, and (2) ὃς εἰ καὶ θείας οὐκ ἠξίωται
μοίρας καθ᾽ αὑτόν, ἀλλά τοι διὰ τὸ φίλῳ θεῷ χρῆσθαι πάντως
ὤφειλεν εὐδαιμονεῖν. His defensiveness, if not embarrassment,
at the brazenness of the claim, reflected in his use of
νεανικώτερον, προσυπερβάλλων, γυμνῆς, ἀπετόλμησεν, perhaps
accounts for the ambiguity of the first disclaimer.[187] Regardless of the ambiguity, perhaps intentional, he is clearly sensitive to the possibility of being misunderstood, and feels compelled to make crystal clear that he does not intend to invade
the domain of τὸ ὄντως ὄν.[188] Granted the fluidity of the term

---

[184]Although it does occur in Prob. 42.

[185]Cf. Diogenes Laertius, 6. 37, 72.

[186]Dio C., Orat. 4. 22, 43. So HÖISTAD, 216.

[187]Colson (Loeb) obviously felt the difficulty in translating the expression, because his translation is equally
unclear: "though, indeed, a god to men, not to the different
parts of nature," presumably meaning, "in the opinion (realm)
of men a god, but not in the opinion (realm) of the parts of
nature." If the genitives were to be taken adverbially, perhaps we could render the phrase "... but, 'god' humanly speaking (i.e. as a human convention), not 'god' insofar as the
components of his nature are concerned, i.e. ontologically
speaking."

[188]The distinction between anarthrous θεός, (cont.)

θεός in Philo's writings,[189] assigning the term to a worshipper (Moses) would not necessarily constitute blasphemy; and yet, evidently he was unsatisfied with the first disclaimer, for he feels compelled to add a second, which is as unambiguous as the first is ambiguous. That it is a genuine denial of Moses' divine status is indisputably proved by the fact that elsewhere Philo uses identical language to describe Gaius' self-appointment to divine status: ... καὶ μὴ κατ' ἄνθρωπον εἶναι, μείζονος δὲ καὶ θειοτέρας μοίρας,[190] although he mentions the claim only to illustrate its incredibility.[191] The clear implication of the second disclaimer is that Philo understands θεός in Ex. 7:1 to mean φίλος (θεοῦ), as if to say, "Even if θεός cannot be taken at face value, at the very least, as an honorific title it implies φίλος θεοῦ."[192]

From these two passages, then, we learn that before a pagan reading-audience Philo is quite unwilling to take Ex. 7:1 at its absolute face value. In both instances, his interpretation has been highly colored by Cynic-Stoic teaching. In Prob. 42-44 the primary scheme is ὁ σοφός = σπουδαῖος = εὐσεβής = φίλος θεοῦ is ἐλεύθερος, whereas in V. Mos. 1. 155ff. we find the extension of the paradox as it is stated in Diogenes Laertius 7. 122, οὐ μόνον δ' ἐλευθέρους εἶναι τοὺς σοφούς, ἀλλὰ καὶ βασιλέας. If our analysis of V. Mos. 1. 155ff. stands, viz. that καὶ βασιλεύς functions as Philo's commentary upon θεός, we discover that in both instances he has interpreted θεός allegorically, in the one to mean βασιλεύς, in the other to mean φίλος θεοῦ.

Turning to the other group of passages, those in which

---

referring to Moses, and articular ὁ θεός in V. Mos. 1. 158 is no doubt intended to protect his flank in the same way.

[189]Cf. WOLFSON, 1. 173.

[190]Leg. ad Gaium 76.

[191]Of course, as DANIÉLOU, 79, points out, there is always the question whether Philo disagreed with the claim in principle, or simply with this particular claimant. Cf. E. M. SMALLWOOD, Legatio ad Gaium. Edited with an Introduction, Translation and Commentary (Leiden, ²1970) 192f., 205ff.

[192]Cf. note 180 above.

Ex. 7:1 is cited in his esoteric writings, i.e. the allegorical
exposition, we get a glimpse of how he explains the passage to
his fellow Jews, or at least converts who had reached the status of initiates and are no longer content with the milk of the
word.

(3) Som. 2. 189 and Mut. 19.

In two of these, Som. 2. 189 and Mut. 19, reference to
Ex 7:1 is more or less straightforward with no attempt at
elucidation. In both instances the titular function of θεός
is central, serving in the former passage to differentiate
between the high priest and Moses, in the latter between God
and Moses. In Som. 2. 189 we are told that the high priest,
although when he enters the Most Holy Place does so "not as a
man,"[193] is nevertheless not called θεός since this is a title
reserved for Moses while still in Egypt. In Mut. 19 there is
a slightly different emphasis. Speaking of God and his respective names and titles, Philo classifies His lordship into three
categories based on the ethical quality of those governed:
(1) He is κύριος and δεσπότης of the evil; (2) He is θεός of
those progressing towards perfection; (3) He is θεός and κύριος
of the perfect. Philo keeps his schema intact by reminding the
reader that God does not call Himself "God of Pharaoh," but
gives that title to Moses.

(4) Sacr. 8ff.

Of the other passages Sacr. 8ff. should be dealt with
first since it is often regarded as one of Philo's more forthright assertions of Moses' divinity.[194] Difficult as it is to

---

[193]See discussion below, pp. 170ff.

[194]GOODENOUGH, Light, 225, "Taken by itself this passage
could only mean that Moses was a deity who was made incarnate
by a special decree of God." MEEKS, Prophet-King, 104f.,
"Furthermore, the analogy between Moses and God implied by this
title θεός is taken so seriously in this passage that it
approaches consubstantiality." TIEDE, 125, "Philo appears to
desert his usual caution of maintaining that Moses is merely
god to the less perfect. Sac. 8 seems to imply a pre-existence
for Moses: "He sent him as a loan to the earthly sphere;" and
the argument in this passage suggests that Moses' nature is
immutable because he is divine." The point that Philo is making
in this context, however, is not exceptional: "Thus you may
(cont.)

decipher all the allegorical subtleties in this passage, a
fairly clear picture of Philo's train(s) of thought can be
sketched, nevertheless. Ostensibly it is a homily on <u>Gen</u>. 4:2,
specifically the word "added" (προσέθηκε), but as is often the
case with Philo, one word can serve as the thread on which to
string a motley assortment of exegetical beads. His real purpose is moralistic: to contrast "two opposite and contending
views of life,"[195] one of which regards as supreme the things
of the mind, i.e. whether we should depend solely upon our
reason (Stoics) or our senses (Epicureans), the other of which
(Judaism) regards ὁ θεός, the Creator, as supreme. Man's soul,
i.e. "Eve," contains both possibilities in its womb, but has
the ability to opt for the virtuous life by leaving behind
"Cain," the self-loving principle, and "adding Abel," the principle which "acknowledges the Cause."[196] On this same
προστίθημι string Philo places another set of pearls: Abraham,
Jacob, and Isaac[197]--examples, in ascending order of importance,
of those who in death are "added" to the "host and people of
God," Isaac being distinguished from the others because "he is
added not to 'people'," but to the "race" or "genus" of the
"imperishable and fully perfect." Above this triad of those
"added" is yet another group "whom God has advanced even
higher, and has trained (them) to soar above species and genus
alike and stationed (them) beside Himself," of whom Moses is
Exhibit A:

---

learn that God prizes the wise man (σοφός) as the world" (<u>Sac</u>.
8). Consequently even when Moses' status as god is elaborated,
it is his possession and representation of virtue that documents his divine stature." CHADWICK, "St. Paul and Philo,"
301, "In a well-known phrase Philo once observed that it would
be easier for God to become man than for man to become God
(<u>Leg</u>. <u>ad Gaium</u> 118). (He regarded both as impossibilities.)
Yet the language that he uses about Moses is incarnational.
The Logos by which God made the cosmos is that same Logos by
which he draws the perfect man to himself. Accordingly, he
sent the Logos to earth in Moses and appointed Moses as God,
placing all earthly things in subjection to him. This is the
reason why no one knows Moses' grave: he was deified."

[195]<u>Sacr</u>. 2.   [196]<u>Sacr</u>. 3.

[197]<u>Sacr</u>. 5-7.

Such is Moses to whom He says "Stand here with Me"
(Deut. 5: 31). And so when Moses was about to die
we do not hear of him "leaving" or "being added"
like those others. No room in him for adding or
taking away. But through the "Word" (ῥήματος) of
the Supreme Cause he is translated (Deut. 34:5),
even through that Word by which also the whole
universe was formed.[198]

It is thus in a passage where Philo details his reasons
for setting Moses at the peak of an allegorically constructed
hierarchy of patriarchs, all of whom exemplify the better of
the two "ways" mentioned in Sacr. 2, that Ex. 7:1 is cited.
Actually, a close examination of this passage reveals that Ex.
7:1 has a double function.

(1) As a prooftext for the "added" homily. Ironically, Philo
departs from the "added" motif when he comes to Moses, who,
instead of being "added" was "translated" (μετανίσταται),
although it seems to matter little to Philo that earlier in
Sacr. 7 Isaac is also said to have been "translated," even less
than an alteration of the LXX of Deut. 34:5, ἐτελεύτησεν, is
required to keep his hermeneutical scheme intact. Even so,
granting that Moses was "translated" instead of "added," Ex.
7:1, along with Deut. 34:6, which mentions that no one knows
the location of his grave, provide Philo with Biblical prooftexts for his "added" homily. Since θεός (whether this refers
to Yahweh, or "deity" in the most general sense, or Moses, is
unclear) is incapable of addition or diminution, and since
Moses is called θεός (Ex. 7:1), ergo, "no room in him for adding or taking away." This same theme is continued in his
description of the actual process of the "translation" of the
perfect soul Moses:

For who has powers such that he could perceive
the passing of a perfect soul to Him that "IS"?
Nay I judge that the soul itself which is passing
thus does not know of its change to better things,
for at that hour it is filled with the spirit of
God. For God does not consult with those whom He
blesses as to the gifts He means to bestow. His
wont is to extend His loving-kindness unstinted
to those who have no thought of them.[199]

(2) As a prooftext for Moses' ἀρετή. Interwoven into this

---

[198] Sacr. 8, Trans. Colson & Whitaker (Loeb).

[199] Sacr. 10, Trans. Colson & Whitaker (Loeb).

"added" homily is the moralistic theme--and this is what Philo
really wishes to emphasize--that Moses is ὁ σοφός, the
possessor of τελεία σοφία, τέλειον ἀγαθόν, ὁσιότης:

> (8b) Thus you may learn that God prizes the Wise
> Man (τὸν σοφόν) as the world,[200] for that same
> Word, by which He made the universe, is that by
> which He draws the perfect man (τὸν τέλειον) from
> things earthly to Himself.[201]
> (9) And even when he sent him as a loan to the
> earthly sphere (ὅτε τοῖς περιγείοις χρήσας αὐτόν)
> and suffered him to dwell therein, He gifted him
> with no ordinary excellence (κοινὴν τινα ἀρετὴν
> ἀνῆπτεν αὐτῷ), such as that which kings and rulers
> have, wherewith to hold sway and sovereignty over
> the passions of the soul, but He appointed him as
> god (ἀλλ' εἰς θεὸν αὐτὸν ἐχειροτόνει), placing all
> the bodily region and the mind which rules it in
> subjection and slavery to him. "I give thee," He
> says, "as god to Pharaoh" (Ex. 7:1); . . .[202]

What is significant here is that Moses' appointment as θεός is
interpreted ethically: for Moses to be called θεός means that
he possessed extraordinary ἀρετή, complete mastery of all
somatic passions, and to a greater degree than any other king, ✓
especially Pharaoh. The real significance Philo sees in Ex.
7:1 is that Moses is set apart from ordinary kings and rulers,
such as Pharaoh, who possess ἀρετὴ κοινή, and who must struggle
to overcome the passions. By contrast, his being appointed
θεός merely testifies to how successfully he has enslaved all
somatic passions and thus exemplifies the one in whom νοῦς
rules the σῶμα, as it should be in the ideal virtuous man.
Thus emerges yet a third line of interpreting Ex. 7:1 allegorically; in addition to θεός being taken to mean βασιλεύς and
φίλος θεοῦ, now it is taken to imply that Moses is ὁ σοφός.

One of the most perplexing phrases in the passage ὅτε
τοῖς περιγείοις χρήσας αὐτὸν εἴασεν ἐνομιλεῖν,[203] commonly
translated "even when He sent him as a loan, and suffered him
to dwell therein," would seem to imply the pre-existence of
Moses, but when seen in the context of Philo's belief in
metempsychosis, is this necessarily such a staggering statement? Since Philo believed that all souls had a prior

---

[200]Cf. Qu. Gen. 3. 39.   [201]Cf. Qu. Gen. 3. 42.

[202]Sacr. 8b-9, Trans. Colson & Whitaker (Loeb).

[203]Sacr. 9.

existence in κόσμος νοητός,[204] including ὁ σοφός,[205] does this imply that Moses was a god in this pre-existent state any more than any other disembodied soul? Thus it must be questioned whether Philo is affirming anything unique about Moses by employing χράω, unless it is the highly personalistic overtones implied in the relationship between God and Moses.

Apart from the question of whether this crucial individual phrase is to be understood in any sense as a unique affirmation about Moses, much less his consubstantiality, there is the larger question of whether we should take these statements in any literal sense at all. Tiede's statement that "this passage suggests that Moses' nature is immutable because he is divine"[206] can only be made if one presupposes the most literal interpretation of the phrase applied to Moses, "no room in him for adding or taking away." Was Moses' nature any more "immutable" than Rebekah's, who, according to Qu. Gen. 4. 97, suffers "neither diminution or increase?" It is at this point that A. J. M. Wedderburn's caveat against an interpreter's moving uncritically between the various levels of interpretation in Philo is especially apropos.[207] The

---

[204] Cf. Plant. 14; Gig. 12ff.; Qu. Gen. 4. 74; Conf. 77-82; on the pre-existence of the patriarchs, especially in Rabbinic thought, cf. WOLFSON, 1. 183; cf. BILLINGS, Platonism, 41ff., 58.

[205] Cf. Qu. Gen. 3. 10.   [206] Cf. note 194 above.

[207] A. J. M. WEDDERBURN, "Philo's Heavenly Man," NT 15 (1973) 301-26, esp. 307ff., where he enumerates the various levels at which Philo's exegesis operates, including: (1) literal, especially in the laws of the Pentateuch; (2) symbolism or typology seen in the literal meaning of the text, e.g. Qu. Gen. 4. 123, 143, 173; (3) allegory to supplement the literal, e.g. Qu. Ex. 1. 15; (4) allegory. It would appear that Sacr. 3ff. belongs to the fourth category. DANIÉLOU, 119ff., classifies Philo's interpretation into literal and allegorical, and subdivides allegorical into cosmological, anthropological, and mystical.

It is also relevant here to mention an observation made by BILLINGS, 11, regarding the way Philo employs different sets of terminology to describe the same event, using now the language of the mysteries, now the language of philosophy, now the language of the Greek Old Testament to describe the same event. He also refers to Conybeare who gave an interesting example to illustrate the point. To adopt or persevere in the Jewish religion is depicted in Philo as (1) a flight from

(cont.)

beginning of this tractate makes it quite clear that the names
and events in the Biblical text, e.g. "Eve," "Cain," and
"Abel," are being used in the most a-historical sense possible;
the level of interpretation is thoroughly allegorical, and the
Biblical names and events have been transferred purely into the
realm of allegorical ideas, such as "So when God added the good
conviction Abel to the soul, he took away the foolish opinion
Cain."[208] In this same connection, Qu. Gen. 4. 137 is worth
mentioning, when Philo asserts, "For the inquiry of the
theologian (Moses) is about characters and types and virtues,
and not about persons who were created and born."[209] Consequently, it must be asked whether Moses in Sacr. 8ff. is being
treated in any historical, literal sense at all, or whether he
has been "translated" to the level of allegorical ideas. If
it is primarily the latter, it is highly debatable how far this
passage can be taken as a statement about Moses' consubstantiality. Sacr. 8ff. thus instead of providing such a clearcut
affirmation of Moses' divinity only provides us with the first
of his several allegorical interpretations of the passage in
his esoteric writings.

(5) Leg. All. 1. 40.

        Whereas in Sacr. 8ff. Philo does not explicitly equate
θεός in Ex. 7:1 with the victorious νοῦς of ὁ σοφός Moses
which has fully conquered the passions, in Leg. All. 1. 40 this
equation is made. Here Philo is engaged in an allegorical
exposition of Gen. 2:7,[210] and at 1. 39 embarks upon a discussion of his psychology, which he regards as interpreting Gen.
2:7 "ethically" (ἠθικῶς), probably simply another way of saying
"allegorically." Thus,

---

idolatry to serve the one true God; (2) in philosophical
language as an ascent from sense to reason; (3) in the language
of ethics, as the victory of reason in the soul; (4) in mystical language, as a transition to the promised land.

    [208]Sacr. 5.

    [209]Also cf. Marcus's note ad loc. (Loeb), referring to
WOLFSON, 1. 125-27. Also, cf. Qu. Gen. 4. 227.

    [210]Leg. All. 1. 31.

As the face is the dominant element in the body,
so is the mind the dominant element of the soul:
into this only does God breathe, whereas He does
not see fit to do so with the other parts, whether
sense or organs of utterance and of reproduction;
for these are secondary in capacity.[211]

The schema--θεός inbreathes νοῦς, which in turn inbreathes the
ἄλογος portion of ψυχή--prevents his having to assert that ὁ
θεός inbreathes ὁ ἄλογος directly, an inconceivable concession
because of the impossibility of ὁ θεός directly contacting anything material. Ex. 7:1 is thus cited in connection with his
assertion that the νοῦς is the ruling faculty of the soul:
ψυχῆς ἡγεμονικόν ἐστιν ὁ νοῦς. To state this proposition
another way, Philo says, νοῦς is θεός ... τοῦ ἀλόγου just as
Moses was asserted to be θεός τοῦ Φαραώ, or Pharaoh's
ἡγεμονικόν. Here we have an example of the way Scripture can
simply provide Philo with a framework of imagery, or an arsenal
of words, for his philosophical theories, for here Ex. 7:1 is
cited merely because it provides a catchword, θεός, which Philo
happens to find appropriate at the moment in delineating his
psychology. It should be observed, however, that θεός here is
more or less a synonym for ἡγεμονικόν, that the significance
Philo sees in θεός is its connotation of "ruling" or "reigning."
In this instance, that which is ruled happens to be ψυχή.

(6) Migr. 84.

Yet another variation of the θεός = νοῦς scheme occurs
in Migr. 84,[212] a passage which forms part of a commentary on
Gen. 12:2, καὶ εὐλογήσω σε, but turns out to be a disquisition[213] on the excellence of Logos (ἐπαινετὸν λόγον),[214]
specifically its two aspects of speech (προφορικὸς λόγος) and
reason (διάνοια/νοῦς), and the necessity of possessing both,
particularly the former, in dealing with Sophists.[215] Whereas
Abel, even though he possessed διάνοια, was deficient in

---

[211]Leg. All. 1. 39. Trans. Colson & Whitaker (Loeb).

[212]Cf. also Qu. Ex. 2. 44 where the same schema occurs.

[213]Migr. 70ff.   [214]Migr. 70.

[215]Migr. 72f.; 82f.; one of Philo's frequent polemics
against Sophists, cf. Qu. Gen. 3. 27.

προφορικὸς λόγος, and therefore was outwitted by Cain, Moses,
because he had both faculties, was able to outwit the Sophists
of Egypt. His access to λόγος, i.e. Aaron, his "mouth" or
"prophet," provided him with a ἑρμηνεύς of his thoughts
(διάνοια). In this discussion the underlying schema is
ὁ θεός ←——→ νοῦς ——→ λόγος. The first arrow is two-
directional, reflecting Philo's conviction that ὁ θεός only
communicates directly with immaterial substance, νοῦς, and con-
versely, that man's νοῦς alone, because of its immateriality,
is capable of apprehending ὁ θεός.[216] Unaided νοῦς he regards
as fully capable of perceiving ὁ θεός, that is, assuming an
incorporeal vacuum in which the mutual communication could
occur; but since νοῦς is inescapably bound to the corporeal
world because of its being housed in σῶμα, and can only express
its thoughts (ἐνθυμήματα) in the corporeal world, a mediating
link between the incorporeal and the corporeal world is
required, viz. λόγος, the ἑρμηνεύς. This schema Philo finds
illustrated in the Moses-Aaron relationship of Exodus 4,
interpreted allegorically. Here, similar to what we found in
Sacr. 8ff., neither Moses nor Aaron is being regarded in any
real historical sense, but rather more or less provide examples
for a disquisition of his views of psychology and epistemology;
the direction of movement of his hermeneutic at this point is
from his exposition of the νοῦς-λόγος schema to the Biblical
text where he detects a similar relationship between νοῦς
(Moses) and λόγος προφορικός (Aaron). When this schema is
applied to the Biblical text, it becomes: immaterial Yahweh
(ὁ θεός) prompts (ὑποβολεύς)[217] Moses (νοῦς) who in turn
prompts Aaron (λόγος) to speak. Stated in a mathematical
formula, ὁ θεός : νοῦς = νοῦς : λόγος. Diagrammatically, the
different levels of Philo's hermeneutic may be sketched as
follows:

$$\begin{array}{ccc}
\text{ὁ θεός} \longleftrightarrow \text{(inspired)} & \text{νοῦς/διάνοια} \longrightarrow & \text{λόγος προφορικός} \\
& | & | \\
& \text{θεός} \longrightarrow & \text{προφήτης} \\
& | & | \\
& \text{Moses} \longrightarrow & \text{Aaron}
\end{array}$$

---

[216]Cf. esp. Migr. 81.

[217]Cf. Migr. 81.

Νοῦς and λόγος are as indissolubly connected as the two
brothers Moses and Aaron;[218] or, again, to state it diagrammatically:

	νοῦς	needs	λόγος
just as	Moses	needs	Aaron
just as	inspired νοῦς	needs	προφήτης
just as	νοῦς	needs	στόμα

This fundamental schema, in which Philo is basically concerned
to demonstrate the praiseworthiness of λόγος (ἐπαινετὸν
λόγον),[219] the faculty which interprets the mind's thoughts, or
which turns out to be a demonstration of the need to be fluent,
employs Ex. 7:1 at one of several levels of interpretation as a
means of illustrating the indissoluble connection between νοῦς
and λόγος. In the process we discover yet a fourth allegorical
interpretation: θεός = ὁ νοῦς ἐπιθειάσας.[220] The motivation
for equating θεός and νοῦς may derive from Philo's conviction
that intercourse between ὁ θεός and νοῦς, because it involves
two incorporeal entities, is to be regarded as a divine (θεῖος)
activity,[221] in which case θεῖος here would function simply as
a synonym for ἀσώματος, as it often does in Philo.[222] It
should be noted that in this particular citation of Ex. 7:1
Moses, strictly speaking, is out of the picture; or at least
he has been left behind at one level of interpretation while
Philo has plunged ahead to another. Unlike the passages
examined so far where the exegetical point of departure is the
Biblical text (i.e. Philo interprets Ex. 7:1 in this manner:
Moses = θεός = βασιλεύς, or φίλος θεοῦ, or ὁ σοφός), here, as
in Leg. All. 1. 40 the exegetical point of departure is a theme
external to the Biblical text (i.e. from Philo's disquisition
on the νοῦς/λόγος schema back to the Moses (θεός)-Aaron (λόγος)
schema).

---

218 Migr. 78.   219 Migr. 70.

220 Migr. 84. Contra A. MÉASSON (Lyon), note on Sacr. 9,
who does not distinguish the allegorical interpretations of
Leg. All. 1. 40 and Migr. 84.

221 Migr. 80.

222 Cf. discussion below, pp. 189ff.

(7) <u>Mut</u>. 125ff.

In <u>Mut</u>. 125ff. Philo is discussing the respective significance of the "many names" (πολυώνυμος) of Moses, three of
which are specified: (1) When he is interpreting and teaching
the oracles of God he is called "Moses;" (2) when he prays and
blesses the people, he is a "man of God" (ἄνθρωπος θεοῦ);[223]
(3) when Egypt is paying the penalty for its impious deeds (i.e.
during the plagues), he is "god of Pharaoh."[224] With regard to
the third name, <u>Ex</u>. 7:1 is not directly cited but is obviously
alluded to. θεός is said to be an appropriate title for two
reasons:

> ... this same person is a god, because[225] he
> is wise and therefore the ruler of every fool
> (θεὸς δὲ ὁ αὐτὸς οὗτος ἅτε σοφὸς ὢν καὶ διὰ τοῦτ'
> ἄρχων παντὸς ἄφρονος), even though that fool boast
> ever so loudly in the support of his royal sceptre.
> And he is a god for this reason in particular (καὶ
> διὰ τοῦτο οὐχ ἥκιστα).[226] It is the will of the
> ruler of all that though there be some doomed to
> punishment for their intolerable misdeeds, they
> should have mediators to make intercession for them,
> who imitating the merciful power of the Father will
> dispense punishment with more moderation and in a
> kindlier spirit. Beneficence is the peculiar pre-
> rogative of a god (θεοῦ δὲ τὸ εὐεργετεῖν [ἴδιον).[227]

The appeal to Moses' being ὁ σοφός as explaining the significance of θεός as his third ὄνομα bears some similarity to <u>Sacr</u>.
8ff., where his appointment as θεός is based upon his extraordinary ἀρετή, especially his mastery of σῶμα, and its
passions. Echoes of <u>V</u>. <u>Mos</u>. 1. 158 and <u>Prob</u>. 42-44 are also
heard, when in both passages the portrait of the ideal σοφός

---

[223]Cf. note on <u>Mut</u>. 128 by R. ARNALDEZ (Lyon), p. 90,
"L'homme est homme de Dieu en tant cu'il agit comme Dieu:
l'adoption divine lui permet de disposer, en faveur des
créatures, des biens du Créateur dont il recoit le dépôt dans
la vertu." Also references to <u>Plant</u>. 67f.; <u>Sir</u>. 21:22ff.;
24:23ff.; <u>Wis</u>. 7:12ff.

[224]Cf. GOODENOUGH, <u>Light</u>, 227:193, who notes that
πολυώνυμος is frequently applied to deities by classical
writers; cf. Diogenes Laertius, 7. 135.

[225]On the ἅτε...ὢν construction, cf. SMYTH, par. 2085.

[226]This phrase seems to point forward; cf. notes by
Colson & Whitaker (Loeb), Arnaldez (Lyon), Heinemann-Adler
(Werke).
[227]<u>Mut</u>. 128b-29. Trans. Colson & Whitaker (Loeb)

is the immediate background even if θεός is not explicitly
equated with ὁ σοφός. But in Mut. 125ff. we have a more explicit enunciation of the Stoic paradox mentioned in Diogenes
Laertius, 7. 122, οὐ μόνον δ᾽ ἐλευθέρους εἶναι τοὺς σοφούς,
ἀλλὰ καὶ βασιλέας, and thus the ἡγεμονικόν-aspect of θεός,
which was adumbrated in the θεός = βασιλεύς identification in
V. Mos. 1. 158, and which we have seen emerging more into the
forefront, such as when θεός = ψυχῆς ἡγεμών, now becomes full-
blown. For Moses to be called θεός Φαραώ means that he is
ἄρχων παντὸς ἄφρονος. The additional phrase, "and even though
that fool (Pharaoh) boast ever so loudly in the support of his
royal sceptre," recalls the delusion of the king of the Per-
sians mentioned in Dio C., Orat. 14. 18, 22ff. where it is
assumed that tiaras and all the trappings of royalty constitute
kingship; the Cynic, of course, knows better.

This θεός = βασιλεύς/ἄρχων identification, which seems
to have been made possible by Philo's thorough acquaintance
with the Stoic paradoxes, provides a plausible explanation for
a related passage, Qu. Gen. 4. 76, where ostensibly in reference to Abraham,[228] ὁ σοφός (or is it ὁ φιλόσοφος?) it is said:

> "And not only (is he regarded) as a ruler but as
> a ruler of rulers and a divine one (emphasis mine)
> and as a king of kings, being excellent and vir-
> tuous, and as being elected, not by men, but by God.[229]

The semi-formal listing of attributes belonging to ὁ σοφός
including "king" (= βασιλεύς), "excellent and virtuous"
(= generosus (Aucher) = σπουδαῖος), "appointed by God"
(= χειροτονηθείς...ὑπὸ θεοῦ) is thoroughly reminiscent of the
character-sketch of ὁ σοφός found in Diogenes Laertius, 7.
117ff. If such a stock list of attributes underlies Philo's
description here, it is possible that "a divine one"[230] may
correspond to θεῖος.[231] This would raise the interesting
possibility that Philo has used θεῖος, the attribute for ὁ
σοφός in the Stoic list, as his point of contact with θεός in
Ex. 7:1. The Stoic σοφός, who according to the list in

---

[228] Gen. 23: 5-6.   [229] Trans. Marcus (Loeb).

[230] Marcus does not propose a Greek word in this instance.

[231] Diogenes Laertius, 7. 117ff.

Diogenes Laertius, is θεῖος καὶ βασιλεύς becomes in Philo, on
the basis of Ex. 7:1 θεὸς καὶ βασιλεύς when, interpreted
ethically, or allegorically, becomes θεὸς καὶ βασιλεὺς παντὸς
ἄφρονος.

In Mut. 129 the second reason given for the appropriateness of θεός as a name for Moses is that he is εὐεργέτης.
Having introduced the ἄρχων motif, it is only natural for Philo
to take up the "king-imitate-King" model, which we have detected earlier,[232] and use it to show Moses' εὐεργεσία.[233] Here
again the Cynic-Stoic conception of the σοφός-βασιλεύς seems to
be looming in the back of Philo's mind.[234]

(8) Det. 160ff.

The most crucial passage for our discussion is Det.
160ff., not only because of its length--it is Philo's most
extended comment upon Ex. 7:1--but because in it he states
explicitly why the passage cannot be taken literally, and further, how it can legitimately be taken. In this sense, it is
the key which helps unlock the passages already mentioned[235]
where we have discovered a consistent pattern in which Philo
feels compelled to interpret the passage allegorically, even
if the exact form of the allegory varies from passage to

_____

[232]Cf. above, p. 119.

[233]On Moses' role as mediator, cf. Heinemann-Adler
(Werke) 5.134:1, who refer to Her. 205; V. Mos. 2. 134; also
Heracleitus, Quaest. Hom. 59.9; John 14:26.

[234]HÖISTAD, 26f., 34, 48, 79, refers to Xenophon, Cyr.
5. 1, 26; 6. 1, 48; 8. 2, 2; 2, 9f.; 2, 12; 2, 7, 13; cf.
Anab. 1. 9, 11; cf. Isocrates, Or. 5. 76; Euripides, Her. Fur.
1252. Mention should also be made of Diodorus Siculus, 1. 13,
5; 17, 1f.; cf. 18, 5; 19, 5; 20, 5; 27, 5, where Osiris is
deified because of εὐεργεσία.

[235]The passage so functions in HEINEMANN (Werke) 5,
note on Migr. 84, to support his contention, "Moses wird
natürlich hierdurch von Philo nicht zur Gottheit erhoben;"
Similarly, COHN (Werke) 3, note on Sacr. 9, "Wenn Moses 'zum
Gott' über den Pharao, d. i. die gottlose und die Leiden-
schaften anführende Anschauung (Leg. All. 3. 13), gesetzt wird,
so ist nach Philo die Erhebung Mosis zu einer Gottheit nicht
etwa wörtlich zu verstehen. Das würde sich mit seinem
Gottesbegriff gar nicht vereinigen lassen. Hier ist zur
Erklärung die Stelle Det. 161 heranzuziehen, wo Philo
entwickelt, dass Moses ein Gott nicht πρὸς ἀλήθειαν sondern
nur δόξῃ genannt wurde."

148

passage. What is more, we have noticed that, whereas for the
most part Philo reserves allegorical interpretation for his
esoteric writings, he resorts to allegory in both instances,
if our interpretation of V. Mos. 1. 155ff. stands, in explaining the passage to pagans.[236] The importance of the passage
demands that the text be cited in full, along with its
translation:

(160) Τὴν δὲ σκηνὴν ταύτην κεκλῆσθαί φησι
μαρτυρίου, σφόδρα παρατετηρημένως, ἵν᾽ ἡ τοῦ
ὄντος ὑπάρχῃ, , μὴ καλῆται μόνον· τῶν γὰρ ἀρετῶν
ἡ μὲν θεοῦ πρὸς ἀλήθειάν ἐστι κατὰ τὸ εἶναι
συνεστῶσα, ἐπεὶ καὶ ὁ θεὸς μόνος ἐν τῷ εἶναι
ὑφέστηκεν· οὗ χάριν ἀναγκαίως ἐρεῖ περὶ αὑτοῦ· "ἐγὼ
εἰμι ὁ ὤν" (Ex. 3:14), ὡς τῶν μετ᾽ αὐτὸν οὐκ
ὄντων κατὰ τὸ εἶναι, δόξῃ δὲ μόνον ὑφεστάναι
νομιζομένων· ἡ δὲ Μωυσέως σκηνὴ συμβολικῶς οὖσα
ἀνθρώπου ἀρετὴ κλήσεως, οὐχ ὑπάρξεως, ἀξιωθήσεται,
μίμημα καὶ ἀπεικόνισμα τῆς θείας ἐκείνης ὑπάρχουσα.
(161) τούτοις ἕπεται καὶ τὸ Μωυσῆν, ὁπότε
χειροτονεῖται "θεὸς τοῦ Φαραώ," μὴ πρὸς ἀλήθειαν
γεγενῆσθαι, δόξῃ δὲ μόνον ὑπολαμβάνεσθαι· θεὸν γὰρ
διδόντα μὲν οἶδα καὶ χαριζόμενον, διδόμενον δὲ οὐ
δύναμαι νοῆσαι, λέγεται δὲ ἐν ἱεραῖς βίβλοις·
"δίδωμί σε θεὸν Φαραώ" (Ex. 7:1), τοῦ διδομένου
πάσχοντος, οὐ δρῶντος· δραστήριον δὲ τὸ ὄντως ὄν,
οὐ πάσχον, ἀναγκαῖον εἶναι. (162) τί οὖν διὰ
τούτων συνάγεται; ὅτι ὁ σοφὸς λέγεται μὲν θεὸς
τοῦ ἄφρονος, πρὸς ἀλήθειαν δὲ οὐκ ἔστι θεός, ὥσπερ
οὐδὲ τὸ ἀδόκιμον τετράδραχμον ἐστι τετράδραχμον·
ἀλλ᾽ ὅταν μὲν τῷ ὄντι παραβάλληται, ἄνθρωπος
εὑρεθήσεται θεοῦ, ὅταν δὲ ἄφρονι ἀνθρώπῳ, θεὸς
πρὸς φαντασίαν καὶ δόκησιν, οὐ πρὸς ἀλήθειαν καὶ
τὸ εἶναι, νοούμενος.[237]

(160) And this tent (Ex. 33:7), he (Moses) says,
has been designated a "tent of testimony"--using
his words with extreme care--so that the (ideal)
tent of the Existent One might truly be said to
exist in fact, not in name only. For, the "tent
of God" exists in actual fact among the "virtues"
(i.e. in the ideal realm), having been constructed

---

[236]It is, of course, impossible to draw hard and fast
lines in Philo's exegetical method, equating literal exposition
with his exoteric writings, allegorical exposition with his
esoteric writings. For example, in Jos. 28, a treatise generally agreed to be addressed to pagans, he employs allegory.
But, it can be said safely, I think, that V. Mos. and Prob.,
one of which was obviously addressed to pagans, the other of
which belongs to a small group of writings devoted solely to
Greek philosophical themes (along with Prov., Alex., Animal.
(cf. WOLFSON, 1. 87)) are generally lacking in allegorical
exposition. Cf. DANIÉLOU, 86.

[237]Loeb text.

out of materials that actually exist (ideas), since
also it is God alone who actually subsists, i.e.
can be said to truly exist--which is why Moses says
of Him--as best as he may--"I am He who is" (Ex.
3:14)--just as if those beings besides Him do not
really exist in actual fact, but can only be regarded
as having a seeming existence. But, the "tent of
Moses" (i.e. in the material realm), since it exists
only symbolically, that is, as a man's "virtue," is
to be so regarded in name only, not in actuality--it
is but a copy and representation--a statue as it
were--of that divine entity. (161) Accordingly, it
also follows that this "Moses," when he was appointed
"god of Pharaoh," did not become so in reality, but
was to be understood (as being god) only seemingly.
My reason for this: I know that God can be conceived
of as "giving" or "bestowing," but "being given"--
this I cannot even conceive of. And so it is said
in the Holy Books: "I give you as god to Pharaoh"
(Ex. 7:1), that which is given (Moses) being passive,
not active; in fact, it is absolutely necessary for
the Truly Existing One to be active, not passive.
(162) What then is to be deduced from these observations? This: the wise man is said to be "god" of
the fool, while in reality he is not a god at all,
any more than a counterfeit tetradrachma is really a
tetradrachma. But, when, however, the wise man is
set side-by-side with the Existent One, he will be
discovered to be a man of God; but, by contrast, when
he is set side-by-side with a fool, one can form an
opinion and imagine that he is a god, though in
actual fact he is really not, even then.

It would be difficult to find a better example, unless
it were Opif. 134ff. and related passages pertaining to the
"earthly/heavenly man," of how Philo superimposes a Platonic
metaphysical framework, especially the κόσμος νοητός-κόσμος
αἰσθητός schema, upon the Scriptures. The structural independence of the whole pericope, Det. 158-62,[238] as well as the fact
that it is Philo's strongest denial that Ex. 7:1 is to be
understood as affirming Moses' divine status raises the question whether we have to do here with a Christian interpola-
tion,[239] but until more evidence is adduced to substantiate
such a notion, it will have to remain as speculative for the
moment.

Abraham and Moses are mentioned as examples of those who

---

[238]N.B. the form of the opening remarks, Det. 158,
Σὺ μὲν οὖν, ὦ καταγέλαστε ... Cf. P. WENDLAND, Philo und die
kynisch-stoische Diatribe (Berlin, 1895) 1-75.

[239]As, for example, in Qu. Ex. 2. 117.

encounter τὸ ὄν, only because they successfully escaped the
shackles of somatic existence--Abraham by departing from his
"father's house," understood allegorically as "the body, sense,
and speech," Moses by setting up the tabernacle "outside the
camp," allegorically understood to mean "beyond the scope of
somatic existence."[240] Arising out of this reference to σκηνή
is a fairly detailed justification of why it can be understood
allegorically, and what follows amounts to two examples of how
an item in the Biblical text can be understood allegorically.
Applying the Platonic metaphysical model to either of those
items, σκηνή or θεός, results in its having a simultaneous dual
existence, one in κόσμος νοητός, the other in κόσμος
αἰσθητός.[241] Thus, in Philo's opinion, an actual object (in
one case a physical object, in the other case non-physical)
mentioned in Scripture may only be a representation (μίμημα καὶ
ἀπεικόνισμα)--and therefore having only seeming existence
(δόξῃ)--of the true (πρὸς ἀλήθειαν) existent, its counterpart
in the ideal world. In this way Scripture is prevented from
obscuring the realities of κόσμος νοητός, thereby enhancing the
status of τὸ ὄν. What we see in this world, thus, is not the
true forms (ἰδέαι), but only copies, or names, and Scripture
points to, rather than obscures them.

The citation of Ex. 7:1 seems to play no other role in
the discussion than merely to provide a second example of how
this Platonic-allegorical model works. Drawing upon the Stoic
distinction between cause and effect,[242] Philo claims that θεός
in Ex. 7:1 must be understood δόξῃ and not πρὸς ἀλήθειαν
because θεός, properly understood, is incapable of being
"given"--and here we are reminded of Sacr. 8ff. where θεός is
said to be incapable of addition or diminution--for then his

---

[240] Det. 159-60.

[241] On the pre-existence of the tabernacle in Rabbinic
thought, cf. WOLFSON, 1. 183. Cf. Qu. Ex. 2. 90 for a similar
treatment of the tabernacle. Also, cf. J. DANIÉLOU, "La
symbolique du temple de Jerusalem chez Philon et Josephe,"
Le symbolisme cosmique des monuments religieux (Rome, 1957)
89-90.

[242] On the Stoic distinction between activity (cause/
force) and passivity (effect/matter), cf. ZELLER, Stoics,
133f.; 141ff.

οὐσία would be diminished and He would no longer be ὁ ὄντως ὤν. And yet, in Ex. 7:1 Moses is boldly asserted to be θεός. To solve this problem, Philo underscores that δίδωμι, the verb used in Ex. 7:1, is active, which would imply that Moses, the object given, is passive. Thus, Moses, being purely passive, is given by ὁ θεός to Pharaoh. If, therefore, it is impossible for θεός in Ex. 7:1 to be understood φυσικῶς,[243] how is it to be understood? Συμβολικῶς: it signifies something else, that ὁ σοφός is θεὸς τοῦ ἄφρονος, not θεός in actual fact (πρὸς ἀλήθειαν δὲ οὐκ ἔστι θεός).[244] Ex. 7:1 therefore must be understood allegorically: Moses is not θεὸς Φαραὼ πρὸς ἀλήθειαν; instead, θεός signifies that ὁ σοφός is θεὸς τοῦ ἄφρονος; he is the fool's ἄρχων. Ex. 7:1 is really telling us something about Moses ὁ σοφός, not Moses θεός.

In a manner similar to Prob. 42-44, where once having issued one disclaimer, Philo issues a second, he buttresses his argument with an even more emphatic statement. Ὁ σοφός, he says, can be viewed from two perspectives: that of ὁ ὄντως ὤν and that of ὁ ἄφρων. If set beside the former, the absolute most that can be said of him is that he is ἄνθρωπος θεοῦ. Apparently, this is exactly the expression Philo needs for underscoring the humanity (or, at least his "other-than-God-ness") of ὁ σοφός, the genitival θεοῦ serving to punctuate the force of his argument: ὁ σοφός may be "man of God," "God's man," or any other phrase the genitive will allow; but not θεός, not even ἀνθρώπων θεός, as in Prob. 43. A similar play upon the genitive occurs in Mut. 128 where the significance of ἄνθρωπος θεοῦ as one of the titles of Moses is being discussed. One who would dare to "procure the good gift for others" and serve as their mediator to God is called "greater, more perfect, truly God-inspired soul," but the most that can be said

---

[243]Cf. Leg. All. 1. 40.

[244]COHN (Werke) 3, note on Det. 162, "Philo wendet sich hier und Spec. Leg. 1. 334ff. gegen die Lehre von der Göttlichkeit des Weisen, die im Widerspruch mit seinem Gefühl des Abstandes zwischen Göttlichem und Menschlichem von hellenistischen Philosophen vertreten wurde." He refers to Seneca, Ep. 31, 11; 53, 11, where the wise man is even placed above God.

of the possessor of such a soul is that he is θεοῦ.[245] Here
again the genitive seems to be Philo's way of contrasting this
title with the third name θεός.

When ὁ σοφός is viewed from the other vantage point,
that of ὁ ἄφρων, i.e. when ὁ σοφός is set beside ὁ ἄφρων,
perhaps, one can speak of him as θεός, if one realizes that
θεός is being used purely as a convention; but, in the final
analysis, even then, ὁ σοφός is not really θεός, Philo reminds
us. By the end of the discussion the term θεός is completely
devoid of any concrete meaning for Philo.

Summary and conclusions.

When we review the instances where Philo deals with Ex.
7:1, we discover the following pattern of uses:

(1) A titular use.

In only two instances, Som. 2. 189 and Mut. 19, is there
anything approaching an interpretation φυσικῶς, and in both
cases Ex. 7:1 is cited to show that the title θεός belongs to
Moses instead of to someone else, viz. the high priest and
Yahweh.

(2) Allegorical interpretation of the single term θεός.

In five passages Philo sees allegorical significance in
the single term θεός, each time interpreting it ethically as a
comment, in one form or another, upon ὁ σοφός. Without doing
too much injustice, I think, to the complexities of his use of
Ex. 7:1 in the various passages, the results may be schematized
as follows:

ὁ σοφός is:

(a) βασιλεύς (φύσεως) = φίλος θεου (V. Mos. 1. 158)

(b) ἐλεύθερος = φίλος θεοῦ (Prob. 42-44)

(c) τέλειος = ὁ ἄρχων τοῦ νοῦ καὶ τοῦ σώματος (Sacr. 9)

(d) (βασιλεύς) = ἄρχων παντὸς ἄφρονος (Mut. 125ff.; Det.
160ff.)

(3) Allegorical interpretation of the relationship.

In Leg. All. 1. 40 and Migr. 84, Ex. 7:1 is cited not
because θεός is interpreted allegorically per se, but primarily

---

[245]Assuming with Colson & Whitaker that θεοῦ should
read, contra C-W, which prints θεός, "though noting that
ἄνθρωπος θεοῦ seems the right reading."

because Philo thinks it illustrates a structural relationship
comparable to a relationship he happens to be discussing.
Again, stated schematically:

	Relationship Philo wishes to express		Comparable Relationship Seen in Ex. 7:1.
Leg. All. 1. 40	νοῦς : ψυχή	=	θεός : Φαραώ
Migr. 84	νοῦς : λόγος	=	θεός : προφήτης
			Moses : Aaron

Or, stated differently,

Leg. All. 1. 40   νοῦς is θεὸς τοῦ ἀλόγου just as
                    Moses is θεὸς τοῦ Φαραώ

Migr. 84   νοῦς needs λόγος just as
                    Moses needs Aaron, or
                    θεός needs προφήτης

We also notice that in the various explanations of Ex.
7:1 it is some peculiar nuance of the term θεός that aids Philo
in his allegorical interpretation, whether it is a text of
Scripture he is explaining or his own philosophical views:

(a) θεός is incapable of addition or diminution (Sacr. 8ff.;
Det. 160ff.)

(b) θεός as a title of distinction (V. Mos. 1. 158)

(c) θεός is characterized by εὐεργεσία (Mut. 125)

(d) The most frequent aspect of θεός Philo capitalizes upon
is the ἡγεμονικός-nuance:

(aa) V. Mos. 1. 158: Moses is θεὸς καὶ βασιλεύς in that he
successfully rules over universal nature.

(bb) Sacr. 9: Moses is σοφός and τέλειος because he successfully rules over the mind and body.

(cc) Mut. 125ff. and Det. 160ff.: Moses is θεός because he
rules over every fool, specifically Pharaoh.

(dd) Prob. 42-44: Moses is ἐλεύθερος and εὐδαίμων because as
φίλος θεοῦ he shares in the rule of the universe, i.e., he ful-
fills the Stoic paradox: not only is the wise man free, but
also king.

(ee) Leg. All. 1. 40: The comparable relationship that Philo
sees between νοῦς:ψυχή and θεός:Φαραώ is that between ruler and
subject.

(ff) Migr. 84: Even though it is not explicitly stated that
the λόγος is subordinate to νοῦς just as Aaron is subordinate

to Moses, this relationship is nevertheless presupposed.

For our purposes, the most important observation is Philo's consistent refusal to interpret Ex. 7:1 literally. Having noticed this propensity, both in his exoteric as well as his esoteric writings, we discovered the key in Det. 160ff. in which he tells us why θεός cannot be taken literally, and suggests at least one other possible option, that ὁ σοφός is ἄρχων παντὸς ἄφρονος. It has also been observed that he issues outright disclaimers about taking the passage literally both in his exoteric and esoteric writings. Or, if we ask whether this was a fleeting conviction, the answer seems to be that he held to it throughout his life. This interpretation was expressed in his younger days in a tractate no doubt written soon after he left the Academy (Prob. 42-44) and occurs in the writings stemming from his later life, especially the allegorical writings, which, according to Bréhier,[246] were the last of his writings. Our examination has also revealed that one of the key passages often cited as evidence for Philo's belief in Moses' divinity, Sacr. 8ff., in fact turns out to be considerably less than a claim that "Moses was a deity who was made incarnate by a special decree of God."[247] If this is the only passage in Philo where one can detect "a pattern of myth in which a heavenly redeemer is essential,"[248] we now have reason to doubt whether there is even one passage. In discussing Det. 160ff. Goodenough remarks, "The point to be decided is not whether Philo contradicts his statements of Moses' divinity, but whether he repeats them often enough so that one may assume that it really represents one of his attitudes towards Moses."[249] Though this statement was made in order to turn Det. 160ff. into a minority view, it actually turns out to have the reverse effect, for if Philo's interpretation of Ex. 7:1 can be taken as any indication of his attitude towards Moses which he evidently held throughout his life and which he expounded both to Greeks and Jews alike, it would strongly suggest that with Det. 160ff. we are very near Philo's heart of hearts on this particular question.

---

[246]BRÉHIER, 9.   [247]GOODENOUGH, Light, 225.
[248]MEEKS, Prophet-King, 104. [249]GOODENOUGH, Light, 226.

What emerges from this investigation is that Philo, when dealing with Ex. 7:1, feels that he is walking through a theological mine-field. Of course, he had the option, which Josephus took, of not quoting Ex. 7:1 at all, which immediately raises the question why he chose to refer to it as many times as he did.

The answer which has been emerging ever since our investigation of V. Mos. 1. 155ff. is that Ex. 7:1 had come to play a crucial role as a passage documenting Moses' status as king. In Philo this "kingship" becomes colored with the Cynic-Stoic philosophical tint which we have seen in varying shades in the passages which we have analyzed. This is confirmed all the more by yet another use of Ex. 7:1 which occurs in the Greek fragment in Qu. Ex. 2. 6, where Philo commenting upon Ex. 22:28b cites Ex. 7:1 in connection with a statement about the proper behavior of a king. Unlike Josephus, Philo was fond of the allegorical method, indeed regarded it as the "scientific" method of exegesis, and by employing it was able to use Ex. 7:1 in a variety of ways, but in most cases to prove the Stoic paradox, "Only the wise man is free, as well as king," in reference to Moses. In other words, Philo is able to appeal to Ex 7:1 repeatedly, and does so to his advantage, because of his consistent ethical-allegorical interpretation of the passage.

Deification and the Divine-Human Encounter.
(1) Qu. Ex. 2. 29.

Qu. Ex. 2. 29 provides the focus for discussing a second cluster of ideas bearing upon our inquiry:

> (29) (Ex. 24:2) Why does He say, "Moses alone shall come near to God, and they shall not come near, and the people shall not go up with them?"
> O most excellent and God-worthy ordinance, that the prophetic mind (τὸν προφητικὸν νοῦν) alone should approach God and that those in second place should go up, making a path to heaven, while those in third place and the turbulent characters of the people should neither go up above nor go up with them but those worthy of beholding should be beholders of the blessed path above. But that "(Moses) alone shall go up" is said most naturally (φυσικώτατα). For when the prophetic mind becomes divinely inspired and filled with God (ἐνθουσιᾷ καὶ θεοφορεῖται, it becomes like the monad, not being at all mixed

with any of those things associated with duality.
But he who is resolved into the nature of unity,
is said to come near God in a kind of family
relation, for having given up and left behind all
mortal kinds, he is changed into the divine, so
that such men become kin to God and truly divine.[250]

Although this passage is not adduced by Windisch as evidence
that θεσπέσιος ἀνήρ and theios aner are equivalent expressions
in Philo[251] (with the implication that the language of prophecy
employed by Philo indicates that he has moved far beyond the
Old Testament view of prophecy, in which there is a great chasm
between the prophet and God, to the point where the prophet
actually becomes deified), it certainly could well have been.
One only has to contrast this portrayal of the prophetic
experience with the graphic portrayal of the prophet's humanity
in Is. 6:1ff. to get some idea of the enormous difference in
these two respective views of prophecy.

In the phrase, "For when the prophetic mind becomes
divinely inspired and filled with God," Philo employs language
that is more or less typical of his descriptions of prophecy.[252]
V. Mos. 2. 250 provides an excellent illustration of the way
προφητεύω, θεοφορέω, θεσπίζω, χράω, ἐνθουσιάζω, (and ἐξίστημι),
and their cognates, tend to cluster. Speaking of Moses at the
destruction of the Egyptian army in the Red Sea, it is said:
ὁ προφήτης ... οὐκέτ᾽ ὢν ἐν ἑαυτῷ (= ἔκστασις) θεοφορεῖται καὶ
θεσπίζει τάδε ... The speech which he delivers is referred to
as τὸ λόγιον; it is further stated, ἀπέβαινε γὰρ τὰ χρησθέντα
θείαις δυνάμεσι.[253] Referring back to the speech, it is said,
τοῦτ᾽ ἐστὶ τῆς κατ᾽ ἐνθουσιασμὸν προφητείας Μωυσέως ἀρχὴ καὶ
προοίμιον.[254] To be sure, this terminology, as well as his use
of other words, such as ὑποβάλλω, ἐπιθειάζω, κατέχω, καταπνέω,

_____

[250]Trans. Marcus (Loeb).   [251]Cf. above, pp. 26ff.

[252]J. LINDBLOM, Prophecy in Ancient Israel (Oxford,
1962) 29, "Philo's description of what a true prophet is is so
exceptionally clear and acute and might very well be taken as
a characterization of the prophetic type in the world of religion as a whole." On Philo's language to describe prophecy,
cf. WOLFSON, 2. 11ff., esp. 25ff.; E. FASCHER, ΠΡΟΦΗΤΗΣ. Eine
sprach- und religionsgeschichtliche Untersuchung (Giessen,
1927) 152-60.

[253]V. Mos. 2. 253.   [254]V. Mos. 2. 258.

μαίνομαι, and their cognates,[255] to depict the prophetic
experience, derives less from the LXX than from the language
of Philo's contemporary Greek world, and in this respect he
has certainly moved beyond the Old Testament.

The prominent position of νοῦς in the discussion of
prophecy in Qu. Ex. 2. 29 and elsewhere is made possible by his
acceptance, with modifications, of a Platonic anthropological
dualism, and it is in this respect that his view of prophecy
most sharply contrasts with that of Old Testament writers who
basically worked from an anthropological monism.[256] The Old
Testament view of prophecy as a man's receiving and proclaim-
ing the "Word of the Lord" or a message from the "Spirit of
the Lord" still remains fundamental to Philo's view, even if he
employs a different language in weaving together the Jewish and
Greek notions of prophecy.[257] Prophecy, at its roots, is for
him a Divine-Human encounter, an event in which an external
divine power, be it God, the divine Spirit, or whoever, invades
the prophet; his anthropological dualism simply allows him to
turn the experience inside out enabling us to see what goes on
inside.[258] What we see primarily is the νοῦς, although unlike

---

[255]Also, cf. Her. 264ff. where, using the metaphor of
the rising and setting of the sun, Philo says that while the
νοῦς shines its noonday beam into the soul, we are "not
possessed" (οὐ κατεχόμεθα), but when it "sets," ecstasy and
divine possession set in: ἔκστασις ... ἡ ἔνθεος ... κατοκωμή
... μανία. A similar cluster of terms is found in Spec. Leg.
1. 64-65: ἀλλά τις ἐπιφανεὶς ἐξαπιναίως προφήτης θεοφόρητος
θεσπιεῖ καὶ προφητεύσει, λέγων μὲν οἰκεῖον οὐδέν -- οὐδὲ γάρ,
εἰ λέγει, δύναται καταλαβεῖν ὃ γε κατεχόμενος ὄντως καὶ
ἐνθουσιῶν, -- ὅσα δ' ἐνηχεῖται, διελεύσεται καθάπερ
ὑποβάλλοντος ἑτέρου· ἑρμηνεῖς γάρ εἰσιν οἱ προφῆται θεοῦ
καταχρωμένου τοῖς ἐκείνων ὀργάνοις πρὸς δήλωσιν ὧν ἂν ἐθελήσῃ.
Cf. Virt. 217ff., where Abraham's departure from Chaldea,
interpreted allegorically, is similarly described.

[256]Cf. E. JACOB, Theology of the Old Testament, Trans.
A. W. Heathcote & P. J. Allcock. (London, 1958) 157f.

[257]Philo's use of non-Biblical terminology to describe
prophecy is the issue underlying the controversy among scholars
whether his view of prophecy is (1) basically Biblical, but
merely couched in non-Biblical terminology, so R. MEYER, art.
προφήτης, TDNT, 6. 822-23; DANIÉLOU, 198; or (2) thoroughly
Greek in word and in deed, so H. THYEN, Der Stil der jüdisch-
hellenistischen Homilie (Göttingen, 1955) 245; BRÉHIER, 185.

[258]G. F. MOORE, Judaism (Cambridge, Mass., 1966) 1. 239.

Plato, who regarded the νοῦς as having an essentially active
role in the prophetic experience, Philo sees it as playing an
essentially passive role.[259]

At this point we detect a certain ambiguity in the
second part of Qu. Ex. 2. 29, where the προφητικὸς νοῦς is said
to "become like the monad, not being at all mixed with any of
those things associated with duality." In Philo's other descriptions of prophecy instead of the νοῦς undergoing a substantial change, i.e. from being dyadic to monadic, it is said to
be evicted or suspended whereupon it is replaced by the divine
Spirit, as, for example, in Her. 265:

> τῷ δὲ προφητικῷ γένει φιλεῖ τοῦτο συμβαίνειν·
> ἐξοικίζεται μὲν γὰρ ἐν ἡμῖν ὁ νοῦς κατὰ τὴν
> τοῦ θείου πνεύματος ἄφιξιν, κατὰ δὲ τὴν μετα-
> νάστασιν αὐτοῦ πάλιν εἰσοικίζεται· θέμις γὰρ
> οὐκ ἔστι θνητὸν ἀθανάτῳ συνοικῆσαι. διὰ τοῦτο
> ἡ δύσις τοῦ λογισμοῦ καὶ τὸ περὶ αὐτὸν σκότος
> ἔκστασιν καὶ θεοφόρητον μανίαν ἐγέννησε.

> This is what regularly befalls the fellowship
> of the prophets. The mind is evicted at the
> arrival of the divine Spirit, but when that
> departs the mind returns to its tenancy. Mortal
> and immortal may not share the same home. And
> therefore the setting of reason and the darkness
> which surrounds it produce ecstasy and inspired
> frenzy.[260]

This last sentence reminds us that the entire prophetic experience, viewed in this way, is "ecstatic"[261] in the most literal
sense of the term, as Qu. Gen. 3. 9 makes clear:

> For ecstasy, as its very name clearly shows, is
> nothing else than the departing and going out of
> the understanding (λογισμοῦ or διανοίας). But
> the race of prophets is wont to suffer this.
> For when the mind is divinely possessed (ἐνθουσι-
> άζει) and becomes filled with God (θεοφόρητος
> γίνεται), and it is no longer within itself, for
> it receives the divine spirit (τὸ θεῖον πνεῦμα)
> to dwell within it.[262]

---

[259]Cf. MEYER, art. προφήτης, TDNT, 6. 822:286; also, E.
R. DODDS, The Greeks and the Irrational (Berkeley, 1968) 217f.

[260]Trans. Colson & Whitaker (Loeb).

[261]A. J. HESCHEL, The Prophets (New York, 1962) 332,
notes that Philo is the first thinker to use the term ἔκστασις
in its technical sense.

[262]Trans. Marcus (Loeb).

The ambiguity is partially, if not wholly explained by Philo's
rather loose use of such terms as νοῦς, διάνοια, λογισμός, ψυχή
in formulating his psychology.[263] In fact, in Her. 55 he himself even distinguishes between a generic and specific use of
ψυχή; in the general sense it is that part of man incarcerated
in the σῶμα, and in this sense it may be subdivided into its
rational and irrational parts; in the specific sense ψυχή can
designate the rational part, which is also referred to as
νοῦς,[264] διάνοια,[265] τὸ ἡγεμονικόν,[266] λόγος,[267] λογικὸν
πνεῦμα,[268] πνεῦμα;[269] it is incorporeal, having as its substance θεῖον πνεῦμα,[270] and is said to be rational (λογικός)
whereas the rest of the ψυχή is irrational (ἄλογος), being
corporeal. In this more restricted sense νοῦς is by definition
incapable of substantial change, since its οὐσία is
ἀγένητος[271] and therefore ἀσώματος.[272] It is in this sense
that the νοῦς is being referred to when prophecy is described
as an invasion by θεῖον πνεῦμα of the ψυχή; the activity of
νοῦς, man's rational faculty, is suspended, or the νοῦς is
evicted, as the case may be, and returns to its normal function
of intellection when the θεῖον πνεῦμα departs.

But in Qu. Ex. 2. 29 the prophetic νοῦς is said to
undergo a substantial change--it is transformed from being
dyadic into monadic. This obviously could not be referring to
νοῦς in the restricted sense mentioned above, since it is by
definition substantially unchangeable; rather, νοῦς is being
employed in the generic sense as a synonym for ψυχή, as in Gig.
15 where ψυχή is equated with νοῦς, and both are set over
against σῶμα.[273] The "dyad-monad" language can only be another

---

[263]On Philo's anthropology and psychology, cf. DRUMMOND,
1. 314ff.; 2. 274ff.; WOLFSON, 1. 360ff.; 413ff.; DANIELOU,
172ff.; FESTUGIÈRE, 541ff.

[264]Cf. Immut. 45.   [265]Cf. Opif. 135.

[266]Leg. All. 2. 6; Post. C. 104, 108, 126.

[267]Cf. Det. 83.   [268]Cf. Spec. Leg. 1. 171.

[269]Cf. Det. 83.   [270]Her. 55; cf. Spec. Leg. 1. 171.

[271]Her. 56.   [272]Opif. 135; Her. 184.

[273]Cf. also Praem. 163, where ἀνθρώπινος νοῦς is (cont.)

way of saying that the ψυχή (in the generic sense) of the
prophet, which under normal circumstances is, let us say, 50%
λογικός and 50% ἄλογος, becomes, in the prophetic experience
100% λογικός. It is in this quintessential rational state that
the prophetic νοῦς is said to be "immortal." The family relationship to God, and the subsequent phrase, "he is changed into
the divine," must therefore be understood to apply to the prophet's ψυχή = νοῦς rather than to the total man as σῶμα + ψυχή.
The deification of the prophet is the incorporealization of the
prophetic νοῦς, "divine" being used here in a fashion similar
to what we find elsewhere as a synonym for "incorporeal."[274]

(2) V. Mos. 2. 188.

V. Mos. 2. 188 is related to Qu. Ex. 2. 29 in two
respects: (1) as a passage illustrating Philo's conception of
the Divine-Human encounter, and (2) as a passage where language
of deification is used to describe this encounter. Here, Philo
classifies divine utterances (τὰ λόγια) into three categories:
(1) those spoken by God Himself, originating under His own
initiative, with the prophet serving as interpreter; (2) those
delivered in the form of questions (to God) and answers (by
God); and (3) those spoken by Moses while in a state of prophetic ecstasy. No. 1 is designated ἑρμηνεία, while Nos. 2 and 3
are προφητεία, and, we are reminded, they are not the same
thing. In connection with No. 1, Moses is referred to as
θεῖος προφήτης : τῶν λογίων τὰ μὲν ἐκ προσώπου τοῦ θεοῦ λέγεται

---

said to be created, which would imply that νοῦς is being used
in its general sense.

[274]Cf. below, pp. 189ff. Also, Philo's use of the
language of deification to describe the prophetic νοῦς should
be contrasted with his extended polemic against the Stoics
(and Epicureans) in Spec. Leg. 1. 333ff., where he condemns
those who elevate the mind to a position of supreme importance
(Stoics, treated in 1. 334-36) and those who similarly treat
the senses (Epicureans, treated in 1. 337-43). In 1. 344 he
specifically states that the proponents of these respective
viewpoints "ascribe divinity to their respective idols" (οἱ
δὲ ταύτας θεοπλαστοῦσιν); also, he designates the two groups
as "one party of whom deify the reason, the other each several
sense" (ὧν οἱ μὲν τὸν λογισμόν, οἱ δ' ἑκάστην τῶν αἰσθήσεων
ἐξεθείωσαν·). Cf. Colson's note (Loeb), pp. 622ff. on par.
327ff.; also compare V. Contemp. 3ff.

δι' ἑρμηνέως τοῦ θείου προφήτου.[275] Unlike <u>Qu</u>. <u>Ex</u>. 2. 29 there
is no hint here that θεῖος is being used in the sense of
"incorporealized," but rather, given the overall context as
one in which forms of prophecy are being discussed, it would
seem to be used as a synonym for ἔνθεος, which, as has already
been noticed,[276] is one of the various meanings of θεῖος. Yet,
if this is the meaning, it is an unusual use of θεῖος for
Philo,[277] who usually uses ἔνθεος itself,[278] or θεσπέσιος
attributively.[279] Thus, if θεῖος is to be understood here as
"inspired," it is an unusual, though by no means impossible,
use by Philo. Another possibility is that reflected in
Colson's translation, where θεῖος is taken to be an expression
equivalent to the genitival τοῦ θεοῦ, a fairly common use in
Philo,[280] and thus his translation "Some are spoken by God in
His own Person with His (θείου) prophet for interpreter."[281]

(3) <u>Qu</u>. <u>Ex</u>. 2. 40.

A slightly different problem is posed by <u>Qu</u>. <u>Ex</u>. 2. 40:

(40) (Ex. 24:12a) What is the meaning of the
words, "Come up to Me to the mountain and be
there"?

This signifies that a holy soul (ψυχὴν ἁγίαν)

---

[275]A similar expression occurs in Josephus, <u>Ant</u>. 18. 64;
cf. 8. 243; 10. 35.

[276]Cf. above, pp. 57ff.

[277]Though, cf. <u>Decal</u>. 175, where ἔνθεος is used where
he normally uses θεῖος : ἐνθέου πνεύματος.

[278]<u>Her</u>. 264; <u>Migr</u>. 35, 84; <u>Mut</u>. 39; cf. <u>Decal</u>. 35, 175;
<u>Conf</u>. 59; <u>Prob</u>. 80; <u>Her</u>. 249; <u>Spec</u>. <u>Leg</u>. 4. 48; <u>Fuga</u> 168; also,
cf. the passages where he uses the contracted form ἔνθους;
<u>Immut</u>. 138; <u>Flacc</u>. 169; <u>V</u>. <u>Mos</u>. 1. 175, 201, 277, 288.

[279]<u>Plant</u>. 29; <u>Migr</u>. 90; <u>Spec</u>. <u>Leg</u>. 1. 8, 314; 3. 178;
<u>Virt</u>. 8; <u>Praem</u>. 43.

[280]Cf. below, pp. 188f.

[281]Similarly, R. ARNALDEZ (Lyon) 22, "parmi les oracles,
les uns viennent de la Personne de Dieu à travers l'interpréta-
tion donnée <u>par son prophète</u>,...." <u>Contra</u> Yonge, 3. 113f.,
"... of the sacred oracles some are represented as delivered
in the person of God by his interpreter, <u>the divine prophet</u>,
...;" also, P. BADT (<u>Werke</u>) 1, "Die Gottesworte wurden teils
von Gott selbst durch Vermittlung <u>des göttlichen</u> Propheten
verkündet."

is divinized[282] by ascending not to the air or
to the ether or to heaven (which is) higher than
all but to (a region) above the heavens. And
beyond the world there is no place but God. And
He determines the stability of the removal by
saying "be there," (thus) demonstrating the
placelessness and the unchanging habitation of
the divine place. For those who have a quickly
satiated passion for reflexion fly upward for
only a short distance under divine inspiration
and then they immediately return. They do not
fly so much as they are drawn downward, I mean,
to the depths of Tartarus. But those who do not
return from the holy and divine city, to which
they have migrated, have God as their chief
leader in the migration.[283]

It is difficult to decide whether this passage is a comment
upon Moses' prophetic experience (which would be probable
assuming Marcus's conjecture that the Armenian translates
θεοφορεῖσθαι), or whether it is referring to the flight of the
soul into the heavens,[284] Philo's characteristic way of depicting the soul's search for the vision of God.[285] In either
case, even if the original word was θεοῦσθαι, the passage
shares with Qu. Ex. 2. 29 its emphasis that the soul (ψυχὴν
ἁγίαν) is under consideration, be it the soul of the prophet
or the soul in search of the vision of God, in which case
astouacanal is probably to be understood as "incorporealized"
or "immortalized."[286] The final sentence suggests that Philo
may be speaking of the flight of the soul at death, which
recalls his fairly typical method of describing death as the

---

[282]Aucher "deificari." Marcus (Loeb) notes, "Arm.
astouacanal usually renders θεοῦσθαι, a word that seems not to
occur elsewhere in Philo. Perhaps the original here was
θεοφορεῖσθαι." Cf. Ebr. 110, where Philo uses θειοῦν.

[283]Trans. Marcus (Loeb).

[284]Though, cf. Qu. Ex. 2. 44 where the prophet Moses,
ready to ascend Sinai, is "about to go on a heavenly journey."
Also, cf. Qu. Gen. 4. 130.

[285]Cf. Cher. 41 where Zipporah is said to have experienced the release from somatic existence to contemplate the
divine essences: "speeding upwards from earth to heaven and
contemplating there the nature of things divine and blessed."
Cf. discussion below, pp. 163ff.

[286]Cf. Qu. Gen. 1. 10 where the mind is said to become
immortal based upon piety. Also, Qu. Gen. 1. 56.

cessation of all somatic, mortal existence and the beginning
(again) of the incorporeal, immortal existence.[287]

Deification and the Human-Divine Encounter.

Philo's classification of prophecy as a type of ἔκστασις
can all too easily lead one to assume that the converse was
also true, viz. that all ἔκστασις was προφητεία. But that this
was manifestly not the case is seen when we come to consider
the other side of the revelatory experience, the Human-Divine
encounter, or what is usually treated under the category of

---

[287]Abraham, Sacr. 5, is said to have "left this mortal
life (ἐκλιπὼν τὰ θνητὰ ...) and inherited incorruption
(καρπούμενος ἀφθαρσίαν), ... becoming like angels;" Isaac's
death is similarly described, Sacr. 7: he was translated
(μετανίστανται) into an incorruptible and most perfect race
(εἰς τὸ ἄφθαρτον καὶ τελεώτατον γένος); (though, on both these
passages, cf. discussion above, pp. 136ff.). Fuga 59 records
the deaths of Nadab and Abihu in the same conventional manner
as a passing from mortal to immortality: θνητῆς ζωῆς ἄφθαρτον
ἀντικαταλλαττόμενοι βίον; they are also spoken of as being
"translated": ἀπὸ τοῦ γενομένου πρὸς τὸ ἀγένητον
μετανιστάμενοι; over them is uttered a proclamation "betoken-
ing immortality" (τὰ σύμβολα τῆς ἀφθαρσίας). Similarly, Enoch's
departure from this life, in Mut. 38: "we read that he was
'translated', that is, changed his abode and journeyed as an
emigrant from the mortal life to the immortal" (τὸ δ᾽ ἐστὶ
μεταναστῆναι καὶ μετοικίαν στείλασθαι τὴν ἀπὸ θνητοῦ βίου πρὸς
τὸν ἀθάνατον); also cf. Qu. Gen. 1. 85; of souls generally, in
Qu. Gen. 3. 11: "Clearly this indicates the incorruptibility
of the soul, which removes its habitation from the mortal body
and returns as if to the mother-city, from which it originally
moved its habitation to this place."
       This raises serious questions about the appropriateness
of the term "apotheosis" or "deification" to describe Philo's
accounts of Moses' death (so, GOODENOUGH, Light, 197, 223;
WINDISCH, 106, "Vergottungsprozess;" GEORGI, 157f.), unless it
be understood that the death of every person, i.e. the wise or
perfect one, is in this same sense a "deification." Thus, V.
Mos. 2. 288, "Afterwards the time came when he had to make his
pilgrimage from earth to heaven, and leave this mortal life for
immortality, summoned thither by the Father Who resolved his
twofold nature of soul and body into a single unity, transforming his whole being into mind, pure as the sunlight" (Trans.
Colson). (Χρόνοις δ᾽ ὕστερον, ἐπειδὴ τὴν ἐνθένδε ἀποικίαν
ἔμελλεν εἰς οὐρανὸν στέλλεσθαι καὶ τὸν θνητὸν ἀπολιπὼν βίον
ἀπαθανατίζεσθαι μετακληθεὶς ὑπὸ τοῦ πατρός, ὃς αὐτὸν δυάδα
ὄντα, σῶμα καὶ ψυχήν, εἰς μονάδος ἀνεστοιχείου φύσιν ὅλον δι᾽
ὅλων μεθαρμοζόμενος εἰς νοῦν ἡλιοειδέστατον ...). Cf. also
Virt. 72ff., esp. 76, "... he began to pass over from mortal
existence to life immortal and gradually became conscious of
the disuniting of the elements of which he was composed" (Trans.
Colson); (... ἤρξατο μεταβάλλειν ἐκ θνητῆς ζωῆς εἰς ἀθάνατον
                                                        (cont.)

"mysticism." While it is true that he frequently employs the religious language of the mysteries,[288] the categories "prophecy" and "mysticism" as representing the two sides of the same coin, or even one side of a single coin, are artificial to the extent that they blur the basic fact that what really is under consideration is the two-directional event of revelation, or illumination, depending upon one's vantage point, and the force that is released as a result of the collision, or interaction, of these two essentially dissimilar planes of reality. This is the reason that both the prophetic event and the so-called "mystical" experience are ecstatic: in both two dissimilar entities meet, the Divine and the Human, the incorporeal and the corporeal, and it is only when the corporeal becomes incorporeal that any genuine meeting of these two forces can occur.

The Divine-Human encounter, in which the direction of the revelatory event is from God to man, is said to occur at various levels, all of which are by definition ecstatic, and all of which can accurately be called prophetic. Philo uses the same language to describe his own inspired moments[289] as that with which he describes the prophetic activity of Abraham, Aaron, Moses, and Isaiah, to name a few, and seems to think that prophecy, in a general sense, is available not merely to select individuals but to the whole group of those who become "wise." It is here that the edges between "prophecy" and "mysticism" begin to blur, for the Human-Divine encounter, in which the direction of movement of the revelatory event is from man to God, and may aptly be called illumination, or as Philo would say, the vision of God, is sometimes described in this same "prophetic" language, as, for example, in Her. 63ff., in which Abraham's departure from Chaldea serves the prototype of the lover of learning (φιλομαθής). In essence, it is a flight from somatic existence to that realm which is

---

βίον κάκ τοῦ κατ' ὀλίγον συνῃσθάνετο τῆς τῶν ἐξ ὧν συνεκέκρατο διαζεύξεως ...).

[288]Cf. A. MÉASSON (Lyon) 4. 202ff. note on Sacr. 14, on mystery language in Philo; also BILLINGS, Platonism, 11.

[289]Migr. 34-35; Cher. 27; Som. 2. 252; though, cf. WOLFSON, 2. 52ff.

unencumbered with "earthly things" (i.e. the material trappings of somatic existence), the realm dominated by the reality of the Truly Existent One. He who makes the trip successfully does so only under divine impulse; he is "possessed with inspiration from above" (ὁ καταπνευσθεὶς ἄνωθεν), has therefore "received a heavenly and divine portion" (οὐρανίου τε καὶ θείας μοίρας ἐπιλαχών), possesses a "mind wholly purified," which has shut out all somatic and sense-perceptions (ὁ καθαρώτατος νοῦς, ἀλογῶν οὐ μόνον σώματος ἀλλὰ καὶ τοῦ ἑτέρου ψυχῆς τμήματος ...). We are told further that only "incorporeal natures inherit intellectual realities" (ἀσώματοι γὰρ φύσεις νοητῶν πραγμάτων εἰσὶ κληρονόμοι). Thus, the heir of these things is he who has successfully escaped the prison of the body--literally--which means that the experience is truly ecstatic. Thus, "like persons possessed and corybants ... filled with frenzy even as the prophets are inspired. For it is the mind which is under the divine afflatus, and no longer in its own keeping, but is stirred to its depths and maddened by heavenward yearning ..." (οἱ κατεχόμενοι καὶ κορυβαντιῶντες βακχευθεῖσα καὶ θεοφορηθεῖσα κατά τινα προφητικὸν ἐπιθειασμόν· ἐνθουσιώσης γὰρ καὶ οὐκέτ' οὔσης ἐν ἑαυτῇ διανοίας ...).[290] Strictly speaking, "prophecy" inappropriately describes this Human-Divine encounter, even though it is ecstatic, and is described with the same basic set of terms.[291] It is not primarily God revealing Himself, or His message, to man, which man in turn passes on; rather it is man's coming to knowledge of God, seeing God. The difficulty arises because in both the Divine-Human and the Human-Divine encounters it is man's νοῦς, the faculty of intellection and the receptacle for comprehending the Divine, that is the basic channel of communication.[292]

The Human-Divine encounter, the quest for the vision of of God, is Everyman's quest,[293] hindered solely by man's

---

[290]Compare Qu. Gen. 4. 140; Qu. Ex. 2. 51.

[291]This distinction is recognized in Her. 69, when the one who experiences the Human-Divine encounter is said to be "like the prophet."

[292]Cf. esp. Her. 63-65, 69.

[293]Cf. Ebr. 124; Qu. Ex. 2. 51; Conf. 145; Fuga 56; (cont.)

inescapable attachment to the corporeal world of reality, both
his own σῶμα and the κόσμος αἰσθητός in which he "sojourns."
Achieving the true vision of God, because it is a purely
rational, intellectual (in the Philonic sense) process and
thus is possible only by complete submission, rather suppres-
sion, of the σῶμα, or by an escape from the world of somatic
existence, can only be "ecstatic,"[294] at least in this life.
Moreover,--and when it is remembered that Philo can be quoted
on both sides of almost any question, this is quite a significant point--Philo adamantly refuses to admit that the true
vision of God is ever actually achieved.[295] Even Moses, the
chief mystagogue, who penetrated into the darkness where God
was, succeeds only in "seeing" the powers that surround God, or
stated philosophically, in comprehending that He is, not what
He is.[296] The impossibility of the quest is grounded both in
Philo's anthropology and his metaphysical dualism, both of
which are, of course, integrally related. Seemingly, the νοῦς,
being θεῖον ἀπόσπασμα,[297] that extraordinarily endowed faculty
which renders the ψυχή capable of receiving immortal ἔννοιαι
and is capable of shattering spatial, temporal, and noetic
boundaries,[298] should be capable of perceiving God, but as long
as it remains shackled in the somatic world the leap of faith
is rendered impossible. This is graphically illustrated in a
most illuminating fragment from Qu. Ex.:

> Ἀμήχανον ἀνθρωπίνῃ φύσει τὸ τοῦ Ὄντος πρόσωπον
> θεάσασθαι. Τὸ δὲ πρόσωπον οὐ κυριολογεῖται,
> παραβολὴ δὲ ἐστιν εἰς δήλωσιν τῆς καθαρωτάτης
> καὶ εἰλικρινεστάτης τοῦ Ὄντος ἰδέας, ἐπειδὴ καὶ
> ἄνθρωπος οὐδενὶ γνωρίζεται μᾶλλον ἢ προσώπῳ κατὰ
> τὴν ἰδίαν ποιότητα καὶ μορφήν. Οὐ γάρ φησιν ὁ

Qu. Gen. 4. 193; Migr. 39; Decal. 35; cf. Her. 111. It can
also be corporate (Israel) as well as individual, cf. Conf. 56,
92; Praem. 43-44; Ebr. 83; Cong. 51; Qu. Ex. 2. 39.

[294]Thus the appropriateness of the "drunkenness" metaphor to illustrate this experience; cf. Ebr. 146-7.

[295]Cf. Qu. Gen. 3. 42; Virt. 215; Det. 89; Abr. 80;
Post. C. 168; Spec. Leg. 1. 40.

[296]Post. C. 169; Fuga 164f.; Mut. 8-10; also, Spec. Leg.
1. 43, 47-53; similarly, Abraham, Qu. Gen. 4. 1; 4. 2.

[297]Cf. Som. 1. 34.   [298]Cf. Det. 86ff.

θεὸς ὅτι "οὐκ εἰμὶ ὁρατὸς τὴν φύσιν"--τίς δὲ
μᾶλλον ὁρατὸς ἢ ὁ τὰ ἄλλα πάντα γεννήσας ὁρατά;--
"πεφυκὼς δὲ τοιοῦτος εἰς τὸ ὁρᾶσθαι ὑπ᾽ οὐδενὸς
ἀνθρώπων ὁρῶμαί" φησι. Τὸ δὲ αἴτιον ἡ ἀδυναμία
τοῦ γενητοῦ. Καὶ ἵνα μὴ περιπλέκων μηκύνω· θεὸν
γενέσθαι δεῖ πρότερον--ὅπερ οὐδὲ οἶόν τε--ἵνα
θεὸν ἰσχύσῃ τις καταλαβεῖν. Ἐὰν δὲ ἀποθάνῃ μέν
τις τὸν θνητὸν βίον, ζήσῃ δὲ ἀντιλαβὼν τὸν
ἀθάνατον, ἴσως ὃ μηδέποτε εἶδεν ὄψεται.[299]

It is impossible for human nature to behold the
face of the Existent One. And "face" is not to
be taken literally, but is an analogy for explaining the purest and absolutely unalloyed form of
the Existent One, since even a man is not recognized by anyone by his shape and form, but rather
by his face. For God does not say, "I am not
visible by nature"--for who is more visible than
he who created all other visible things? He says,
"Being such a one who has created, in order to be
seen, I am seen by no man." But the fault lies in
the inability of the creature. And so as not to
prolong the discussion and further complicate
matters: in order for one to be able to comprehend
Deity, it is first necessary to become Deity--the
very thing which is impossible.[300] But if someone
dies in respect to the mortal life, he will live,
receiving in exchange the immortal (life), and
likewise he will see what he had never seen.

Thus, the νοῦς, man's only receptacle capable of κατάληψις of
τὸ ὄν, struggles to see τὸ ὄν, to penetrate the heavenly realm,
to rise above somatic, corporeal existence imposed upon man,
but shackled in the σῶμα, it cannot; the Human-Divine encounter
is, strictly speaking, an impossibility.

Summary.

Having looked at both sides of the Divine-Human
encounter, we must now briefly summarize by considering the
question of deification and the appropriateness of the expression theios aner to describe this phenomenon.

We have noticed that in speaking of both the Divine-
Human and Human-Divine encounters Philo employs the language of
deification primarily in terms suggesting that the soul or mind
becomes divine, immortal, or incorporeal. The language of
deification is used to describe the ecstatic experience, for it

---

[299]Marcus (Loeb, Suppl. 2, p. 258).

[300]Contra Yonge 4. 249, "... it is inevitable that God
must first be created (which is not possible) in order for any
one to be able to comprehend God."

is only when one is literally outside one's corporeal existence, either when receiving a divine revelation or when allowing one's soul to fly into the heavens in search of the true
vision of God, that such language is appropriate. The νοῦς or
ψυχή during the encounters can be called θεῖος, but the
expression theios aner is not employed in describing either
encounter. θεσπίζω and cognates are used in describing the
prophetic experience, but in no instance does the explicit
language of deificiation occur. Philo's use of non-LXX
language, borrowed from assorted sources ranging from Plato to
the mysteries, does not per se bear testimony one way or the
other, but as Wolfson has convincingly shown, merely indicates
his superimposition of Greek categories upon his concept of
prophecy derived from Scripture.

The real question is whether, in his adoption of non-LXX
language to describe the Divine-Human encounter, especially the
deification language, Philo represents a major shift in thought
from the Old Testament point of view which disallowed deification of human beings.[301] A fully satisfactory answer to this

---

[301]Two examples of an argument in the affirmative can be
mentioned. WINDISCH, 102, sees in Philo's treatment of Elijah
signs of a major conceptual change in Israel's understanding of
divinity. In Immut. 138ff., Philo quotes the LXX (1 Kings 17:
18) which refers to Elijah as ἄνθρωπος θεοῦ, whereas Philo goes
ahead to describe him as ἔνθους, attributing to him the generally understood experience of ecstatic frenzy. From this
Windisch concludes, "Schon hier wird klar, wie Philo den
biblischen Gottesmann mit dem altgriechischen theios aner
zusammenschmilzt." In a somewhat similar vein, A. DEISSMANN,
"Die Hellenisierung des semitischen Monotheismus," Neue Jahrbücher für das klassische Altertum 11 (1903) 175, cites Hos.
1:2 as an example of the Hellenizing of Jewish monotheism in
the LXX, and argues that the LXX rendering of the MT ב as ἐν
illustrates the contrast between God speaking to the prophet
and God speaking in the prophet: "... im Effekt ist aus dem
Worte Gottes 'zu' dem Propheten ein Wort Gottes 'in' dem
Propheten geworden, die realistische Derbheit ist gemildert
und das Gott im Propheten ist der Welt verständlich, die voll
war von gotterfüllten Sehern und Seherinnen, in denen der Gott
war und sie in dem Gott."
On the other side stands E. FASCHER, ΠΡΟΦΗΤΗΣ, still one
of the basic works on the subject, who, in spite of the fact
that Windisch appeals to him in support of his case ("Über die
Unterschiede, die zwischen dem jüdischen Nabi und dem
griechischen Ekstatiker bestehen und die Philo auswischt, vgl.
etwa Fascher, Prophetes, S. 151f"), maintains that, in spite
of Philo's use of Greek terminology, he still does not

(cont.)

question would require an exhaustive investigation of the
entire complex question of Philo's conception of prophecy.
But, with reference to the passages we have examined, the most
significant finding is that Philo invariably speaks of the
νοῦς/ψυχή, and applies language of deification to it. But, as
we have seen, his use of this language, because of his adoption
of a modified Platonic metaphysics and anthropology, can be
nothing more than another way of stating that the νοῦς/ψυχή
becomes incorporeal in the prophetic experience. In this
respect, of course, his concept of prophecy is different from
that of the Old Testament, but one cannot facilely speak of
this phenomenon in Philo as "deification" without further   ∨
qualification. Such qualification must give adequate account
of the complexities of Philo's anthropology, psychology, metaphysics, as well as his complicated use of three, sometimes
four, sets of terminology to describe the same event.

As to the Human-Divine encounter, its elusiveness,
indeed its impossibility, stands out as the most striking
feature, as the quotation from the Qu. Ex. fragment shows.[302]
We have seen that the pervasiveness of Philo's anthropological
dualism lies at the root of this problem, and that the central
faculty involved is the νοῦς, and that in both cases, σῶμα
provides the major obstacle to realization of the goal. We
have also simply noted the unusual use of "divine" to mean
"incorporeal," a point which we shall consider in more detail
later.

---

transform the Old Testament "prophets" into the Greek mold:
"Späterhin tritt immer das Pneuma als Vermittler ein, der
Mensch sucht den Sitz der Offenbarung, je mehr er sein Inneres
kennen lernt, in sich selbst, aber ein Eingehen Jahwes in die
Menschen, ein "ἔνθεος γενέσθαι" ist undenkbar. Die israel-
itische Religion hat keinen Plato gehabt, der für sie Ähnliches
geleistet hätte, ist doch selbst Philo von dieser Linie nicht
abgewichen trotz alles griechischen Einflusses" (pp. 151f.);
further, summing up his discussion of Philo, "Aber in der
Wahrung des Abstandes zwischen Gott und Mensch ist er--trotz
aller griechischen Anleihen--Jude geblieben. Aufs N.T. hat
Philo, wie sich zeigen wird, mit seiner neuen Terminologie und
seinen eklektischen Vorstellungen nicht eingewirkt, dieses
liegt in der Linie der Septuaginta" (p. 160). Also, cf. MEYER,
art. προφήτης, TDNT, 6. 822-23.

[302]Cf. above, pp. 166f.

On the basis of these observations, we would be inclined to agree with E. R. Dodds's assessment of Philo when he denies that the language of ecstasy in Philo implies any real mystical union between man and God.[303] A further observation worth making is that the Divine-Human and the Human-Divine encounters are temporary experiences. In Gig. 20 we are reminded that πνεῦμα θεοῦ does not abide among the mass of men, but comes and goes. Apparently, the only exception is Moses, who enjoys the distinct advantage of having θεῖον πνεῦμα as his constant companion, whereas it does not abide with others permanently.[304] He is able to shed the somatic veil, enter the darkness, and learn the secrets of the most holy mysteries. "He then ever has the divine spirit at his side, taking the lead in every journey of righteousness."[305]

The High Priest.

Philo's conception of the nature of the high priest must also be mentioned because of the remarkably forthright language employed in several passages. In the Old Testament high standards had been laid down for the high priesthood,[306] but, as R. A. Stewart remarks, "It is quite clear, from Lev. 4:3; 9:7; 16:6, and 17, and numerous other contexts, that the Old Testament never so much as contemplated a sinless High-priest."[307] Much of Philo's language more or less is a restatement of the Biblical requirements for the ethical and ritual purity of the high priest: he must be blameless, perfect, the husband of a virgin;[308] according to V. Mos. 2. 139 the lustrations are symbolic of his blameless life. Moving slightly beyond this,

---

[303] E. R. DODDS, Pagan and Christian in the Age of Anxiety (Cambridge, 1968) 71.

[304] Gig. 54f.   [305] Gig. 55.

[306] Lev. 21-22.

[307] R. A. STEWART, "The Sinless High-Priest," NTS 14 (1967-68) 126. This article also contains an excellent analysis of this theme in other Jewish sources and the New Testament, both contrasted with Philo's view. Also, cf. the same author's article, "Creation and Matter in the Epistle to the Hebrews," NTS 12 (1965-66) 284-93, for a useful discussion of Philo's metaphysical views and their relation to Plato and Hebrews.

[308] Som. 2. 185ff.

however, Spec. Leg. 1.116 asserts that the Law desires him to
be "endued with a nature higher than the merely human"
(μείζονος ... φύσεως ἢ κατ' ἄνθρωπον) and "to approximate to
the Divine" (ἐγγυτέρω προσιόντα τῆς θείας), to become as it
were "on the borderline between the two" (μεθόριον, εἰ δεῖ
τἀληθὲς λέγειν). Given Philo's propensity for hyperbole, this
language by itself could be understood as merely restating
these high ethical requirements, especially when it is recalled
that he often uses the μεθόριος metaphor of man in general as
"on the borderline between heaven and earth."[309] Fuga 108 goes
yet further:

> We say, then, that the High Priest is not a man,
> but a Divine Word (οὐκ ἄνθρωπον ἀλλὰ λόγον θεῖον)
> and immune from all unrighteousness whether
> intentional or unintentional.[310]

But the force of this claim is diminished by Philo's prefacing
remarks that he is no longer considering the high priest
historically but is "looking for the hidden meaning of the
literal words."[311] This becomes all the more obvious when the
high priest is said to be "the child of parents incorruptible
and wholly free from stain, his father being God . . . and his
mother Wisdom."[312]

But, in addition to these statements about the general
demeanor and position of the high priest, Philo, by a most
unusual exegesis of Lev. 16:17, asserts that something extraordinary happens to the high priest when he enters the Most
Holy Place. According to the LXX of Lev. 16:17, καὶ πᾶς
ἄνθρωπος οὐκ ἔσται ἐν τῇ σκηνῇ τοῦ μαρτυρίου εἰσπορευομένου
αὐτοῦ ἐξιλάσασθαι ἐν τῷ ἁγίῳ, ἕως ἂν ἐξέλθῃ. Whether Philo
altered the text to suit his exegetical whims or whether he
had before him a different text[313]--both of which are entirely

---

[309] Cf. Leg. All. 3. 161; Opif. 135; Det. 84-85; Conf.
176ff.; Her. 283; Decal. 134; Plant. 14, 20-22; Som. 1. 146.

[310] Trans. Colson & Whitaker (Loeb).

[311] Fuga 108.   [312] Fuga 109.

[313] On this complex problem, cf. P. KATZ, Philo's Bible.
The Aberrant Text of Bible Quotations in Some Philonic Writings
(Cambridge, 1950), esp. 3ff. on Lemma alterations; also review
by G. D. KILPATRICK, JTS 2 (1951) 87ff.; neither Lev. 16:17 nor
Som. 2. 188-89; 2. 231; Her. 84 is listed in Katz's   (cont.)

possible--, the fact remains that three times, in Som. 2. 188-
89; 2. 231, and Her. 84, the text no longer speaks of the
exclusive privilege of the high priest to be alone in the
tabernacle while he makes atonement in the Holy Place. Instead
it elicits from Philo two, possibly three, different allegorical interpretations.

In Som. 2. 188-89, where the high priest is treated as
symbolic of the Logos,[314] the "father of holy intelligences"
(πατὴρ λόγων ἱερῶν),[315] and "a being whose nature is midway
between (man and) God, less than God, superior to man"
(μεθόριός τις θεοῦ [καὶ ἀνθρώπου] φύσις, τοῦ μὲν ἐλάττων,
ἀνθρώπου δὲ κρείττων)[316] Philo's rendition of Lev. 16:17 is
appealed to for its supposed reference to this μεθόριος-
character of the high priest. In Som. 2. 231, it is the Perfect man who is under consideration, and the text is cited as
proof that ὁ σοφός/ἀστεῖος stands on the borderline between God
and man: "neither God nor man, but ... on the borderline
between the uncreated and the perishing form of being" (...
οὔτε θεὸν οὔτε ἄνθρωπον ... ἀλλ' ... μεθόριον τῆς ἀγενήτου καὶ
φθαρτῆς φύσεως).[317] A similar ethical allegorical interpretation occurs in Her. 84 where Philo seeks to show that the soul
of ὁ σοφός is not necessarily confined to somatic existence, in
spite of its attachment to σῶμα (σῆμα). In this instance Lev.
16:17 offers proof that the high priest, while in the Most Holy
Place, is:

> οὐ (ἄνθρωπος) σωματικῶς, ἀλλὰ ταῖς κατὰ ψυχὴν
> κινήσεσιν. ὁ γὰρ νοῦς, ὅτε μὲν καθαρῶς λειτουργεῖ
> θεῷ, οὐκ ἔστιν ἀνθρώπινος, ἀλλὰ θεῖος· ὅτε δὲ
> ἀνθρωπίνῳ τινί, τέτραπται καταβὰς ἀπ' οὐρανοῦ,
> μᾶλλον δὲ πεσὼν ἐπὶ γῆν ἐξέρχεται, κἂν ἔτι μένῃ
> τὸ σῶμα ἔνδον αὐτῷ.

---

index; C. SIEGFRIED, "Philo und der überlieferte Text der LXX,"
ZWT 16 (1873) 531f., classifies Lev. 16:17 among those passages
"in which Philo bases an interpretation upon a certain expression in the text which we do not find in our texts of the LXX."
H. E. RYLE, Philo and Holy Scripture (London, 1895) 212f.,
merely notes the difference without attempting an explanation.

[314]So, note by Colson & Whitaker (Loeb), ad loc., p. 524.

[315]Som. 2. 185   [316]Som. 2. 188.

[317]Som. 2. 234.

... no man, that is, in the movements of his soul
though in the bodily sense he is still a man. For
when the mind is ministering to God in purity, it
is not human, but divine. But when it ministers
to aught that is human, it turns its course and
descending from heaven, or rather falling to earth,
comes forth, even though his body still remains
within.[318]

Even though in all three instances the entry of the high
priest into the Most Holy Place has been allegorized, it is
quite clear that Philo conceives the Most Holy Place on at
least two levels of reality corresponding to his Platonic metaphysics. In Qu. Ex. 2. 94, 95, 96, 106, where he delineates
the Holy Place = αἰσθητὸς κόσμος/Most Holy Place = νοητὸς
κόσμος schema, the objects and activities within the Most Holy
Place are necessarily understood to be incorporeal in their
οὐσία, which makes it understandable why the high priest's
entry into and exit from the Most Holy Place serves as an
excellent prototype for communication between κόσμος αἰσθητός
and κόσμος νοητός, whether it is the Logos or ὁ σοφός who
happens to be regarded as standing on the borderline.

We thus find again that the language of deification in
reference to the "mind," in this case of the high priest interpreted allegorically as the Logos and ὁ σοφός, corresponds
directly with the language of incorporealization, made possible
by a Platonic view of the world.

Theios Aner and Virt. 177.

Having looked at the main group of passages in that
stream of Philo's though which suggests a tendency on his part
to deify mortals,[319] we now turn to his actual use of the

---

[318]Her. 84. Trans. Colson & Whitaker (Loeb).

[319]I.e. those passages which have usually been adduced
in this connection, as, for example, GOODENOUGH, Light, 223ff.
Philo's use of υἱὸς θεοῦ has been omitted from this discussion,
primarily because it is not used of historical individuals to
suggest their divinity. In Mut. 131, for example, "Isaac," who
is "laughter of the heart," ἱs υἱὸς θεοῦ; Adam, being the first
created man, was God's son in a unique sense (Virt. 204); often,
it is primarily a moral term to designate the righteous man
(Spec. Leg. 1. 318; Qu. Gen. 1. 92) and it is in this sense
that it is said that those who live in the knowledge of God are
υἱοὶ θεοῦ (Conf. 145; so Deut. 14:1; 32:6, 18). It is used of
the κόσμος (Immut. 31f.; cf. V. Mos. 2. 134), the wise man

(cont.)

expression <u>theios</u> <u>aner</u> itself. The most well-known passage is
<u>Virt</u>. 177:

τὸ μὲν γὰρ μηδὲν συνόλως ἁμαρτεῖν ἴδιον θεοῦ
τάχα δὲ καὶ θείου ἀνδρός, τὸ δὲ ἁμαρτόντα
μεταβαλεῖν πρὸς ἀνυπαίτιον ζωὴν φρονίμου καὶ
τὸ συμφέρον εἰς ἅπαν οὐκ ἀγνοήσαντος.

For absolute sinlessness belongs to God alone,
or possibly to a divine man;[320] conversion
from sin to a blameless life shows a man of
wisdom who has not been utterly ignorant of
what is for his good.[321]

In contrast to Josephus who explicitly designates ὁ νομοθέτης
as <u>theios</u> <u>aner</u>, Philo does not directly attach the label to
Moses even though he is being discussed in this context[322] and
in spite of Goodenough's confidence that the referent is
"obviously Moses."[323]

(1) <u>Moses</u> <u>and</u> <u>Sinlessness</u>.

It is certainly undeniable that if, in Philo's opinion,
any mortal man ever attained sinless perfection, it was Moses,
whom he designates in <u>V</u>. <u>Mos</u>. 2. 192 as "the holiest of men
ever yet born" (ὁσιώτατον τῶν πώποτε γενομένων) and in <u>Ebr</u>. 94
as "the most perfect of men" (... Μωυσῆν τὸν τελειότατον).[324]
It is not surprising, therefore, that in <u>V</u>. <u>Mos</u>., where Moses
is depicted as the embodiment of the Stoic Sage, we discover

(<u>Som</u>. 2. 273), the Logos (<u>Som</u>. 1. 215; <u>Conf</u>. 146), and of
angels (<u>Qu</u>. <u>Gen</u>. 1. 92). Cf. E. SCHWEIZER, art. υἱός, <u>TDNT</u>
8. 355f.; also DRUMMOND, 2. 281f.

[320]YONGE, 3. 454, "For absolutely never to do anything
wrong at all is a peculiar attribute of God, and perhaps one
may also say of <u>a</u> <u>God-like</u> <u>man</u>." COHN (<u>Werke</u>) 2. 364, "Denn
überhaupt nicht zu sündigen kommt nur Gott zu, vielleicht auch
einem <u>gottbegnadeten</u> <u>Manne</u> ..." M-R. SERVEL (Lyon) 26. 127f.,
"Ne commettre absolument aucune faute n'appartient qu'à Dieu
ou peut-être bien à quelque homme divin."

[321]Trans. Colson (Loeb).   [322]Cf. <u>Virt</u>. 175, 178.

[323]GOODENOUGH, <u>Light</u>, 233; TIEDE, 108, "an apparent
reference to Moses."

[324]Cf. also <u>Leg</u>. <u>All</u>. 3. 134-35; <u>Qu</u>. <u>Ex</u>. 2. 27. The
extensive list of epithets (with references) attributed to
Moses by Philo has been conveniently compiled by J. W. EARP,
(Loeb) 10. 386ff. On the Rabbinic debate about the sinlessness of the patriarchs, cf. WOLFSON, 1. 451f., esp. 451:85.

that Philo has considerably censored the Biblical narrative which candidly relates Moses' foibles and shortcomings, such as his murder of the Egyptian.[325] In V. Mos. 1. 83 he does mention that Moses tries to refuse the mission to Egypt, but in 1. 210ff., describing the Meribah incident, he follows the account in Ex. 17:1ff. where no blame is imputed to Moses, making no mention of the tradition recorded in Num. 20:10ff. where Moses' conduct is censured.[326] At 1. 196 he omits to mention Moses' grumbling and doubting prior to the (second) miraculous quail feast.[327] Interestingly, between 1. 219 and 220 he omits Jethro's suggestion for improving judicial procedures, presumably thinking it would detract from Moses' all-sufficiency.[328] At 2. 1, reviewing Book I, he notes that the life of Moses presented therein was "not merely blameless but highly praiseworthy" (ἔτι δὲ παιδείας καὶ ἀρχῆς, ἣν οὐ μόνον ἀνεπιλήπτως ἀλλὰ καὶ σφόδρα ἐπαινετῶς ἦρξε ...). At 2. 5 we are told that as high priest Moses was equipped with "perfect rites and perfect knowledge of the service of God," yet at 2. 6 he concedes that Moses, in spite of embodying king, lawgiver, and high priest in one person, is nevertheless, by virtue of his being a created being, but a mortal creature (γενητὸς γὰρ οὐδὲν ἧττον καὶ θνητός ἐστιν). His ritual purity is mentioned at 2. 68-69. At 2. 167 where Moses' descent from Sinai and the golden calf incident are mentioned, no mention is made of the breaking of the tablets.[329] As noted above, he is called the "holiest of all men yet born" in 2. 192. At 2. 288ff. there is no mention of Moses' being prohibited to enter the promised land.[330]

Yet, in the middle of this portrayal of Moses, at 2. 147, we are reminded that sin is congenital to every human being, even ὁ σπουδαῖος, by virtue of his being a created

---

[325] Ex. 2:12.

[326] Cf. also Num. 27:14; Deut. 32:48ff.; 34:4; also Deut. 1:37; 3:26f.; 4:21; Ps. 106:32-33.

[327] Num. 11:11-23; cf. Ex. 17:2-4.

[328] Ex. 18:13ff.   [329] Ex. 32:19f.

[330] Cf. Deut. 32:51; also references in note 326.

being.[331] Evidently Philo sees no inconsistency in praising Moses (and the other patriarchs) as the paragon of the virtues, even to an excessive degree, while at the same time allowing that he fell short of the mark. In Abr. 4ff. where he extols the patriarchs as οἱ ἔμψυχοι καὶ λογικοὶ νόμοι ἄνδρες ἐκεῖνοι γεγόνασιν, who were αὐτομαθεῖς and αὐτήκοοι, and gladly conformed to φύσις, it is obvious that he still does not regard them as sinless, although he shifts the blame from them to τύχη:

> They committed no guilty action of their own
> free will or purpose, and where chance led them
> wrong they besought God's mercy and propitiated
> Him with prayers and supplications, and thus
> secured a perfect life guided aright in both
> fields, both in their premeditated actions and
> in such as were not of freely-willed purpose.[332]

In Mut. 50 he asserts that "the complete acquisition of the virtues is impossible for man, as we know him," and in Qu. Gen. 4. 203 quotes Epicharmus approvingly, "Whoever transgresses the least is the best man, for no one is sinless and no one is without blame."

Because of the conflict between Philo's panegyric on the one hand and his denials of the possibility of living a sinless life, it has to remain an open question[333] whether he felt that Moses possessed "absolute sinlessness" in the sense mentioned in Virt. 177. Even if he did, that by no means proves that he has Moses in mind when he mentions the outside chance of a theios aner becoming absolutely sinless. In Virt. 177 the theios aner is, and must remain, anonymous.

---

[331]Cf. YONGE, 4. 260, Fragments, "I think it absolutely impossible that no part of the soul should become tainted, not even the outermost and lowest part of it, even if the man appeared to be perfect among men;" also, p. 266, "Perfection and an absence of deficiency are found in God alone. But deficiency and imperfection exist in every man." Similarly, Spec. Leg. 1. 252; Immut. 75-76; Mut. 48ff.; Sacr. 15; though cf. Spec. Leg. 3. 134f. Commenting on Virt. 177, ZELLER, Philosophie (3.2) 450:1, says, "Wenn (Virt. 177) die Möglichkeit offen gelassen wird, dass ein göttlicher Mann fehlerfrei bliebe, so ist diess eine Inkonsequenz, welche sich Philo aus Rücksicht auf die Heroën des jüdischen Volkes erlaubt."

[332]Abr. 6. Trans. Colson (Loeb).

[333]Cf. WOLFSON, 1. 451.

The more important question is to determine as precisely
as we can the meaning of the expression, and here we face the
same task which confronted us in Ant. 3. 180--assessing the
lexicographical data bearing upon the meaning of θεῖος, and
trying to establish whether it is a terminus technicus, and if
so, in what sense.

(2) θεῖος in Philo.[334]

An examination of the lexicographical data reveals a
pattern of diversity insofar as the actual meaning of θεῖος is
concerned. It is used of aspects and activities, e.g. speaking,
influencing, etc., or anything directly stemming from or
relating to God, the Existent One, or activities, etc. for
which He can be said to be ultimately responsible. Philo can
speak of the "divine origin" (θεία ἀρχή) of all things,[335] an
obvious reference to God's creation by fiat. The Decalogue was
spoken by the "divine voice" (θεία φωνή) of God.[336] When Moses
tells Aaron about God's revelation in the burning bush, he
calls it "the divine message" (τὰ θεῖα λόγια).[337] In

-----

[334] The lack of a complete concordance on Philo makes any
exhaustive treatment of this question impossible. Efforts are
being made to remedy this unfortunate lack of such a basic tool,
notably by P. BORGEN and his team at the Institute of Religion,
University of Bergen, who have compiled the data on computer
cards, but as yet it is unpublished. The new index by G. MAYER,
according to a personal letter from him, has been completed and
is scheduled to appear shortly. Although the difficulties
arising from the diverse fragments, some of which exist only in
Armenian, with Aucher's Latin translation, present a formidable
task, a concordance of the scope and admirable quality of that
on Josephus produced by the Institutum Judaicum Delitzschianum
under the direction of K. H. RENGSTORF is a desideratum. For
our purposes, therefore, the LEISEGANG index, in spite of its
deficiencies, has been used.
We shall omit the many uses of τὸ θεῖον as a designation
for God/deity in this discussion.

[335] Leg. All. 1. 9.   [336] Decal. 36; Spec. Leg. 4. 132.

[337] V. Mos. 1. 85. Other "divine communications" designated by θεῖος include ἀκοαί: Fuga 208; ἄκουσμα: Mut. 209;
ἀποφθέγματα: Jos. 95; δόγματα: Mut. 202; Det. 133; λόγια:
Jos. 95; Spec. Leg. 4. 50; λόγοι: Conf. 81; Migr. 129;
προστάγματα: Abr. 275 (= Gen. 26:5); πρόσταξις: V. Mos. 1. 99;
προστάξεις: V. Mos. 2. 60, 70; ῥήματα καὶ λόγοι: Migr. 80;
ὑποσχέσεις: Her. 101; Mut. 54; Som. 1. 175; χρησμός: Migr. 29,
66 (Gen. 3:14); χρησμοί: Fuga 21.

discussing the serpent-rod miracle of Aaron, Philo specifies
that God was responsible for these "signs and wonders," and
therefore they were brought about by some "more divine power"
(δύναμιν θειοτέραν) which makes every feat easy.[338] The fore-
fathers who participated in the Exodus did so under "divine
guidance" (θείᾳ πομπῇ).[339] God's "divine favors" (αἱ θεῖαι
χάριτες) always precede His judgments.[340]

---

[338]V. Mos. 1. 94. In several passages δύναμις θεία
seems to be used as a synonym for ὁ θεός; cf. Post. C. 27;
Virt. 54; Conf. 115; Spec. Leg. 2. 2; Abr. 26; cf. V. Mos.
2. 253, 255; Det. 83.

[339]Spec. Leg. 2. 158; also of ἐπιφροσύνη: Det. 61;
Migr. 171; Her. 278; Som. 2. 25; Abr. 18, 235; Jos. 37; V. Mos.
1. 132, 211; 2. 5, 32, 58, 154, 278; ἐπιφροσύναις θείαις: V.
Mos. 2. 261; πρόνοια: Conf. 115; Mut. 25; V. Mos. 1. 162;
Flacc. 125; also, ὄψις: V. Mos. 2. 254; Praem. 165; φροντίς:
Abr. 70.

[340]Qu. Gen. 1. 89. Other uses of θεῖος to denote a
specific quality, aspect, act, etc. of God include: ἀγαθά:
Ebr. 37; Her. 69, 76, 240; Fuga 20; V. Contemp. 39; cf. Sacr.
22; Det. 156; Mut. 219; ἀκοή: Cher. 72; Immut. 111; ἀρεταί:
V. Mos. 2. 189; ἀρχή: Leg. All. 1. 9; γνώμη (upon Sodom):
Abr. 141; γονή: Immut. 137 (re Tamar); Mut. 255 (re Leah);
γοναί: Det. 147; Immut. 5 (re Hannah); γράμμα: Migr. 85;
γράμματα: Her. 176; δικαστήριον: Decal. 111; Spec. Leg. 4.
34; Virt. 171; Praem. 69; δόγματα: Conf. 51; Migr. 131;
δυνάμεις: V. Contemp. 6; δωρεά: Opif. 23; Som. 1. 113;
δωρεαί: Cong. 96; Mut. 142; εἰκών: Opif. 25; Conf. 62; Her.
57; Mut. 223; Spec. Leg. 1. 171; 3. 207; ἐκκλησία = ἐκκλησία
κυρίου (Deut. 23:2): Conf. 144; ἐναύγασμα: Leg. All. 3. 7;
ἐνδιαίτημα = σκηνή: Cong. 116; ἐπιφροσύνη: cf. note 339 above;
ἔργον: Her. 216; Mut. 223; Aet. 69; ἔργα: Immut. 106; Praem.
9; ἔρως: Plant. 39; Her. 14; Som. 2. 232; Abr. 170; Virt. 55;
Prob. 43; ἔρωτες: Som. 1. 165; εὐδαιμονία: Cher. 19; θεωρία:
Migr. 150; ἵμερος: Migr. 157; κρίσις: Spec. Leg. 3. 121;
κριτήρια: Virt. 66; λογιότης (as opposed to Moses' eloquence):
V. Mos. 1. 83; λόγος = ὁ κύριος (Gen. 18:11f.): Leg. All. 3.
218; λόγοι: Spec. Leg. 3. 1; Virt. 108; μηνύματα: V. Mos.
1. 119; μοῖρα: Spec. Leg. 2. 261; Prob. 44; Leg. ad Gaium 76;
νόμισμα: Det. 152; Immut. 105?; νομοθεσία, νόμος, νόμοι: cf.
note 341 below; ὁμολογία: Ebr. 39; ὄνομα: Post. C. 101; Mut.
13; V. Mos. 2. 208; Spec. Leg. 4. 40 (= Lev. 19:11-12);
ὄργανον: Migr. 52; V. Mos. 2. 103?; οὖς: Spec. Leg. 1. 272;
ὄψις: V. Mos. 1. 272; 2. 254; Praem. 165; παραίνεσις: Praem.
83; πεντάς (= first five commandments of Decalogue): Decal.
121; σοφία: Det. 117; cf. Post. C. 138; πλοῦτος: Post. C. 139;
πόμα: Som. 2. 248; πράγματα: Her. 1; πρόνοια: Conf. 115;
Mut. 25; V. Mos. 1. 162; Flacc. 125; σπέρματα: Cher. 46 (re
Leah); Post. C. 170; Mut. 134 (re Tamar); V. Mos. 1. 279 (re
Israel); σποραί: Abr. 101?; σπόρος: Praem. 160?; συμμαχία:
Som. 1. 227; τέχνη: Spec. Leg. 1. 266; τροφή: Sacr. 86;
(cont.)

Derivatively, the words spoken by God, and therefore the utterances, commands, precepts of the Law, specific passages of Scripture, and the Torah as a whole are called θεῖος.[341] The Spirit of God of Gen. 6:3 is πνεῦμα θεῖον.[342] God's "breath" or "spirit" which He breathed into earthly man (i.e. as opposed to the "heavenly man" who was created first) is called the "divine breath" (πνεῦμα θεῖον),[343] as well as the Spirit who inspires prophecy,[344] and initiates the Human-Divine encounter;[345] the composition of νοῦς is also said to be πνεῦμα θεῖον.[346]

The Logos, since it is the supreme emanation from God, the Existent One, is constantly referred to as θεῖος.[347]

Det. 116; Cong. 100; ὑποσχέσεις: Her. 101; Mut. 54; Som. 1. 175; φροντίς: Abr. 70; φύσις: Abr. 144; φῶς: Her. 264; Som. 2. 74; χάρις: Immut. 5, 104; Ebr. 145; Cong. 96; χάριτες: Post. C. 42; χερσὶ θείαις (re creation of First Man): Opif. 148; Virt. 203; χορηγίαι: Som. 1. 186. Related to this is the use of θεῖος as "God-sent": κατοικωκή: Sacr. 62; κατοχή: Plant. 39; λόγος (= manna): Her. 79; cf. Sacr. 86; Det. 116; Cong. 100; τροφαί: Leg. All. 3. 152; 161?.

[341] ἐντολαί: Praem. 79; λόγος (= Scripture): Leg. All. 3. 8 (Num. 5:2; Deut. 23:2); 3. 217 (Gen. 17:15f.); Mut. 169; Virt. 108?; λόγοι: Leg. All. 3. 14; Conf. 59 (cf. Conf. 81; Migr. 129); Decal. 13; νομοθεσία: Cong. 120; V. Mos. 2. 51; νόμος: Opif. 143; Leg. All. 3. 167; Abr. 275; Jos. 174; Spec. Leg. 2. 129; 3. 137; νόμοι: V. Mos. 2. 12; Spec. Leg. 2. 163; ὁμολογία: Ebr. 39; παραίνεσις: Praem. 83; πρόσταγμα: Opif. 168; προστάγματα: Abr. 275; πρόσταξις: V. Mos. 1. 99; προστάξεις: V. Mos. 2. 60, 70; ῥήματα καὶ λόγοι: Migr. 80; σύνταξις: Fuga 139 (Ex. 16:16); χρησμός: Migr. 29, 66; χρησμοί: Fuga 21; Mut. 7 (Ex. 20:21); cf. Leg. All. 3. 142.

[342] Gig. 29; Immut. 2; cf. Gig. 47, "divine spirit of Wisdom" = God.

[343] Leg. All. 1. 33; Opif. 135 (2x); Plant. 18.

[344] Gig. 23 (Bezaleel, Ex. 31:2f.), 27, 28?, 29?, 53?, 55; Immut. 2?; Her. 265; Fuga 186; Jos. 116; V. Mos. 2. 265; Spec. Leg. 4. 49; Virt. 217; cf. Plant. 24, where νοῦς of ὁ σοφός is lifted up by πνεῦμα θεῖον.

[345] Gig. 28?, 53?, 55?; Plant. 24; Her. 57; Virt. 217.

[346] Her. 55; Spec. Leg. 4. 123; also cf. Opif. 135 (2x); Leg. All. 1. 33; Plant. 18.

[347] Opif. 20, 31, 36, 146; Leg. All. 3. 171, 208; Cher. 36?; Sacr. 66?; Det. 118; Immut. 176?, 180?, 182?; Plant. 10;

(cont.)

Wisdom, hypostatized, is referred to as "that divine spring"
(ἡ θεία πηγή).[348] The other heavenly beings,[349] since they are
θεοί, are understandably called θεῖοι; this is true of
"angels,"[350] the stars, who are "mind throughout,"[351] the
"potencies,"[352] and the heavenly beings (bodies?) in general.[353]
Philo can speak of a "divine being" generically, as a being who
is neither man nor an inanimate thing, yet not ὁ θεός: he who
is not susceptible to getting drunk, Philo says, would be an

_____

Migr. 67, 83?, 130 (2x), 174; Her. 119, 188, 191, 225, 234, 235;
Fuga 5?, 13, 94, 97, 101, 108?, 137; Mut. 114, 116; Som. 1. 62,
65, 66, 68, 71, 85, 118 (2x), 119, 128, 147, 190, 215; 2. 242,
245, 247; Abr. 244?; Other instances where λόγος is θεῖος, but
in what appears to be a less philosophical-technical sense
include: Post. C. 32, 122?, 129?; Immut. 134; Her. 79 (manna);
Mut. 114, 116; Som. 1. 118 (2x), 128; V. Mos. 2. 124.

[348]Post. C. 138; Her. 126, 127, 129, 199; Fuga 195;
Prob. 13; also Det. 117.

[349]Though in what sense they are to be regarded as
"beings" is disputed. Cf. WOLFSON, 1. 363ff. I am using the
term in the most general sense which it will allow to include
any entity which exists between God and the earth, whether this
is conceived spatially or philosophically. The imprecision is
Philonic.

[350]Som. 1. 148; Fuga 5; Abr. 107, 115; Conf. 28; cf.
Som. 1. 140f.; also 1. 190; Cher. 3; also Cher. 23?.

[351]Gig. 8; Aet. 47; cf. Plant. 12; Opif. 73, 144; Som.
1. 135.

[352]Her. 312; Spec. Leg. 1. 209.

[353]In fact, in a number of passages, θεῖος is probably
best translated as "heavenly," in the sense of "belonging to
the heavens," either to apply to an entity in that realm or
stemming from that realm. Thus, ἀγάλματα: Opif. 55; Abr. 159;
ἄθροισμα (= the "divine assemblage" of Deut. 32:1): Virt. 73;
ἀρετή (sent from heaven): Her. 112?; περίοδοι (of planetary
movements): Migr. 64; στράτευμα (of the planets, heavens,
etc.): Conf. 174; στρατόπεδον: Ebr. 143; Decal. 104; στρατός:
Som. 2. 119; Also, σύλλογος: Post. C. 177?; φύσεις (=heavenly
beings): Leg. All. 2. 23; Conf. 154; also Cher. 41; Immut.
151; Conf. 133, 154; Her. 176; Mut. 219?; Abr. 115; Aet. 47;
also cf. Decal. 104, where planets are said to share in the
divine φύσις; χορεία: Cher. 23; in Migr. 184 heavenly bodies
are said to have a diviner portion (μοῖρα); also, Abr. 162
speaks of θεία οὐσία of heaven; also Opif. 45. Those passages
where he refers to χορὸς θεῖος belong together: Leg. All. 1.
61; 3. 7, 242; Ebr. 31; Her. 241; Fuga 62, 74; Spec. Leg.
2. 249 and Prob. 13 (= Phaedr. 247a).

"inanimate thing or a divine being, certainly not a man"
(ἄψυχόν ἐστιν ἢ θεῖον, ἄνθρωπος δὲ οὐκ ἂν εἴη τὸ παράπαν).[354]

This brings us to another category, those passages where
θεῖος is used derivatively to mean "inspired,"[355] "holy" or
"sacred,"[356] "extraordinary" or "excellent."[357] At this stage
the word tends to shade off into a rather banal usage where it
has lost its specificity for the most part. Philo often talks
of two categories of things as "divine and human" (τὰ θεῖα καὶ
τὰ ἀνθρώπινα)[358] simply as a convenient way of categorizing;
similarly, θεῖος can function as an antonym of ἀνθρώπειος.[359]

But there still remains a large group of passages which
do not easily fit into any of the categories mentioned so far.
Although they vary considerably as to their subject matter,
many of them have in common a use of θεῖος which roughly
corresponds to "incorporeal," "a-somatic," "immortal."[360]

---

[354]Plant. 177.

[355]Mut. 169, λόγος ... καὶ χρησμός ἐστι θεῖος ...; Leg.
All. 3. 14, διὰ λόγων θεῖων (of Moses); Virt. 108?; Fuga 21?,
χρησμοί; Mut. 7?, χρησμοί.

[356]ἄγαλμα: Spec. Leg. 1. 23; βωμός: Sacr. 138;
λειτουργία: Virt. 54; ὄργανον: V. Mos. 2. 103; ὄργια: Sacr.
60; Fuga 85; ὄρος (= Sinai): Leg. All. 3. 142; περίβολοι:
Abr. 128; πόμα: Som. 2. 248?; σύλλογος: Leg. All. 3. 81;
Post. C. 177; τελεταί: Cher. 42; Praem. 121; τόπος: Som. 1.
127?; cf. χορός references, note 353.

[357]Cf. Aet. 112?, κόσμος is θεῖος in its size; V.
Contemp. 67; cf. V. Mos. 2. 12; Plant. 177, ὁ σοφός, immune
to drunkenness.

[358]Cf. Spec. Leg. 2. 231.

[359]As in Som. 2. 291; cf. V. Mos. 1. 27.

[360]ἀγάλματα: Cher. 93; Abr. 159; ἀγέλη: Mut. 105;
ἀνατολαί: Leg. All. 1. 61; ἀπόσπασμα (ἡ ψυχή): Leg. All.
3. 161; ἀπόσπασμα (νοῦς): Som. 1. 34; ἀρετή: Her. 179; Som.
2. 277; ἀρεταί: Agr. 119; Migr. 158; V. Mos. 2. 189; Prob. 74;
V. Contemp. 26; ἀρετῶν αὐγαί: Som. 1. 84; βίος: Ebr. 100;
βλάστημα: Migr. 140; Som. 2. 173; βλαστήματα: Cong. 57; γένη
(opp. φθαρτός): Leg. All. 2. 95; γένος: Som. 1. 256; γένος:
Fuga 168; γένος: Her. 183ff.; τὰ θεῖα (opp. τὰ θνητὰ γένη):
Leg. All. 1. 16; τὸ δέκατον: Cong. 106; δύναμις: Det. 83;
ἐννοήματα: Immut. 120; ἐπίπνοιαι: Som. 1. 129; ἐπιστήμη:
Her. 128; ἐπιστῆμαι: Her. 132; θεάματα καὶ ἀκούσματα: Gig.
31; τὸ καλόν: Sacr. 63; κάλλη: V. Mos. 1. 190; κατασκευή:
Plant. 14; Conf. 108, 122; κρατήρ: Som. 2. 190; λογισμός:
(cont.)

Although it would be most interesting, and probably most revealing, to investigate closely each of the uses of θεῖος in this last catch-all category, it is not necessary at this point to find a pigeon-hole for every use, although in the next section we shall examine some of these passages. But, several observations can be made before proceeding further:

(1) Out of these approximately 400 occurrences of θεῖος, it is conjoined with ἀνήρ once; with ἄνθρωπος not at all. It is never applied to a named individual attributively, and is rarely used of historical persons at all, the major exception being προφήτης in V. Mos. 2. 188. One important passage, Qu. Ex. 2. 54, where Philo refers to "the divine and holy Moses," was not considered simply because it is one of those instances where only the Armenian is preserved.[361] Generally, when it is used with reference to a person, either specifically, such as the high priest in Her. 84, or Moses in V. Mos. 1. 27, or generally in referring to man, it is in reference to νοῦς/ψυχή. No instance was discovered where Philo applies the term to man, thought of as a combination of σῶμα and ψυχή; moreover, no instance was discovered where the term is applied to σῶμα.

(2) Arising out of the last point is a second observation. The term is rarely, if ever, applied to things in the corporeal world. Apart from those instances where it seems to mean "holy" or "sacred" as when applied to the tabernacle or altar, etc., it is difficult to find examples where Philo uses the term in reference to objects or entities in κόσμος αἰσθητός.

(3) The great variety of shades of meaning cannot be

Opif. 67; Post. C. 184; λόγοι: Post. C. 18, 89; μέθη: Leg. All. 3. 82; μοῖρα: Opif. 84; Migr. 46; Her. 64; Mut. 185; νοῦς (high priest): Her. 84; (Moses): V. Mos. 1. 27; ὄργανον: Virt. 74; ὁ κατὰ διάνοιαν ὀφθαλμός: Conf. 100; παιδιὰ τῆς ψυχῆς: Plant. 169; παιδιαί: Cher. 8; παράδεισος (Eden-noetic): Opif. 153; περίοδοι: Her. 88; πράγματα: Her. 63; προφήτης: V. Mos. 2. 188; σκηνή: Det. 160; στρατός (of virtues): Agr. 79; φαντασία: Mut. 3; φέγγος τῆς ἀρετῆς: Leg. All. 1. 18; φύσις: Spec. Leg. 1. 116, 269; 2. 225 (2x); 3. 178; φύσεις: Opif. 144; Leg. All. 2. 10; Immut. 46; Fuga 162, 163; ζῷα (opp. θνητός): Agr. 51; φῶς: Leg. All. 1. 17; Migr. 39; Som. 2. 74; χαρακτήρ: Virt. 52; ψυχή: Cher. 93; Det. 90; also cf. Sacr. 109; Prob. 24.

[361]Cf. further discussion below, p. 195.

overlooked, a factor which must be taken into consideration in determining the meaning of _theios_ _aner_ and deciding whether it is a _terminus_ _technicus_. We have noticed in addition to the standard categories of uses a large group of passages which are extremely difficult to classify under the conventional meanings. As we shall see later, many of them occur in allegorical expositions or in contexts where the complexities of Philo's philosophical thought are being expounded.

(3) _Terminus_ _Technicus_?

As noted earlier, direct application of the expression _theios_ _aner_ to Moses does not occur in Philo as it does in Josephus _Ant_. 3. 180. But whereas it remained impossible to determine for sure whether Josephus uses _theios_ _aner_ in any technical sense, simply because it is a _hapax_ _legomenon_, this is not the case with Philo, who uses the expression in at least two generally overlooked passages in _De_ _Providentia_: 2. 39 and 2. 48.[362]

_De_ _Providentia_ is a treatise from Philo's younger days[363] set in the form of a dialogue between Philo and one Alexander, presumably Tiberius Julius Alexander, his nephew, who, Josephus tells us rather ruefully, "did not remain (true) to the customs of his fathers."[364] In the dialogue Philo affirms that the world is governed by Providence, while Alexander ventilates his doubts by playing the _advocatus_ _diaboli_. The flavor of the dialogue is Greek throughout; there is not a single allusion to the Old Testament, nor any mention of Moses, and as Colson remarks, "the one and only fact which suggests that the writer is a Jew is the personal allusion to his visit

---

[362]Mentioned neither by BIELER nor GOODENOUGH, _Light_. ZELLER, _Philosophie_, 390: 4, and WOLFSON 1. 100: 67, mention _Prov_. 2. 48, but as yet I have not seen 2. 39 adduced in this connection. (The system of numeration is that found in _Werke_. Since both passages occur in sections not preserved by Eusebius, _Praep_. _Evang_. VII & VIII, they are omitted in the Loeb ed.)

[363]Cf. L. FRÜCHTEL, Introduction, in _Werke_ 7. 269; according to WOLFSON, 1. 87, it belongs to a group of four treatises which are devoted to special philosophical problems. Cf. note 236. Cf., however, NOCK, _Essays_, 2. 561f.

[364]_Ant_. 20. 100.

to Jerusalem via Ascalon (par. 64)."[365] In the course of the
dialogue the expression "divine men" is mentioned twice, once
in a speech by Alexander, once in a speech by Philo. In the
course of his objections to a belief in Providence, Alexander
says:

> Furum enim Mercurius refugium est tutissimum,
> adulterorum Mars; omnium vero dux Juppiter: et
> omnes sunt mendaces; quandoquidem vera de Diis
> Poëtarum nemo dicit: quia semper qui consimiles
> perpetrant injurias, apologiae loco eadem referunt
> de supremo quoque atque optimo. Non ita tamen
> Xenophanes, aut Parmenides, aut Empedocles, sive
> alii, quicumque theologi a poësi capti sunt divini
> viri, sed potius theoriam naturae jucunde sibi
> accommodantes, et vitam omnem ad pietatem laudemque
> Deorum dedicantes, optimi quidem viri comperti sunt,
> poëtae tamen non felices: quos oportebat divinitus
> spiritum sortiri, gratiamque de caelo, metrum,
> carmen, digitumque caelestem ac divinum, ut poëmata
> vera relinquerent velut prototypum libri perfectum:
> et pulchrum cunctis exemplar (sive indicium,
> argumentum).[366]

> And certainly, Mercury is the safest refuge of
> thieves, and Mars of adulterers; the leader of them
> all is Jupiter; and they are all liars; seeing that
> none of the poets tells the truth about the gods,
> for those who commit similar offences always, by
> way of self-defense, recount the same also of the
> highest and best. Not so, however, [is it with]
> Xenophanes, or Parmenides, or Empedocles, or any
> other theologians, that is, divine men, who are
> captivated by poetry,[367] but rather they joyfully
> accommodate to themselves a theory of nature; and,
> those who dedicate all their life to the worship
> and praise of the gods are discovered to be the
> best men, but not happy poets. It was they who
> ought to attain a spirit in a divine way, and favor
> from heaven, metre, song, and rhythm both heavenly
> and divine, in order that they might leave behind
> true poetry as a perfect prototype of a book, and a
> beautiful model to all men (or mark, argument).

---

[365] COLSON (Loeb) 9. 448; cf. LEISEGANG, art. "Philon,"
PWRE 20.1 (1941) 8f.; also L. FRÜCHTEL, Introduction in Werke
7. 269. Not surprisingly, the authenticity has been questioned,
but not seriously after P. WENDLAND, Philos Schrift über die
Vorsehung (Berlin, 1892) established it as genuinely Philonic.

[366] Prov. 2. 39 = Aucher p. 74, lines 24ff.

[367] Compare L. FRÜCHTEL (Werke) 7. 343, "Nicht ebenso
machen es Xenophanes, Parmenides, Empedokles oder andere von
der Poesie ergriffene göttliche Männer, die Theologen sind ..."

After a brief interchange, Philo, in his reply, says:

> Age, interim ponamus inter nos, universum ingenitum
> ac sempiternum, juxta illud quod suggerit sermo
> celeberrimorum philosophantium, sicut conscribunt
> Parmenides, Empedocles, Zeno, Cleanthes, aliique
> divi homines, ac velut verus quidam proprieque
> sacer coetus. Atqui ex ingenita materia, quid
> miramur, si pars aliqua generetur, aut corrumpatur,
> partim per Providentiam Dei, partim ob rerum
> ordinem?[368]

> Well then! Let us, for the moment, assume between
> ourselves that the universe is uncreated and eternal,
> as the language of the more celebrated of those who
> philosophize suggests, such as Parmenides, Empedocles,
> Zeno, Cleanthes, and other divine men, a company, so
> to speak, true and properly sacred.[369] And yet, of
> the uncreated matter, we wonder whether some part is
> begotten or some part destroyed, partly through God's
> providence, partly because of the ordinary course of
> events?

Between these two exchanges there occurs yet another statement
where Philo expresses his reservations about the possibility of
man's becoming a god:

> At quare Empedocles, Parmenides, Xenophanes,
> aemulatorque istorum chorus non sortiti sunt
> spiritum Musarum, quum theologiam exercuerunt?
> Ideo scilicet, o vir optime, quia non decebat
> hominem Deum esse, quasi omnia integre in se
> condentem, sed remanere hominem participem generis
> humani, cui error et deliquium cognata sunt.
> Oportebat itaque eos ultimo loco in veri investi-
> gatione contentos esse: ad illud autem, ad quod
> non erant ex natura destinati, minime satagere
> pervenire.[370]

> But, why did not Empedocles, Parmenides, Xenophanes,
> and that group imitating them obtain the spirit of
> the Muses when they practised theology? Because,
> obviously, O excellent man, it was not fitting for
> man to be God, as if containing all things within
> himself; but (it was fitting) for him to remain man
> sharing in the human race to which error and trans-
> gression are inborn. And so, it was necessary for

---

[368]Prov. 2. 48 = Aucher p. 79, lines 14ff.

[369]Compare FRÜCHTEL (Werke) 7. 347, "Wohlan, wollen wir
vorderhand unter uns annehmen, das Weltall sei ungeworden und
ewig, entsprechend jener Behauptung, die uns die Lehre der
hervorragendsten Philosophen an die Hand gibt, wie sie von
Parmenides, Empedokles, Zenon und Kleanthes und anderen göttlichen Menschen, einer geradezu wahrhaften und in eigentlichem
Sinn heiligen Versammlung, niedergeschrieben ist."

[370]Prov. 2. 42 = Aucher p. 76, lines 26ff.

them to be content, in the last analysis, in their
investigation of the truth; however, least capable
of arriving at that level to which they were not
destined by nature to attain.

In spite of these reservations, it is undeniable that the use
of "divine men" in these dialogues reflects Philo's familiarity
with a more technical use of the expression as it was known
from Greek authors, such as that found in Dio Chrysostom, Orat.
33. 4, when θεῖος ἄνθρωπος is used as a term to mean
"philosophers":

> Well then, let me state my own suspicions. You
> seem to me to have listened frequently to
> marvellous men (θείων ἀνθρώπων), who claim to
> know all things, and regarding all things to be
> able to tell how they have been appointed and
> what their nature is, their repertoire including,
> not only human beings and demigods, but gods, yes,
> and even the earth, the sky, the sea, the sun and
> moon and other stars--in fact the entire universe--
> and also the processes of corruption of generation
> and ten thousand other things.[371]

And, in fact, it is precisely this indisputable familiarity by
Philo with Greek authors, particularly Plato, that makes his
infrequent use of the expression all the more striking.
Philo's familiarity with Plato's writings cannot reasonably be
disputed.[372] Yet when we turn to those writings, we not only

---

[371]Trans. J. W. Cohoon (Loeb).

[372]As evidenced by the proverb "current among the
Greeks," cited by Jerome, De viris Illustribus, ch. 11, ἢ
Πλάτων φιλωνίζει ἢ Φίλων πλατωνίζει, cited by BILLINGS,
Platonism, 2. The Index to Werke, 7. 391, lists the following
quotations or allusions to Plato (* = Plato mentioned by name):
Eryxias 397e: Plant. 171; Leg. 770a: Her. 307; Menexenus
238a: Opif. 133*; Phaedr. 236d: Spec. Leg. 2. 2; Phaedr.
245a: Prov. 2. 43*; Phaedr. 247a: Spec. Leg. 2. 249; Prob.
13*; Phaedr. 259c: Prob. 8; V. Contemp. 35; Resp. 473d: V.
Mos. 2. 2; Theaet. 176a: Fuga 63*; Theaet. 176c: Fuga 82;
Theaet. 191c: Her. 181; Tim. 24e: Aet. 141*; Tim. 25c-d:
Aet. 141*; Tim. 28b-c: Prov. 1. 21*; Tim. 29a: Plant. 131;
Tim. 29b: Prov. 1. 21*; Tim. 29e: Opif. 21; Tim. 32cff.:
Aet. 25*; Tim. 33b: Prov. 2. 56*; Tim. 33c-d: Aet. 38*; Tim.
37e: Aet. 52*; Tim. 38b: Prov. 1. 20*; Tim. 41a: Aet. 13*;
Her. 246 (Decal. 58); Tim. 49a: Ebr. 61; Tim. 50d: Ebr. 61;
Tim. 75d: Opif. 119*; Tim. 90a: Plant. 17 (Det. 84f.);
Phaedr. 91c; Crito 46b; V. Arist. vulg. 9: cf. Prov. 2. 52*;
also, COLSON (Loeb), 9. 232:a and 521:59, mentions: Symp.
206c?: Aet. 69; Symp. 209: V. Contemp. 68. Cf. also V.
Contemp. 57ff. (Plato and Xenophon); Prov. 2. 42*; Prov. 1.
21*; Spec. 1. 48. Cf. esp. BILLINGS, Platonism, esp. 88ff. on
(cont.)

discover θεῖος to be one of Plato's favorite words[373] just as it is in Philo, but we also discover his willingness to attach it to named individuals, past and present, including Homer,[374] Pindar (along with many of the other poets),[375] Socrates,[376] Tyrtaeus;[377] participants in his dialogues including Ion,[378] Phaedrus,[379] Clinias;[380] the Platonic philosopher in the technical sense,[381] a pupil aspiring to the life of a philosopher,[382] lawgivers,[383] guardians of the ideal city-state,[384] man as compared with animals;[385] twice to refer to men who are in some way more than human.[386]

Moreover, _theios aner/theios anthropos_, though the two words are not always juxtaposed in this exact form (an important point to remember) frequently occur: three times _theios anthropos_ is a general reference to humanity, or at least three

---

Plato's influence upon Philo's phraseology; on the larger question of the influence of philosophical thought on Philo, cf. DANIÉLOU, 16, 57ff., who cites _Spec. Leg._ 3. 1-2 to illustrate the thoroughly Platonic flavor found in some passages in Philo; cf. also BRÉHIER, 14ff., esp. 17; also POHLENZ, "Philon," 478, "Von den Originalwerken der grossen Philosophen hat er allerdings wohl nur die wichtigsten Dialoge Platos gründlich studiert."

[373]F. AST, _Lexicon platonicum sive Vocum platonicarum Index_, 3 vols. (Leipzig, 1835-38); cf. also R. MUGNIER, _Le sens du mot_ θεῖος _chez Platon_ (Paris, 1930); cf. below, note 414.

[374]_Ion_ 530b; _Phaedo_ 94e. By contrast, Philo, so far as I have been able to find, never calls Homer θεῖος, although he can speak of him in superlative tones: _Conf._ 4, ὁ μέγιστος καὶ δοκιμώτατος τῶν ποιητῶν ... φησι; _Qu. Gen._ 4. 2, "clever and considerably learned;" cf. also _Abr._ 10; _Leg. ad Gaium_ 80; _V. Contemp._ 17ff.; _Prob._ 31; _V. Mos._ 1. 61; _Jos._ 2.

[375]_Meno_ 81b.

[376]_Phaedr._ 238c; _contra_ TIEDE, 30, "Plato does not refer to Socrates nor himself as θεῖος ..."

[377]_Leg._ 1. 629c.   [378]_Ion_ 542b.

[379]_Phaedr._ 234d, 242a.   [380]_Leg._ 1. 626c.

[381]_Resp._ 6. 500c-d; _Soph._ 216b-c.

[382]_Epis._ 7. 340c.   [383]_Leg._ 4. 704d.

[384]_Resp._ 7. 540c.   [385]_Polit._ 271e.

[386]_Leg._ 2. 657a; _Resp._ 5. 469a.

passages imply that mankind can become θεῖος;[387] twice it has a more specific connotation, although exactly what that connotation is, is not clear.[388] Theios aner (again, not always in this exact form) occurs twelve times; it is used with reference to Prodicus,[389] Ion,[390] Simonides,[391] Epimenides,[392] an Elean stranger,[393] prophets,[394] good men,[395] "the oldest and wisest men,"[396] poets,[397] heroes and demigods,[398] once, possibly, of a hero,[399] and "godlike" men as opposed to other men.[400]

Philo's divergence from Plato with regard to his use of θεῖος and theios aner should also be viewed against the background of his use of θεῖος to render the genitival τοῦ θεοῦ, or similar constructions. Numerous instances can be cited where Philo employs θεῖος as a substitute for the genitival τοῦ θεοῦ.[401] This can be seen, first, in his use of the LXX, as when τὰς ἐντολὰς κυρίου τοῦ θεοῦ ὑμῶν[402] becomes θείας ἐντολάς;[403] ἐκκλησίαν κυρίου[404] becomes ἐκκλησία θεία;[405] νόμος μου (i.e. God)[406] becomes θεῖος νόμος;[407] τὰς ἐντολάς μου καὶ τὰ δικαιώματά μου (of God)[408] becomes θεῖος νόμος καὶ θεῖα πρόσταγμα;[409] or, even when merely varying his own style

---

[387]Resp. 2. 383c; 6. 500c-d; Leg. 7. 818c.

[388]Phileb. 18b; Leg. 12. 951b.

[389]Protag. 315e. [390]Ion 542a-b.

[391]Resp. 1. 331e. [392]Leg. 1. 642d.

[393]Soph. 216b. [394]Meno 99c.

[395]Meno 99d. [396]Leg. 2. 666d; cf. 665a.

[397]Leg. 7. 817a. [398]Critias 110c.

[399]Leg. 1. 630e (textual variant).

[400]Epis. 2. 311d.

[401]Cf. discussion above, pp. 177ff., esp. note 340.

[402]Deut. 11:26. [403]Praem. 79.

[404]Deut. 23:2. [405]Conf. 144.

[406]Ex. 16:4. [407]Leg. All. 3. 167.

[408]Gen. 26:5. [409]Abr. 275.

as when ὁ θεοῦ λόγος becomes θεῖος λόγος.[410] But, given this propensity, it seems never to occur to Philo to turn ἄνθρωπος θεοῦ into θεῖος ἄνθρωπος;[411] on the contrary, ἄνθρωπος θεοῦ becomes a special means for him to underscore the humanity of Moses vis à vis God.[412]

We are faced, therefore, with this situation: Philo knows the term as used by Greek authors; he uses it in what was evidently a conventional sense to refer to Empedocles, Epimenides, Zeno, Cleanthes;[413] he uses the expression once to refer to a potentially sinless (human) being; but, never, so far as I can determine, does he apply the term to Moses, nor to any of Israel's heroes; in fact, he seems consciously and deliberately to avoid it.

(4) Philosophical Role of θεῖος.

When we begin to look for possible explanations for this seemingly deliberate refusal to use the expression theios aner as well as the refusal to apply θεῖος to named individuals, even to individuals at all--a refusal noticed, but ignored, by Windisch--, the most promising answer has been made possible by the research of J. van Camp and P. Canart, whose detailed examination of θεῖος in the writings of Plato was prompted by his variegated use of the term as well as the integral role which it plays in his thought.[414] After examining each usage in its own context and fitting it into what was felt to be the proper stage of the development of Plato's thought, they conclude that the word is used in three senses, which more or less correspond to the ones we have noticed in both Josephus and

---

[410] Leg. All. 3. 171.

[411] Cf. Gig. 60, 61, 62, 63; Her. 57; Immut. 139; Conf. 41; Mut. 24, 26, 125.

[412] Mut. 125, 128.

[413] That he is using the term conventionally is seen by the fact that in the same context where he uses the term twice, he explicitly denies the possibility of a man's becoming a god; he could thus use "divine man" without understanding it as an affirmation of the divinity of the man so designated.

[414] J. VAN CAMP & P. CANART, Le sens du mot θεῖος chez Platon (Louvain, 1956). A useful table of references is provided in MUGNIER (cf. note 373).

Philo.

(1) The popular religious sense, designated as "étymologique" and "mythologique," roughly meaning "pertaining to God or the gods":

> La signification religieuse de theios se rattache directement a l'étymologie: theios désigne ce qui se rapport aux dieux. Sens parfaitement clair, mais dont il est impossible de rien conclure: quoi de plus commun que les dieux dans le langage de la Grèce du IVᵉ siècle?[415] . . . . Le sens étymologique banal ou mythologique renvoie aux divinités populaires.[416]

(2) The hyperbolic or metaphorical sense:

> Quant au sens métaphorique de theios, il peut se rattacher indirectement à l'étymologie: il marque une supériorité quelconque avec une nuance d'excès ou d'admiration (d'où l'appellation: sens "hyperbolique" ou "emphatique" ...)[417]

In this sense θεῖος means "superior," "extraordinary," "wonderful," "more than human."

(3) In the sense of "inspired":

> Au point de départ, c'est un cas particulier du sens étymologique. L'homme inspiré est "divin" parce que possédé par le dieu. Nulle part, pensons-nous, Platon n'approfondit ce thème dans le sens religieux, ou ne vise à formuler une théorie philosophique de l'inspiration. Constamment, d'ailleurs, la nature de la divinité inspiratrice reste dans la pénombre. A ce point de vue, le sens de theios inspiré reste un sens populaire, traditionnel.[418]

This use of θεῖος is closely related with ἔνθεος, and is frequently used in connection with one of Plato's favorite expressions, θεία μοῖρα, as well as with θεία δύναμις.

The most significant finding of their research, however, is establishing that Plato capitalizes upon the fluidity of the term, using it to his advantage as his thought becomes more highly developed in the later dialogues where the theory of Ideas takes more definite shape and where, they argue convincingly,[419] θεῖος comes to play a crucial philosophical role

---

[415] VAN CAMP & CANART, 413. [416] Ibid., 414.

[417] Ibid., 413. [418] Ibid., 414.

[419] Cf. reviews by D. J. ALLAN, Classical Review N.S. 9 (1959) 170-71; H. KOLLER, Gnomon 29 (1957) 466-68; W. J. VERDENIUS, Mnemosyne 14 (1961) 51-4; O. GIGON, Museum Helveticum 17 (1960) 44.

functioning in dialectical fashion as a type of connecting link
between the world of forms and the world of sense:

> En d'autres termes, si l'on recherche le contenu
> philosophique de theios, l'on s'apercoit qu'il est
> inséparable du mouvement de la pensée. Theios n'a
> pas de contenu philosophique, mais plutôt un rôle
> philosophique . . . . L'étude a montré que le
> qualificatif theios, appliqué à des réalités
> d'intérêt philosophique, n'apporte jamais à la
> définition de celles-ci un complément indispensable.
> Il est impossible de lui assigner un contenu précis
> et technique. Mais, grâce à son imprécision, à sa
> souplesse même, il évoque à l'esprit d'un lecteur
> moyen une atmosphere et un niveau. L'atmosphère
> est celle que suggère le theios religieux défini
> plus haut: il confère aux réalités philosophiques
> qu'il détermine le prestiqe qui entourait, pour un
> homme normal, la sphère du divin.[420] . . . . Mais,
> nous l'avons vu, si theios n'a pas de contenu
> philosophique, il joue un rôle philosophique au
> sein du procédé platonicien de la transposition.[421]

It is precisely this emergent meaning that we saw
occurring in several of the passages in Philo which we examined,
where θεῖος is inadequately translated by the standard meanings
such as "divine," "heavenly," "inspired," or "extraordinary,"
but instead more nearly approximates "incorporeal" or
"noumenal."[422] Philo's discourse on the "Tenth," in Cong. 105-
6 is most revealing in this respect, for there θεῖος is
directly equated with νοητός, and both are contrasted with
αἰσθητός, as seen in the following diagram illustrating his
analysis:

---

[420]VAN CAMP & CANART, 416. This observation was made
much earlier by WINDISCH, 27ff.

[421]VAN CAMP & CANART, 419.

[422]WOLFSON 1. 365, refers to this "special sense" of
θεῖος in discussing Opif. 144, where it seems to mean "imperishable," as in Leg. All. 2. 95.

Not only does this vertical representation of reality remind us
of Plato's analogy of the Line, but this use of θεῖος parallels
Plato's use of the term as applicable to ἰδέαι. It will be
immediately noticed, however, that many of the components of
the "nine parts" constituting ὁ κόσμος are elsewhere called
θεῖος by Philo, such as the stars,[423] as well as other heavenly
beings.[424] On the surface, this would seem to be contradictory,
since obviously both κόσμος αἰσθητός and κόσμος νοητός cannot
be θεῖος in the same sense. But, if θεῖος plays a philosophical role in Philo very much as it does in Plato, whereby at
times it can be applied to the intelligible world while at
other times to the sensible world, then its usage makes sense.
Further examination of Philo's use of θεῖος, particularly in
the group of passages mentioned in note 360, reveals that this
is precisely the role it plays in Philo. Many of the bridges
Philo builds between ὁ θεός and the created order are worked
out in terms of θεῖος terminology. His epistemology, for
example, focuses upon the νοῦς, which is θεῖος and is the
receptacle which is capable of perceiving ἔννοιαι from ὁ
θεός.[425] It will also be recalled that were it not for σῶμα,
the νοῦς would be capable of perfectly perceiving ὁ θεός; their
common incorporeality is the means of communication between
them. His anthropology directly hinges upon his cardinal
belief that the νοῦς is ἀπόσπασμα θεῖον, because of its having
been stamped with the εἰκὼν θεία.[426] Similarly, the Logos,
being θεῖος, is the prototype for the εἰκὼν θεία. In each of
these instances θεῖος plays the philosophical role of designating those entities within the chasm separating ὁ θεός and the
created order, and in each instance can appropriately be
rendered "incorporeal." Accordingly, it becomes extremely useful when Philo is discussing the οὐσία of a given entity, such
as τὸ ἡγεμονικόν, the rational part of the soul. In contrast
to the irrational part, whose οὐσία is "blood," and therefore
corporeal, the rational part has θεῖον πνεῦμα as its οὐσία, i.e.
an incorporeal οὐσία, partaking of the same οὐσία as the κόσμος

---

[423]Cf. Aet. 47.   [424]Cf. note 353 above.

[425]Cf. discussion of Migr. 84 above, pp. 142ff.

[426]Cf. BRÉHIER, 541f.; cf. Leg. All. 3. 161; Mut. 223.

νοητός, and ultimately of God. Also, the οὐσία of heavenly
beings, which are incorporeal, are described in terms of their
having a "diviner constitution."[427] It is hardly surprising,
then, to discover that it is virtually impossible to find
instances in Philo where θεῖος is used of anything corporeal,
the only apparent exceptions being Spec. Leg. 1. 23, where he
refers to a "divine image" (ἄγαλμα) in a sanctuary; Cong. 116,
where he mentions the "divine dwelling place" (ἐνδιαίτημα), the
tabernacle; Her. 216, the sacred candlesticks, a work of art
"approved and divine;" Leg. All. 3. 142, where Sinai is the
"holy mount" (θεῖον ὄρος); Agr. 51 where he lists land, water,
air and fire and all plants and animals ... whether "mortal or
divine." As mentioned above, the first four probably are to be
taken as "sacred;" the last instance is another case where
θεῖος is to be understood as "immortal;" by dividing animals
into "mortal and divine," he is probably distinguishing between
men, who possess θεῖον ἀπόσπασμα, and beasts, who do not.

A large number of instances turn out to be allegorically
understood realities: Mut. 105, "the divine herd" (ἀγέλη);
Leg. All. 1. 61, "divine sunrising" (ἀνατολαί, i.e. Eden,
understood noetically); Migr. 140, "divine sapling" (βλάστημα)
= Isaac; Cong. 57, "divine saplings," (βλαστήματα) = those
seeking virtue; Sacr. 138, "divine altar" (βωμός) of Abel; Som.
2. 190, "divine mixing bowl" (κρατήρ) which God fills with
virtue; Det. 152, "divine coinage" (τὸ θεῖον νόμισμα); V. Mos.
2. 103, "musical and divine instrument" (ὄργανον) harmonized by
the "sun;" Conf. 100, "divine eye" (ὀφθαλμός) of understanding;
Opif. 153, "divine Garden" = Eden in the ideal world; Som. 2.
248, "divine draught" (πόμα) mixed in a bowl; Cher. 46, "divine
seed" (σπέρματα) in Leah conceived virtue;[428] Ebr. 143, Samuel's
rank in the "divine army" (στρατόπεδον);[429] Som. 1. 127, "the
divine place" (τόπος) = location of Jacob's dream, which, as
seen from Som. 1. 161-64, 68, τόπος is not being understood as
a literal place; Sacr. 86, "divine food" (τροφή) =

---

[427]Plant. 14.

[428]Cf. Post. C. 170; Mut. 134; V. Mos. 1. 279; Abr. 101;
Praem. 160.

[429]Cf. Decal. 104; Agr. 79; Som. 2. 119.

manna;[430] Opif. 148, "divine hands" (χερσὶ θείαις).[431] The one
major exception is Philo's designation of the stars, which he
generally regards as incorporeal,[432] and thus θεῖος,[433] but
which in one passage are said to be corporeal.[434]

It is, of course, too much to expect to find invariable
patterns in Philo's usage of θεῖος. Because his writings span
several decades and cover a host of different subjects, we must
look for overall trends, while at the same time not overlooking
the exceptions, but nevertheless treating them as exceptions.
Given the diversity of usage of the term θεῖος in Philo, what
we fail to find is Philo ever applying θεῖος to σῶμα, and
especially to ἄνθρωπος, who was by definition, at least one-
half σῶμα (that is, earthly man), and this is the direction
toward which our analysis has been pointing.

(5) Summary and Conclusions.

Philo's mention of theios aner in Virt. 177 may very
well have been a use of the expression in the semi-technical
sense to refer to philosophers, as we found him using it in De
Providentia. But, there is no hint of this. Given Philo's
frequent use of θεῖος to mean "incorporeal" or "immortal," it
is also possible that he is thinking of a man whose νοῦς has
reached the vision of τὸ ὄν, but had that been the case he is
more likely to have spoken of a ψυχὴ θεία. Because of the
strong moralistic overtones, evidenced by the primacy of the
topic of sinlessness, and because the passage after all occurs
in a context where he is discussing the virtues, it seems
reasonable to suggest that Philo is being influenced by the
Stoic ideal of the Wise Man, who was regarded as incapable of
wrongdoing. At the same time, however, it was generally conceded that the Stoic Wise Man was an unattainable goal. Thus

---

[430]Cf. Det. 116; Cong. 100.

[431]Cf. Virt. 203.   [432]Opif. 73.

[433]WOLFSON, 1. 364:38, notes that COHN, Werke, attempts
to resolve the apparent contradiction by taking "such as the
stars" to refer to "the incorporeal and perceptible only by
mind." WOLFSON seems to accept Opif. 144 (as it stands) as
Philo's own view, viz. that stars had "bodies."

[434]Opif. 144.

when Philo looks for examples of "absolute sinlessness," which
is alone an attribute of God, he adduces the Stoic Wise Man,
perhaps half jestingly, as one who "perhaps" (τάχα) has reached
the goal. But, at the same time, it must be noted again, that
in this passage theios aner is not attached to Moses, at least
not explicitly.

Another passage, Qu. Ex. 2. 54, where Philo calls Moses
"holy and divine," must be regarded as an instance where θεῖος
(?) is directly applied to Moses, but since "divine and holy"
becomes something of a cliché, as when the Most Holy Place is
said to be "holy and truly divine,"[435] or when the Decalogue is
called the "holy and divine law,"[436] one wonders how far this
can be taken as an ascription of divinity to Moses.

Given the frequency of the term θεῖος in Philo, as well
as his highly creative use of it modelled after Plato, these
few stray references are conspicuous primarily because they are
exceptional rather than typical. Even though he knows the
expression theios aner in a seemingly semi-technical sense used
by the Greeks, he does not attach the term to Moses, nor to any
other of Israel's heroes. Even though he most likely knows of
Plato's frequent application of the term to named individuals,
historical persons, past and present, he but rarely applies
θεῖος to a person, in any sense. Even though he frequently
employs θεῖος for the genitival expression τοῦ θεοῦ, he never
transforms ἄνθρωπος θεοῦ into θεῖος ἄνθρωπος; rather, he uses
it to underscore Moses' humanity vis à vis God.

Philo never uses theios aner as a synonym for miracle-
worker, nor is miracle-working ever mentioned in the contexts
where theios aner occurs. Although he exercises considerable
freedom in reportraying Israel's heroes in terms of non-
Biblical models, such as the Stoic Wise Man, or the Cynic-Stoic
σοφός-βασιλεύς, he does not recast Moses, nor other Jewish
figures, into miracle-workers. In fact, as Tiede notices,[437]
he actually de-emphasizes Moses' role as miracle-worker as compared with the Biblical account. Although he constantly
employs the language of deification at various levels of

---

[435]Qu. Ex. 2. 91; cf. 2. 37; 2. 39.

[436]Cong. 120.   [437]TIEDE, 134ff.

interpretation and exposition, he exhibits no corresponding
tendency to accent the miraculous in those same passages. If
our interpretation of V. Mos. 1. 156 is correct, I have not
discovered a single instance where reference to miracle-working,
either in reference to Moses, to any specific person, or to man
in general, is adduced as a means of authenticating a claim to
divinity, or even mentioned in connection with the language of
deification.

In attempting to explain why Philo seems deliberately to
avoid the use of theios aner, and the application of θεῖος to
individuals, especially in its literal sense, we have argued
that both his anthropological and metaphysical dualism constitute the root causes. His unswerving conviction that there is
a vast chasm between Creator and creature as well as his view
of man as composed of σῶμα/ψυχή, combined with his modified
Platonic metaphysical view of the world, often conceived of
vertically, but always in terms of the κόσμος νοητός/κόσμος
αἰσθητός schema, all of which was formulated in terms of
Biblical theology derived from the Greek Scriptures, made it
impossible for him to conceive of Moses, or any other human
being as θεῖος in any real, concrete sense of the term. For
Philo ever to have conceded that man, conceived of as a combination of σῶμα and ψυχή/νοῦς, the man of flesh and blood who
walks upon the earth and inhabits the sensible world, and
therefore enextricably bound with somatic existence, is θεῖος
in anything but the most derivative sense of the term would
have meant the total collapse of his philosophical and theological system. Deification, in Philo, takes place only insofar
as detachment from the sensible world is possible, whether it
has to do with the Wise Man who rules every fool, the Divine-
Human encounter, the Human-Divine encounter, or the high priest
who enters the Most Holy Place.

Philo's tendency to overstate cannot be denied. His
language of praise, particularly of Moses, is often excessive.
There are instances where he uses language of deification in
reference to Moses, but there are as many references where he
uses the same language of man in general. Even if it could be
shown that Philo in Virt. 177 calls Moses theios aner, and even
if it could be shown that by the expression he means divine man

in the literal sense of the term, could it be claimed, on the basis of this _single_ reference amidst _forty-six_ treatises (in the Loeb series) that Philo exhibits a _tendency_ to deify Israel's heroes?

Before we can speak of the deification of Israel's heroes in Philo, therefore, we must at least do so in terms of his own thought. The complexities and intricacies of his thought have been severely obscured and distorted by uncritically paralleling his use of θεῖος and related language of deification with the claims of other figures of the Hellenistic world, such as Empedocles or Apollonius of Tyana. On the basis of the foregoing analysis of his use of such language, especially with its focus upon the νοῦς/ψυχή, it is untenable simply to treat the claims of Empedocles and Apollonius together with Philo's statements about Moses without noticing, and respecting, the vast difference between the respective points of view. To wrench passages from their context in Philo and lift them from his complex and often incoherent system of thought only serves to complicate and distort an already complicated picture, and, above all, results in attributing to Philo convictions and beliefs at which he would have been appalled. The irregularities in his thought indeed must remain; they cannot and should not be harmonized by tendentious exegesis. Yet, passages must be seen and understood in their own context, and his statements about theios aner, Moses, and deification--supposed, claimed, or real--must be understood and stated, first, in terms of his own system of thought, and, second, in terms true to that system of thought. His was a system of thought in which the impossibility of a somatic, corporeal human being's becoming incorporeal, and therefore divine, in this life was a conviction which he held from his youth until his old age, and which seems to have been hardened by the ruthless audacity and incredible tactlessness of Gaius Caligula. Our analysis has tended to confirm, rather than overturn, the assessment of Philo by C. H. Dodd:

> True to his Jewish upbringing, Philo keeps the distinction between God and man. He has no doctrine of rebirth by which the human becomes divine, nor does he ever say that by knowing God man is deified .... For Philo God is eternally other than man. There is indeed in man a divine (cont.)

element by virtue of his creation in the image of
God, and in this sense God may be called the Father
of men, as indeed of all things; but in no way can
man become God, or the son of God in an absolute
sense. At his best he is the adopted son of God.
Philo is here in harmony with the whole biblical
tradition, in both Testaments, though later
Christian writers allowed themselves to speak of
man as being deified through the incarnation of the
Son of God.

Here we come at once upon the ambiguity of duality
which runs through all Philo's thought. Up to a
point he will use the language which is natural to
the Hermetists, but it does not always mean exactly
the same thing to him. On the one hand he shares
the religious outlook of Greek thinkers from Plato,
whose God was the metaphysical Absolute, the One
beyond the many. On the other hand, he is deeply
influenced by the piety of the Old Testament, which
no amount of allegorical exegesis can wholly resolve
into a mystical absorption into the One. Up to a
point he is able to reconcile the two ways of religion, but in the end they remain unassimilated.[438]

---

[438]C. H. DODD, The Interpretation of the Fourth Gospel
(Cambridge, 1954) 60-61.

So far, we have looked at the two most important representatives of Hellenistic Judaism, apart from the LXX itself.
One other group of writings also deserves attention: those
Greek-speaking Jewish authors whose works have only been preserved in fragments.[1] Although each of these has been examined

---

[1]F. JACOBY, Die Fragmente der Griechischen Historiker
(= FGrH) (Leiden, 1958, repr. 1969) Teil III C, Bd. 2, remains
the standard collection of the "historical" texts, having super-
seded C. MÜLLER, Fragmenta Historicorum Graecorum (= FHG)
(Paris, 1849) Bd. 3. A collection of the texts of the historians only (omitting Pseudo-Hecataeus) is included in J.
FREUDENTHAL, Alexander Polyhistor und die von ihm erhaltenen
Reste jüdaischer und samaritanischer Geschichtswerke
[Hellenistische Studien, Heft 1 & 2] (Breslau, 1875) 219-36,
which still remains the most comprehensive treatment of critical questions (I have not yet seen N. WALTER'S Habilitationsschrift Untersuchungen zu den Fragmenten der jüdischen-
hellenistischen Historiker (Halle, 1967-68) apud ThLZ 94 (1969)
394; it was unavailable on request.) W. N. STEARNS, Fragments
from Graeco-Jewish Writers (Chicago, 1908), is primarily a
collection of the texts with brief introductions and annotations; it improved upon Jacoby by including Ezekiel the
Tragedian and Aristobulus (though omitting Pseudo-Hecataeus),
but failure to use Freudenthal, unconcern for textual critical
questions, and the generally poor method employed considerably
reduces the value of the work (cf. the scathing review by L.
COHN, Berliner Philologische Wochenschrift 30 (1910) 1401-05;
also N. WALTER, Der Thoraausleger Aristobulos (Berlin, 1964)
7:2; Helikon 3 (1963) 791. Because most of these fragments are
preserved in Eusebius, Praeparatio Evangelica, Bk. IX, the
edition by E. H. GIFFORD, Eusebii Pamphili Evangelicae
Praeparationis Libri XV, 5 vols. (Oxford, 1903), which includes
Greek text with apparatus criticus (2 vols.), English translation (2 vols.), and a volume of notes, is indispensable; also,
the new critical edition by K. MRAS, Die Praeparatio Evangelica
[GCS] Part I: Einleitung, Bks. I-X (1954); Part II: Bks. XI-XV
(1956). The most convenient recent collection of all the
fragments is A.-M. DENIS, Fragmenta Pseudepigraphorum Quae
Supersunt Graeca Una Cum Historicorum et Auctorum Judaeorum
Hellenistarum Fragmentis (pub. with Apocalypsis Henochi Graece,
ed. M. Black) (Leiden, 1970), which reproduces the GCS text
(wherever possible) and the Naber text of Josephus. It should
be used in conjunction with his companion-volume Introduction
aux Pseudépigraphes Grecs d'Ancien Testament (Leiden, 1970),
esp. 241-83. The only satisfactory translation which brings
(cont.)

in connection with our inquiry, rather than attempting to
examine them as a group, and therefore each one superficially,
it has been decided to concentrate upon Artapanus, the most
important witness from this group who is most often adduced as
proof that Greek-speaking Jewish authors transformed Moses and
other Jewish heroes into _theioi_ _andres_. This decision arises
out of the conviction that until an earnest attempt is made to
assess the relevant evidence in depth and to understand each of
these authors within his own _Sitz_ _im_ _Leben_, our understanding
of what happened in Hellenistic-Judaism insofar as the _theios_
aner question is concerned will remain confused and unclear.

---

all the fragments together is P. RIESSLER, Altjüdisches
Schrifttum ausserhalb der Bibel (Heidelberg, ²1966), which
contains brief, but often helpful annotations in an appendix.
Cf. the forthcoming translation (according to a letter from the
author) of the fragments by N. WALTER, in Jüdisches Schrifttum
aus hellenistisch-römischer Zeit (Gütersloh: Verlag G. Mohn,
1974).
        Deciding which text of the Hellenistic-Jewish authors to
use for our study is complicated by several factors. The lack
of any standard system of numeration for the fragments makes
reference and cross-reference both cumbersome and confusing,
particularly when there is no single critical edition contain-
ing all the authors. JACOBY and FREUDENTHAL contain an
apparatus criticus but exclude the "non-historians," such as
Aristobulus and Ezekiel the Tragedian (though, oddly enough,
JACOBY includes the poets Philo the Elder (No. 729) and
Theodotus (No. 732)). GIFFORD AND MRAS contain an apparatus
criticus but the fragments are not collected together and
systematically numbered as in JACOBY. All of the fragments are
contained in DENIS, but there is no apparatus criticus; his
decision to shift the order of arrangement (of JACOBY) of some
of the fragments, and therefore alter the numeration (e.g.,
Eupolemus, F 4 & 5), is all the more confusing. Since the
corrupt state of the fragments requires the use of an apparatus
criticus in discussing certain points and since it is desirable
to have all the fragments collected and numbered, JACOBY has
been chosen as the basis for this study.
        In general, the most useful secondary treatments for
getting into the fragments are: FREUDENTHAL, Polyhistor; E.
SCHÜRER, Geschichte des jüdischen Volkes im Zeitalter Jesu
Christi (Hildersheim, 1964, repr. of ³1909 ed.) 3. 420-633;
SCHMID-STÄHLIN, Geschichte der griechischen Literatur (München,
⁶1959) 2. 588-624; P. DALBERT, Missionsliteratur, 27-123; DENIS,
Intro., 241-83; P. M. FRASER, Ptolemaic Alexandria (Oxford,
1972) 1. 687-716 (with the immensely valuable corresponding
notes in vol. 2). Apart from the standard encyclopedia
articles, mention should also be made of G. DELLING,
Bibliographie zur jüdisch-hellenistischen intertestamentarischen Literatur 1900-1965 (Berlin, 1969).

Artapanus: Jew or Greek?[2]

Scholars have always been baffled by the highly syncretistic flavor of Artapanus' treatment of Old Testament themes,
and it is hardly surprising that a wide variety of interpretations of him has resulted. Simply put, the problem is: a Jew
could not have made the concessions which he made to paganism
and have remained a Jew;[3] and yet, the preposterous propagandistic claims which he made in behalf of Judaism could not have
been made by a pagan or an apostate Jew. To the older scholars,
such as Dähne and Ewald, who conceive of Judaism primarily in
terms of pure strains, this seemingly incompatible mixture can
only be explained if Artapanus were a pagan;[4] or, a Samaritan,

---

[2]In addition to the literature cited in SCHÜRER, 3.
479f. and DENIS, Intro., 241, 255ff., add: BOUSSET-GRESSMANN,
20f., 486, 494f.; M. BRAUN, History and Romance in Graeco-
Oriental Literature (Oxford, 1938) 26ff.; P. M. FRASER,
Ptolemaic Alexandria (Oxford, 1972) I. 704ff., 714; 2. 983:177-
986:201; M. FRIEDLÄNDER, Geschichte der jüdischen Apologetik
(Zürich, 1903) 122ff.; J. GEFFCKEN, Zwei griechische Apologeten
(Leipzig/Berlin, 1907) xiiiff.; J. GUTMAN, Ha-Sifrut ha-Yehudit
ha-Hellenistit (Jerusalem, 1963) 2. 109ff.; M. HADAS,
Hellenistic Culture (London, 1959) 96ff.; I. HEINEMANN, art.
"Moses," PWRE 16.1 (1935) 365ff.; M. HENGEL, Judentum und
Hellenismus (Tübingen, ²1973) 166f.; 170f.; "Anonymität,
Pseudepigraphie und 'Literarische Fälschung' in der jüdisch-
hellenistischen Literatur," in Pseudepigrapha I [Entretiens sur
L'Antiquité Classique, Tome 18] (Genève, 1972) 231-329, esp.
239ff.; K. J. MERENTITES, "Ο ΙΟΥΔΑΙΟΣ ΛΟΓΙΟΣ ΑΡΤΑΠΑΝΟΣ ΚΑΙ ΤΟ
ΕΡΓΟΝ ΑΥΤΟΥ," Ἐπετηρὶς τῆς Ἑταιρείας Βυζαντινῶν Σπουδῶν
(= Annuaire de l'Association d'Etudes Byzantines) 27 (1957)
292-339; 29 (1959) 273-321; 30 (1960-61) 281-350 (pub. as
single work, Athens, 1961, reviewed by N. WALTER, Helikon 3
(1963) 789ff.); A. SCHALIT, art. "Artapanus," E Jud 3 (1971)
645f.; W. N. STEARNS, Fragments from Graeco-Jewish Writers
(Chicago, 1908) 42ff.; D. L. TIEDE, The Charismatic Figure as
Miracle Worker (Missoula, Mont., 1972) 146ff.; 317ff.; G.
VERMÈS, "La figure de Moïse au tourant des deux testaments,"
in Moïse, l'homme de l'alliance (Paris, 1955) 68ff.; O.
WEINREICH, "Gebet und Wunder. Zwei Abhandlungen zur Religions-
und Literaturgeschichte," Genethliakon W. Schmid (Stuttgart,
1929) 298ff. For a summary of the fragments, cf. DALBERT, 43;
also FRASER, 1. 704ff.

[3]Cf. R. REITZENSTEIN, Poimandres. Studien zur
griechisch-ägyptischen und frühchristlichen Literatur (Leipzig,
1904), 182:5, "Ein Jude konnte nicht erfinden, dass Moses den
Tierdienst begründet hat; nur wenn ihm dies gegeben war, konnte
er ihn durch eine neue Offenbarung Gottes den reinen Kult
lernen lassen."

[4]FREUDENTHAL, 148.

which amounted to the same thing.[5] Freudenthal, by contrast,
convinced that no pagan could have been motivated to produce
such a chauvinistic piece of Jewish propaganda, and that the
"foreign" elements could not be explained as interpolations or
as traceable to a pagan redactor or to the pagan Polyhistor as
he extracted the work, reckons that the author was a Jew using
"Artapanus" as a pseudonym,[6] but writing his account in ventriloquist fashion, describing Moses as an Egyptian priest
would have done. Any improprieties are the fault of the dummy
not the ventriloquist.[7] Schürer fully acknowledges that
Artapanus was a Jew and that he depicted Moses as the founder
of Egyptian cults, but argues that his reason for doing so is
simply to show that all culture, including religion, is traceable to Moses; no approval is given to the cults; they are
really dedicated τῷ θεῷ.[8] Schlatter, also defending Artapanus,
justifies Moses' conduct as a masterstroke of political genius:
he does not recognize animal worship in the least, but, like
all good politicians, is a pragmatist who does anything to keep
the peace and gain favor.[9] Arguing in the same vein, Heinemann
points out that it was not at all unusual for Jews to apply
Egyptian legends to Biblical heroes.[10] More importantly, he

---

[5]So, Grätz and Herzfeld, apud FREUDENTHAL, 146.

[6]FREUDENTHAL, 150ff., argues that the author of Ep.
Aris. is also the author of the Artapanus fragments. He relies
heavily upon a single piece of circumstantial evidence, Ep.
Aris. 6, and never satisfactorily explains why "Artapanus"
would be chosen as a pseudonym. Accordingly, this part of his
analysis of Artapanus has never been accepted by scholars. Cf.
A. GUTSCHMID, Kleine Schriften (Leipzig, 1890) 2. 184f.;
SCHÜRER, 3. 479; DALBERT, 44; MERENTITES, 10 (cf. WALTER
review, 790).

[7]FREUDENTHAL, 143ff.; cf. summary statement, 169.

[8]SCHÜRER, 3. 479. Followed by DALBERT, 52. M.-J.
LAGRANGE, Le judaïsme avant Jésus-Christ (Paris, 1931), 500,
incorrectly states SCHÜRER'S view as being that Artapanus
attacks idolatry no less than Ep. Aristeas and Sib. Or. On the
difference between Artapanus and Ep. Aris., cf. WALTER, review
791.

[9]SCHLATTER, Geschichte, 195f.

[10]HEINEMANN, 368, notes that the Osiris sagas were
applied to Rabbinic narratives of Joseph. He refers to

(cont.)

thinks it significant that Artapanus is heavily dependent upon
Hecataeus of Abdera, since the latter's emphasis that the animals are consecrated because of their usefulness (θέσις) as
opposed to their inherent nature (φύσις), to use a Stoic
distinction,[11] reflects a cool attitude to the Egyptian cults,
which is equivalent to disapproval.[12] His dependence upon
Hecataeus' attitude to the gods only illustrates how one can
draw upon critical arguments used in one religious system without realizing the potentially dangerous implications they have
for one's own religion. M. Friedländer is representative of
those scholars who freely admit certain improprieties in
Artapanus, but argue that the exigencies of the Egyptian-Jewish
polemical battle justified his fighting fire with fire.[13] L.
Ginzberg, on the other hand, chides him for his "mistaken
apologetic zeal" and failure to recognize "what was truly great
in Judaism."[14] O. Weinreich, and his pupil[15] K. J. Merentites,
who, so far as I know, has written the only extended (if ver-
bose) commentary on the Artapanus fragments, stress the heavy
pagan influence discernible in Artapanus.[16] Scholarship in the

---

G. KITTEL, Die Probleme des palästinischen Spätjudentums und
das Urchristentum (Stuttgart, 1926) 169ff.; cf. Jubilees
4:17ff.; 11:23.

[11]Cf. Origen, C. Celsum I. 24 (= SVF 2. 146).

[12]HEINEMANN, 368. Cf. F. JACOBY, art. "Hekataios (4),"
PWRE 7.2 (1912) 2750ff. on Hecataeus' critical stance towards
Greek μυθολογία. HEINEMANN'S statement "dass schon in
Hekataios' Darstellung keine Zustimmung zum ägyptischen Kultus
lag" (368) is difficult to square with such passages as
Diodorus Siculus 1. 12, 9; 21, 6, 9-11; 83.1-90.4, in which
Hecataeus, unlike other ancient authors who often treat the
animal cults disdainfully, takes pains to establish the reasons
that animals are worshipped, and does so apologetically.

[13]FRIEDLÄNDER, 112f. Also cf. I. LEVY, "Moïse en
Éthiopie," Revue des études juives 53 (1907) 201ff.; VERMES,
68ff., besides stressing Artapanus' apologetic stance, cautions
(contra J. JEREMIAS, art. Μωυσῆς, TDNT 4. 850, 856) against
using Artapanus as a typical representative of Hellenistic-
Judaism.

[14]GINZBERG, art. "Artapanus," JE 2 (1902) 145.

[15]MERENTITES, 30 (1960) 295:1.

[16]WEINREICH, 298ff.; of MERENTITES'S commentary, FRASER,
(cont.)

last half-century, with its understanding of Judaism, especially in the Diaspora, broadened by research on such discoveries as those at Elephantine and Dura Europas, has learned more about the syncretistic complexion of Judaism, and has consequently been more willing to see Artapanus as a concrete example of how much Jews did in fact accommodate their religion to a pagan culture. N. Walter thus contends that what Freudenthal sought to evade cannot be evaded, and that "die Verwischung des ausschliessenden Gegensatzes zwischen jüdischem Glauben und ägyptischem Tierkult war die eigene Meinung des Artapanus."[17]

Artapanus' Syncretistic Portrait of Moses.

Our particular interest is to investigate the nature and implications of this accommodation in terms of Artapanus' understanding of Israel's heroes, specifically the appropriateness of the expression theios aner, which he does not use, to describe them. Are the modifications and reinterpretations of Israel's heroes which we find in Artapanus adequately and properly explained by analyzing them in terms of this concept? Is there discernible a tendency to ascribe divinity to them for propagandistic reasons?

A number of references which tend to answer in the affirmative have been proposed.[18] The first group consists of those which identify Moses with figures of Greek mythology. Moses, we are told, was called Musaios by the Greeks,[19] and on reaching manhood became the teacher of Orpheus,[20] thus reversing the usual order that Orpheus was the teacher of Musaios.[21]

---

2. 983:177, says, " ... a lengthy discussion of, and commentary on, Artapanus--the only one in recent years-- ... consisting of detailed discussions of exegetical and textual points, many useful, some otiose, with lengthy but sometimes antiquated bibliographical notes." The review by WALTER (cf. note 2) is highly critical.

[17]WALTER, review, 791.

[18]Cf. BIELER, 2. 30f.; GEORGI, 149.

[19]F 3. 3.   [20]F 3. 4.

[21]Cf. W. K. C. GUTHRIE, The Greeks and Their Gods (Boston, 1955) 310.

Moreover, he was deemed by the Egyptian priests worthy of the same honor as a god and consequently was called Hermes because of his interpretation (ἑρμηνεία) of the sacred writings.[22] The rod with which he performed the miracles before Pharaoh is displayed in every temple in Upper Egypt right along with Isis.[23] A second group of passages asserts his approbation, indeed his consecration, of Egyptian polytheistic cults. He assigned the god to be worshipped in each nome;[24] he also consecrated the animals worshipped by the Egyptians.[25] Third, in a category to itself, is the account of Moses' miraculous escape from imprisonment by Pharaoh,[26] which is regarded by Weinreich as a thaumaturgic demonstration of his divinity.

Moses' Miraculous Escape (F 3. 23-36).

Since the case for a theios aner interpretation of Artapanus has been most forcefully put by Weinreich, we shall take the groups of references mentioned above in reverse order and examine his argument "dass der späthellenistische Moses-roman des Artapanos die jüdische Mosestradition zum Bios eines Gottmenschen im antiken Sinne umgestaltet."[27] Briefly stated, Weinreich argues that the escape-miracle in F 3. 23-26, particularly the motif of the prison-door opening automatically (αὐτομάτως), has no Biblical nor Jewish parallel,[28] but finds its closest counterpart in pagan sources, specifically Euripides, Bacchae 509ff. and Philostratus, Vita Apollonii 7. 38; 8. 30. Since the latter is several centuries later, we shall concentrate upon the former. The Euripides passage records Dionysus' miraculous escape from prison by which his claim to be παῖς Διός is vindicated. According to Weinreich, Artapanus incorporates a similar prison-escape scene into his Moses romance, replaces Dionysus with Moses, allowing the

_____

[22]F 3. 6.   [23]F 3. 32.

[24]F 3. 4.   [25]F 3. 12; possibly 3. 4, 9.

[26]F 3. 23-26.

[27]WEINREICH, 298; the argument is spelled out on pp. 298-309.

[28]He dismisses Isa. 45:1ff. and Ps. 107:10ff. as possible parallels.

reader to draw the obvious conclusion. Merentites basically
reproduces the same view, but especially calls attention to the
Dionysus traditions current in Ptolemaic Egypt: Artapanus
includes the scene to prove indisputably to a non-Jewish reader
familiar with such traditions that Moses was a superior _theios
aner_.[29]

The force of Weinreich's argument is clear and cannot be
lightly dismissed.[30] It assumes, of course, Artapanus'
acquaintance with sophisticated Greek literature, either
directly or indirectly; there is always the possibility that
the scene may simply be Artapanus' own invention.[31] There is
a strong likelihood that the Dionysus cult was a live threat
to Judaism in Egypt at this time, and may very well partially
constitute the _Sitz im Leben_ out of which Artapanus writes.[32]
If Fraser is correct that Artapanus probably wrote during the
reign of Ptolemy VI Philometor (ca. 180-145 B.C.),[33] this would
lend credibility to Cerfaux's fascinating suggestion that the
famous decree of Ptolemy V Philopator (ca. 221-203 B.C.) pro-
mulgating the Dionysus cult in the _chora_ around Alexandria
provides the immediate background for the cryptic reference in
F 3. 26.[34] Independent of this conjecture, however, Ptolemaic

---

[29]MERENTITES, 30 (1960) 294-97. He especially distinguishes the miracle from those mentioned in Josephus, _Bel._
6. 293; Tacitus, _Hist._ 5. 13; _Psalm_ 23 (24):7.

[30]TIEDE, 165ff., though recognizing the cruciality of
the prison-escape scene in Weinreich's argument, refuses to
admit the force of the point, but his refusal is inadequately
substantiated. He adduces Sesostris' miraculous escape from a
dangerous situation, and thus suggests that at this point
Artapanus is still being influenced by the hero romance tradition. But, the parallel is farfetched. Daniel also escaped
miraculously from a lion's den death (_Dan._ 6:16ff.)

[31]So, FRASER, 1. 705.

[32]Cf. FRASER, 2. 342:96; M. P. NILSSON, _The Dionysiac
Mysteries of the Hellenistic and Roman Age_ (Lund, 1957)11f.;
JANE E. HARRISON, _Prolegomena to the Study of Greek Religion_
(Cambridge, [3]1922) 362-453; A. D. NOCK, "Notes on the Ruler-
Cult," in _Essays on Religion and the Ancient World_ (Oxford,
1972) 1. 143f.

[33]FRASER, 1. 704.

[34]L. CERFAUX, "Influence des Mystères sur le Judaïsme
(cont.)

patronage of the Dionysus cult, especially by Philopator, is
well-known and indisputable.[35] If, therefore, the Jewish cult
was being threatened by a resurgence of interest in the
Dionysus cult, and if Artapanus is incorporating a scene from
Bacchae into his Moses narrative, as Weinreich suggests, the
results are most revealing.

It will be recalled that Pentheus, king of Thebes, wish-
ing to arrest the growth of the Dionysus cult, incarcerates
(unknowingly) Dionysus, who had come to Thebes in human form.[36]
With the exception of Pentheus, everyone, including the reader,
knows Dionysus' true identity. His divinity is repeatedly, if
not excessively, asserted: he is θεός,[37] μέγας θεός,[38] ὁ Διὸς
παῖς,[39] δαίμων,[40] ὁ δαίμων ὁ Διὸς παῖς,[41] δεσπότης,[42] Διὸς
γόνος.[43] This claim is jeopardized by his imprisonment,[44] and
great stress is laid upon the security measures taken by
Pentheus.[45] But, alas, it is a futile attempt to imprison a
god, and by his escape his divinity as Διὸς γόνος is verified.[46]

Alexandrin avant Philon," in Recueil L. Cerfaux (Gembloux,
1954) 1. 105. The decree = Pap. No. 1211, BGU 6 (1922), also
quoted in FRASER, 2. 345-46:114. It is a matter of considerable controversy whether the decree intends to promote or
arrest the growth of the Dionysus cult. Cf. discussion in
FRASER, 1. 204 and W. SCHUBART, Einführung in die Papyruskunde
(Berlin, 1918) 352, both of whom cite extensive bibliography;
also additional bibliography in BGU.

[35]Cf. FRASER, 1. 202; NILSSON, Dionys., 11.

[36]Bacch. 432ff.

[37]Bacch. 47, 100, 157, 180, 182, 192, 194, 242-47, 284,
300, 312, 330ff., 342, 635, 712, 769, 789, 1347.

[38]Bacch. 329.

[39]Bacch. 1, 4, 84, 550-1, 581, 605, 859-61, 1340-3; cf.
466.

[40]Bacch. 22, 219, 256, 272, 298, 498, 769.

[41]Bacch. 416.   [42]Bacch. 582.

[43]Bacch. 603.

[44]Cf. Bacch. 550, 581, 582, 589.

[45]Bacch. 609-41.   [46]Bacch. 603; cf. 635-36.

When we compare Artapanus' prison-escape scene,[47] we
find some rather striking contrasts. First, it should be noted
that Artapanus' scene falls into the half of the Moses narrative[48] in which ὁ θεός figures as a major character, and thus
the most striking fact is that the scene is incorporated into
Artapanus' Moses romance precisely at the point where Yahweh,
not Moses, has been thrust into the center of the stage. In
F 3. 1-20 Moses is featured alone, whereas in 3. 21-39 he is
paired with ὁ θεός.[49] Immediately prior to the escape scene
Moses informs Pharaoh that he has been commissioned by ὁ
δεσπότης τῆς οἰκουμενῆς to set the Jews free.[50] Whereas
Dionysus in Bacchae is hailed as δεσπότης while imprisoned,[51]
in Artapanus' narrative Yahweh, not Moses, is δεσπότης, and ὁ
δεσπότης τῆς οἰκουμενῆς at that, which suggests that rather
than Moses' being presented by Artapanus as a νέος Διόνυσος,[52]
it is Yahweh who is being introduced as the real competitor of
Dionysus. In both instances the kings are equally blind: but
Pentheus is blind to Dionysus, while Pharaoh is blind to
Yahweh.[53] Moreover, it is the name of Yahweh, not Moses, which
has magical powers.[54] If, therefore, Artapanus is incorporating the escape scene into his narrative from a pagan source,
his reshaping of the scene is successful only in allowing
Yahweh of the Jewish cult to be pitted against the god of the
Dionysus cult. Incorporating a scene from Bacchae would certainly have aroused the interest of Dionysus adherents, and
shifting Yahweh into the center of the stage would have
achieved tactical advantage and thus have served his propagandistic ends, but it would presuppose an intellectual subtlety
not everyone is willing to grant Artapanus. Apart from the
question of whether he is influenced by Euripides, the escape
scene as it stands, with its emphasis upon the power of Yahweh
and the power of his name, fits in well with the rest of

---

[47] F 3. 23-26.   [48] F 3. 21-39.

[49] N.B. F 3. 21, 22, 24, 26, 36, 38.

[50] F 3. 22.   [51] Bacch. 582.

[52] Cf. NOCK, "Ruler-Cult," Essays, 144ff.

[53] F 3. 24.   [54] F 3. 26.

F 3. 21-39 where this theme is predominant. Regardless of its
origins, it is obviously intended to underscore the power of
Yahweh, not Moses.

Moses and Greek Mythology.

As to the first two groups of references,[55] it has been
known for a long time that Artapanus, particularly in his portrait of Moses in F 3. 1-20, has drawn upon non-Biblical traditions such as those found in Herodotus, Hecataeus of Abdera (as
preserved in Diodorus Siculus, Book I), and Plutarch.[56] It was
the fact that virtually every feature of his portrait could be
paralleled in these traditions that enabled M. Braun to trace
the "Moses Romance" found in Artapanus to the same Sitz im
Leben that produced romantic literature celebrating the deeds
of such national heroes as Ninus, Semiramis, Sesostris,
Nectanebus, Amenophis, and Alexander the Great.[57] His reasons

---

[55]The first two groups of passages belong together in
the sense that they derive from a common set of traditions
celebrating the deeds of deities and national heroes. But, in
another sense, they are to be kept distinct. Those passages
which portray Moses as the founder of pagan cults may reflect
Artapanus' syncretism, even his heterodoxy, but per se they do
not relate to the question of whether Artapanus considers Moses
a supra-human, semi-divine, or divine person. It is the first
group of passages which bears on this question, and to this
extent the two sets of claims being made are to be kept
separate. Generally, those passages portraying Moses as the
founder of pagan cults have posed greater difficulties for
interpreters of Artapanus (cf. FREUDENTHAL, 146; REITZENSTEIN,
Poimandres, 182). Now, it may be that if Artapanus is willing
to allow that Moses is the father of the Egyptian cults, he
would be more willing to allow that he is divine, but that
constitutes a separate question.

[56]FREUDENTHAL, 148, 153f.; E. SCHWARTZ, art. "Artapanos,"
PWRE 2 (1895) 1306; H. WILLRICH, Judaica. Forschungen zur
hellenistisch-jüdischen Geschichte und Litteratur (Göttingen,
1900) 111ff.; I. LEVY (cf. note 13) 207ff. compiles parallel
profiles of Artapanus' Moses and Hecataeus' traditions about
Sesostris, Osiris, et al., and argues that the attribution of
these traditions to Moses had been made by Ps.-Hecataeus, a
Jewish author, upon whom Artapanus has drawn in compiling his
Moses narrative; J. GEFFCKEN, xiii; SCHLATTER, Geschichte, 195;
HEINEMANN, 367.

[57]BRAUN, 26ff., assembles the Moses portrait of
Artapanus, documenting parallels with the hero-romances
circulating about Ninus, Semiramis, Sesostris, Nectanebus,
and Alexander the Great. Followed by TIEDE, 151ff. Cf.
parallel profiles in LEVY (cf. note 56).

for including these non-Biblical traditions are clearly propagandistic: "Not only does he (Moses) surpass each one
individually, but also all of them combined."[58] D. L. Tiede
unpacks this statement of Braun's in his lucid delineation of
how Artapanus, in his utilization of these traditions, the
Sesostris legends in particular, always skillfully manages to
let Moses emerge as the frontrunner.[59]

While it cannot be doubted that features of the
Sesostris legends have filtered into Artapanus' portrait of
Moses, these should not be stressed to the neglect of other
elements.[60] The only indisputable points of contact between
Artapanus' Moses portrait and the Sesostris legends are the
following: Moses' division of Egypt[61] into 36 nomes,[62] and
the duration of the battle with the Ethiopians.[63] Most of the
other features are common to other cycles of legends. For
example, the benefactor motif[64] is common in Osiris[65] and
Isis[66] legends. Similarly, the establishment of worship in
each nome, whether building a temple or appointing the deity,

---

[58] BRAUN, 26.

[59] TIEDE, 151-77.

[60] As, e.g., in TIEDE, 151ff.

[61] N.B. that Artapanus employs the unusual designation
πόλις, which, although it can denote "country" (cf. LSJ), is
not the usual way of referring to Egypt. One would have
expected χώρα, the more usual way of referring to Egypt as
opposed to Alexandria. Cf. OGIS 56.5; PHib. 1.27.167, apud
LSJ; cf. also MOULTON-MILLIGAN, 695. SCHALIT, 646, takes it
to be "city." If we are to understand πόλις as "city" in the
more narrow sense, the most likely candidate would be Memphis,
in which case, Artapanus' concern may be more parochial than
is usually assumed. Cf. FRASER, 1. 706.

[62] F 3. 4 = Diod. S. 1. 54, 3.

[63] F 3. 8 (ten years) = Diod. S. 1. 55, 10 (nine years);
thus even here there is a discrepancy.

[64] F 3. 4, δ' αὐτὸν πολλὰ τοῖς ἀνθρώποις εὔχρηστα
παραδοῦναι.

[65] Diod. S. 1. 13, 5; 17, 1f.; cf. 18, 5; 19, 5; 20, 5;
27, 5.

[66] Diod. S. 1. 22, 1; cf. 27, 1; 27, 3-4.

is affirmed of Osiris,[67] Isis,[68] and Hermes.[69] An Ethiopian
campaign also belongs to the Osiris legends[70] as well as to the
Semiramis romance.[71] Further, the founding of cities is an
activity of both Osiris[72] and Isis.[73]

Some features of Artapanus' portrait of Moses, on the
other hand, are unique to cycles of legends other than the
Sesostris cycle, or the national romance cycles generally.
The εὑρετής-topos,[74] in which a list of εὑρήματα are attributed
to a single individual, does not figure in the Sesostris
legends,[75] whereas it is a prominent feature of the Osiris
cycle,[76] the Isis cycle,[77] and especially the Hermes cycle.[78]
Some of the features belong exclusively to the Isis legends:
the consecration of animals;[79] the apportionment of a special
land allotment to priests.[80] It might be argued that Isis'
assigning the parts of Osiris' body remodeled into statues to
be worshipped in each nome[81] is more like Artapanus F 3. 4 than
Sesostris' temple building activities.[82]

---

[67]Diod. S. 1. 15, 3.   [68]Diod. S. 1. 21, 5ff.

[69]Diod. S. 1. 16, 1.

[70]Diod. S. 1. 17, 1; 18, 3.

[71]Diod. S. 2. 14, 4. On the Ethiopian campaign,
especially in Targumic and Midrashic literature, cf. VERMES,
69:27 (cf. note 2); also, cf. Josephus, Ant. 2. 238ff.

[72]Diod. S. 1. 15, 1; 18, 6; 19, 7.

[73]Diod. S. 1. 27, 4.   [74]F 3. 4.

[75]The claim that Sesostris was the first Egyptian to
build warships (Diod. S. 1. 55, 2; cf. Herod. 2. 102) is
hardly parallel, though it may echo the εὑρετής-topos. Cf.
TIEDE, 153.

[76]Diod. S. 1. 14, 1; 15, 8; 17, 4; 27, 5.

[77]Diod. S. 1. 14, 1 (cf. 14, 3); 25, 2; 25, 6; 27, 4.

[78]Diod. S. 1. 15, 9; 16, 1-2. Note the similarity of
the formal structure with Artapanus F 3. 4.

[79]F 3. 4 = Diod. S. 1. 21, 6; 21, 9ff.

[80]F 3. 4 = Diod. S. 1. 21, 7.

[81]Diod. S. 1. 21, 5ff.   [82]Diod. S. 1. 56, 2.

Clearly, we are forced to conclude that Artapanus'
portrait of Moses comprises diverse strands from a variety of
traditions, some of which are unique to certain cycles of
legends, while others overlap each other. The resultant portrait is uniform only in its favorable depiction of Moses.
The problem arises, for our inquiry, when it is recognized that
from these diverse traditions Artapanus ascribes to Moses
qualities and achievements which in the other traditions are
ascribed to the deities Isis, Osiris, Hermes-Thot, or to figures on the borderline between heroes and gods--Alexander the
Great, Sesostris, et al.[83] By doing so, does Artapanus intend
to transfer Moses into this same class of beings? Or, does he
presuppose the transfer? Or, is he even able to distinguish
between the levels of tradition insofar as they partake of myth
and history?[84] These questions must be analyzed in the light
of: (1) the Sitz im Leben of Artapanus, (2) the literary genre
of his work, (3) the pro-Egyptian cast of the Moses portrait,
and (4) a certain restraint discernible in Artapanus.

Sitz im Leben.

Artapanus' indiscriminate inclusion of popular legends
as well as his familiarity with local traditions,[85] including
priestly traditions, has led Fraser to suggest that "it is most
natural to see in him not a member of the influential Jewish
circles around Philometor or a later Ptolemy, but (as his

---

[83]Plutarch, De Is. et Osir. 360b-e testifies to the
fluidity of such categories in antiquity. His comments are
evidence that the ancients disputed about what constituted
legitimate and illegitimate claims to divinity. He classifies
Typhon, Osiris, and Isis as δαίμονες--"demigods"--those who
were stronger than men yet not possessing divine qualities
unmixed and undiluted, although they were later transferred
from being "good demigods" to "gods" because of their virtues,
as were Heracles and Dionysus later (361e).

[84]BRAUN, 33, speaks of "... the common people who
cannot clearly and consciously differentiate between truth
(ἀλήθεια), lies (ψεῦδος) and literary fiction (πλάσμα) and
therefore willingly accept the myth, especially the written
myth, above all when this myth appeals to their wishes and
ideals, as members of a particular social group." In passing,
it may be asked whether Braun is overly sceptical of the
critical faculties of the ordinary man.

[85]N.B. "the Memphians say," "the Heliopolitans say,"
F 3. 35.

Persian name might suggest) as a Jew of mixed descent, possibly
resident in another centre such as Memphis, where the residence
of Jews from an early date exacerbated a problem which was
still only nascent in the capital."[86] This _Sitz_ _im_ _Leben_ can
be delineated more precisely in at least two respects: (1) the
Manethonian traditions relating to the Jews and Moses,[87] and
(2) the mystery cults in Egypt.[88]

Many scholars agree with Fraser in thinking that
Artapanus must be viewed _vis_ _à_ _vis_ Manetho, or, at least, the
traditions preserved by him.[89] It is not difficult to imagine
how the melting-pot character of the lower-class social setting
mentioned above could produce a situation in which ethnic mis-
conceptions abounded, and one can easily conceive how the

_____

[86]FRASER, 1. 706. By locating Artapanus within this
lower social class, Fraser is in agreement with Braun, 3ff.,
who, after distinguishing between the two sociological levels
at which Graeco-Oriental romance narratives flourished (viz.
the literary, e.g., Manetho, Josephus, and the popular), dis-
cusses Artapanus within the latter group.

[87]For the Manethonian treatment of the Jews, cf.
Josephus, _Ap_. 1. 227ff.

[88]Cf. chapter 5 on "The Cults of Alexandria," in FRASER,
1. 189ff.

[89]FRASER, 1. 705f., 714; BRAUN, 27:1; FREUDENTHAL, 161;
cf. SCHALIT, 646. TIEDE, 175f., doubts that Artapanus is
responding to anti-Jewish polemics such as those found in
Manetho, primarily because the theft by the Jews of Egyptian
goods (F 3. 34-35) is so openly acknowledged. While we must
agree with VERMES, 74:33, that F 3. 34-35 is a "curieux oubli
dans un écrit apologetique," Artapanus' attempt to tone down
the brazenness of the theft cannot be overlooked. If Josephus
softened the Old Testament version (Ex. 12:35-36) which reports
that the Jews despoiled (ἐσκύλευσαν) the Egyptians, surely the
same must be said for Artapanus who uses χρησαμένους. It is
by no means certain that "appropriated" (TIEDE, 175, 324) is
the best rendering (VERMES, 74, chooses "empruntèrent"). Its
more usual meaning is "furnish," and it is not impossible to
translate F 3. 34, "After they had been furnished many drinking
vessels by the Egyptians ...," which would not be very different from Josephus, _Ant_. 2. 314. F 3. 35, however, cannot be
sensibly translated in any fashion other than "appropriated"
or "took," although its force is softened by its being part of
the Heliopolitan tradition. But even if χρησαμένους in F 3. 34
must be taken in the same sense as F 3. 35 and translated
"appropriated," considerable edge has been taken off the
Biblical account in any case, which would suggest Artapanus'
apologetic intentions.

distorted picture of the Jews and Jewish history which is
preserved in Manetho could have arisen, circulated as a general
Egyptian stereotype of the Jews, and occasioned a response such
as we find in Artapanus. Whether his primary intention, however naive, is to refute Manetho (or, the traditions preserved
by him) for the sake of the upper-class literati,[90] or for the
sake of his fellow Jews resident in Memphis is a moot question.
Neither is automatically precluded, since propaganda causes
people to do and say strange things. The important point, for
our discussion, is whether in either situation ascribing
divinity to Israel's heroes would have any propagandistic value
to Artapanus in countering the uncomplimentary portrait of
Moses and the Jews which was evidently circulating in Egypt.

Artapanus' liberal inclusion of features from the Isis
and Osiris legend-cycles into his portrait of Moses, particularly the former, coupled with his irresistible urge to upstage
Isis at every conceivable opportunity[91] suggests that the
Jewish cult is in serious competition with local mystery
cults.[92] In fact, since Manetho was instrumental in establishing the Sarapis cult in Egypt,[93] Artapanus' countering the
Manethonian traditions may be serving the additional purpose
of taking a slap at the Sarapis cult.

---

[90]Scholars usually admit Artapanus' apologetic stance,
though there is some difference of opinion whether he is
responding on a literary level, and if so, what level. Cf.
TIEDE, 148f.; 174f. Also, cf. V. TCHERIKOVER, "Jewish
Propaganda Literature Reconsidered," Eos 48 (1956) 169ff.
FREUDENTHAL, 144, 150, is convinced that Artapanus' intention
is to arouse admiration for Moses among pagan readers.

[91]Cf. F 3. 16, 32.

[92]E. BAMMEL, review of M. GREEN, Evangelism in the Early
Church in ThLZ 98 (1973) 530, refers to J. LEIPOLDT, Dionysos
(Leipzig, 1931) 1-48; L. VIDMAN, Sylloge Inscriptionum
religionis Isiacae et Sarapiacae (Berlin, 1969); Isis und
Sarapis bei den Griechen und Römern (Berlin, 1970); R. E. WITT,
Isis in the Graeco-Roman World (London, 1971); also, cf. F.
DUNAND, Le culte d'Isis dans de basin oriental de la
Méditerranée (Leiden, 1973) 3 vols.

[93]His exact role with regard to the establishment of
the Sarapis cult is disputed. Cf. FRASER, 1. 246ff.; 505f.;
also, OCD[2], 951. Also, J. E. STAMBAUGH, Sarapis Under the
Early Ptolemies (Leiden, 1972).

Literary Genre.

Scholars usually make two mistakes in treating Artapanus, the second deriving from the first: (1) treating the Moses fragment in isolation from the Abraham and Joseph fragments, and (2) classifying the Moses fragment as a specific literary genre. Obviously, as Weinreich's earlier argument has shown, the proper identification of the literary genre is essential to our inquiry. Tiede is rightly sceptical about classifying F 3 as a "Moses Romance," or even as an "aretalogy" or a "βίος of a theios aner."[94] Such classifications can be made only if F 3 is isolated from F 1 & 2. Certainly, F 3 is the longest fragment, but it is not the only fragment. When F 3 is isolated from F 1 & 2, the features common to all three fragments are camouflaged. There is far more justification for classifying Artapanus' work as a whole as a "national romantic history"[95] (assuming that it should be dignified with the name "history" at all) in the same category as Hecataeus' On the Egyptians than for classifying F 3 as a "Moses Romance."[96]

It is also a mistake simply to equate Artapanus himself with the popular legends and traditions which he incorporates into his Moses narrative.[97] The fact that he stems from a humble milieu does not ipso facto make his work non-literary, though it may help explain why it is sub-literary. Unlike the popular national romances, Artapanus' work is not anonymous, and, however miserably he fails in his literary efforts and however comical his literary pretentiousness, his work On the Jews (Περὶ ᾿Ιουδαίων),[98] both because of its title and

---

[94]TIEDE, 146f.; cf. especially 147:69.

[95]Perhaps "ein erbaulicher Tendenzroman," WACHSMUTH'S designation for Hecataeus' Αἰγυπτιακά would be more appropriate. Cf. K. WACHSMUTH, Einleitung in das Studium der Alten Geschichte (Leipzig, 1895) 330.

[96]It must be noted, in all fairness, that unlike Hecataeus' Aegyptiaka, Artapanus' work seems to have consisted of a recital of deeds of individuals—Abraham, Joseph, and Moses. But F 1 implies that his concerns were broader. He has evidently attempted to trace the origins and development of the Hebrew race, in which Abraham naturally played a central role.

[97]So TIEDE, 151ff., esp. 174.

[98]The actual title is variously reported. Cf.

(cont.)

contents, must be placed on the same literary category as
Hecataeus' On the Egyptians, Manetho's On the Egyptians, and
Berossus' On the Babylonians. It may be true that in Artapanus
legends, myth, and history flow together and at times are
indistinguishable,[99] but certainly no more so than in Hecataeus,
whose work is every bit as tendentious and "romantic" as
Artapanus--and, understandably so, since both are engaged in
writing national romantic propaganda,[100] which is by definition
eclectic. Manetho, strictly speaking, is engaged in writing a
propagandistic treatment of the Egyptians in the course of
which he includes an uncomplimentary portrayal of the Jews
insofar as they relate to the Egyptians. By the same token,
Artapanus' sole task is not merely to refute this Manethonian
account of the Jews. Like Hecataeus and Manetho, he intends to
glorify his national heritage and adopts the same method of
argument which they used: to demonstrate the superiority of
that heritage by documenting its priority (i.e. antiquity) and
cultural contributions.[101] But, at the same time he wants to

---

DENIS, Intro., 255. B. Z. WACHOLDER, "Pseudo-Eupolemus' Two
Greek Fragments on Abraham," HUCA 34 (1963) 85:19, notices that
"the title Περὶ Ἰουδαίων is credited by Jacoby to the following authors: Pseudo-Hecataeus of Abdera, Aristeas, Artapanus,
Cleodemus-Malchus, Alexander Polyhistor, Damocritus, Nicharcus
of Ammonius, Theodotus, Philo of Byblus. The variety of the
subject-matter treated in these works, such as Damocritus'
diatribe against the Jews or Aristeas' Job, suggests that in
some cases Περὶ Ἰουδαίων merely denotes a generic name rather
than an actual title."

[99] Cf. FREUDENTHAL, 148f.

[100] Cf. WACHSMUTH, Einleitung, 330f.; WALTER, review,
791, is sceptical about classifying Artapanus as either
"apologetic" or "missionary" literature.

[101] While Artapanus does mention that Joseph was the
first (πρῶτον) person to divide the land and mark it off with
boundaries (F 2. 2), the priority-topos is fairly subdued
(contrast Eupolemus F 1). Nor is stress put upon the
dependence-topos. It appears, instead, that Artapanus has
employed the εὑρετής-topos, both in respect to Joseph (F 2. 2)
and Moses (F 3. 4) somewhat creatively. Whereas it normally
functioned to demonstrate priority, dependence, and superiority,
in Artapanus it functions to demonstrate Jewish benevolence
towards Egypt. In this respect, he is similar to those traditions in which εὑρήματα function as a means of documenting
εὑεργεσία (cf. Diod. S. 1. 13, 5; 17, 1ff.), but he evidently
(cont.)

counter the negative Manethonian portrait of Moses and the
Jews. These two themes, thus, not only parallel each other
but intersect. By demonstrating the dependence of Egyptian
culture upon the Jews, he not only establishes the priority of
the latter, but at the same time proves their benevolent as
opposed to their malevolent posture.

Artapanus' work, therefore, whatever else it is, is a
literary attempt, patriotically motivated. Far from being a
creative piece of work, it merely assembles traditions and
legends indiscriminately. But in it we get a glimpse of a
type of popular Jewish propaganda capable of being produced
within the lower classes where competition with local cults
was no less real than the tension and uneasiness of Jewish-
Egyptian, Jewish-Greek relationships. May we speculate further
and suggest that it is conceivable that the Moses narrative in
F 3 once constituted part of a synagogue sermon, assuming that
preachers then as now often strayed from their text (i.e. Ex.
2-16)? The Biblical text is retold tendentiously with the aim
of countering traditions like those associated with Manetho.
In the retelling there is a vivid imagination at work, in
σπερμολόγος fashion, picking up bits and pieces of Isis,
Osiris, Orphic, and national hero romance (Sesostris) legends,
as well as bits of magic and superstition, plus elements suit-
able for countering Dionysiac traditions. The end-result is a
Jewish leader re-portrayed as the benefactor of Egypt who combined in one man the sum total of all the best that the
Egyptian cults had to offer. In semi-rhetorical fashion[102]
the preacher acknowledges variant local explanations of his
story, but mentions them only in order to detach himself from
them. The influence of popular philosophic schools is to be
detected in the strongly Euhemeristic strain in Artapanus.
The strong cultic emphasis may suggest connections with
Leontopolis. Any excess of claims by Artapanus can be probably
explained by the excesses on Manetho's part.

Or, we may simply be witnessing propaganda at an

---

sees no benefit in taking the next step of deducing ἀθανασία
from εὐεργεσία (cf. Diod. S. 1. 17, 1-2; 20, 5; 22, 1ff.).

[102]F 3. 35.

individual level,[103] where we see an unrefined, though not
necessarily un-ingenious, way of setting one's own religious
heroes over against those like Sesostris, Alexander the Great,
or Osiris, whose deeds were celebrated in Egypt. The legends
are taken over, turned bottom-up, applied to Moses (or Joseph,
or Abraham) all for the glory of God--and Judaism. At least it
demonstrates that not all propaganda was as untactfully forthright as Wisdom of Solomon 13-15 or Sibylline Oracles Book III,
even if the price was incredibility.

Pro-Egyptian Cast.

It will be recalled that the account of Jewish history
preserved in Manetho focused upon three aspects of the Jews'
relationship with Egypt: (1) their anti-Egyptian activities,
especially the destruction of the sacred animals and
temples;[104] (2) their leader;[105] (3) the circumstances of
their departure from Egypt.[106] We see these three themes
being countered, not only in Artapanus' Moses fragment, but
in certain respects in all three fragments. The single
feature which Artapanus' Abraham, Joseph, and Moses share in
common is their pro-Egyptian cast, specifically their benefac-
tion of Egyptian culture. The origin of astrology, a most
significant feature of Egyptian life,[107] is traceable to
Abraham, who taught it to Pharaoh.[108] In the second fragment
the features of the Joseph narrative selected by Artapanus are
thematically pro-Egyptian. Although the Joseph "romance" lent
itself to being developed along moralistic lines,[109] in F 2
this tendency is totally absent. Only those aspects of his
career which benefited Egypt are narrated.[110]

Taken together with F 1 & 2, F 3 is seen to possess

---

[103]Cf. A. D. NOCK, Conversion (Oxford, 1965) 77f.

[104]Josephus, Ap. 1. 243-44; 248-50.

[105]Josephus, Ap. 1. 238, 250.

[106]Josephus, Ap. 1. 229; 233-36.

[107]Cf. Diod. S. 1. 28, 1; 81, 3.

[108]F 1; cf. Anonymous (= FGrH No. 724), F 1. 3.

[109]Cf. BRAUN, 44ff.   [110]F 2. 2-4.

these same contours. Braun has outlined how Artapanus' portrait of Moses "forms a counter-picture, pro-Jewish in tendency, to an anti-Jewish Egyptian account."[111] Artapanus has a special predilection for portraying the Jews in general, and Moses in particular, as temple builders and cult benefactors.[112] His references to their external origins and to their Syrian homeland[113] and his reminder that when they came to Egypt they brought along their own possessions[114] serves to buttress his point that they were not a blight to the Egyptians.

Structurally, the Moses fragment falls into two clearly definable sections: 3. 1-20 and 3. 21-39. Both sections accomplish the same end by different means. In F 3. 1-20 Artapanus incorporates non-Biblical legends current in popular circles in order to depict Moses as the benefactor of the Egyptians. This is accomplished by utilizing the conventional device of the hero romance in which the hero is pitted against an antagonist, who in the end is bested. In this case, the romance develops as a contest between Moses and Chenephres, Moses' foster-father and one of the petty kings of Lower Egypt. Moses the hero is introduced as the embodiment of everything the Egyptians prized and revered.[115]

The first section is characterized particularly by the presence of non-Biblical traditions. Reflections of the Biblical narrative are infrequent, brief, and allusive. Behind F 3. 2-3 stands Ex. 1:8-14 and Ex. 2:1-10; F 3. 17 possibly recalls Ex. 2:15, while F 3. 18 may be an intentional modification of Ex. 2:12.[116] Ex. 2:15-22 is condensed into a couple of lines at the beginning of F 3. 19. There is no mention of Yahweh, unless ὁ θεός in F 3. 4 is so interpreted. It becomes obvious that in this first section Artapanus is not even attempting to present a Biblical portrait of Moses, nor even a modified Biblical portrait. His preoccupation instead is to present a Moses favorable to Egyptians. Strictly speaking,

---

[111]BRAUN, 26f. [112]F 2. 3; 3. 4, 9, 12.

[113]F 1; F 2. 1. [114]F 2. 3.

[115]F 3. 4.

[116]Cf. VERMÈS, 70:29, who refers to the Targumic explanations of Moses' murder of the Egyptians.

F 3. 1-20 could be called a "Moses Romance," for it is a self-contained unit consisting almost exclusively of legends and traditions which were stock features of the national hero romances. It matters little to Artapanus whether those heroes were legendary figures (Sesostris), deities (Isis and Osiris), or demigods (Hermes).[117] The fact that his mosaic consists of such an indiscriminate selection raises some serious doubts about whether he is consciously transposing the Moses of the Biblical tradition into any one category such as a theios aner in the so-called Hellenistic sense.

Εὑρετής-Topos.

Structurally, F 3. 3-6 is not an independent unit, but belongs to the larger "Moses Romance," of F 3. 1-20.[118] Since the εὑρετής-topos does not figure prominently in the national hero romances, it appears that Artapanus has incorporated it at this point as a means of glamorizing his hero Moses who thereby contrasts the more sharply with the antagonist Chenephres, whose jealousy is triggered by Moses' fame (ἀρετή).[119] There can be little doubt that in F 3. 3-4 Artapanus has incorporated and reshaped to suit his own needs the thoroughly Greek εὑρετής-topos whose development can be traced to 7th-6th century Greece.[120] Its usefulness for Jewish apologetic is

---

[117]On the fluidity of these categories, cf. note 83.

[118]The charge that the Jews had produced no contributions to civilization (Josephus, Ap. 2. 135, 148) may lie behind F 3. 3-6. For a discussion of F 3. 3-6, cf. R. EISLER, Orphisch-dionysische Mysterien-Gedanken in der christlichen Antike (Leipzig/Berlin, 1925) 6ff.

[119]Ἀρετή is a crucial term in determining whether F 3 is an "aretalogy" (Cf. GEORGI, Gegner, 150; TIEDE, 156ff. On the problem of defining "aretalogy," cf. TIEDE, 1ff.). TIEDE, 156ff., understands it to point to the military prowess of Moses as it is unfolded in F 3. 7ff. The sense of the passage, it seems to me, demands that ἀρετή be understood primarily in terms of F 3. 3-6, which can be done without committing the post hoc fallacy as Georgi does. The irony, of course, is that Chenephres' jealousy is precipitated by the host of pro-Egyptian benefactions accomplished by Moses. The same literary technique occurs again in F 3. 12-13.

[120]In the following remarks I am dependent upon K. THRAEDE, art. "Erfinder II (geistesgeschichtlich)," RAC

(cont.)

due in large measure to Plato and Herodotus,[121] who were
largely responsible for impressing upon Greece the antiquity
and therefore the priority of the Orient, especially Egypt,
vis à vis Greece. In a sense, this is only a continuation of
a process begun by Ionian rationalistic criticism. Local
mythographic traditions had explained all worthwhile cultural
achievements (εὑρήματα) by assigning them to gods and heroes of
Greek mythology. Unsatisfied with these explanations, subsequent rationalistic thinking, of which Sophism and Euhemerism
were direct heirs, sought to give more scientific, empirical
reasons for the origin and rise of civilization. Once the
mythographical explanations were suspect, Greece had to come
to terms with history, in particular with the greater antiquity
of Egypt. Herodotus, who regarded the Egyptians as the oldest
and wisest of all peoples,[122] illustrates as well as anyone the
dawning of this Greek awareness, but also the cultural pride
which makes a Greek reluctant to capitulate totally.[123] In
Herodotus there occurs on an international scale a type of
argument which was deeply rooted in earlier local and national
traditions. When there was an encounter between two conflicting cultural traditions (e.g. Athens vs. Sicyonians,[124] or
Greece vs. Egypt), the resolution could take the form of claim
and counter-claim. The proponents of each culture could assert
that it was responsible for the greatness of the other. This
claim[125] in turn led to a claim to priority or antiquity, on
the natural assumption that the younger copied the older. One
solution to this set of claims and counter-claims developed
along the lines of the εὑρετής-topos. Claims to antiquity were

---

5. 1191-1278; also, "Das Lob des Erfinders. Bemerkungen zur
Analyse der Heuremata-Kataloge," Rheinisches Museum für
Philologie N.F. 105 (1962) 158ff.

[121]THRAEDE, RAC, 1204. Cf. specifically Plato, Phaedr.
274e; Herodotus 2. 4, 15f., 43f., 49ff., 58.

[122]Herodotus 2. 2, 77, 121; apud THRAEDE, 1204.

[123]Cf. THRAEDE, 1211f., on "Interpretatio graeca."

[124]Herodotus 5. 67; cf. Aristotle, Poet. V. 3-6,
1449a-b; apud THRAEDE, 1200.

[125]THRAEDE refers to it as "Mimesis-Topos."

buttressed by positing εὑρεταί πρῶτοι of certain universally
acknowledged τέχναι. Such claims could either be denied outright, or they could be admitted while at the same time
disparaged by counter claims of greater importance.

By the time Artapanus writes (mid-2nd century B.C.) this
topos was well established in both literary and non-literary
circles as a highly fluid propagandistic device useful in
various contexts including encomium, ethnography, universal
history, local history, comedy, and elegy.[126] Far from being
the exclusive property of literati, it flourished, naturally
enough, in popular circles, which makes its presence in
Artapanus not at all surprising. By employing this topos, he
brings into the service of Judaism a well-developed argument
of acknowledged propagandistic value for any well-meaning
patriot.

Our knowledge of the topos from other sources enables
us to see more clearly the significance of the list of εὑρήματα
which Artapanus attributes to Moses. The formal structure of
such lists varied, depending upon the purpose for which they
were used.[127] At least three patterns were known:
(1) A single εὑρετής (either a person, people, city, or
country) to whom πολλὰ εὑρήματα are ascribed.[128]
(2) An enumeration of a list of εὑρεταί (again, either of a
single person, a people, etc.) with corresponding εὑρήματα for
which each had become famous.[129]
(3) A εὑρήματα-catalog: a random recitation of εὑρήματα with
the one or more εὑρεταί to which each was traceable.[130]

Artapanus' list conforms to No. 1 and is selective
rather than comprehensive. Actually, Moses' εὑρήματα are
meagre when compared with the all-encompassing list attributed

---

[126]THRAEDE, 1192.   [127]THRAEDE, 1203.

[128]Cf. Aeschylus, Prometheus 500-506; Diod. S. 1. 16,
1-2 (of Hermes). Also Diogenes Laertius 9. 50-56 (of
Protagoras).

[129]Cf. Critias, Elegy Diehl 1. For a recent English
translation, cf. R. S. SPRAGUE (ed.), The Older Sophists. A
Complete Translation by Several Hands of the Fragments in Die
Fragmente der Vorsokratiker, edited by Diels-Kranz (Columbia,
S.C., 1972) 250.

[130]Cf. Pliny, nat. hist. 7. 191ff. Cf. THRAEDE, Lob.

to Prometheus,[131] Apollo,[132] or even Hermes.[133] Unlike
Prometheus, for whom πᾶσαι τέχναι are claimed,[134] Moses only
transmitted πολλὰ τοῖς ἀνθρώποις εὔχρηστα. Even then they are
all εὑρήματα which are singularly beneficial to Egypt. Πλοῖα[135]
and τὰ ὄργανα τὰ ὑδρευτικά immediately call to mind the Nile,
while μηχανὰς πρὸς τὰς λιθοθεσίας[136] would have special appeal
for pyramid-builders. Αἰγύπτια ὅπλα and πολεμικά foreshadow
the military role which Moses is to play in the Moses romance.
Since military technology was such a common feature of the
εὑρήματα-catalogs, Artapanus felt inclined to specify
Αἰγύπτια.[137] The inclusion of φιλοσοφία indicates how
thoroughly the notion that Egypt was the source of philosophical thought had penetrated the Hellenistic world.[138] It also
testifies to the degree to which ἀνὴρ σοφός had come to replace
the gods and heroes in the εὑρετής-topos.[139]

It is difficult to assess the precise significance of

---

[131]Aeschylus, Pr. 442-506; though, cf. Plato, Polit.
frg. 274c-d. Note also Palamedes, although his εὑρήματα are
fewer than Prometheus', became more firmly established in
heurematography. Cf. THRAEDE, 1199; also cf. Pliny, nat. hist.
7. 202; on Palamedes, cf. Loeb ed. of Aeschylus, vol. 2, pp.
441f.

[132]Cf. Pindar, Pyth. 5, 60ff.; Plato, Symp. 197a, et al.

[133]Diod. S. 1. 16, 1-2.   [134]Aeschylus, Pr. 506.

[135]Cf. Pliny, nat. hist. 7. 206ff.; cf. Herodotus 1.
171; Thucydides 1, 4; on Athena as inventor of ships, cf.
PRELLER-ROBERT 1. 217.

[136]Cf. especially Herodotus 2. 125; possibly the reference to the crowbar in Pliny nat. hist. 7. 195 provides the
parallel. STEARNS, 54, suggests "hurling engines." Cf.
Manetho, F 12 (also F 11) Loeb.

[137]Compare Καρικὰ ὅπλα, Pliny, nat. hist. 7. 200; cf.
Pindar, frg. 281B; Schol. Ven. Homer Il. 10, 439; Strabo,
10.3.19; Hellanicus, frg. 71b, 189 (Jacoby, FGrH No. 4); for
a military technology catalog, cf. Servius, Comm. Ver. Aen.
9. 503ff. Apud THRAEDE, 1208.

[138]Cf. Plato, Phaedr. 274c-e; Plutarch, quaest. conv.
9. 3, 2; Isocrates, Or. 11. 11-14, 17-20, 28, 30, apud THRAEDE,
1205; cf. also 1209f.; Diod. S. 1. 96. Competing traditions
also existed, e.g. for Mesopotamia, cf. THRAEDE, 1207f.

[139]THRAEDE, 1209f.

Artapanus' inclusion of φιλοσοφία in the list.[140] Probably it is to be connected with the Mousaios-Moses-Orpheus equation in F 3. 3b-4. Doubtless within the spheres of popular propaganda mirrored in Artapanus the orthographical resemblance between Μώυσος and Μουσαῖος[141] had been noticed, and since it was a commonplace for Orpheus and Musaios to be mentioned together,[142] there was sufficient basis for attaching the name of Orpheus to Moses traditions. In some traditions Orpheus is the father,[143] in others the master (teacher),[144] of Musaios; in either case, Musaios was usually subordinate to Orpheus. Reversing this traditional order was a small price to pay for the associational value attaching to the name Orpheus.

The prominent role which Orpheus plays in the εὑρετής-topos may be explained by Thraede's suggestion that the Kulturbringer-motif had its origins in Orphic-Pythagorean circles.[145] He early functions as the fulcrum around which priority claims are made: to establish the priority of Crete vis à vis Greece, Ephorus asserts that the Dactyls, from Mt. Idê on Crete, had taught Orpheus his mysteries.[146] In the early dawn of Greek historical writing Hellanicus, attempting to trace the genealogy of Homer and Hesiod, does so with

---

[140]TIEDE, 152, attaches little significance to it.

[141]Cf. Eusebius, H.E. 7. 32. 16.

[142]Cf. Aristophanes, Ra. 1030ff.; Hippias, apud Clem. Alex., Strom. 6. 15. 1-2 [II 434. 19 Stählin]; Strom. 1. xxi. 103. 5.

[143]Justin, Cohort. ad Gent. 15. Cf. Kern, Orph. Fragm., p. 256, No. 245; Papyr. Berol. 44 Saec. IIa. Chr. Diels FVS², 478, 24ff. References cited in EISLER, Orph.-Dion., 6:5.

[144]The point was not undisputed. Tatian, ad Graec. 41, τοῦ δὲ Ὀρφέως μαθητής Μουσαῖος (Migne); τοῦ δὲ Ὀρφέως Μουσαῖος μαθητής (Gebhardt-Harnack); Clement Alex., Strom. I. xxi. 131. 1 (GCS Früchtel) Ὀρφεύς δὲ, ὁ συμπλεύσας Ἡρακλεῖ, Μουσαίου διδάσκαλος (cf. app. crit. for additional textual variants; also cf. discussion in Migne, Clem. loc. cit. note 82); Euseb., P.E., X. 11. 30 (GCS Mras) τοῦ δ' Ὀρφέως Μουσαῖος μαθητής; cf. Kern, Orph. Fragm. No. 15, p. 5.

[145]THRAEDE, 1224. Cf. also W. JAEGER, Paideia, 3. 180ff.

[146]Ephorus, frg. 104 = Diod. S. 5. 64. 4.

reference to Orpheus, reckoning that Homer was ten generations
removed from Orpheus.[147] In a slightly different connection,
Hecataeus mentions that Orpheus was responsible for trans-
mitting the Dionysus cult to Greece.[148] To the ancient mind
Orpheus denoted a religio-philosophic-mystical figure associated with a strict, ascetic system of religious teaching.[149]
If one needs to find a concrete associational point to explain
the motivation for Artapanus' identification of Orpheus and
Moses, the ιεροί λόγοι may provide the answer.[150] These "holy
writings" were as significant a feature of the Orphic system
as the "holy writings" of Moses were to the Jews. Orphism was
not only ancient and widespread,[151] but in Egypt was a serious
competitor of the Dionysus cult.[152] By asserting that Moses
is the teacher of Orpheus, Artapanus may very well be taking
an indirect slap at the Dionysus cult while at the same time
asserting the priority, and therefore the superiority of
Judaism over Orphism as a religious system possessing "holy
writings." He also may have been keenly aware that the list
of εὑρήματα which he attributes to Moses were not those usually
associated with Orpheus,[153] and after tailoring the list to fit
his specific purposes, concluded by including φιλοσοφία to call
attention to the Orpheus-Moses connection made earlier.

There are some rather conspicuous omissions from the
list. Considering the crucial role which laws played in

---

[147]Hellanicus, frg. 5 (Jacoby, FGrH No. 4); cf. also
E. ROHDE, Kleine Schriften (Tübingen/Leipzig, 1901; repr.
Hildesheim/New York, 1969) 1. 5ff.; 16ff.

[148]Diod. S. 1. 23, 2ff.

[149]Cf. W. K. C. GUTHRIE, The Greeks and Their Gods
(Boston, 1955) 307ff.

[150]Cf. NOCK, Conversion, 31.

[151]Plato, Resp. 2. 364e; cf. Plutarch, Coniugalia
praecepta 140 (19); apud W. JAEGER, Early Christianity and
Greek Paideia (London, 1969) 8.

[152]Cf. OCD², 759; NOCK, Conversion, 27; NILSSON, Diony.,
12.

[153]Cf. THRAEDE, 1210; Mallius Theodorus, On Meters VI,
589, 220 Keil (Cf. Diels-Kranz 68 B 16) apud SPRAGUE, 250;
though, Orpheus as the inventor of ships, cf. EISLER, Orph.-
Diony., 7:3.

ancient societies and the prominent role which they played in
εὑρήματα-catalogs and propaganda,[154] it is most surprising that
Artapanus makes not a single allusion to the laws of Moses,
unless they are to be seen behind ἱερὰ γράμματα in F 3. 4; cf.
3. 6. The agricultural motif often common in such lists is
also absent.[155] In vivid contrast to the εὑρήματα attributed
to Osiris and Isis,[156] none of the items has cultic significance, with the possible exception of πλοῖα.

It becomes obvious that Artapanus' list has been
compiled to fit with the rest of his portrait of Moses as
cult benefactor[157] and political leader who establishes
harmonia successfully.[158] Little wonder that he was beloved
by the people[159] and that the priests deemed him worthy of
honor befitting a god.[160] The choice of the Hermes appellation
was singularly appropriate in light of the associations it had
in the Egyptian mind with Thoth.[161] If there is an explicit
ascription of divinity to Moses in Artapanus, this is it. In
the ancient Greek pantheon Hermes was a son of Zeus, and unlike
Luke,[162] Artapanus relates the tradition without demur, but
like Josephus[163] he places the claim in the mouth of the

---

[154]Cf. Ephorus, frg. 147, 149 (Jacoby, FGrH No. 70);
also Isocrates, Or. 4. 39.

[155]Of Osiris: Diod. S. 1. 14, 1; 15, 6; 15, 8; 18, 6;
Of Isis: Diod. S. 1. 14, 1; of Demeter: Euripides, Suppl.
28f.; Isocrates, Or. 4. 28.

[156]Cf. Diod. S. 1. 14ff.   [157]F 3. 4b.

[158]F 3. 5.   [159]F 3. 6.

[160]Rather than an ascription of divinity, what we have
here is a conventional method of encomium current in Egypt.
Note the formal structure of Manetho F 11, F 12, where he is
praising the achievements of Tosorthros (Sesorthos): οὗτος
Ἀσκληπιὸς ⟨παρὰ τοῖς⟩ Αἰγυπτίοις κατὰ τὴν ἰατρικὴν νενόμισται
... (Loeb). On ἰσοθέου (F 3. 6) cf. NOCK, "Notes on Ruler-
Cult," Essays 1. 135:5; also compare Phil. 2:6.

[161]Cf. Diod. S. 1. 16; Philo, V. Mos. 1. 1; Clem. Alex.,
Strom. 1. xxi. 150. 4; VERMÈS, 69:26; HEINEMANN, 368; EISLER,
Orph.-Diony., 7:2, "Der Verfasser will Moses also auch als
Autor oder Inspirator der Hermes-Trismegistos-Literatur
hinstellen!"

[162]Acts 14:12ff.   [163]Ap. 1. 279.

Egyptians. Freudenthal rightly notices that the blatancy of
the claim is mitigated by the strong Euhemeristic influence
prevalent in Ptolemaic Egypt and discernible in Artapanus.[164]
It is also worth noticing that the claim, rather than being
based upon or authenticated by thaumaturgic activity, arises
from his skill as an exegete.

The antagonist Chenephres, whose jealousy is triggered
by the fame (ἀρετή)[165] of Moses, begins a series of abortive
attempts to kill him. The tradition relating Moses' victory
over the Ethiopians,[166] whose invincibility was legendary, not
only served to demonstrate Moses' military prowess, but
represents the first in a long line of futile attempts by
Chenephres to dispose of Moses. It provides Artapanus with
an occasion to note that Moses could be beloved even by his
fiercest enemies.[167] In the remaining paragraphs[168] a second
plot unfolds against Moses, again triggered by a beneficial
deed performed by him in behalf of the Egyptians. The
Egyptians are alienated from Moses at the instigation of
Chenephres, an Egyptian.[169] The Egyptian Chanethothes is
killed by Moses in self-defense.[170] Even when Moses is safely
removed in Arabia, his concern for the Egyptians is undiminish-
ed: he dismisses without a second thought the proposal of
Raguel, his father-in-law, to invade Egypt.[171] The
antagonist--an Egyptian--comes to a bad end because of his
own vile deeds.[172]

There is a clear transition in F 3. 21, where the Exodus
narrative is resumed. With the exception of the prison-escape
scene,[173] every paragraph is either a summary, distortion, or

---

[164]On Euhemerism in Hecataeus, cf. Diod. 1. 13, 3f.
cf. WACHSMUTH, Einleitung, 330; FREUDENTHAL, 146, 154, 160;
Here, possibly Artapanus reflects his dependence upon ethno-
graphic literary tradition going back to Leon of Pella, who
had described the gods as human beings (cf. OCD[2], 595).

[165]F 3. 6, 9.   [166]F 3. 7-11.

[167]F 3. 10.   [168]F 3. 12-20.

[169]F 3. 13.   [170]F 3. 18.

[171]F 3. 19.   [172]F 3. 20.

[173]F 3. 23-26.

jumbling of the Biblical account. With some qualifications
F 3. 21-39 can be called a summary of the events recorded in
Exodus 2:23-16:36. The suffering of the Jews in Egypt is taken
for granted, having been mentioned previously only briefly.[174]
If the first section has been directed at countering the
Manethonian portrait of Moses, the second section surely
focuses upon clarifying the circumstances relating to the
departure of the Jews from Egypt. Basically, Artapanus
attempts to show in this section that the Exodus was accomplished under the auspices of ὁ θεός and therefore was necessary and unavoidable. For the first time Yahweh becomes a
participant in the narrative. Generally speaking, the events
of the Exodus are done at His behest. Moses decides to fight
against Egypt only at the behest of the φωνή θεία, and even
then reluctantly.[175] He informs Pharaoh that he had been
commanded to set the Jews free by ὁ δεσπότης τῆς οἰκουμένης.[176]
That his commander is no ordinary deity is seen by the fact
that anyone who treats his name lightly suffers fatal conse-
quences.[177] The powers of the rod responsible for all the
plagues done against the Egyptians derive ultimately from
Isis.[178] Thus all these malevolent acts perpetrated against
the Egyptians are traced indirectly to an Egyptian goddess!
The crossing of the Red Sea, as well as the stay in the desert,
is accomplished under divine impulse, approval and guidance.[179]
In the Manethonian account the Jews are depicted as ruthless
pillagers; it is no surprise that a second time[180] Artapanus
counters this view.[181]

In both sections, therefore, we see the same themes as
we found in F 1 & 2: the Jews, viewed properly, have been a

---

[174]Cf. F 3. 2.   [175]F 3. 21-22.

[176]F 3. 22.   [177]F 3. 24-26.

[178]F 3. 32. Is it possible that the phallic symbol,
which was a feature of Isis epigraphy (cf. Diod. S. 1. 22,
6-7) as well as Dionysus epigraphy (cf. NILSSON, Dionys.)
provided the basis for Artapanus' identifying Moses' rod with
the Isis cult?

[179]F 3. 36-38.   [180]F 3. 34; cf. F 2. 3.

[181]Cf. note 89 above.

boon, not a bane, to Egypt. Egypt has always been the better
for having had them in its borders.

Restraint of Artapanus.

Although scholars often assert, without qualification,
that Artapanus identifies Moses with Hermes, Orpheus, etc., a
closer examination of the fragments suggests that at least some
qualifications should be made when setting forth Artapanus'
theological views. Although Freudenthal's view that Artapanus
was affecting an Egyptian priestly point of view is generally
rejected,[182] it is based upon a perceptive perusal of the
evidence, as Freudenthal's views usually are. The element of
truth in his thesis is the manner in which Artapanus detaches
himself from many of the claims made for Moses. Walter may be
right that Artapanus himself actually holds the views expressed
in his work,[183] but at least the extent to which he qualifies
his statements should be noticed.[184] Once we begin to assemble
these qualifiers, the list becomes fairly impressive. Taking
the Moses fragment, since that is where the issue rises most
sharply, we are told that Moses was called Musaios by the
Greeks;[185] he was deemed worthy of honor befitting a god by
the (Egyptian) priests[186] and it is implied that he was called
Hermes by them, or, at least, by the Egyptians. Although it is
fairly certain that his assertion that Moses assigned the god

---

[182]Cf. HEINEMANN, 368; SCHWARTZ, 1306.

[183]WALTER, review, 791.

[184]Since the evidence is fragmentary and third-hand, it
resists dogmatic interpretation. It is impossible to know, for
example, the significance of the fact that the events of Ex.
17-40 are telescoped into two dozen words (F 3. 38); is the
omission of this section of Moses' life by summarizing it in a
few words to be taken as a reflection of Artapanus' anti-cultic
bias, or simply of his lack of interest in Moses the lawgiver
and his legislation? Or, is φησι in F 3. 39 the telltale sign
of editorial activity by Polyhistor, or Eusebius, or both?
Even with the fragments as they stand, the interpreter is con-
tinually aware that he is more than likely dealing with a
summary (cf. WALTER, review, 791, who comments on the large
number of infinitives as evidencing redactorial activity).
Failure to remember this only results in oversubtle analyses
of words and syntax.

[185]F 3. 3. [186]F 3. 6.

to be worshipped in each nome[187] is a reference to Egyptian gods, it is by no means an unambiguous statement.[188] No less ambiguous is the phrase "there were cats, dogs, and ibises."[189] In this connection it should be remarked that the only unambiguous statement that Moses consecrated the Egyptian's animals is found in F 3. 12. But, even so, may not F 3. 5 represent Artapanus' attempt to justify this as an act of political expediency? It is often overlooked that in F 3. 9 the ibis is consecrated not by Moses, but by his associates. And, rather than F 3. 12 making Moses indirectly responsible for the Apis cult,[190] he is only made responsible for the brilliant suggestion as to why the bull was useful to mankind. Chenephres--not Moses--is explicitly named as the one who named the bull Apis and commanded the masses to consecrate the temple for it. The reference to animals consecrated by Moses in F 3. 35 is part of the "Heliopolitan tradition" which he cites, thus purposely detached from himself, as is the "Memphian tradition," which gives a rationalized explanation of the Red Sea crossing. The statement in F 3. 16 that Merris, Moses' foster-mother, was the eponym of Meroe, and that she was revered by the inhabitants not one whit less than Isis, if intended to imply that Moses was a son of a god, is significant, if anything, for its indirectness.[191] If the structure of the Moses narrative bears any resemblance to the structure of the original work, is it not possible that the second section as a

---

[187]F 3. 4.   [188]Cf. TIEDE, 161:103.

[189]LAGRANGE, 500, thinks that the ambiguity is intentional.

[190]So TIEDE, 161.

[191]Contra Weinreich, 302, who thinks that this incident was an aetiology explaining Jewish acceptance of the ruler cult. Cf. HENGEL, Judentum u. Hellenismus, 58f.; 519ff., who cites epigraphical evidence bearing on the question of how the Jews accommodated to imperial requirements while at the same time maintaining their religious integrity. Cf. W. S. FERGUSON, CAH 7. 13ff.; A. D. NOCK, CAH, 10. 481ff.; REITZEN-STEIN, Poimandres, 182, opines "dass der jüdische Gesetzgeber in der Tat schon im zweiten Jahrhundert v. Chr. in bestimmten Kreisen Ägyptens Verehrung genoss."

whole, in which ὁ θεός[192] and ὁ δεσπότης τῆς οἰκουμενῆς[193]
figure prominently, was intended to offset any concessions
which may have been made in the first section? In the second
section Artapanus would have easily passed any ordination test,
assuming that the examiners recognized F 3. 35 as the
Memphians' opinion, and not Artapanus'.[194] The prominence of
magical power attached to the divine name[195] and evident in
the narrative of the plagues only brings honor to Yahweh, not
Moses.

One could perhaps argue that these qualifiers belong to
Eusebius, if Clement's modification of the prison-escape scene
is any indication that Christian writers tended to correct
apparent heterodox tendencies in their sources.[196] It appears,
however, that Eusebius, for the most part, has simply extracted
his materials from Polyhistor and his conscientious use of φησι
indicates that he was not entirely irresponsible in his method.

Summary and conclusion.

When we view the aims of Artapanus in the light of all
three fragments, we are forced to conclude that he is writing
a work On the Jews in the same vein as Hecataeus' On the
Egyptians, in which his aim is to glorify Judaism--for whatever
reasons. Basically, he accomplishes this (or attempts to do
so) by the same line of argument current in Alexandria:
antiquity (priority) proves superiority. Cult and culture
were not really that inseparable in this milieu, so that
superiority of both stood or fell together.

We have seen that Artapanus freely depicts and reinterprets Israel's heroes, particularly Moses, to suit his propagandistic fancy, but that in doing so he is not entirely
without theological scruples. He demonstrates no proclivity
to ascribe divinity to Moses in any way approaching what we
find in Euripides' Bacchae; in fact, he seems to be countering
Dionysiac traditions by shifting Yahweh to the center of the

---

[192]F 3. 21.   [193]F 3. 22.

[194]Cf. DALBERT, 52.   [195]F 3. 25-26.

[196]The two versions are paralleled in Jacoby, FGrH;
cf. discussion by WEINREICH, 302f.

stage vis à vis Dionysus. The theios aner concept is alien to the Sitz im Leben out of which Artapanus springs. The potency of his propaganda is not proportionate to, nor even dependent upon, the degree to which he can remodel Israel's heroes after the so-called Hellenistic model of the theios aner. He was not interested in a theios aner Moses (or Abraham, or Joseph) but a pro-Egyptian Moses, and it seems never to have occurred to him that designating any of Israel's heroes as theios aner would have any propagandistic value. The syncretistic flavor of his work, his accommodation to non-Jewish ideas and traditions, are indisputable. Efforts to indict him or exonerate him are misguided; we have attempted neither to bury him nor to praise him, but to understand him. Whether one sees him as an over-patriotic Jew whose zeal outran his knowledge, or a faithful Jew who either made no significant concessions to paganism, or made some concessions for a higher cause, our analysis has demonstrated that he was not totally without scruples, and that his faith imposed some restrictions upon what he would allow. Indeed, his faith is the only plausible explanation of why he attempted what he did.

CHAPTER FIVE

CONCLUSION

Apologetic intentions pervade Hellenistic-Jewish writing throughout the three centuries beginning with our earliest source Demetrius the Chronographer until the time of Josephus. Jews, both in the Diaspora and Palestine, whenever they commingled with non-Jews, be they Babylonians, Egyptians, Macedonians, Greeks, or Romans, inevitably found themselves in a defensive posture. The many contributory causes ranged from a deeply ingrained superiority complex whose basis lay in their consciousness of having been elected by God--a consciousness capable of breeding an uncompromising exclusiveness--to their peculiar practices which excited curiosity and antipathy. Even if they found themselves aliens in a strange land, they, nevertheless, could equalize, if not elevate their position vis à vis other peoples by resorting to and cultivating, by a rather complex mental chemistry, a solidarity nurtured by the consciousness of their unique relationship to the only true God. The price was high, however, for fidelity to an exclusive religious system inevitably entails defense of that system. Since exclusiveness engenders counterattack, persons who by chance happened not to belong to the Elect would understandably retaliate, seeking to isolate the chinks in the Jewish armor, and resorting to any means available, would seize upon the most vulnerable points of the system and there direct their criticism, accusations, and innuendo. It was essentially a matter of survival. An exclusivistic group, religious or otherwise, which aims to engulf what it regards as the rest of humanity into its fold, either ideologically or realistically, throws down the gauntlet whether the outsider wishes it so or not.

The sweep of Alexander the Great across the East had married two (at least two) enormously dissimilar cultures, and the Hellenistic Age tells the story of how that marriage fared. At times, and in some places, it was fairly blissful, while at other times and in other places the only reasonable solution proved to be divorce on the grounds of mutual incompatibility. Much of the story has to be deduced. The sources are often

fragmentary and piecemeal, and often allusive. Not everyone
likes to air his marriage problems before the public, though
there are times when it eventually must be done. The literature therefore can range from the cryptically apologetic
Demetrius, who ostensibly is writing a chronicle of Biblical
history, but is in fact countering charges that have been
levelled against the Chosen People and their newly published
Bible in Greek, to the openly apologetic Josephus, who, in
Contra Apionem has judged that public confrontation is the only
feasible solution, and is more than willing to call names. To
be sure, the situation has changed substantially within the
three centuries separating these two ends of the spectrum, so
the contrast is not entirely fair. Even so, we are witnessing
a different degree of apologetic writing in each case. In
fact, the same differences are discernible even with Josephus
himself. In Contra Apionem the fight is open; in Antiquitates
it is being carried on between the lines for the most part.
Philo is often more subtle, but his apologetic intentions are
obvious on almost every page of his writing.

Since these spokesmen for Judaism exhibit great variety,
it is necessary to assess them in terms of certain variables.
The debate occurs in different historical circumstances,
conditioned by geographical no less than political, economic,
and religious factors; the participants have personalities as
vastly different as that of Josephus and Philo, or of Artapanus
and Demetrius. It also occurs at various sociological levels
ranging from the popular romance novel of Artapanus to the more
sophisticated literary level of a Josephus or Philo. As to the
basic motivation, there is no essential difference; they are
all engaged in the same enterprise: they are heirs of the
promise seeking to defend themselves and the validity of their
claims to now hostile, now unsympathetic, now apathetic
audiences, whose knowledge of them is more often than not
grossly misinformed.

Our aim has been to investigate one aspect of this
debate--the role which the theme of Israel's heroes, either
collectively or individually, played within the literary battle
that went on. It has involved the question of how the Jews
interpreted their own national history as they came to be

Hellenized, but we have primarily examined how these figures of Israel's past began to be interpreted and reinterpreted as Jews established their position vis à vis non-Jews. Specifically, we have looked at the question of whether the Jews, as they reacted and interacted with non-Jews, began to conceive of and to portray these heroes in terms suggesting divinity and whether the evidence suggests that ascribing divinity to their heroes had any value as propaganda, and, if so, what. The specific focus of our inquiry has been upon the expression theios aner, its meaning as used by Hellenistic-Jewish authors, its function within this apologetic setting, and the related questions which the expression raises. Some of the crucial passages within this literature have been examined with a view to determining not only what precisely the author is claiming but also whether such claims recur with sufficient regularity to enable us to speak of a tendency, or to speak of these as a major or significant feature of Hellenistic-Jewish propaganda. At the same time, some attempt has been made to set this single theme within the larger context of Hellenistic-Jewish propaganda in order to see whether its relationship to other themes is direct or indirect, central or peripheral.

As to the question of whether in Hellenistic-Judaism it became easier for Jews to conceive of a divine man because the line of demarcation between man and God had become blurred, we have seen evidence that suggests that Hellenization among Jews, rather than bridging the gap, only widened it. As surprising as it may sound, Philo offers the best proof of this--the radical dualism between Creator and creature, between God and man, if anything became more deeply entrenched in Philo. At the same time, in the course of our investigation we had occasion to notice the tendency to deify Israel's heroes in circles of Judaism not normally classed as Hellenistic-Judaism. Although it falls beyond the scope of this study, apocalyptic Judaism offers some of the best examples of this, not to mention some of the Rabbinic passages which have been noted in passing. The hagiographical tendency seems to have been common to all groups, and we have noted its presence within Hellenistic-Jewish sources.

There seems to be no direct correlation, therefore,

between the extent of Hellenization and a willingness or propensity to deify human beings.

It is certainly true that within Hellenistic-Judaism there was the willingness, on the part of some, Artapanus, for example, to incorporate Greek mythological traditions into the Biblical account. Philo's willingness to allegorize is also an indication of the degree of his accommodation to non-Biblical modes of thought. In all three of the authors which we examined, a considerable amount of Hellenization has occurred, both in language and thought. Philo honestly believes in Platonic metaphysics. Moreover, this Hellenization affected the categories in which Hellenistic-Jews began to conceive of their past heroes, but in their reinterpretation and portrayal of those heroes it cannot be said that the tendency to deify such persons constituted a major feature of their apologetic. While it is true that Philo uses "language of deification," he does so in a highly qualified sense, and, we have argued, that even when allowance is made for the idiosyncratic complexion of his theology, the line of demarcation between man and God still exists, in the end. It cannot be denied that these authors, at times, incorporated hagiographical traditions, and even spoke of their heroes in suprahuman terms, but one must make allowance for a certain amount of hyperbole. What is more, as we have already had occasion to notice, to isolate is to exaggerate. Due account must be given to the fact that in perhaps the best single example of Hellenistic-Jewish apologetic which we have, Contra Apionem, but for a single, offhand allusion which mentions that the Egyptians considered Moses as theios, this tendency is non-existent. It may be true, therefore, that during the Hellenistic era there occurs a significant shift in Jewish thinking which enables Jews more easily to attribute divinity to their Biblical heroes for propagandistic purposes, but the evidence for supporting such a contention does not seem to be forthcoming from Hellenistic-Jewish apologetic, at least, in the sources which we have examined.

A word should also be said about the relation between the expression theios aner and miracle working. Our investigation has shown that there is even less reason, on the basis of the sources examined, to use the expression theios aner as an

equivalent of "miracle-worker." In none of the four instances
where theios aner occurs in the sources examined does the
expression carry this meaning. Apart from the expression
theios aner itself, in those passages where "language of
deification" was employed, there was no visible tendency to
authenticate such claims by appeals to miracles or miracle
traditions.

This study began as an inquiry into New Testament
Christology, but, as sometimes happens, one small detour became
the main road. The decision to concentrate on extra-Biblical
sources arose from the conviction that until this single area
of the theios aner hypothesis had been examined--and hopefully
clarified--, the New Testament question would inevitably remain
clouded.

Our fundamental criticism of the use of the expression
theios aner in Christological discussions arises from its
intrinsic ambiguity. Long before this study, several scholars
had already begun to express doubts about the legitimacy and
propriety of using theios aner as a terminus technicus or as a
concrete, well-defined category, but this study has tended to
reinforce those doubts. The obvious again needs pointing out:
the single word theios was capable of at least four distinct
meanings, with room for intermediate shades, and this fluidity
has been amply attested with the Hellenistic-Jewish authors,
specifically Josephus and Philo. Thus, because theios aner is
automatically capable of at least four meanings, including
"divine man," "inspired man," "a man, in some sense, related
to God," and "extraordinary man," it is less possible to speak
without further ado of a theios aner Christology, as if theios
aner had only one meaning, especially as if the two notions of
divinity and miracle-working were essential ingredients.
Unlike υἱὸς θεοῦ in which the Father-son model remains constant, even though the expression itself may be taken meta-
phorically or literally, theios aner has no such built-in
control. As to its use as a terminus technicus, in the case
of an expression such as ἐν Χριστῷ, which occurs repeatedly in
the New Testament, the question is one of deciding from among
many uses whether a given use is a technical expression. But,
theios aner, not only does not occur in the Greek Old Testament

or New Testament, but only rarely occurs in Jewish sources at all. Its usefulness therefore, is extremely questionable, for using it in Christological discussions merely introduces into an already confused field of study yet another ill-defined, if not undefinable category, at a time when precision and clarity of meaning should be sought, not sacrificed.

One is made to ask whether the Christological question has often been wrongly framed. At one time it seemed appropriate to account for the ascription of the title υἱὸς θεοῦ as well as miracle traditions to Jesus by pointing to the Hellenistic milieu as having produced the necessary catalyst, having been prepared for by Hellenistic-Judaism where Jews in similar Hellenistic milieux had made similar claims about their heroes. The underlying assumption was that a Hellenistic milieu produced the catalyst for producing a chemical change which was otherwise impossible in a purely Jewish setting. Not only has our study pointed up the difficulties of analyzing Christology with such air-tight categories as "Hellenistic" and "Jewish," but it has suggested that the time now seems ripe to seek for answers to the two-pronged question of Jesus' divine sonship and his miracles along lines other than Hellenistic Sitze im Leben or in terms of a process of Hellenization. The fact is that Hellenization seems, in some instances, to have made it more difficult for Jews to conceive of a divine man.

The same point applies to the question of miracles and miracle traditions within the Gospels. Our study has failed to produce evidence to substantiate the position that Hellenistic-Jews, in an effort to propagate their faith to Gentiles, tended to heighten thaumaturgic motifs, either in their portrayals of Israel's heroes or in their own understanding of history. Philo actually tones down Moses' miracle working activity as compared with the Biblical account. Both Philo and Josephus carve Israel's heroes into figures besides miracle-workers; for all of Artapanus' embellishments of the Moses traditions, he seems little concerned to turn him into a miracle-worker. This raises the inevitable question of just how attractive the miracle-worker motif was to pagans, and may explain why this aspect of the Jesus tradition is non-existent in the apostolic fathers. The end-product in Josephus, Philo, and even

Artapanus, turns out to be vastly dissimilar to the commonly adduced miracle-worker type, such as Apollonius of Tyana. To account, therefore, for the presence of miracles and miracle traditions within the Gospels on the basis of a Hellenistic Sitz im Leben, particularly that of missionary preaching, as the earlier form critics did, seems to be a highly dubious exercise. The preoccupation to focus attention upon the miracles as primarily means of attesting the divinity of the miracle worker, either compared with the Rabbinic or the Hellenistic miracle-worker, obscures the more fundamental line of continuity with the Old Testament, and the corollary understanding of miracles in terms of Salvation-history, particularly their eschatological implications.

The point can also be made another way. A look at the sermons in Acts, particularly the motif of Jesus as miracle-worker, reveals exactly the opposite tendency. As the sermons become more "Hellenistic" in texture, the portrayal of Jesus as miracle-worker diminishes; it is present in Acts 2:22 and Acts 10:38, but absent in Acts 17.

As to the question of missionary preaching, the question of the exact relationship between Hellenistic-Judaism, its sources, its theology, its sociological complexion, and early Christian missionary preaching is still unresolved. The first question is whether the sources are adequate enough to construct the picture of Hellenistic-Jewish missionary activity that Georgi does. To assemble all the references to supposed missionary activity within the mystery religions and add to them the occasional pieces of evidence for travelling Jews, from which is elaborated a detailed picture of Hellenistic-Jewish missionaries is a highly questionable method of approach. Even more, can one speak so confidently about Hellenistic-Jewish theology as if it were homogeneous? It must not be forgotten that the Diaspora was capable of considerable theological diversity; the same Diaspora produced Philo and the Sibylline Oracles.

Our criticism of the use of the expression theios aner as a Christological category also applies to the question of heresies and heretical tendencies in early Christianity. Efforts to extend our knowledge about the nature of heresies within early Christianity can, of course, only be applauded, but can they be benefited by the continual use of a category as fluid as _theios aner_? We believe that there is even less reason to analyze opponents of Paul, either at Corinth or Thessalonica, or elsewhere, as _theioi andres_, if this is taken to mean that they are miracle-workers, or experts in pneumatic demonstrations, whatever that might mean. Is there not greater need for more precise categories with which to treat these persons? The term becomes even less useful if it is meant to imply the _divinity_ of these persons. As to the "orthodox" stream, _Acts_ 10:26 and _Acts_ 14:15ff., among other passages, make it clear that the apostles shunned the notion that _they_ were divine. If there is evidence that in "heterodox" streams some Christian missionaries began to conceive of themselves as divine, an effort should be made to determine the precise nature of this self-understanding; and, even if it is found that they actually conceived of themselves in other than human terms, it is questionable whether _theios aner_ is the most desirable term to use.

The historiographical implications of our investigation have been briefly alluded to. Whatever else the expression _theios aner_ does, it provides a concrete example of the difficulties one encounters in trying to sketch the growth and development of primitive Christianity. Especially does it illustrate the near impossibility of sketching Christological development along a neatly defined scheme. It is becoming more and more difficult to speak with confidence about "Palestinian Christianity" or "Hellenistic Christianity," or even "Hellenistic-Jewish Christianity," as if these were clearly defined entities. Even less can we suppose that certain Christological categories were by definition impossible to conceive of within each of these categories. What cannot be doubted is that a given Christological title or category was understood differently with a given _Sitz im Leben_, for various reasons; but asserting the impossibility of a given Christological title as having been used or understood within a given setting, merely because it was "Jewish" or "Hellenistic" seems unwarranted.

Our study, thus, has concentrated upon evidence bearing

upon the appropriateness of the expression _theios aner_ as a
Christological category. We have especially concentrated upon
this concept as it relates to Hellenistic-Jewish apologetic
because that represents the most crucial link in the _theios
aner_ hypothesis, as we have analyzed it. We have argued that
it is an unsuitable expression for Christological discussions,
mainly because of its imprecision, and especially when it is
assumed to be a static, well-defined category in which the two
notions of divinity and miracle-working are essential, prominent features. What has especially become clear is the
untenability of the _theios aner_ = miracle-worker equation.
We have found that as long as _theios aner_ is used as a generic
term for a type of individual in antiquity who was in some way
"of God," it has a certain usefulness, although its generality
and fluidity more often obfuscate than clarify, because it
allows a variety of types to be categorized within a single
class, a conglomeration that easily results in the blending of
otherwise distinct lines. Used as an expression in the more
strict sense of a "_divine_ man," i.e. a man who is a god, either
by his own claims or by those of others, the term has little
applicability to the circumstances obtaining within Judaism,
particularly within the sources which we have examined--
Josephus, Philo, and Artapanus. We have noticed a marked
reluctance within these various strata of Hellenistic-Judaism
to ascribe divinity to human beings in any real sense, and, in
fact, have argued that such a claim did not constitute a major
feature of Jewish propaganda addressed to pagans. To be sure,
Israel's heroes were remodeled to fit pagan notions, sometimes
with almost total disregard for Old Testament traditions, but
the general thrust of the reshaping was not in the direction of
ascribing divinity to these figures. They are often described
in highly laudatory terms, but nothing like the rather blatant
claims one finds in Philostratus with reference to Apollonius
of Tyana. Even when these authors incorporate mythological
traditions into their narratives, they do not do so for the
purpose of transforming these heroes into Greek gods. To be
sure, passages from the Old Testament which would strongly
support such a view are not taken up and used as one would
expect if this had been a major preoccupation of Hellenistic-

Jewish apologists. Jews were always rather gifted in reinterpreting the Old Testament to suit their present needs, even if considerable rejuggling was necessary, but that is precisely what we do not find in this connection. Philo's use of Ex. 7:1 has provided a case in point. The implications of these findings are that regardless of the theological shifts that occurred in Judaism through the penetration of Hellenism, the chasm between God and man still remained real, at least, in these circles of Judaism which we have examined. Their heroes remained men--glorified men whose deeds and accomplishments were embellished--but men all the same.

Our study has concentrated upon a single expression, theios aner, and a few bits of data--the occurrence of this expression four times in the sources which we have examined. A. D. Nock once remarked, "A fact is a holy thing, and its life should never be laid down on the altar of generalization."[1] It is hoped that our study has served as a corrective, in a small sense, to the temptation to transform the fact of the theios aner into a generalized figure who meets us at every turn in New Testament scholarship.

---

[1]A. D. NOCK, Essays, 1. 333.

BIBLIOGRAPHY

SOURCES

I. JOSEPHUS.

   A. Editions.

      Dindorfius, Guilelmus. Flavius Josephus. Opera.
        Graece et Latine. Recognovit Guilelmus
        Dindorfius. Paris, 1845-57. 2 vols.

      Hudson, J. Flavius Josephus. Opera Omnia Graece et
        Latine, cum notis & nova versione J. Hudsoni ...
        Adjiciuntur in fine Caroli Danbuz libri duo pro
        testimonio Fl. Josephi de Jesu Christo ...
        Sigebertus Havercampus. Amsterdam, 1726.

      Niese, B. Flavii Iosephi Opera. Editio maior.
        Berlin, 1887-95. 7 vols.

      Thackeray, H. St. J., Ralph Marcus, Allen Wikgren, &
        L. H. Feldman. Josephus with an English Transla-
        tion. (The Loeb Classical Library) London/
        Cambridge, Mass., 1926-65. 9 vols.

   B. Translations.

      Dutch:

      Séwel, W. Alle De Werken van Flavius Josephus.
        Amsterdam, 1704.

      English:

      Anonymous. The Works of Josephus, with great diligence
        revised and amended, according to the excellent
        French translation of M. Arnauld d'Andilly.
        London, 1676; 1683; 1693.

      Anonymous. Works of the Learned and Valiant Josephus
        Epitomized from the Greek Original. 2nd ed. rev.
        London, 1701.

      Court, John. The Works of Flavius Josephus. Transla-
        ted by J. Court from the original Greek according
        to Dr. Hudson's edition. London, 1733.

      L'Estrange, Sir Roger. The Works of Flavius Josephus.
        Translated into English by Sir Roger L'Estrange.
        All carefully revised & compared with the original
        Greek. London, 1702; Dundee, 1766.

      Lodge, Thomas. The Famous and Memorable Workes of
        Josephus, A Man of Much Honour and Learning Among
        the Jews. Trans. fr. Latin and French by Tho.
        Lodge. London, 1609; 1640; 1670.

      Maynard, George Henry. The Genuine & Complete Works of
        Flavius Josephus, the Celebrated Warlike, Learned
        and Authentic Jewish Historian. Trans. from the

original in the Greek language ... George Henry
Maynard. London, 1785; New York, 1792; Philadelphia, 1795.

Thackeray, H. St. J., Ralph Marcus, Allen Wikgren, &
L. H. Feldman. Josephus with an English Translation. (Loeb) London/Cambridge, Mass., 1926-65.
9 vols.

Thompson, Ebenezer & William Charles Price. The Works
of Flavius Josephus. The Whole Newly Translated
from the Original Greek by Ebenezer Thompson &
William Charles Price. London, 1777. 2 vols.

Whiston, William. The Genuine Works of Flavius
Josephus the Jewish Historian. Translated from
the original Greek according to Havercamp's
accurate edition by William Whiston. London,
1737. Other editions appeared in 1793, 1806,
1812, 1815, 1825, 1840, 1841, 1843, (1850?),
1864, 1865, 1867, 1873, 1875-76, 1878-79, 1884,
1889-90 (rev. by A. R. Shilleto), 1893, 1906
(newly rev. ed. by D. S. Margoliouth), 1963.

Wilson, James. A Collection of the Genuine Works of
Flavius Josephus. Faithfully translated from the
original Greek by James Wilson, with explanatory
notes, and a copious index. London, 1740.

French:

Bourgoing, François. Histoire de Fl. Iosèphe
Sacrificatevr Hebriev. Escrite premierement par
l'auteur en langue Grèque, & nouvellement traduite
en François par F. Bourgoing. Lyon, 1558. 2 vols.
in 1.

D'Andilly, Arnauld. Histoire des Ivifs Ecrite par
Flavius Ioseph. Sous le Titre de Antiqvitez
Ivdaiqves. Tradvite sur l'original Grec M.
Arnavld D'Andilly. Troisième Ed. Paris, 1670;
rev. ed., 1680; new ed. incl. Bel. & Vita:
Amsterdam, 1700.

Genebrard, G. Histoire de Fl. Josèphe ... Mise en
françois. Reueuë sur le Grec, & illustrée de
chronologie ... par G. Genebrard. Paris, 1588;
1616 (2 vols. in 1).

Gillet, R. P. Nouvelle Traduction de L'Histoire
Joseph. Faite sur le Grec avec des notes
critiques & historiques ... R. P. Gillet. Paris,
1756-67. 4 vols.

Reinach, Th. Oeuvres complètes de Flavius Josèphe,
Traduites en Français, sous la direction de Th.
Reinach. (Publ. de la Soc. des études juives)
Paris, 1900-32. 7 vols.

German:

Cotta, Johann Friderich. Jos. Fl. Sämmtliche Wercke.
Ausgefertigt von Johann Friderich Cotta.
Tübingen, 1736.

Hedion, Caspar. Jos. Fl. Josephus Teütsch ... Caspar
Hedion. Strassburg, 1531. 2 pts.

Martin, R. Die jüdischen Alterthümer des Flavius
Josephus übersetzt und mit Anmerkungen versehen.
Köln, 1852. 2 vols.

Ott, Johann Baptist. Jos. Fl. Sämtliche Wercke.
Erläutert von Johann Baptist Ott. Zürich, 1736.

Hebrew:

Schalit, Abraham. [פלביוס יוספוס] יוסף בן מתתיהו
קדמוניות היהודים
Jerusalem/Tel Aviv, 1955-63. 3 vols.

II. PHILO

A. Editions and Translations.

Arnaldez, R., J. Pouilloux, C. Mondésert, et al. Les
oeuvres de Philon d'Alexandrie. (Lyon ed.)
Paris, 1961- . 27 vols. pub. to date.

Aucher, J. B. Philonis Judaei. Sermones Tres Hactenus
Inediti. Venice, 1822.

Cohn, L. & P. Wendland. Philonis Alexandrini Opera
Quae Supersunt. Berlin, 1896-1930. 7 vols.

Cohn, L., I. Heinemann, M. Adler, & W. Theiler. Philo
von Alexandria. Die Werke in deutscher
Übersetzung. Breslau, 1909-38; repr. Berlin,
1962; Bd. 7, 1964.

Colson, F. H., G. H. Whitaker, & R. Marcus. Philo with
an English Translation. (Loeb series) London/
Cambridge, Mass., 1949-61. 12 vols.

Yonge, C. D. The Works of Philo Judaeus. London,
1854-55. 4 vols.

III. OTHER JEWISH SOURCES.

Denis, Albert-Marie (collegit et ordinavit). Fragmenta
Pseudepigraphorum Quae Supersunt Graeca Una Cum
Historicorum et Auctorum Judaeorum Hellenistarum
Fragmentis. (Along with Apocalypsis Henochi
Graece, ed. M. Black). (Pseudepigrapha Veteris
Testamenti Graece, edd. A-M. Denis et M. De Jonge,
vol. 3). Leiden, 1970.

Etheridge, J. W. The Targums of Onkelos and Jonathan
ben Uzziel on the Pentateuch with the fragments of
the Jerusalem Targum. New York, 1968. 2 vols.
in 1.

Freudenthal, J. Alexander Polyhistor und die von ihm
erhaltenen Reste judäischer und samaritanischer
Geschichtswerke (Hellenistische Studien, Heft 1 &
2) Breslau, 1875. 219-36.

Jacoby, F. Die Fragmente der griechischen Historiker.
Leiden, 1958; repr. 1969. III C, Bd. 2.

Müller, C. Fragmenta Historicorum Graecorum collegit, disposuit, notis et prolegomenis illustravit, indicibus instruxit. Paris, 1841-72. 5 vols. Esp. vols. 2-3.

Riessler, P. Altjüdisches Schrifttum ausserhalb der Bibel. Heidelberg, ²1966.

Stearns, W. N. Fragments from Graeco-Jewish Writers. Chicago, 1908.

IV. CLASSICAL SOURCES.

   A. Collections, etc.

De Vogel, C. J. Greek Philosophy. A Collection of Texts with Notes and Explanations. III: The Hellenistic-Roman Period. Leiden, 1964.

Diels, H. & W. Kranz. Die Fragmente der Vorsokratiker. Berlin, ⁵1934-37. 3 vols.

Dittenberger, W. (ed.). Orientis Graeci Inscriptiones Selectae. Leipzig, 1903-05.

Jacoby, F. Die Fragmente der griechischen Historiker. Leiden, 1957-1969.

Kern, O. (ed.). Orphicorum Fragmenta. Berlin, 1922.

Schubart, W. & E. Kühn (edd.). Papyri und Ostraka der Ptolemäerzeit (Ägyptische Urkunden aus den Staatlichen Museen zu Berlin. Griechische Urkunden. VI. Band) Berlin, 1927.

Sprague, R. S. (ed.). The Older Sophists. A Complete Translation by Several Hands of the Fragments in Die Fragmente der Vorsokratiker, edited by Diels-Kranz. Columbia, S. C., 1972.

Von Arnim, H. Stoicorum Veterum Fragmenta. Leipzig, 1903-24; repr. Stuttgart, 1964. 4 vols.

   B. Individual Authors Most Frequently Cited.

Aeschylus. Works. Trans. H. W. Smyth. (Loeb series) London/Cambridge, Mass., 1922-26. 2 vols.

Aristotle. Nicomachean Ethics. Trans. H. Rackham. (Loeb series) London/Cambridge, Mass., 1934.

Dio Chrysostom. Discourses. Trans. J. W. Cohoon. (Loeb series) London/Cambridge, Mass., 1932-51. 5 vols.

Diodorus Siculus. Library of History. Trans. C. H. Oldfather, et al. (Loeb series) London/Cambridge, Mass., 1933-63. 12 vols.

Diogenes Laertius. Lives of Eminent Philosophers. Trans. R. D. Hicks. (Loeb series) London/Cambridge, 1925; vol. 2 rev. 1938. 2 vols.

Epictetus. Works. Trans. W. A. Oldfather. (Loeb series) London/Cambridge, Mass., 1925-28. 2 vols.

Euripides. Works. Trans. A. S. Way. (Loeb series) London/Cambridge, Mass., 1912. 4 vols.

Heracleitus. Quaestiones Homericae. Ed. & trans. F. Buffière. (Budé) Paris, 1962.

Herodotus. Works. Trans. A. D. Godley. (Loeb series) London/Cambridge, Mass., 1920-26. 4 vols.

Isocrates. Works. Trans. G. Norlin and LaRue Van Hook. (Loeb series) London/Cambridge, Mass., 1928-1945. 3 vols.

Manetho. Aegyptiaca, etc. Trans. W. G. Waddell. (Loeb series) London/Cambridge, Mass., 1940.

Plato. Works. Trans. Paul Shorey, et al. (Loeb series) London/Cambridge, Mass., 1914-35. 12 vols.

Pliny. Natural History. Trans. H. Rackham, W. H. S. Jones, et al. (Loeb series) London/Cambridge, Mass., 1938-1963. 11 vols.

Plutarch. Moralia. Trans. F. C. Babbitt, et al. (Loeb series) London/Cambridge, Mass. 1927-69. 16 vols.

Stobaeus. Anthologium. Ed. K. Wachsmuth and O. Hense. Berlin, 1884-1912. 5 vols.

V. CHRISTIAN SOURCES.

Eusebius:

Gifford, E. H. Eusebii Pamphili Evangelicae Praeparationis. Libri XV. Oxford, 1903. 5 vols.

Mras, K. Die Praeparatio Evangelica. (GCS). Berlin, 1954-56. 2 vols.

OTHER WORKS

Achtemeier, Paul J. "Gospel Miracle Tradition and the Divine Man." Interpretation 26 (1972) 174-97.

_____. "The Origin and Function of the Pre-Markan Miracle Catenae." JBL 91 (1972) 198-221.

_____. Review of D. L. Tiede, Charismatic Figure. CBQ 35 (1973) 559-60.

_____. "Toward the Isolation of Pre-Markan Miracle Catenae." JBL 89 (1970) 265-91.

Allan, D. J. Review of Canart & Van Camp. Θεῖος chez Platon. Classical Review N.S. 9 (1959) 170-71.

Ambrozic, A. M. The Hidden Kingdom. A Redaction-Critical Study of the References to the Kingdom of God in Mark's Gospel. (CBQ Monograph Series, 2) Washington, D.C., 1972.

Armstrong, A. H. "Plotinus," in The Cambridge History of Later Greek and Early Medieval Philosophy. Ed. A. H. Armstrong.

Cambridge, 1967. 193-268.

Arnaldez, R. "Introduction Générale (Philon)," Les oeuvres de Philon d'Alexandrie. Paris, 1961. 1. 17-112.

Ast, F. Lexicon platonicum sive Vocum platonicarum Index. Leipzig, 1835-38. 3 vols.

Bammel, E. Review of M. Green, Evangelism in the Early Church. ThLZ 98 (1973) 529-32.

Bardy, G. "Apologetik." RAC, 1. 533-43.

✓ Barrett, C. K. "Paul's Opponents in II Corinthians." NTS 17 (1970-71) 233-54.

✓ Baur, F. C. Apollonius von Tyana und Christus. Tübingen, 1832.

Becker, Jürgen. "Wunder und Christologie, zum literarkritischen und christologischen Problem der Wunder im Johannesevangelium." NTS 16 (1969-70) 130-48.

Behm, J. "προνοέω, πρόνοια." TDNT, 4. 1009-17.

Betz, Hans Dieter. "Jesus as Divine Man," in Jesus and the
✓   Historian. (Colwell Festschrift, Ed. F. T. Trotter)
       Philadelphia, 1968. 114-33.

_____. Lukian von Samosata und das Neue Testament,
✓   religionsgeschichtliche und paränetische Parallelen.
       (Ein Beitrag zum Corpus Hellenisticum Novi Testamenti)
       Berlin, 1961.

_____. (ed.). Christology and a Modern Pilgrimage. A Discussion with Norman Perrin. Claremont, 1971.

Betz, Otto. "The Concept of the So-called 'Divine Man' in
✓   Mark's Christology," in Studies in New Testament and Early
       Christian Literature. (Wikgren Festschrift, Ed. D. E.
       Aune; Novum Testamentum, Supplements, 33) Leiden, 1972.
       229-40.

✓ Bieler, Ludwig. ΘΕΙΟΣ ΑΝΗΡ. Das Bild des "Göttlichen
       Menschen" in Spätantike und Frühchristentum. Wien, 1935
       (Bd. 1); 1936 (Bd. 2); repr. Darmstadt, 1967, 2 vols. in L

Bieneck, J. Sohn Gottes als Christusbezeichnung der
       Synoptiker. (Abh. z. Theol. d. Alten u. Neuen Testaments,
       21) Zürich, 1951.

Billings, T. H. The Platonism of Philo Judaeus. Chicago,
       1919.

Bluck, R. S. H. Plato. Meno. Cambridge, 1961.

Bousset, Wilhelm. Kyrios Christos. A History of the Belief in
       Christ from the Beginnings of Christianity to Irenaeus.
       Trans. John E. Steely of 5th & 6th(?) Ger. edd. New York,
       1970.

_____. and H. Gressmann. Die Religion des Judentums im
       Späthellenistischen Zeitalter [Handbuch zum Neuen
       Testament, 21] 4. Auflage. Tübingen, 1966.

Bowker, John. The Targums and Rabbinic Literature. An
       Introduction to Jewish Interpretations of Scripture.
       Cambridge, 1969.

249

Braun, H. "The Meaning of New Testament Christology." JThC 5 (1968) 89-127.

Braun, M. History and Romance in Graeco-Oriental Literature. Oxford, 1938.

Bréhier, E. Les idées philosophiques et religieuses de Philon d'Alexandrie. (Études de philosophie médiévale, 8) Paris, ²1925.

Brüne, B. Flavius Josephus und seine Schriften in ihrem Verhältnis zum Judentume, zur griechisch-römischen Welt und zum Christentume mit griechischer Wortkonkordanz zum Neuen Testamente und 1. Clemensbriefe. Gütersloh, 1913.

Bultmann, Rudolf. The Gospel of John. Trans. G. R. Beasley-Murray of 1964 printing of Das Evangelium des Johannes, with the supplement of 1966. Oxford, 1971.

_____. History of the Synoptic Tradition. Trans. John Marsh. 2nd ed. with corrections and additions from 1962 supplement. Rev. ed. Oxford, 1972.

_____. Theology of the New Testament. Trans. Kendrick Grobel. New York, 1951 (vol. 1); 1955 (vol. 2).

Cerfaux, L. "Influence des Mystères sur le Judaïsme Alexandrin avant Philon," in Recueil Lucien Cerfaux, études d'exégèse et d'histoire religieuse de M. Cerfaux. Gembloux, 1954. 1. 65-112.

Chadwick, H. "Philo," in Cambridge History of Later Greek and Early Medieval Philosophy. Ed. A. H. Armstrong. Cambridge, 1967. 137-57.

_____. "St. Paul and Philo of Alexandria." BJRL 48 (1965-66) 286-307.

Cohn, L. "Einleitung und Chronologie der Schriften Philos." Philologus, Suppl. 7 (1899) 387-435.

_____. Review of W. N. Stearns, Fragments from Graeco-Jewish Writers. Berliner Philologische Wochenschrift 30 (1910) 1401-05.

Cohon, Samuel S. "Theology of Judaism according to Josephus," Review of Schlatter, Theologie. JQR N.S. 26 (1935-36) 152-57.

_____. "The Unity of God. A Study in Hellenistic and Rabbinic Theology." HUCA 26 (1955) 425-79.

Colpe, C. Die religionsgeschichtliche Schule. Darstellung und Kritik ihres Bildes vom gnostischen Erlösermythus. (FRLANT, N.F. 60) Göttingen, 1961.

Conzelmann, H. An Outline of the Theology of the New Testament. Trans. J. Bowden. of 2nd Ger. ed. New York, 1969.

Cornford, F. M. Principium Sapientiae. The Origins of Greek Philosophical Thought. Ed. W. K. C. Guthrie. New York, 1965; orig. pub. 1952.

Corradi, G. Studi Ellenistici. Torino, 1929.

Cowley, A. E. (ed.). The Samaritan Liturgy. Oxford, 1909.

Cullmann, Oscar. The Christology of the New Testament. Trans. S. C. Guthrie & C. A. M. Hall of 1957 Ger. ed. London, 1959.

Dalbert, P. Die Theologie der hellenistisch-judischen Missionsliteratur unter Ausschluss von Philo und Josephus. (Theologische Forschung wissenschaftliche Beiträge zur kirchlich-evangelischen Lehre) Hamburg-Volksdorf, 1954.

Daniélou, J. Philon d'Alexandrie. Paris, 1958.

_____. "La symbolique du temple de Jérusalem chez Philon et Josephe." Le Symbolisme cosmique des Monuments religieux [Série Orientale Roma, 14. Actes de la Conference Internationale qui a eu lieu sous les auspices de L'Istituto Italiano per il Medio ed Estremo Oriente avec la collaboration du Musée Guimet à Rome, 1955.] Rome, 1957. 83-90.

Deissmann, A. "Die Hellenisierung des semitischen Monotheismus." Neue Jahrbücher für das klassische Altertum 11 (1903) 161-77.

De Kruijf, T. Der Sohn des lebendigen Gottes. Rome, 1962.

Delling, Gerhard (ed.). Bibliographie zur jüdisch-hellenistischen und intertestamentarischen Literatur, 1900-65. (TU, 106) Berlin, 1969.

_____. "Josephus und die heidnischen Religionen." Klio 43-45 (1965) 263-69.

_____. "Josephus und das Wunderbare," in Studien zum Neuen Testament und zum hellenistischen Judentum. Gesammelte Aufsätze, 1950-68. Ed. F. Hahn, T. Holtz, N. Walter. Göttingen, 1970. 130-45.

Denis, Albert-Marie. Introduction aux Pseudépigraphes Grecs d'Ancien Testament (Studia in Veteris Testamenti Pseudepigrapha, 1) Leiden, 1970.

Dibelius, Martin. Die Formgeschichte des Evangeliums. Ed. G. Bornkamm. Tübingen, ⁶1971.

_____. From Tradition to Gospel. Trans. B. L. Woolf of 2nd rev. Ger. ed. London, 1934.

Dirlmeier, F. "ΘΕΟΦΙΛΙΑ-ΦΙΛΟΘΕΙΑ." Philologus 90 (= N.F. 44) (1935) 57-77.

Dodd, C. H. The Interpretation of the Fourth Gospel. Cambridge, 1954.

Dodds, E. R. The Greeks and the Irrational. Berkeley, 1968.

_____. Pagan and Christian in an Age of Anxiety. Some Aspects of Religious Experience from Marcus Aurelius to Constantine. Cambridge, 1968.

Drummond, James. Philo Judaeus. The Jewish-Alexandrian Philosophy in Its Development and Completion. London, 1888. 2 vols.

Dunand, F. Le culte d'Isis dans de basin oriental de Méditerranée. Leiden, 1973. 3 vols.

Edersheim, A. "Josephus " Dictionary of Christian Biography. London, 1882. 3. 441-60.

Eisler, Robert. Orphisch-dionysische Mysterien-Gedanken in der christlichen Antike. (Vorträge der Bibliothek Warburg, 2. Vorträge, 2. Teil, Ed. F. Saxl.) Leipzig/ Berlin, 1925.

Fabricius, Joannes A. Bibliotheca Graeca. Ed. G. C. Harles. 4th ed. Hamburg, 1790-1809. 12 vols.

Fascher, Erich. ΠΡΟΦΗΤΗΣ. Eine sprach- und religions- geschichtliche Untersuchung. Giessen, 1927.

Feldmann, Louis H. "Hellenizations in Josephus' Portrayal of Man's Decline." Religions in Antiquity (Goodenough Festschrift, Ed. J. Neusner. Studies in the History of Religion, 14.) Leiden, 1968. 336-53.

_____. Studies in Judaica. Scholarship on Philo and Josephus (1937-62). New York, n.d.

Ferguson, W. S. "Deification." Cambridge Ancient History. 7. 13-22.

Festugière, A. J. Contemplation et vie contemplative selon Platon. Paris, 1936.

_____. La revelation d'Hermès Trismégiste. Vol. 2: Le dieu cosmique. Paris, 1949. 519-85.

Foakes-Jackson, F. J. Josephus and the Jews. The Religion and History of the Jews As Explained by Flavius Josephus. London, 1930.

Forbes, Mansfield D. (ed.). Clare College. 1326-1926. Cambridge, 1928-30. 2 vols.

Fraser, Peter Marshall. Ptolemaic Alexandria. Oxford, 1972. 3 vols.

Freudenthal, J. Alexander Polyhistor und die von ihm erhaltenen Reste judaischer und samaritanischer Geschichtswerke. (Heft 1 & 2 in Hellenistische Studien) Breslau, 1875.

Friedländer, M. Geschichte der jüdischen Apologetik als Vorgeschichte der Christentums. Zürich, 1903.

Früchtel, U. Die kosmologischen Vorstellungen bei Philo von Alexandrien. Ein Beitrag zur Geschichte der Genesis- exegese. Leiden, 1968.

Fuller, Reginald H. The Foundations of New Testament Christology. London, 1965.

_____. Review of G. Minette de Tillesse, Le secret messianique dans l'évangile de Marc. CBQ 31 (1969) 109-12.

Gärtner, Bertil. The Areopagus Speech and Natural Revelation. Uppsala, 1955.

Gager, John. Moses in Greco-Roman Paganism. New York, 1972.

Geffcken, Johannes. Zwei griechische Apologeten. (Sammlung wissenschaftlicher Kommentare zu griechischen und römischen Schriftstellern) Leipzig/Berlin, 1907.

Georgi, Dieter. Die Gegner des Paulus im 2. Korintherbrief. Studien zur religiösen Propaganda in der Spätantike.

(Wissenschaftliche Monographien zum Alten und Neuen
Testament, 11) Neukirchen-Vluyn, 1964.

Geyer, F. "Lysimachos." PWRE 14.1 (1928) 1-31.

Gigon, O. Review of Canart and Van Camp, θεῖος chez Platon.
Museum Helveticum 17 (1960) 44.

Ginzberg, L. "Allegorical Interpretation." JE 1. 403-11.

_____. "Artapanus." JE 2. 145.

Goodenough, Erwin, R. By Light, Light. The Mystic Gospel of
Hellenistic Judaism. New Haven, 1935; repr. Amsterdam,
1969.

_____. An Introduction to Philo Judaeus. Oxford, ²1962.

_____. Jewish Symbols in the Greco-Roman World. New York,
1953-68. 13 vols.

_____. "Philo's Exposition of the Law and his De vita
Mosis." HTR 27 (1933) 109-25.

_____. "The Political Philosophy of Hellenistic Kingship."
Yale Classical Studies 1 (1928) 55-102.

_____. "Wolfson's Philo." JBL 67 (1948) 87-109.

Grässer, E. "Jesus in Nazareth (Mark VI. 1-6a). Notes on the
Redaction and Theology of St. Mark." NTS 16 (1969-70)
1-23.

Grundmann, W. Die Gotteskindschaft in der Geschichte Jesu und
ihre religionsgeschichtlichen Voraussetzungen (Studien
zur deutschen Theologie und Frömmigkeit, 1) Weimar, 1938.

_____. "Sohn Gottes." ZNW 47 (1956) 113-33.

Guthrie, W. K. C. The Greeks and Their Gods. Boston, 1955.

Gutman, J. ספרות היהודית-ההלניסטית היהדות וההלניות
(Jerusalem, 1963) בראשית תקופת החשמונאים

Gutschmid, Alfred von. Kleine Schriften. Ed. Franz Rühl.
Leipzig, 1889-94. 5 vols.

Habicht, C. Gottmenschentum und griechische Städte.
(Zetemata, 14) München, ²1970.

Hadas, Moses. Hellenistic Culture. Fusion and Diffusion.
London, 1959.

Hahn, Ferdinand. The Titles of Jesus in Christology: Their
History in Early Christianity. Trans. H. Knight & G. Ogg.
London, 1969.

Hanson, R. P. C. Allegory and Event. A Study of the Sources
and Significance of Origen's Interpretation of Scripture.
London, 1959.

Harrison, Jane Ellen. Prolegomena to the Study of Greek
Religion. Cambridge, ³1922.

Heinemann, I. "Antisemitismus." PWRE, Suppl. 5 (1931) 3-43.

_____. "Moses (1)." PWRE 16.1 (1933) 359-75.

Hempel, J. Untersuchungen zur Überlieferung von Apollonius
von Tyana. (Beiträge zur Religionswissenschaft, 4)
Leipzig/Stockholm, 1920.

Hengel, Martin. "Anonymität, Pseudepigraphie und 'Literarische Fälschung' in der jüdisch-hellenistischen Literatur." Pseudepigrapha I (Entretiens sur L'Antiquité Classique, Tome 18) Vandoeuvres-Genève, 1972. 231-329.

_____. Judentum und Hellenismus. Studien zu ihrer Begegnung unter besonderer Berücksichtigung Palästinas bis zur Mitte des 2. Jh. v. Chr. (Wissenschaftliche Untersuchungen zum Neuen Testament, 10) Tübingen, 21973.

Hennecke, E. & W. Schneemelcher (edd.). New Testament Apocrypha. Trans. R. McL. Wilson. London, 1963-65. 2 vols.

Heschel, A. J. The Prophets. New York, 1962.

Höistad, Ragnar. Cynic Hero and Cynic King. Studies in the Cynic Conception of Man. Uppsala, 1948.

Hölscher, G. "Josephus." PWRE 9.2 (1916) 1934-2000.

Holl, K. The Distinctive Elements in Christianity. Trans. N. V. Hope. Edinburgh, 1937.

_____. "Die schriftstellerische Form des griechischen Heiligenlebens." Neue Jahrbücher für das klassische Altertum 29 (1912) 406-27.

Jacob, E. Theology of the Old Testament. Trans. A. W. Heathcote & P. J. Allcock. London, 1958.

Jacoby, F. "Hekataios (4)." PWRE 7.2 (1912) 2750-69.

Jaeger, W. Early Christianity and Greek Paideia. London, 1969.

_____. Paideia: The Ideals of Greek Culture. Trans. G. H. Highet from 2nd Ger. ed. Oxford, 1939-45. 3 vols.

Jeremias, J. "Abba." ThLZ 79 (1954) 213-14.

_____. "Μωυσῆς." TDNT 4. 848-73.

Jewett, R. "Enthusiastic Radicalism and the Thessalonian Correspondence." SBL Proceedings. Los Angeles, 1972. 1. 181-232.

Joosen, J. C. and J. H. Waszink. "Allegorese." RAC 1. 283-93.

Katz, P. Philo's Bible. The Aberrant Text of Bible Quotations in Some Philonic Writings and Its Place in the Textual History of the Greek Bible. Cambridge, 1950.

Keck, Leander. "Mark 3: 7-12 and Mark's Christology." JBL 84 (1965) 341-58.

Kee, Howard Clark. Jesus in History: An Approach to the Study of the Gospels. New York, 1970.

_____. "Aretalogy and Gospel." JBL 92 (1973) 402-22. ✓

_____. Review of F. Hahn, Christologische Hoheitstitel. JBL 83 (1964) 191-93.

_____. "The terminology of Mark's Exorcism Stories." NTS 14 (1967-68) 232-46.

Kelber, Werner H. The Kingdom in Mark. A New Place and a New Time. Philadelphia, 1974.

Kilpatrick, G. D. Review of P. Katz, Philo's Bible. JTS 2 (1951) 87-9.

Kittel, G. Die Probleme des palästinischen Spätjudentums und das Urchristentum. (Beiträge zur Wissenschaft vom Alten und Neuen Testament, 3. Folge, 1) Stuttgart, 1926.

Klein, J. A Commentary on Plato's Meno. Chapel Hill, N.C., 1965.

Kleinknecht, H. "νόμος (Greek and Hellenistic World)." TDNT, 4. 1023-35.

Knigge, H-D. "The Meaning of Mark." Interpretation 22 (1968) 53-70.

König, E. "Tabernacle." JE 11. 653-56.

Koester, Helmut. "Häretiker im Urchristentum." RGG³ 3. 17-21.

_____. "ΝΟΜΟΣ ΦΥΣΕΩΣ. The Concept of Natural Law in Greek Thought." Religions in Antiquity. (Goodenough Festschrift, Ed. J. Neusner. Studies in the History of Religion, 14) Leiden, 1968. 521-41.

_____ and James M. Robinson. Trajectories through Early Christianity. Philadelphia, 1971.

Koller, H. Review of Canart and Van Camp, θεῖος chez Platon. Gnomon 29 (1957) 466-68.

Kortenbeutel, H. "Philos." PWRE 20. 1 (1941) 95-103.

Krüger, Paul. Philo und Josephus als Apologeten des Judentums. Leipzig, 1906.

Kuby, A. "Zur Konzeption des Markus-Evangeliums." ZNW 49 (1958) 52-64.

Kümmel, Werner G. The New Testament: The History of the Investigation of Its Problems. Trans. S. McLean Gilmour & Howard C. Kee. London, 1973.

Lagrange, M.-J. Le judaïsme avant Jésus-Christ. (Études Bibliques) Paris, 1931.

_____. "Socrate et Notre-Seigneur Jésus-Christ." Revue Biblique 44 (1935) 5-21.

Lampe, G. W. H. "Miracles in the Acts of the Apostles." Miracles. Cambridge Studies in Their Philosophy and History. Ed. C. F. D. Moule. London, 1965. 163-78.

Laqueur, Richard. Der jüdische Historiker Flavius Josephus. Ein biographischer Versuch auf neuer quellenkritischer Grundlage. Giessen, 1920.

Lauterbach, J. Z. "The Ancient Jewish Allegorists in Talmud and Midrash." JQR N.S. 1 (1910-11) 291-333; 503-31.

Leipoldt, J. Dionysos. [ΑΓΓΕΛΟΣ. Archiv für neutestamentliche Zeitgeschichte und Kulturkunde, Beiheft 3] Leipzig, 1931.

Leisegang, Hans. "Der Gottmensch als Archetypus." Eranos-Jahrbuch, 18. (Jung Festschrift, Ed. Olga Fröbe-Kapteyn) Zürich, 1950. 9-45.

_____. Indices ad Philonis Alexandrini. Berlin, 1926.

_____. "Philon (41)." PWRE 20. 1 (1941) 1-50.

Levy, Isidore. "Moïse en Éthiopie." Revue des études juives 53 (1907) 201-11.

Lieberman, Saul. Hellenism in Jewish Palestine. Studies in the literary transmission, beliefs and manners of Palestine in the I century B.C.E.-IV century C.E. (Texts and Studies of the Jewish Theological Seminary in America, 18) New York, 1950.

Liddell, H. G., R. Scott, H. S. Jones, & R. McKenzie. A Greek-English Lexicon. Oxford, 1948.

Liefeld, W. L. "The Hellenistic 'Divine Man' and the Figure of Jesus in the Gospels." JETS 16 (1973) 195-205.

Lindblom, C. J. Prophecy in Ancient Israel. Oxford, 1962; repr. 1963.

Luz, U. "Das Geheimnismotiv und die markinische Christologie." ZNW 56 (1965) 9-30.

MacDonald, John. Memar Marqah. The Teaching of Marqah. 2 vols. BZAW 84 (1963).

_____. "The Samaritan Doctrine of Moses." SJT 13 (1960) 149-62.

_____. The Theology of the Samaritans. London, 1964.

Manson, William. Jesus the Messiah: the Synoptic Tradition of the Revelation of God in Christ: with Special Reference to Form-criticism. London, 1943.

Marshall, I. Howard. "Palestinian and Hellenistic Christianity: Some Critical Comments." NTS 19 (1972-73) 271-87.

Massebieau, L. and E. Bréhier. "Essai sur la chronologie de la vie et des oeuvres de Philon." Rev. Hist. Rel. 53 (1906) 25-64.

Maurer, C. "Knecht Gottes und Sohn Gottes im Passionsbericht des Markusevangeliums." ZTK 50 (1953) 1-38.

Meeks, Wayne A. "Moses as God and King." Religions in Antiquity. (Goodenough Festschrift, Ed. J. Neusner. Studies in the History of Religion, 14) Leiden, 1968. 354-71.

_____. The Prophet-King: Moses Traditions and the Johannine Christology. (Novum Testamentum, Supplements, 14) Leiden, 1967.

Merentites, K. J. "Ο ΙΟΥΔΑΙΟΣ ΛΟΓΙΟΣ ΑΡΤΑΠΑΝΟΣ ΚΑΙ ΤΟ ΕΡΓΟΝ ΑΥΤΟΥ (Γλωσσικὸν, φιλολογικὸν καὶ θρησκειολογικὸν ὑπόμνημα εἰς κείμενα τῆς ἑλληνιστικῆς γραμματείας)." Ἐπετηρὶς τῆς Ἑταιρείας Βυζαντινῶν Σπουδῶν (= Annuaire de l'Association d'Études Byzantines) 27 (1957) 292-339; 29 (1959) 273-321; 30 (1960-61) 281-350.

Meyer, Rudolf. Hellenistisches in der rabbinischen Anthropologie. Rabbinische Vorstellungen vom Werden des Menschen. (Beiträge zur Wissenschaft vom Alten und Neuen Testament, 4. Folge, Heft 22) Stuttgart, 1937.

_____. "προφήτης (Judaism in Hellenistic-Roman Period)." TDNT, 6. 812-28.

Momigliano, Arnaldo. Review of M. Hengel, Judentum und Hellenismus. JTS N.S. 21 (1970) 149-53.

Montgomery, J. A. "The Religion of Flavius Josephus." JQR N.S. 11 (1920-21) 277-305.

Moore, G. F. History of Religions. Edinburgh, 1914-20. 2 vols.

_____. Judaism in the First Centuries of the Christian Era; the Age of the Tannaim. Cambridge, Mass., 1966. 3 vols.

Moulton, J. H. & G. Milligan. The Vocabulary of the Greek Testament. London, 1930.

Mugnier, R. Le sens du mot θεῖος chez Platon. (Bibl. d'hist. de la philos.) Paris, 1930.

Murray, Oswyn. "Aristeas and Ptolemaic Kingship." JTS 18 (1967) 337-71.

Neumark, H. Die Verwendung griechischer und jüdischer Motive in den Gedanken Philons über die Stellung Gottes zu seinen Freunden. Würzburg, 1937.

Niese, Benedictus. "Josephus." HERE, 7. 569-79.

Nilsson, Martin P. The Dionysiac Mysteries of the Hellenistic and Roman Age. Lund, 1957.

_____. Geschichte der griechischen Religion. München, 31967 (vol. 1); 21961 (vol. 2).

Nock, Arthur Darby. Conversion. Oxford, 1965.

_____. Early Gentile Christianity and Its Hellenistic Background. New York, 1964.

_____. Essays on Religion and the Ancient World. Ed. Zeph Stewart. Oxford, 1972. 2 vols.

_____. "The Institution of Ruler Worship." Cambridge Ancient History. 10. 481-89.

Oepke, A. "ἀποκαλύπτω." TDNT, 3. 563-92.

Palmer, Henrietta R. List of English Editions and Translations of Greek and Latin Classics Printed Before 1641. London, 1911.

Patai, R. Man and Temple in Ancient Jewish Myth and Ritual. New York, 1947.

Pembroke, S. G. "Oikeiōsis." Problems in Stoicism. Ed. A. A. Long. London, 1971. 114-49.

Perrin, Norman. "The Christology of Mark: A Study in Methodology." JR 51 (1971) 173-87.

_____. Christology and a Modern Pilgrimage. Ed. H. D. Betz. Claremont, 1971.

_____. What is Redaction Criticism? London, 1970.

Peterson, E. "Der Gottesfreund. Beiträge zur Geschichte eines religiösen Terminus." ZKG 42 (N.F. 5) (1923) 161-202.

Petzke, G. Die Traditionen über Apollonius von Tyana und das Neue Testament (Studia ad Corpus Hellenisticum Novi Testamenti, 1) Leiden, 1970.

Pfister, F. "Kultus." PWRE 11.2 (1922) 2106-92.

Pohlenz, M. "Philon von Alexandreia." Nachrichten von der Akademie der Wissenschaften in Göttingen (Philologisch-historische Klasse). Fasc. No. 5. Göttingen, 1942. 409-87.

Preisker, H. Wundermächte und Wundermänner. Halle-Wittenberg, 1952/3.

Preller, L.-C. Robert. Griechische Mythologie. 4. Aufl. Berlin, 1894-1926. 3 vols.

Prümm, Karl. Religionsgeschichtliches Handbuch für den Raum der altchristlichen Umwelt; hellenistisch-römische Geistesströmungen und Kulte mit Beachtung des Eigenlebens der Provinzen. Rome, 1954.

_____. "Zur Früh- und Spätform der religionsgeschicht-lichen Christusdeutung von H. Windisch." Biblica 42 (1961) 391-422; 43 (1962) 22-56.

Raven, John. Plato's Thought in the Making. A Study of the Development of His Metaphysics. Cambridge, 1965.

Reinhardt, K. "Herakleitos (12)." PWRE 8.1 (1912) 508-10.

Reitzenstein, Richard. Die hellenistischen Mysterien-religionen, ihre Grundgedanken und Wirkungen. 1. Aufl. Leipzig/Berlin, 1910. 3. Aufl. 1927.; repr. Darmstadt, 1956.

_____. Hellenistische Wundererzählungen. Darmstadt, 1963; repr. of 1906 ed.

_____. Poimandres. Studien zur griechisch-ägyptischen und frühchristlichen Literatur. Leipzig, 1904.

Rengstorf, Karl Heinrich (ed.). A Complete Concordance to Flavius Josephus. Vol. 1: A - Δ. Leiden, 1973.

Richards, G. C. "The Composition of Josephus' Antiquities." Classical Quarterly 33 (1939) 36-40.

Richardson, A. An Introduction to the Theology of the New Testament. New York, 1958.

Richardson, W. "The Philonic Patriarchs as Νόμος ῎Εμψυχος." Studia Patristica, vol. 1, pt. 1 (TU, 63) Berlin, 1957. 515-25.

Robinson, James M. & Helmut Koester. Trajectories through Early Christianity. Philadelphia, 1971.

Rohde, E. Kleine Schriften. Tübingen/Leipzig, 1901; repr. Hildesheim/New York, 1969.

Ryle, H. E. Philo and Holy Scripture, or the Quotations of Philo from the Books of the Old Testament. London, 1895.

Sandmel, Samuel. Philo's Place in Judaism. A Study of Con-ceptions of Abraham in Jewish Literature. New York, ²1971.

Schalit, Abraham. "Artapanus." E Jud. 3. 645-46.

_____. Namenwörterbuch zu Flavius Josephus. Leiden, 1968.

Schlatter, Adolf. Geschichte Israels von Alexander dem Grossen bis Hadrian. Stuttgart, ³1925.

_____. Die Theologie des Judentums nach dem Bericht des Josefus. (Beiträge zur Förderung christlicher Theologie. 2. Reihe. Bd. 26) Gütersloh, 1932.

Schlier, H. "ἐλεύθερος." TDNT, 2. 487-502.

Schmid, W. & O. Stählin. Geschichte der griechischen Literatur. München, 61961. 2 vols.

Schreiber, J. "Die Christologie des Markusevangeliums: Beobachtungen zur Theologie und Komposition des zweiten Evangeliums." ZTK 58 (1961) 154-83.

_____. Theologie des Vertrauens. Eine redaktions-geschichtliche Untersuchung des Markusevangeliums. Hamburg, 1967.

Schubart, W. Einführung in die Papyruskunde. Berlin, 1918.

_____. "Das hellenistische Königsideal nach Inschriften und Papyri." Archiv für Papyrusforschung 12 (1937) 1-26.

Schürer, Emil. Geschichte des jüdischen Volkes im Zeitalter Jesu Christi. Hildesheim, 1964. Repr. of: vol. 1: 1901 (= 3. & 4. Aufl.); vol. 2: 1907 (= 4. Aufl.); vol. 3: 1909 (= 4. Aufl.).

_____. "Josephus." Realencyklopädie für protestantische Theologie und Kirche (31901). 9. 377-86.

Schulz, S. Die Stunde der Botschaft. Einführung in die Theologie der vier Evangelisten. Hamburg, 1967.

Schwartz, E. "Artapanus." PWRE 2 (1895) 1306.

Schweizer, E. "υἱός (New Testament)." TDNT, 8. 363-92.

_____. Jesus. Trans. D. E. Green. London, 1971.

_____. "Neuere Markus-Forschung in U.S.A." Evangelische Theologie 33 (1973) 533-37.

Scott, C. A. A. Review of H. Windisch, Paulus und Christus. JTS 36 (1935) 85-6.

Shutt, R. J. H. Studies in Josephus. London, 1961.

Siegfried, C. Philo von Alexandria als Ausleger des Alten Testaments an sich selbst und nach seinem geschichtlichen Einfluss betrachtet. Jena, 1875.

_____. "Philo und der überlieferte Text der LXX." Zeitschrift für wissenschaftliche Theologie 16 (1873) 217-38; 411-28; 522-40.

Skemp, J. B. "Plato's Concept of Deity." Zetesis. Bijdragen op het Gebied van de klassieke Filologie, Filosofie, Byzantinistiek Patrologie en Theologie. (Festschrift Emile de Strijcker) Antwerp/Utrecht, 1973.

Smallwood, E. Mary. Philonis Alexandrini. Legatio ad Gaium. Edited with an Introduction, Translation and Commentary. Leiden, 21970.

Smith, Morton. "The Image of God. Notes on the Hellenization of Judaism, with especial reference to Goodenough's work on Jewish Symbols." BJRL 40 (1958) 473-512.

_____. "Prolegomena to a Discussion of Aretalogies, Divine Men, the Gospels and Jesus." <u>JBL</u> 90 (1971) 174-99.

_____. Review of D. L. Tiede, <u>Charismatic Figure</u>. <u>Interpretation</u> 28 (1974) 238-40.

Smyth, Herbert Weir. <u>Greek Grammar</u>. Cambridge, Mass., 1956.

Sprödowsky, Hans. <u>Die Hellenisierung der Geschichte von Joseph in Ägypten bei Flavius Josephus</u>. (Greifswalder Beiträge zur Literatur- und Stilforschung) Greifswald, 1937.

Stambaugh, J. E. <u>Sarapis Under the Early Ptolemies</u>. Leiden, 1972.

Stewart, R. A. "Creation and Matter in the Epistle to the Hebrews." <u>NTS</u> 12 (1965-66) 284-93.

_____. "The Sinless High-Priest." <u>NTS</u> 14 (1967-68) 126-35.

Strack, H. L. & P. Billerbeck. <u>Kommentar zum Neuen Testament aus Talmud und Midrasch</u>. München, 1922-61. 5 vols.

Stuhlmacher, Peter. <u>Das paulinische Evangelium. I: Vorgeschichte</u>. (FRLANT, 95) Göttingen, 1968.

Tcherikover, Victor. <u>Hellenistic Civilization and the Jews</u>. Trans. S. Applebaum. Philadelphia, 1966.

_____. "Jewish Apologetic Literature Reconsidered." <u>Eos</u> 48 (1956) 169-93.

Thackeray, H. St. J. "Josephus." <u>HDB</u>, 5. 461-73.

_____. <u>Josephus. The Man and the Historian</u>. New York, 1929.

_____ and Ralph Marcus. <u>A Lexicon to Josephus</u>. Paris, 1930-55. 4 pts.

Thraede, Klaus. "Erfinder II (geistesgeschichtlich)." <u>RAC</u>, 5. 1191-1278.

_____. "Das Lob des Erfinders. Bemerkungen zur Analyse der Heuremata-Kataloge." <u>Rheinisches Museum für Philologie</u> N.F. 105 (1962) 158-86.

Thyen, Hartwig. <u>Der Stil der jüdisch-hellenistischen Homilie</u>. (FRLANT, N.F. 47) Göttingen, 1955.

Tiede, David Lenz. <u>The Charismatic Figure as Miracle Worker</u>. (SBL Dissertation Series, 1) Missoula, Montana, 1972.

Van Camp, J. & P. Canart. <u>Le sens du mot θεῖος chez Platon</u>. Louvain, 1956.

Verdenius, W. J. Review of Canart & Van Camp, θεῖος chez Platon. <u>Mnemosyne</u> 14 (1961) 51-4.

Vermès, G. "La figure de Moïse au tournant des deux testaments." <u>Moïse, l'homme de l'alliance = Cahiers Sioniens</u> 8 (1954) 63-92.

Vidman, L. <u>Isis und Sarapis bei den Griechen und Römern; epigraphische Studien zur Verbreitung und zu den Trägern des ägyptischen Kultes</u>. Berlin, 1970.

_____. <u>Sylloge Inscriptionum religionis Isiacae et Sarapiacae</u>. (Religionsgeschichtl. Versuche und Vorarbeiten, 28) Berlin, 1969.

260

Vielhauer, P. "Erwägungen zur Christologie des Markusevangeliums." Zeit und Geschichte (Festschrift
Bultmann. Ed. E. Dinkler.) Tübingen, 1964. 155-69.

Von Martitz, W. "υἱός (Classical Greek)." TDNT, 8. 335-40.

Wacholder, Ben Zion. "Pseudo-Eupolemus' Two Greek Fragments
on the Life of Abraham." HUCA 34 (1963) 83-113.

Wachsmuth, Kurt. Einleitung in das Studium der Alten
Geschichte. Leipzig, 1895.

Walter, Nikolaus. Review of K. J. Merentites, ΑΡΤΑΠΑΝΟΣ.
Helikon 3 (1973) 789-92.

_____. Der Thoraausleger Aristobulos. Untersuchungen zu
seinen Fragmenten und zu pseudepigraphischen Resten der
jüdisch-hellenistischen Literatur (TU, 86) Berlin, 1964.

_____. Untersuchungen zu den Fragmenten der jüdisch-
hellenistischen Historiker. Unpub. Habilitationsschrift.
Halle, 1967/68.

Watson, G. "The Natural Law and Stoicism." Problems in
Stoicism. Ed. A. A. Long. London, 1971. 216-38.

Wedderburn, A. J. M. "Philo's Heavenly Man." NT 15 (1973)
301-26.

Weeden, T. J. "The Heresy That Necessitated Mark's Gospel."
ZNW 59 (1968) 148-58.

_____. Mark: Traditions in Conflict. Philadelphia, 1971.

Weinacht, H. Die Menschwerdung des Sohnes Gottes im Markusevangelium. Studien zur Christologie des Markusevangelium.
Tübingen, 1972.

Weinreich, Otto. "Antikes Gottmenschentum." Neue Jahrbücher
für Wissenschaft und Jugendbildung 2 (1926) 633-51.

_____. "Gebet und Wunder. Zwei Abhandlungen zur Religions-
und Literaturgeschichte." (1. Abhandlung: "Primitiver
Gebetsegoismus," 169-99; 2. Abhandlung: "Türöffnung im
Wunder-, Prodigien- und Zauberglauben der Antike, des
Judentums und Christentums," 200-452.) Genethliakon
Wilhelm Schmid. Edd. F. Focke et al. [Tübinger Beiträge
zur Altertumswissenschaft, Heft 5] Stuttgart, 1929.

Welles, C. Bradford. Royal Correspondence in the Hellenistic
Period. A Study in Greek Epigraphy. New Haven, 1934.

Wendland, Paul. Die hellenistisch-römische Kultur (Handbuch
zum Neuen Testament) Tübingen, ⁴1972.

_____. Philo und die kynisch-stoische Diatribe. (Beiträge
zur Geschichte der griechischen Philosophie und Religion)
Berlin, 1895.

_____. Philos Schrift über die Vorsehung. Berlin, 1892.

Wenschkewitz, Hans. "Die Spiritualisierung der Kultusbegriffe:
Tempel, Priester und Opfer im Neuen Testament," ΑΓΓΕΛΟΣ.
Archiv für neutestamentliche Zeitgeschichte und
Kulturkunde 4 (1932) 70-230.

Wetter, G. P. "Der Sohn Gottes." Eine Untersuchung über den
Charakter und die Tendenz des Johannes-Evangeliums.

Zugleich ein Beitrag zur Kenntnis der Heilandsgestalten
der Antike. (FRLANT, N.F. 9) Göttingen, 1916.

Williamson, G. A. The World of Josephus. London, 1964.

Willrich, Hugo. Judaica. Forschungen zur hellenistisch-
jüdischen Geschichte und Litteratur. Göttingen, 1900.

Windisch, Hans. Paulus und Christus. Ein biblischreligions-
geschichtlicher Vergleich. (Untersuchungen zum Neuen
Testament, Heft 24) Leipzig, 1934.

Witt, R. E. Isis in the Graeco-Roman World. London, 1971.

Wolfson, H. A. Philo. Foundations of Religious Philosophy in
Judaism, Christianity, and Islam. Cambridge, Mass.,
1947. 2 vols.

Zeller, Eduard. Die Philosophie der Griechen in ihrer
geschichtlichen Entwicklung. Leipzig, ⁴1903. 3 vols.

_____. Stoics, Epicureans, and Sceptics. Trans. O. J.
Reichel. London, 1880.

INDEX

I. Modern Authors

263

A. Old Testament

B. Josephus

B. Josephus

B. Josephus

B. Josephus

Bellum (cont.)		Agr.	
6.47	64:114	51	182:360, 193
6.59	65.119	79	182:360, 193:429
6.252	65:119	119	181:360
6.293	206:29		
6.296	65:128	Alex.	148:236
6.303	65:119		
6.429	64, 65:129	Animal.	148:236
7.120	65:130		
7.150	90:278		
7.159	65:131	Cher.	
7.162	90:278	3	180:350
7.185	64:118	8	182:360
7.318	64:111	19	178:340
7.343	60:68	23	180:350, 180:353
7.344	62:86, 105:8	27	164:289
8.45	64:115	36	179:347
		41	162:285, 180:353
Vita		42	181:356
402	64:112	46	178:340, 193
		72	178:340
		93	181:360, 182:360
	C. Philo	127	118:99
Abr.		Conf.	
4ff.	176	4	187:374
6	176:332	28	180:350
10	187:374	41	189:411
18	178:339	51	178:340
26	178:338	56	166:293
70	178:339, 179:340	59	161:278, 179:341
75	118:99	62	178:340
78	118:99	77ff.	140:204
80	166:295	81	177:337, 179:341
101	178:340, 193:428	92	166:293
107	180:350	100	182:360, 193
115	180:350, 180:353	108	181:360
128	181:356	115	178:338, 178:339, 178:340
141	178:340	122	181:360
144	179:340	133	180:353
159	180:353, 181:360	144	178:340, 188:405
162	180:353	145	165:293, 173:319
170	178:340	146	174:319
235	178:339	154	180:353
244	180:347	174	180:353
261	114:66	176ff.	171:309
275	177:337, 179:341, 188:409		
Aet.		Cong.	
13	186:372	11	111:46
25	186:372	15ff.	111:40
38	186:372	50	166:293
47	180:351, 180:353, 192:423	57	181:360
52	186:372	79f.	111:46
69	178:340, 186:372	96	178:340, 179:340
112	181:357	100	179:340, 194:430
141	186:372	105f.	191

C. Philo

Cong. (cont.)		Flacc.	
106	181:360	125	178:339, 178:340
116	178:340, 193	169	161:278
120	179:341, 195:436	**Fuga**	
140ff.	111:46	5	180:347, 180:350
155f.	111:46	13	180:347

Decal.		Fuga	
13	179:341	20	178:340
32	105:12	21	177:337, 179:341, 181:355
35	161:278, 166:293	56	165:293
36	177:336	59	163:287
58	186:372	62	180:353
90	118:99	63	186:372
104	180:353, 193:429	74	180:353
111	178:340	82	186:372
121	178:340	85	181:356
134	171:309	94	180:347
175	161:277, 161:278	97	180:347
		101	180:347
Det.		108	171, 171:311, 180:347
61	178:339	109	171:312
83	159:267, 159:269, 178:338,	137	180:347
	181:360	139	179:341
84f.	171:309, 186:372	162	182:360
86ff.	166:298	163	182:360
89	166:295	164f.	166:296
90	182:360	168	161:278, 181:360
116	179:340, 194:430	186	179:344
117	178:340	195	180:348
118	179:347	208	177:337
133	177:337		
147	178:340	**Gig.**	
152	178:340, 193	8	180:351
156	178:340	12ff.	140:204
158	149:238	15	159
158ff.	149	20	170
159f.	150:240	23	179:344
160ff.	147ff., 152, 153, 154, 182:360	27	179:344
161	147:235	28	179:344, 179:345
162	151:244	29	179:342, 179:344
		31	181:360
Ebr.		36ff.	114:70
30	105:12	47	179:342
31	180:353	53	179:344, 179:345
37	178:340	54f.	170:304
39	178:340, 179:341	55	170:305, 179:344, 179:345
61	186:372	60	189:411
83	166:293	61	189:411
94	174	62	189:411
100	181:360	63	189:411
110	105:10, 162:282		
124	165:293	**Her.**	
143	180:353, 193	1	178:340
145	179:340	14	178:340
146f.	166:294	55	159, 159:270, 179:346
		56	159:271

C. Philo

C. Philo

C. Philo

V. Mos. (cont.)	
1.154	113, 121:119
1.155	115, 115:76, 115:77, 118, 122
1.155ff.	129, 133, 134, 135, 148, 155
1.156	76:205, 121, 128, 129, 196
1.157	114:72, 115:78, 121:116
1.158	108ff., 114, 115:79, 118:100, 120:106, 126:138, 127:146, 133, 133:177, 135:188, 145, 146, 152, 153
1.158f.	117:94, 128
1.160ff.	114:71
1.162	117:90, 178:339, 178:340
1.175	161:278
1.190	181:360
1.196	175
1.201	161:278
1.210ff.	175
1.211	178:339
1.219f.	175
1.272	178:340
1.277	161:278
1.279	178:340, 193:428
1.283	105:12
1.288	161:278
2.1	109:29, 175
2.2	109:30, 186:372
2.2ff.	68:138
2.5	175, 178:339
2.6	175
2.12	114:73, 179:341, 181:357
2.19ff.	105:12
2.20	114:73
2.32	178:339
2.51	179:341
2.58	178:339
2.60	177:337, 179:341
2.68f.	175
2.70	177:337, 179:341
2.74ff.	82:260
2.88	83:262
2.98f.	83:262
2.102	83:262
2.103	178:340, 181:356, 193
2.124	180:347
2.131	114:66
2.134	147:233, 173:319
2.139	170
2.154	178:339
2.167	175
2.188	160ff., 182:360
2.189	178:340, 181:360
2.192	174, 175
2.208	178:340
2.250	156

V. Mos. (cont.)	
2.253	156:253, 178:338
2.254	178:339, 178:340
2.255	178:338
2.258	156:254
2.261	178:339
2.265	179:344
2.278	178:339
2.288	108:24, 163:287
2.288ff.	28, 175

Fragments

Gen. Gk. frag. 1.55		105:12
	2.54	105:12
Frag. P 362 E		114:70

D. Artapanus

Fragments

1 & 2	215
1	215:96, 218:108, 219:113
2	218
2.1	219:113
2.2	216:101
2.2ff.	218:110
2.3	219:112, 219:114, 228:180
3	215, 217
3.1ff.	209, 219, 220
3.2	228:174
3.2f.	219
3.3	204:19, 229:185
3.3f.	220, 224
3.3ff.	220, 220:118, 220:119
3.4	204:20, 205:24, 205:25, 210:62, 210:64, 211, 211:74, 211:78, 211:79, 211:80, 216:101, 219, 219:112, 219:115, 226, 226:157, 230:187
3.5	226:158, 230
3.6	205:22, 226, 226:159, 227:165, 229:186
3.7ff.	227:166
3.8	210:63
3.9	205:25, 219:112, 227:165, 230
3.10	227:167
3.12	205:25, 219:112, 230
3.12f.	220:119
3.12ff.	227:168
3.13	227:169
3.16	214:91, 230
3.17	219
3.18	219, 227:170
3.19	219, 227:171

IV. Ancient Sources - Classical

IV. Ancient Sources - Classical